The Exchange-Traded Funds Manual

The Exchange-Traded Funds Manual

Gary L. Gastineau

JOHN WILEY & SONS

The information, opinions, data and statements contained herein are those of the author, and not necessarily those of Nuveen Investments, and should be interpreted, acted on and represented as such.

This publication is designed to provide accurate and authoritative information in regard to the subject matter covered. It is sold with the understanding that the publisher is not engaged in rendering professional services. If professional advice or other expert assistance is required, the services of a competent professional person should be sought.

ISBN: 0-471-21894-4

Printed in the United States of America.

10 9 8 7 6 5 4 3 2 1

About the Author

Gary Gastineau joined Nuveen Investments in March 2000, where he is Managing Director of Exchange-Traded Fund Product Consulting. Gastineau oversees the creation and development of equities-based and taxable fixed-income exchange-traded funds and related products, building on Nuveen's recognized leadership position in exchange-traded municipal bond funds.

Gastineau is a recognized expert on open-end exchange traded funds. Prior to joining Nuveen he directed product development at the American Stock Exchange for approximately five years. As Senior Vice President in New Product Development, Gastineau was instrumental in the introduction of many of the popular index share products (such as Sector SPDRs, WEBs, and DIAMONDs), which have attracted more than $65 billion in assets since their first appearance in 1993. Previously, he held senior positions in research, product development, and portfolio management at major investment banking firms.

During his career, Gastineau has also specialized in risk management and derivatives applications. He has prepared and published institutional research for S. G. Warburg, Swiss Bank, Salomon Brothers and Kidder, Peabody. Gastineau is the author of *The Options Manual* (Third Edition, McGraw-Hill, 1988), and co-author of the *Dictionary of Financial Risk Management* (Fabozzi, 1999) and *Equity Flex Options* (Fabozzi, 1999), as well as numerous journal articles.

Gastineau is a frequent speaker on financial innovations, risk management, and regulatory issues. He serves on the editorial boards of *The Financial Analysts Journal*, *The Journal of Derivatives*, *The Journal of Portfolio Management*, *Contemporary Finance Digest*, and *Financial Practice and Education*. Gary is a member of a number of advisory boards, including the Review Board for the Research Foundation of the Association for Investment Management and Research (AIMR). He is an honors graduate of both Harvard College and Harvard Business School.

Preface

Exchange-traded funds (ETFs) are the most important—and potentially the most versatile—financial instruments introduced since the debut of financial futures 30 years ago. Like other newcomers to the financial stage, ETFs are finding some starring roles, other roles where they will be an important part of an ensemble cast and, of course, others where they will have merely a "walk-on" part to play.

Press coverage of ETFs has been extraordinary by any standard; but in the fund world, results are measured by asset growth. ETF assets grew at a 132% average annual rate from 1995 through 2000. Growth slowed in 2000 and 2001 because of a less ebullient market environment and some important new product delays, but eventually the market will stabilize, the rate of ETF innovation will accelerate and assets will grow rapidly again. I suspect that most readers would have agreed with this growth forecast before they bought the book. I am confident that most will agree before they finish reading.

A casual reader of popular ETF articles might conclude that ETFs are simply more flexible, lower-cost and highly tax-efficient equity index funds. The existing ETFs fit that description, but we expect to see ETFs with fixed-income and actively managed equity portfolios and with risk management features among their investment objectives.

This book was written primarily for relatively sophisticated individual investors and for the advisors who work with them. As Chapter 1 explains, I believe that few investors can make full and economically efficient use of important ETF features without the support and infrastructure an advisor can provide. At issue are the complexity of the tax, risk management, record maintenance, investment policy, fund evaluation, and portfolio integration decisions that need to be made in implementing an ETF-oriented investment program.

If an investor or advisor wants to compare an ETF with a conventional mutual fund, HOLDRs, or a Folio account, Chapters 2 and 4 will show the way. If day trading is of interest, Chapter 8 should be more helpful to traders than most such market structure descriptions and analyses prove to be. If you want to understand the strengths and weaknesses of conventional and ETF index funds, Chapter 6 will almost certainly tell you more than you want to know. Chapter 6 and part of Chapter 9 combine to offer some new perspectives on the perennial performance debate between indexers and active managers. Among other points, we demonstrate that the cost advantages of indexing, as it is practiced today, are less than they have been.

No discussion of ETFs would be complete without consideration of HOLDRs and Folios and how they compete with and, in the case of Folios, incorporate ETFs. A number of Folio investors and advisors using FOLIO*fn*'s advisor infrastructure are active users of ETFs and this usage will continue to grow. In fact, HOLDRs with ETFs as constituent securities are not unthinkable—just improbable.

Another important topic is the analysis and comparative evaluation of ETFs, partly on the basis of total operating and transaction costs. Mutual fund analysis and evaluation has been a fuzzy activity at its best. It is easy enough to calculate the return for a fund and to "pick" the best-performing funds from last year. In fairness to some diligent fund analysts, the problem of how to analyze mutual fund performance more usefully has not been a lack of will, but a lack of data. With conventional funds reporting their portfolios only twice a year, well after the statement date for the report has passed, it is impossible to determine what trades the funds made and when, whether good performance came from a few inspired (or lucky) positions, and whether the fund's trading desk was effective or a source of excess trading costs. It will take time, but analysts can do far more and far better fund evaluations with the data that will be available to reveal the ETF management process. Most ETFs will provide enough information to permit analysts to evaluate (1) the trading cost efficiency of any index used; (2) the trading costs associated with an active portfolio management process; (3) the information which triggers changes in an active account; and (4) how the actual portfolio would have compared to a portfolio that was changed only to replace stocks acquired for cash in mergers. These are only some early stages in the development of analytical and risk management possibilities.

This book is purposely not titled "Introduction to Exchange-Traded Funds," "Everything You Need to Know About ETFs," "How to Triple Your Money with Exchange-Traded Funds," or even "The Only ETF Book You Will Ever Need." If the publisher had insisted on one of those titles, I would have chosen the last one, but with reluctance. I have tried to cover all the important topics in reasonable depth and I have tried to anticipate new fund structures and applications, but, like others who have participated in the development and growth of these funds, I recognize the limitations on anyone's ability to anticipate the course of change. I have tried to approach the topical coverage and level of analysis that characterized my earlier book, *The Options Manual*.[1] Most examples are drawn from the U.S. experience, because I am most familiar with that market. At present, regulatory and market structures are both diverse and relatively unsettled outside the United States.[2]

ENDNOTES

1. Gastineau (1988).

2. See, for example, the diverse viewpoints expressed and products described in Rutter (2001).

Acknowledgements

Several times in the past, I have found writing a book to be a useful way to clarify my own thinking about a subject. In that respect, this book has been the most useful of all. ETFs have more pervasive and more significant effects on cash and derivative securities markets, investor objectives and behavior, tax and estate planning, regulatory policies, performance measurement and evaluation, and individual investor portfolios than any other financial instrument I have ever worked with. In the process of writing and learning, I have had a great deal of help and advice from many people. Of course, I remain responsible for residual errors.

I owe a special debt to Michael Carty, Wayne Wagner, Jim Wiandt, and two Nuveen colleagues cited below who read the entire manuscript and gave me invaluable comments and criticisms.

Most helpful comments, suggestions, and data have come from Michael Babel, Jay Baker, Henry Belusa, Scott Ebner, Gary Eisenreich, A. Michael Lipper, Albert Madansky, Burton Malkiel, Kevin McNally, Richard Michaud, Kathleen Moriarty, Esq., Nathan Most, James Novakoff, Robert Tull, Seth Varnhagen, Clifford Weber, and Steve Winks.

Help on specific issues is also gratefully acknowledged from James Bicksler and his MBA Students at Rutgers, Diane Garnick, Mary Joan Hoene, Esq., Steve Kim, Lawrence Larkin, Ron Ryan, and George "Gus" Sauter.

Five of my Nuveen colleagues have been extraordinarily helpful. Richard Harper developed the asset allocation model described in Chapter 1 and provided useful comments on the organization of the book. David Kuenzi developed data for a number of the exhibits and commented extensively on the entire text. Steven Lotz prepared the diagrams in Exhibits 3-1 through 3-6. Ranga Nathan provided his trademarked critique of the text, both line by line and overall. Michael Piszczek gave me extensive comments on various aspects of taxation.

Other Nuveen colleagues who have provided useful comments and/or important information are Tom Baranowski, Paul Berejnoi, Bruce Bond, Doris Cheng, Jessica Droeger, Esq., Kenneth

Fincher, Steven Foy, John Gambla, Brian Kosek, John Nersesian, and Gifford Zimmerman, Esq.

Colleagues who have provided valuable insights on specific issues are William Adams IV, John Amboian, Bill Fitzgerald, Benjamin Fulton, Larry Martin, Timothy Schwertfeger, and Paul Williams.

Tina Lazarian not only searched the Internet for data and citations, she analyzed and digested data and provided a host of editorial suggestions. Without her help, the book would not exist. Stacey Morales provided invaluable help on production of some of this material when I was at the American Stock Exchange, and my Nuveen colleagues James Kearney and Dorothy Anderson provided important assistance at critical points.

My daughters, Gayle and Nicole, provided invaluable research assistance and editorial commentary, including assistance on the content and structure of the exhibits.

I owe a special debt to my wife, Nancy. She tolerated, with reasonable grace, the time I committed to this project and the limitations it forced on other activities. I am reasonably sure that she would have been tolerant if I had delayed past the deadline she set for me to pack up the book materials that have dominated our dining room for the past year. Prudence suggests that her tolerance is something I do not need to be absolutely sure about.

Gary L. Gastineau
Thanksgiving Eve, 2001

Table of Contents

Chapter 1

Introduction

The purpose of this book is to help a wide range of investors use "open-end" exchange-traded funds (ETFs) intelligently and effectively. Even before I began work on this project, it was clear that the book had to be more than a detailed description of "open-end" exchange-traded funds and how they worked. It had to do more than highlight the principal characteristics of these funds and explain why they have become the most popular new investment vehicle for individual investors in the past half-century. (The decisions of Vanguard and other conventional mutual fund managers to add exchange-traded share classes to existing index funds will help ensure that a high rate of growth in ETF assets and trading volume continues.) The principal objectives of this book are to help the reader (1) to understand the reasons for ETF growth and, more importantly, (2) to use ETFs profitably. In this Introduction we focus on the investor's need for help on three topics that will recur throughout the book: asset allocation and risk management, taxation and financial planning, and ETF selection and evaluation.

THE CHANGING STRUCTURE OF THE FINANCIAL SERVICES INDUSTRY

The early development and growth of "open-end" exchange-traded funds coincided with a period of dramatic change in the financial markets. Part of the reason for the success of ETFs has been that they are a favorite toy of the poster child of the financial market revolution: the on-line trader.[1] Share prices near or over $100 on some of the most successful funds and tight bid-asked spreads in a period of high share-price volatility have made ETFs a compelling choice for the on-line trader who pays only nominal per share brokerage commissions and—correctly—sees the percentage bid-asked spread

1

as his principal transaction cost. High (and highly visible) trading volume, competitive market makers, and active arbitrage pricing, often enhanced by the presence of related derivative products, have made ETFs a logical and sensible choice for active traders and any-one else who wants to participate in short-term stock price moves. At the other end of the trading spectrum, long-term investors have become increasingly sensitive to the issue of fund tax efficiency after large taxable capital gains distributions by conventional mutual funds in the wake of the strong equity markets of the 1990s and the weak markets of 2000 and 2001. The better-managed[2] "open-end" ETFs have succeeded in keeping most of their share-holders' capital gains in unrealized and, hence, tax-deferred form. Both short- and long-term investors are attracted by the low expense ratios of these funds, which are largely a result of eliminating unnecessary shareholder accounting at the fund level.

But there is a disturbing side to the ETF story. An important feature of recent markets is the relative isolation of many individual investors. Since the introduction of negotiated commissions in 1975, we have seen a steady change in brokerage firm economics from the fee-for-service model (i.e., the traditional commission charge) to an earnings model for many financial firms that is based on fees for assets gathered. Payments made to brokers for customer order flow have often been more valuable to the traditional broker than the small remaining brokerage commission.[3] Increasingly, the advisor or repre-sentative who has been the investor's contact with a full-service bro-kerage firm shares in a fee linked to the value of the assets in an account. This asset-based charge may be in the form of a service fee associated with a traditional equity or money market fund, or a WRAP fee, where the investor pays an asset-based fee in return for the right to make trades or receive advice without a commission on each transaction. The asset-gathering and the account-servicing func-tions may be handled by different employees of a firm. Employees often work in teams to coordinate customer service. If coordination among team members is not done well, an investor's relationship with important members of the team may be transitory and unsatisfying.

The discount and deep-discount brokerage model where the SEC-registered firm employee has become an order taker or account statement troubleshooter often eliminates any relationship an investor might have with an individual who would have been a financial advisor or consultant in a full-service brokerage firm. The investor using a discount broker may place orders with an anonymous telephone voice. In this case, the relationship is remote and purely transactional. Aggressive on-line traders may enter orders on a screen without any human contact at all in the order entry process, making trading an extremely solitary activity. Commissions are very low, making transactions appear very cheap. In a low-transaction-cost environment, it is easy to overlook some of the risk exposures linked to more active trading.

As their stock positions turn over more quickly in response to lower trading costs, active traders need a greater understanding of personal risk management and a relationship with someone whose knowledge of markets and securities is complementary to their own. They need this support more than ever before. But, just as the need for interaction is increasing, changing industry economics make appropriate personal/business relationships harder to achieve and maintain.

The information resources of the Internet are often cited as a replacement for the broker-client relationship; but the investor needs to digest and apply information, not just obtain it. Information is not wisdom. ETFs put the power of instant diversification into the hands of investors who need the context of Harry Markowitz's Nobel Prize–winning work to understand the significance of diversification and tools like those William Sharpe, another Nobel Laureate, has developed for his firm, Financial Engines, to put diversification, asset allocation, and risk management to work for them.[4]

Far more people should, and will, be using these exchange-traded funds than are using them today. But one purpose of this book is to provide a broader perspective and a more useful frame of reference for the risks and rewards of common investment strategies and tactics. This volume is designed to be a useful companion for the on-line trader as well as the long-term investor, but it is not a substitute for regular interaction with a mentor/advisor/alter ego with an appropriately complementary skill set to the trader's or investor's own areas of competence.

The mutual fund revolution centered on ETFs has just begun. Many new variations on the exchange-traded fund theme will appear over the next few years. The opportunity for investors to earn improved after-tax returns and to create tax-efficient risk-reward patterns not possible with other financial instruments makes the case for ETFs compelling relative to conventional funds. In subsequent chapters, we will take a brief look at the history and early development of the prototype products that evolved into the "open-end" exchange-traded fund. We will examine the critically important investment characteristics of the existing exchange-traded funds. Most of these characteristics will still be key features of the new ETF products under development. We will discuss these funds in the context of dramatic changes in financial market structure and in the way investors interact with the markets and with each other. In this context, we will look at changing profit models for financial institutions as they affect the individual investor. We will look at the "maturation" of the index fund revolution. The existing "open-end" exchange-traded funds are, after all, equity index funds. We will see that indexing has at least a few more generations of development ahead. Reports of indexing's full maturity, let alone its demise, are off the mark; but some radical changes need to be made to keep faith with the principles behind the development of index funds. On the other hand, ETF offerings will soon encompass far more than index funds, and we look as carefully as possible at the shape of future funds.

This introductory chapter includes brief examinations of several of the eternal verities of investing. One purpose in discussing these often-neglected core principles of investing is that they can help the new on-line investor as much as they have helped institutional investors improve after-tax returns and control risks. An important purpose in introducing these topics is to emphasize every investor's need for qualified interactive advice and support from appropriate investment experts. After a brief discussion of the changing economics of share trading, we will turn to an illustration of some of the things every investor needs to know about asset allocation, taxation, and fund selection—and how knowledge of these topics should be integrated into an ETF investment program.

This relatively high-level investment policy discussion is designed to persuade every investor who correctly perceives the attractiveness of "open-end" exchange-traded funds that venturing into the financial arena without readily available, high-quality assistance and support is like an early Christian volunteering to go unarmed into a Roman arena with a pride of hungry lions. It requires more faith than most of us are able to muster. Investors and speculative traders alike can enhance their probabilities of success and approach the market with greater confidence if they are backed by a solid, high-quality support network. This network, centered on an investment advisor, will provide the investor with help in evaluating the characteristics and relative attractiveness of the exchange-traded funds offered in the market. The network will provide a frame of reference for personal risk management with positions structured to take advantage of the tax treatment accorded different financial instruments held in different types of accounts. Many readers will find some elements of this discussion familiar, but thinking about these elements from the perspective of the investor in "open-end" exchange-traded funds should be both interesting and useful.

THE ECONOMICS OF SHARE TRADING

Exhibit 1-1 illustrates the change in a typical retail investor's common stock transaction costs since the elimination of fixed commissions in 1975. Over a period of 25 years, the cost of trading 100 shares of a typical $40 stock declined by more than 75%.

In 1975, trading volume on the New York Stock Exchange was an average of 18.5 million shares per day. For the year 2000, New York Stock Exchange volume averaged 1,041,600,000 shares per day, an increase of more than 50 times since 1975.[5]

Exhibit 1-1: Comparison of Stock Transactions (Per Share/Pre-1975 versus 2000)

Assume a share price of $40 (The share price mattered in commission calculations before 1975) and a trade of 100 shares

	Pre-1975	2000
Commissions (round trip)	$0.78	$0.16
Typical Bid-Asked Spread	$0.25	$0.09
Total Transaction Cost:	$1.03	$0.25

Individual investor commissions are assumed to be $8.00 per side in 2000. This is the extreme low end for 100 shares, but many discount brokers charge a fixed dollar amount for any trade up to 5,000 shares, or sometimes more.

Two features of these cost and volume numbers are most significant. First, buying and selling shares over a relatively short time with a reasonable probability of profit after transaction costs is a far more attractive idea in 2002 than it was in 1975. The cost of the 100-share trade in 1975 was over 2.5% of the value of the trade, and the cost of the trade in 2000 was only a quarter of that, or about 0.625% of the value of the trade. This comparison is based on and limited to small trades. The cost of large institutional trades, which have a market impact beyond the quoted bid-asked spread, has not declined as much.[6] The second point of significance is that, using the figures in Exhibit 1-1 as an approximation, NYSE consolidated total trading revenue (volume times total net customer cost per share) in the year 2000 was more than 13½ times the total trading revenue for 1975. This increase suggests that revenues of stock market–oriented financial institutions have grown substantially over the period. Wall Street has learned to cut prices and make it up on volume. Arguably, both the financial institution and its individual investor/customer should be better off in the new environment.

Corresponding to the development of the modern, increasingly electronic market place has been the growth of portfolio indexation. Promoted by a small number of firms and a large number of journalists—and championed most vocally by John Bogle, Founder-Chairman of Vanguard, and Burton Malkiel, Princeton professor and author of *A Random Walk Down Wall Street*—indexing has become almost a mantra for many investors. Some inconsistency between the active day trading of exchange-traded index funds and the cost-saving, long-term investing focus of most indexation literature is not necessarily a cause for great concern. ETFs are not the first financial instrument to appeal to both conservative and aggressive investors. The focus on one or more diversified stock index funds as the repositories for a large fraction of an individual's portfolio has great merit, but the admonition to invest in an index fund is an incomplete lesson in the findings of modern portfolio theory and risk management. Bogle, Malkiel, and other supporters of indexing have long and correctly argued that widespread emphasis on the Standard & Poor's 500 Stock Index as the index of choice is greatly overdone. As most advocates of diversification have argued, an investor should have exposure to smaller companies, to foreign equity markets, and to domestic asset classes like fixed income not represented in the S&P 500. Additional asset classes can provide useful diversification and improve a portfolio's risk/return structure. Diversifying an equity portfolio beyond the S&P 500 and moderating the downside of equities with debt instruments can lead to a better risk-adjusted return and, in some circumstances, a better average long-term return. Although the S&P 500 is the traditional index for broad market U.S. index funds, we will find in Chapter 6 that the S&P 500 is actually not a particularly good template for an index fund. Nonetheless, we use it occasionally to illustrate risk-reward trade-offs and some of the benefits of diversification.

DIVERSIFICATION AND RISK/RETURN TRADE-OFFS

A simple example of an improved risk-reward structure with diversification will illustrate the value of diversification in improving an investor's compound rate of return. Exhibit 1-2 illustrates the risk and compound rates of return of several types of portfolios over the 20-year period 1981–2000. The top line shows results for a portfolio with a varying mix from 100% long-term municipal bonds (lower-left end of the line) to 100% in the S&P 500 (upper-right end of the line). The lower line shows a similar relationship for a portfolio with a mix varying from 100% long-term Treasury bonds (lower left) to 100% in the S&P 500 (upper right). After-tax return is measured on the vertical (y) axis and risk or standard deviation of return is measured on the horizontal (x) axis.

We want to make two key points with this diagram:

1. An investor who has all his investments in bonds can improve his expected return materially and simultaneously reduce risk by replacing, say, 20% of the bonds with equities.

2. An investor who has all her investments in equities can materially reduce risk without much sacrifice in expected return by replacing some of the equities with bonds.

Exhibit 1-2: The Risk-Return Trade-Off of Bonds and Stocks in the United States (1981–2000)

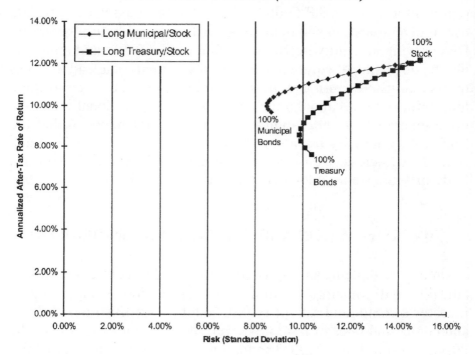

Methodology:

All investment income generated by the portfolio is reinvested, along with the after-tax proceeds of the 20% annualized turnover rate. The allocation between the two assets is allowed to roam within a 5% band around its target before re-balancing. Investment income was taxed at representative rates of an individual earning $100,000 in 2000 dollars; with net capital gains deducted at the rate appropriate for the period. At the end of 2000, the portfolios were fully liquidated to recognize the existing tax liability. The asset class returns were proxied by the returns of representative indices.

MUNICIPAL BONDS: Lehman Brothers Long Municipal Index
TREASURY BONDS: Lehman Brothers Long Treasury Index
S&P 500 STOCKS: Ibbotson Associates Large Company Stock Index

---

The efficient frontiers of attainable portfolios, which the curved lines in Exhibit 1-2 illustrate, measure the effect of diversification on risk-return enhancement. This trade-off is the first of a number of features we will use to illustrate the need most investors have for outside help—in this case help in evaluating the scope of diversification and risk control that is appropriate for the investor's attitude toward risk. The help need not be in the form of a complex mathematical model. It can easily be based on the experience and common sense of a trusted financial counselor who has helped other investors deal with diversification and risk management decisions in the past.

The fact that fixed-income securities add diversification because of imperfect correlation between bond risk and returns and the risk and returns in an equity portfolio suggests that most investors should have some exposure to longer-term bonds. This does not mean that short-term borrowings to lever a portfolio are necessarily bad. However, the astute investor should keep the effect of leverage in mind because it increases the possibility of catastrophic loss and becomes counterproductive at some level. Most aggressive traders have heard stories of on-line traders whose brokers sold out their securities without even giving them notice of the need to meet a margin call. While this may be an extreme example of the opportunities for ruin, the accompanying graph of compound returns from 12% and 20% arithmetic returns at various standard deviation (risk or volatility) levels illustrates the effect of return volatility on long-term investment results.

Exhibit 1-2 (Continued)
Effective Marginal Federal Rates on Income and Capital Gains, 1981–2000[1]

Year(s)	Marginal Rate on Income	Effective Marginal Rate on Capital Gains
1981	63.0%	25.2%
1982–83	50.0	20.0
1984–86	48.0	19.2
1987	39.0	28.0
1988–90	39.0	28.0
1991–96	31.0	28.0
1997	31.0	28.0–22.0[2]
1998–2000	31.0	20.0

[1] These historical tax rates before 1997 were obtained from the 1998 version of the Commerce Clearing House Inc.—Standard Federal Tax Reporter and are representative of those experienced by an investor who earned $100,000 in 2000 dollars throughout the period.
[2] The Taxpayer Relief Act of 1997 imposed tax rates of 20% on long-term capital gains and 28% on intermediate-term gains. Beginning in May, when the Act became effective, the 22% rate represented a composite of the two rates, given recent market performance and portfolio activity rate. In 1998, the intermediate bracket was eliminated.
Source: Harper (2001)

Exhibit 1-3: The Effect of Volatility on the Compound Return of a Portfolio

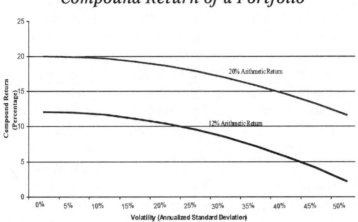

Assumption: Arithmetic return is compounded annually for 40 years. Results are not very sensitive to use of a shorter period or a higher compounding frequency.

Source: Richard Michaud

Most investors who are familiar with the implied standard deviations imbedded in the prices of options and with the levels of volatility reported for many underlying stocks and portfolios in the markets of recent years will recognize that annualized standard deviations in the range of 30% to 50% were common for equity positions in some recent years. When volatility gets this high, the risk increases that substantial losses cannot be recouped even in the long run. As the right-hand side of the graph shows, the compound return at high levels of volatility drops sharply. The 20% average return provides a compound return of less than 12% at a 50% volatility and the 12% average return gives a compound (or geometric) return of only slightly more than 2% at a 50% volatility level. Volatilities of individual stocks and portfolios of stocks with similar risk characteristics often measure over 50%. The technology stock–heavy NASDAQ 100 index and the QQQ ETF based on it have traded at 50% volatility levels for long stretches in recent years. Regardless of one's average return expectations, this high risk level reduces longer-term expected returns. Actually, the risk is greatest with single stocks or baskets of highly correlated stocks like the technology-based QQQs because a catastrophic loss can nearly eliminate the chance to recover in the long run.

To recapitulate, the point of this graph is that, beyond a certain point, leverage and volatility *reduce* expected return to the vanishing point. This graph is based on the return pattern of a diversified portfolio. Single stocks, like some of the dot-coms, had recorded volatilities off the right side of the graph, and their prices dropped so far that recovery is hard to imagine in some cases. Simple tools to measure diversification—and, hence, the concentration of risk—can improve long-term return expectations and reduce risk.[7]

TAX-EFFICIENT INVESTING AND FINANCIAL PLANNING

Professional financial counselors regularly point out to their clients that most investors have at least two kinds of accounts with two very different tax structures: their personal account where long-term capital gains, particularly unrealized long-term capital gains that can be deferred indefinitely, are the most valuable form of investment return, and deferred-taxation retirement accounts, such as 401(k)s and IRAs, where all returns are tax-deferred until the investor makes a withdrawal from the account. When money is withdrawn from the retirement account, it is all taxed at ordinary income rates, the same rates that apply to dividends and interest for most taxpayers.[8]

The significance of this two-account tax model is that all investors should plan the investment asset distribution between *at least* these two types of accounts.[9] A long-term investor who uses ETFs but trades only rarely should have some of his equity investments in his taxable personal account where they have the opportunity for a favorably taxed long-term capital gain *and the possibility of deferring realization of that gain indefinitely.* Fixed-income positions, unless they are tax-advantaged like a municipal bond portfolio, should be in a tax-deferred retirement account because the return from a taxable fixed-income instrument or portfolio compounds untaxed in these accounts until the investor begins to make withdrawals, typically after retirement. An active trader, whether she uses ETFs or individual stocks, might do better by trading equities in a tax-deferred account because long-term capital gains will be rare and, in any event, quickly realized and taxed. If the equity-trading account uses all the assets in the retirement account(s), she should usually hold any remaining fixed-income positions as tax-exempt bonds in her taxable account.[10]

As the table in Exhibit 1-4 illustrates, the economics of a tax-deferred account such as an IRA, 401(k) or other qualified defined contribution retirement plan are often very different from the economics of a taxable account. The tax rates assumed in Exhibit 1-4 are the current top brackets for an individual investor. These rates—including the estate tax rate—are scheduled to change dramatically and in both directions over the next 10 years. Many readers will be subject to lower rates and/or state and city income taxes and some readers will have special concerns like an outsized position in the stock of their present or a former employer in either a tax-deferred or taxable account that affects the risk and tax characteristics of their entire portfolio and constrains their asset allocation decisions. The variations among investors in their risk exposures and tax concerns is too diverse to cover adequately here, but this exhibit does illustrate a number of interesting features of tax-deferred and taxable accounts that are of general interest to users of ETFs.

As the numbers in line (a) indicate, an investor in the top tax bracket will have to earn about $16,556 to pay federal taxes and have $10,000 left over to go into a taxable investment account. As line (e) indicates, the tax on the deferred income (and its investment gains) will usually be higher than taxes paid on distributions from the taxable account when the assets of the deferred account are distributed after retirement. Some of the gains in the taxable account are taxed as long-term capital gains and the original basis of the investment and accumulated dividends have already been taxed. The advantage of the deferred account is in compounding the pre-tax contribution for many years before taxes must be paid.[11] Ordinarily, an investor should elect to defer the tax on as much income as possible for as long as possible to let returns compound tax free. It usually makes sense to take full advantage of tax-deferred retirement plans.

Exhibit 1-4: *Simplified Tax Effects of Savings and Distributions— Tax-Deferred and Taxable Accounts*

| | Tax-Deferred Accounts | | | | | | Taxable Accounts | | |
| | Corporate Bonds | | Equities | | Municipal Bonds | | Equities | | |
Description of Step	Amount	Tax Rate	Amount	Tax Rate	Amount	Tax Rate	Amount		Tax Rate
Accumulation									
(a) Pretax Salary to Make $10,000 Contribution to Account	$10,000	0.0%	$10,000	0.0%	$16,556	39.6%	$16,556		39.6%
(b) Available to Invest	$10,000	0.0%	$10,000	0.0%	$10,000	0.0%	$10,000		
(c) Average Annual Return on $10,000 Pre-tax	$650	0.0%	$1,000	0.0%	$500	0.0%	$1,000		
(d) After Tax	$650	0.0%	$1,000	0.0%	$500	0.0%	$91	Dividends	39.6%
							up to $680	LTCG	20.0%
							up to $850	Unrealized capital gains	0.0%
Distribution									
(e) Needed to Provide $10,000 After Tax	$16,556	39.6%	$16,556	39.6%	$10,000	0.0%	$10,000	Principal	0.0%
							$16,556	Dividends	39.6%
							$12,500	LTCG	20.0%
Residual— To Distribute $10,000 to Next Generation									
(f) Pre-Estate Tax	$36,791	55.0%	$36,791	55.0%	$22,222	55.0%	$22,222		55.0%
(g) Pre-Income Tax	$16,556	39.6%	$16,556	39.6%	$10,000	0.0%	$10,000		0.0%
(h) Available to Beneficiary	$10,000	0.0%	$10,000	0.0%	$10,000	0.0%	$10,000		0.0%

Federal Taxes only: Income Tax   39.6%
                        LT Cap Gains   20.0%

Assumed Returns: Corporate Bonds: 6.5%
                     Municipal Bonds: 5.0%
                     Equities Dividends: 1.5%
                     Capital Gains: 8.5%
                     Equities Total: 10.0%
                     Inflation Rate: 3.4%

High-tax-bracket investors usually have *relatively* fewer of their assets in longer term tax-deferred accounts like 401(k)s and IRAs than middle-income taxpayers, simply because of the contribution limits imposed by the tax code. Even if a taxpayer does not plan to live off these tax-deferred accounts, they offer a limited safety net that even a wealthy investor should use; they can shelter some income from taxation and they can increase the value of a charitable contribution after the deaths of the taxpayer and spouse. Because of the limit on annual contributions, the relative value of the tax shelter provided by these accounts is not as great to a high-tax-bracket investor as to an investor who is not subject to the top estate tax bracket. Unless an additional shelter mechanism is added, the combination of the estate tax and the income tax on distributions makes it difficult to pass much of the value of these accounts to the next generation. To see this, look at the cost of passing tax-deferred account assets to the next generation (lines (f), (g), and (h) of Exhibit 1-4).

An interesting feature of allocating investments between taxable and tax-deferred accounts is the sensitivity of the decision to the tax treatment of the positions involved. There is very different tax treatment of taxable equity positions (lines (d) and (e) of Exhibit 1-4) depending on holding period and ability to defer realization of long-term capital gains. It can be important to allocate assets and trading strategies carefully between taxable and tax-deferred accounts. In general, an active equity-trading account that is even modestly successful should be in a tax-deferred account if possible. Even an account that realizes only long-term gains should be on the tax-deferred side relative to a portfolio that accumulates *unrealized* long-term gains. Unrealized long-term gains are relatively more valuable in a taxable account (lines (d), (e), (f), and (g)). If equity returns are high, the ability of well-managed ETFs to defer capital gains taxes indefinitely is extremely valuable to high-bracket investors because of the tax reduction during their lifetime and the value to their heirs of the step up in basis of the fund shares.[12]

Most investors have an intuitive grasp of the value of putting long-term equity investments in a personal account where the tax advantage of deferred long-term capital gains can be significant and putting taxable fixed-income positions in retirement accounts. The correct allocation policy for an investor who uses ETFs or other funds as well as individual stocks is a function of fund type and tax management policy and the investor's trading style. It is clear that investors as a group do not pay enough attention to where they carry various asset classes. Many investors need expert advice on the nuances of taxation and the tax-efficient location of investment positions.

This discussion centered on Exhibit 1-4 does not address the employee stock options and employer stock holdings in many investors' accounts. Even after the market decline from early 2000 levels, many of these stock positions dominate investors' net worth calculations, frustrate attempts at diversification and inhibit tax planning. ETFs are one logical answer to the question of what to do with whatever cash an investor can extract from these dominant positions, but the investor needs specialized advice on how to manage the diversification and tax issues these positions present. Many investors who do not have large positions in their employer's shares have made successful investments in one or a few stocks that now dominate their portfolios. In general, the older and more successful an investor, the more difficult it is to achieve and maintain a diversified portfolio without paying some capital gains taxes. Some advisors specialize in the needs of such investors. Appropriate solutions vary greatly, but an investor in this circumstance should spare no more than a few moments for self-congratulations on the skill or good fortune that led to this "problem" before addressing possible paths to increased diversification and risk reduction that can be followed without a substantial tax penalty.[13]

As an exercise in integrating some of these observations about asset allocation, risk, taxation, and compound interest, we turn to Exhibit 1-5, which examines some of the choices an affluent 30-year-old couple might make in saving and investing for retirement. Readers are encouraged to consider additional scenarios, but we focus here on a small number of cases with financially significant differences. Our choices of scenarios reflect issues we will raise elsewhere in the book. Our investors—a married couple, both of whom are employed—earn real (inflation-adjusted) pre-tax income of $350,000 per year after saving an inflation-adjusted $50,000 per year, pre-tax. Some of this $50,000 usually goes into tax-deferred accounts and some into taxable accounts after the necessary taxes have been paid on it. In our base scenarios, we use the tax rates and asset class returns from Exhibit 1-4. Ignoring such major outlays as the cost of college educations and investment/expenditure combinations like residential real estate, we assume each year's savings are invested in a specified split between tax-deferred and taxable accounts and that nothing is withdrawn for 35 years. At age 65, they begin to withdraw funds (in a tax-efficient way) to obtain an after-tax income equivalent to 80% of their disposable real income during their working careers. All asset choices and placements are appropriate to an account's tax status, e.g., municipal bonds in taxable accounts.

Exhibit 1-5 covers four pages and takes the initial income tax and long-term capital gains rates of 39.6 and 20.0%, respectively, from the bottom of Exhibit 1-4, combined with the average return assumptions for each asset from Exhibit 1-4. We assume corporate bonds will return an average of 6.5%, municipal bonds an average of 5.0%, and equities an average total of 10.0% consisting of 1.5% from dividends and 8.5% from realized or unrealized capital gains.

Table 1 of Exhibit 1-5 shows the expected results of seven different savings and investment plans. As noted, we assume that our married couple saves the equivalent of $50,000 out of their annual pre-tax income. The first number filled in under the various scenario headings in Exhibit 1-5, Table 1, shows the percentage of that $50,000 annual pre-tax amount allocated to tax-deferred accounts. About 50% of the gross savings of $50,000 is the maximum that this couple could allocate to such tax-deferred accounts under current tax laws, but there is reason to believe that the maximum contribution will continue to escalate over the long term, as it does under current law.

Scenarios A and B assume that none of the savings are placed in tax-deferred accounts; Scenarios C, D, and E assume that 25% of the available total is placed in tax-deferred accounts, and Scenarios F and G assume that 50% of the total is placed in tax-deferred accounts. The second line under each scenario shows the equity/debt mixture in each account. The mix ranges from 100% equities and nothing in debt in Scenarios A, C, and F to 40% equities and 60% in debt securities in Scenario E. The next three lines show the equity return volatility at 17.5% annually and the return volatility (standard deviation of return) for municipal bonds and taxable bonds at 4.9% and 5.5%, respectively.

Exhibit 1-5: Impact of Taxation and Equity Return Levels on the Results of Savings and Investment Plans

Table 1: 10% Average Annual Equity Returns

	Scenario A	Scenario B	Scenario C	Scenario D	Scenario E	Scenario F	Scenario G
Percentage of Savings– Tax Deferred	0	0	25	25	25	50	50
Equity/Debt Mix	100%/0%	70%/30%	100%/0%	70%/30%	40%/60%	100%/0%	70%/30%
Equity Return Volatility (ann. std. dev.)	17.5%	17.5%	17.5%	17.5%	17.5%	17.5%	17.5%
Debt Return Volatility							
Municipal	4.9%	4.9%	4.9%	4.9%	4.9%	4.9%	4.9%
Taxable	5.5%	5.5%	5.5%	5.5%	5.5%	5.5%	5.5%
10% Return—No gain realization before retirement							
Year 35 Account Value (in millions)							
5 Percentile	$3.45	$2.73	$4.08	$3.81	$3.48	$4.70	$4.93
50 Percentile	9.61	5.73	11.39	8.09	6.21	13.23	10.52
95 Percentile	24.07	11.07	28.85	15.73	10.16	33.63	20.41
Probability of having assets after							
10 years retirement	86.2%	68.8%	88.0%	81.8%	68.0%	89.6%	89.4%
20 years retirement	62.0%	27.6%	66.6%	47.6%	16.4%	70.8%	60.2%
25 years retirement	56.4%	18.6%	60.6%	37.4%	8.6%	64.0%	51.6%
10% Return—Realizing gains over 5 years							
Year 35 Account Value (in millions)							
5 Percentile	$3.15	$2.59	$3.84	$3.72	$3.42	$4.54	$4.88
50 Percentile	8.05	5.10	10.26	7.69	6.03	12.34	10.28
95 Percentile	18.21	9.21	24.08	14.36	9.74	30.24	19.55
Probability of having assets after							
10 years retirement	84.2%	65.4%	87.2%	80.0%	67.2%	89.0%	89.0%
20 years retirement	57.0%	20.0%	62.6%	32.4%	8.2%	70.4%	59.8%
25 years retirement	47.2%	12.4%	57.2%	23.6%	1.8%	62.0%	50.6%
10% Return —Realizing gains each year as long-term capital gains							
Year 35 Account Value (in millions)							
5 Percentile	$2.99	$2.44	$3.73	$3.63	$3.36	$4.46	$4.83
50 Percentile	7.05	4.65	9.48	7.32	5.88	11.85	9.97
95 Percentile	14.48	8.02	21.52	13.51	9.43	28.58	18.91
Probability of having assets after							
10 years retirement	80.0%	58.8%	86.0%	78.2%	64.6%	88.2%	88.6%
20 years retirement	49.8%	12.8%	60.4%	40.4%	13.6%	67.0%	58.6%
25 years retirement	38.4%	6.4%	52.8%	29.6%	6.0%	60.8%	48.6%
10% Return—Realizing gains each year as short-term capital gains							
Year 35 Account Value (in millions)							
5 Percentile	$2.68	$2.24	$3.51	$3.51	$3.28	$4.31	$4.74
50 Percentile	5.56	3.90	8.40	6.79	5.57	11.19	9.60
95 Percentile	10.13	6.19	18.12	12.12	8.76	26.31	18.02
Probability of having assets after							
10 years retirement	70.4%	34.2%	80.0%	74.4%	56.4%	87.0%	87.0%
20 years retirement	23.4%	1.0%	52.2%	29.8%	7.2%	62.4%	55.0%
25 years retirement	14.4%	0.6%	43.4%	21.2%	2.8%	56.8%	43.8%

The first series of numbers in the body of the table shows the range of assets accumulated over a 35-year accumulation period for that scenario with an average 10% pre-tax return on the equity positions and with no capital gains realized in the taxable account. Keep in mind that we have assumed an inflation rate of 3.4%; so the nominal amount of each year's contribution grows by 3.4% each year. The spread between the fifth and 95th percentile accumulation totals simply reflects the range of possible outcomes after 35 years, given the relatively typical 17.5% annualized standard deviation for the equity return and the equally typical annualized standard deviations for the fixed-income returns. Clearly, with an average return of 10%, the amount of money accumulated at the end of 35 years could be relatively small or quite large depending upon whether individual annual returns ended up closer to the 5% or the 95% percentile level. The second set of numbers under the assumption of 10% equities/zero gains realization in the taxable account shows the probability that the investors will have assets left for future use after 10 years of retirement on the assumption that they take money out to provide 80% of their working years' real disposable income during retirement.

In one specific case, Scenario G has a 50% allocation to tax-deferred accounts, a 70%/30% equity/fixed-income split, a 17.5% standard deviation of the equity return, and 4.9% and 5.5% annualized standard deviations for municipal and taxable debt returns, respectively. The 5% percentile value of the portfolio after 35 years is $4.93 million, and the 95% percentile level is $20.41 million. The 50th percentile is $10.52 million. After the 35th year, we assume that the investors retire and begin living off their retirement accounts. What becomes important at this point is: What is the probability that they will have assets remaining in their retirement accounts after a specific number of years of retirement? To state the issue in a traditional way, what is the probability that they will not run out of money?

Under the assumption of 10% equity return/no taxable gains until withdrawals begin, there is an 89.4% probability that they will have assets remaining in the account for future withdrawals after a retirement period of 10 years. At 20 years after retirement, there is a 60.2% chance they will have assets remaining, and after 25 years of retirement, there is still a 51.6% chance of assets remaining. It is useful to keep an eye on the changes in these percentages as we look at changes in the assumptions.

The remaining groups of numbers as we go down the columns on Table 1 of Exhibit 1-5 show identical changes of assumptions for each column. The change is in the capital gains tax assumption for the equities in the taxable account. The second set of numbers assumes realization of all available long-term capital gains every five years. The third set assumes that all long-term capital gains are realized annually as soon as the gain goes long term to take advantage of the 20% tax rate. The fourth set of numbers in each column assumes that all transactions in the taxable account are executed by a short-term trader, and none of the gains benefit from the 20% long-term gains tax rate. In a comparison of either the value of the portfolios at the end of 35 years of accumulation or a comparison of the percentages associated with the probability of having assets left after a consistent number of years of retirement, there is a decrease in both numbers as the tax efficiency of the portfolios declines and taxes consume a larger portion of the gains. To examine just one example in detail, for Scenario F, the 50th percentile assets at the 35-year mark drops from $13.23 million in the no-taxable-gains case to $11.19 million in the short-term gains tax case.

The second page of Exhibit 1-5 is based on identical assumptions relative to comparable positions on page 1 with the exception of the fact that we assume an 8% average equity return, 1.5% from dividends and 6.5% from capital gains—realized or unrealized as the case requires. The relatively small apparent difference between the 10% and 8% return has a very significant impact on the value of the portfolio in various cases at the 35-year retirement point and after periods of 10, 20, or 25 years.

Exhibit 1-5 (Continued)
Table 2: 8% Average Annual Equity Returns

	Scenario A	Scenario B	Scenario C	Scenario D	Scenario E	Scenario F	Scenario G
Percentage of Savings— Tax Deferred	0	0	25	25	25	50	50
Equity/Debt Mix	100%/0%	70%/30%	100%/0%	70%/30%	40%/60%	100%/0%	70%/30%
Equity Return Volatility (ann. std. dev.)	17.5%	17.5%	17.5%	17.5%	17.5%	17.5%	17.5%
Debt Return Volatility							
Municipal	4.9%	4.9%	4.9%	4.9%	4.9%	4.9%	4.9%
Taxable	5.5%	5.5%	5.5%	5.5%	5.5%	5.5%	5.5%
8% Return—No gain realization before retirement							
Year 35 Account Value (in millions)							
5 Percentile	$2.32	$2.04	$2.73	$2.85	$2.78	$3.14	$3.67
50 Percentile	6.43	4.28	7.59	6.07	5.08	8.77	7.88
95 Percentile	16.05	8.37	19.16	11.90	8.32	22.27	15.34
Probability of having assets after							
10 years retirement	65.8%	39.8%	68.6%	59.4%	38.8%	73.0%	73.2%
20 years retirement	32.6%	7.0%	37.2%	17.0%	3.6%	42.2%	32.2%
25 years retirement	25.6%	3.4%	29.8%	9.8%	1.4%	33.2%	21.4%
8% Return—Realizing gains over 5 years							
Year 35 Account Value (in millions)							
5 Percentile	$2.24	$2.02	$2.66	$2.83	$2.78	$3.10	$3.67
50 Percentile	5.56	3.97	6.94	5.80	5.00	8.37	7.71
95 Percentile	12.58	7.21	16.35	11.04	8.04	20.36	14.83
Probability of having assets after							
10 years retirement	63.2%	35.8%	67.8%	58.4%	37.6%	72.4%	72.4%
20 years retirement	26.8%	4.2%	33.8%	15.2%	3.4%	39.8%	31.6%
25 years retirement	16.6%	2.2%	25.2%	8.6%	1.2%	32.0%	19.6%
8% Return—Realizing gains each year as long-term capital gains							
Year 35 Account Value (in millions)							
5 Percentile	$2.15	$1.94	$2.61	$2.74	$2.74	$3.06	$3.62
50 Percentile	5.06	3.69	6.52	5.59	4.91	8.08	7.55
95 Percentile	10.60	6.46	14.99	10.41	7.77	19.44	14.44
Probability of having assets after							
10 years retirement	57.6%	30.8%	65.8%	54.2%	36.8%	69.8%	70.8%
20 years retirement	19.2%	3.0%	30.8%	12.4%	3.0%	37.8%	29.6%
25 years retirement	10.6%	1.2%	22.4%	7.0%	1.2%	30.6%	19.2%
8% Return—Realizing gains each year as short-term capital gains							
Year 35 Account Value (in millions)							
5 Percentile	$2.00	$1.82	$2.52	$2.66	$2.70	$3.00	$3.57
50 Percentile	4.31	3.23	5.94	5.30	4.72	7.67	7.31
95 Percentile	7.92	5.18	12.84	9.47	7.33	18.05	13.78
Probability of having assets after							
10 years retirement	41.4%	13.4%	58.2%	45.6%	28.2%	67.2%	69.0%
20 years retirement	4.8%	0.2%	21.8%	8.0%	1.4%	33.8%	25.6%
25 years retirement	3.0%	0.0%	12.2%	4.0%	0.8%	25.8%	12.8%

Exhibit 1-5 (Continued)
Table 3: 12% Average Annual Equity Returns

	Scenario A	Scenario B	Scenario C	Scenario D	Scenario E	Scenario F	Scenario G
Percentage of Savings—Tax Deferred	0	0	25	25	25	50	50
Equity/Debt Mix	100%/0%	70%/30%	100%/0%	70%/30%	40%/60%	100%/0%	70%/30%
Equity Return Volatility (ann. std. dev.)	17.5%	17.5%	17.5%	17.5%	17.5%	17.5%	17.5%
Debt Return Volatility							
Municipal	4.9%	4.9%	4.9%	4.9%	4.9%	4.9%	4.9%
Taxable	5.5%	5.5%	5.5%	5.5%	5.5%	5.5%	5.5%
12% Return—No gain realization before retirement							
Year 35 Account Value (in millions)							
5 Percentile	$5.04	$3.60	$6.03	$5.04	$4.28	$7.00	$6.49
50 Percentile	14.65	7.64	17.40	10.39	7.72	20.13	14.13
95 Percentile	37.39	14.90	44.60	21.62	12.79	51.80	28.44
Probability of having assets after							
10 years retirement	95.0%	86.8%	96.8%	93.2%	85.2%	97.2%	97.2%
20 years retirement	84.4%	58.0%	88.2%	73.6%	42.4%	90.0%	83.6%
25 years retirement	80.6%	48.6%	83.6%	66.0%	30.2%	86.8%	77.8%
12% Return—Realizing gains over 5 years							
Year 35 Account Value (in millions)							
5 Percentile	$4.41	$3.32	$5.55	$4.81	$4.16	$6.64	$6.33
50 Percentile	11.42	6.67	15.08	10.13	7.48	18.65	13.58
95 Percentile	26.39	12.13	36.93	19.62	12.15	46.73	27.09
Probability of having assets after							
10 years retirement	93.8%	84.6%	95.6%	92.6%	84.6%	97.2%	97.2%
20 years retirement	80.2%	49.6%	85.0%	71.6%	41.0%	89.0%	82.4%
25 years retirement	73.8%	38.6%	81.0%	63.4%	29.2%	85.0%	76.0%
12% Return—Realizing gains each year as long-term capital gains							
Year 35 Account Value (in millions)							
5 Percentile	$4.13	$3.09	$5.29	$4.66	$4.07	$6.45	$6.24
50 Percentile	9.71	5.94	13.76	9.62	7.23	17.69	13.31
95 Percentile	20.32	10.25	32.02	18.04	11.69	43.44	26.10
Probability of having assets after							
10 years retirement	92.6%	79.6%	94.6%	92.2%	83.6%	96.8%	96.4%
20 years retirement	75.0%	39.0%	82.6%	69.6%	39.0%	88.2%	81.4%
25 years retirement	67.0%	27.4%	79.0%	60.8%	26.2%	83.4%	75.4%
12% Return—Realizing gains each year as short-term capital gains							
Year 35 Account Value (in millions)							
5 Percentile	$3.51	$2.72	$4.88	$4.45	$3.97	$6.17	$6.02
50 Percentile	7.22	4.71	11.79	8.82	6.75	16.48	12.77
95 Percentile	13.19	7.49	26.56	15.93	10.72	39.79	24.62
Probability of having assets after							
10 years retirement	87.2%	61.6%	93.0%	90.4%	79.6%	95.2%	95.6%
20 years retirement	52.0%	11.0%	77.0%	60.0%	28.6%	85.2%	77.6%
25 years retirement	40.0%	4.2%	69.4%	49.2%	16.2%	80.6%	69.6%

Exhibit 1-5 (Continued)
Table 4: Variation in Average Annual Equity Returns

	Scenario A	Scenario B	Scenario C	Scenario D	Scenario E	Scenario F	Scenario G
Percentage of Savings—Tax Deferred	0	0	25	25	25	50	50
Equity/Debt Mix	100%/0%	70%/30%	100%/0%	70%/30%	40%/60%	100%/0%	70%/30%
Equity Return Volatility (ann. std. dev.)	17.5%	17.5%	17.5%	17.5%	17.5%	17.5%	17.5%
Debt Return Volatility							
Municipal	4.9%	4.9%	4.9%	4.9%	4.9%	4.9%	4.9%
Taxable	5.5%	5.5%	5.5%	5.5%	5.5%	5.5%	5.5%
8% Return—No gain realization before retirement							
Year 35 Account Value (in millions)							
5 Percentile	$2.32	$2.04	$2.73	$2.85	$2.78	$3.14	$3.67
50 Percentile	6.43	4.28	7.59	6.07	5.08	8.77	7.88
95 Percentile	16.05	8.37	19.16	11.90	8.32	22.27	15.34
Probability of having assets after							
10 years retirement	65.8%	39.8%	68.6%	59.4%	38.8%	73.0%	73.2%
20 years retirement	32.6%	7.0%	37.2%	17.0%	3.6%	42.2%	32.2%
25 years retirement	25.6%	3.4%	29.8%	9.8%	1.4%	33.2%	21.4%
10% Return—No gain realization before retirement							
Year 35 Account Value (in millions)							
5 Percentile	$3.45	$2.73	$4.08	$3.81	$3.48	$4.70	$4.93
Median	9.61	5.73	11.39	8.09	6.21	13.23	10.52
95 Percentile	24.07	11.07	28.85	15.73	10.16	33.63	20.41
Probability of having assets after							
10 years retirement	86.2%	68.8%	88.0%	81.8%	68.0%	89.6%	89.4%
20 years retirement	62.0%	27.6%	66.6%	47.6%	16.4%	70.8%	60.2%
25 years retirement	56.4%	18.6%	60.6%	37.4%	8.6%	64.0%	51.6%
12% Return—No gain realization before retirement							
Year 35 Account Value (in millions)							
5 Percentile	$5.04	$3.60	$6.03	$5.04	$4.28	$7.00	$6.49
Median	14.65	7.64	17.40	10.89	7.72	20.13	14.13
95 Percentile	37.39	14.90	44.60	21.62	12.79	51.80	28.44
Probability of having assets after							
10 years retirement	95.0%	86.8%	96.8%	93.2%	85.2%	97.2%	97.2%
20 years retirement	84.4%	58.0%	88.2%	73.6%	42.4%	90.0%	83.6%
25 years retirement	80.6%	48.6%	83.6%	66.0%	30.2%	86.8%	77.8%

The significance of the 8% equity return assumption is that in spite of the market decline since the first quarter of 2000, common stocks are not cheap by historic valuation standards. Arnott and Bernstein (forthcoming) and Arnott and Ryan (2001) make the case that the historic equity risk premium—the incremental return that equity investors have received as compensation for the presumed added risk

of holding equities—is likely to be at or close to zero in the period
ahead. If this assumption is correct and interest rates stay near current
levels, even the assumption of an 8% average pre-tax return on equities is probably too high. In performing analyses of the sort developed
in the tables of Exhibit 1-5, it is not common to include scenarios as
pessimistic as this 8% average equity return, including 3.4% expected
inflation. Nonetheless, if historical *values* of stocks are more meaningful than historical *returns* from stocks, a significant period of
returns in this range or lower is a high-probability scenario.

On the brighter side, the third page of Exhibit 1-5 shows
results with a 12% equity pre-tax return. The difference between 8%
and 10% and, even more, the difference between 8% and 12% average pre-tax equity returns is quite significant both in terms of the
value of the account after 35 years of accumulation and the probability of having assets remaining after various retirement periods.
To provide a clean comparison along the average return dimension,
the most important comparison of this discussion, on the final page
of Exhibit 1-5, assembles the results of the basic 8%, 10%, and 12%
equity return scenarios with no realization of taxable returns during
the accumulation years and gains realization only to facilitate withdrawals during retirement years.

Readers are encouraged to examine the assumptions in these
tables with a view toward their implications for personal retirement
saving. Several observations may be useful to stimulate this examination of the assumptions. First, a 12% average equity return is closest
to 20th century historic results. A more conservative assumption
seems more realistic at today's share values that are still close to the
highs for the past century. Second, the results are quite sensitive to the
assumed average equity return.[14] The 50th percentile accumulation in
Scenario G in Table 4 is $7.88 million with an 8% pre-tax equity
return, $10.52 million with a 10% pre-tax equity return, and $14.13
million with a 12% pre-tax equity return. Third, the results are sensitive to the amount of money allocated to the various asset classes.
Comparing Scenarios F and G in Table 4, the 50th percentile 35-year
accumulation in the 12% pre-tax equity return case in Scenario F is
$20.13 million, versus $14.13 million under the 70.0% equity allocation of Scenario G. If the average pre-tax equity return is only 8%, the

Scenario F average 35-year 50th percentile value is only $8.77 million versus $7.88 million for the lower equity allocation of Scenario G. In the latter case, the lower equity return is more important than the difference in allocation. Fourth, failure to defer the tax on capital gains can be costly, especially if equity returns are high. In the 12% average pre-tax equity return case for Scenario F on Table 3, the 95th percentile value at the end of 35 years is $51.80 million with capital gains taxes deferred as long as possible, versus $43.44 million if gains are allowed to go long term but are realized as soon as they are eligible for the preferential tax rate. The difference here is entirely due to the value of compounding the returns longer before paying the tax.

Our investors clearly plan to maintain a comfortable living standard in retirement. To meet this goal, they are saving a higher fraction of their pre-tax income than most U.S. families. Even with the higher savings rate, the numbers in the accounts after 35 years of accumulation will seem large to most of today's investors—even to those who are in high tax brackets and who have a high net worth. Few 65-year-old retiring couples have a $10 million retirement fund today. The concern one must have in looking at these portfolio values is that they reflect the compounding effect of 3.4% a year in inflation over the next 35 years. Each generation looks at larger income and net worth numbers than its parents, but not necessarily increased buying power. On an inflation-adjusted, standardized basis, the most relevant numbers are clearly the percentage probabilities that the investor will still have assets left after a particular period of retirement.

Investors who have used Financial Engines' or Fidelity's asset allocation software through their 401(k) plans or similar software through other connections will not be particularly surprised at these numbers or relationships. Investors comparing across assumptions in different cases will see that the results are highly sensitive to a number of variables. References to the importance of some of those variables will appear in later chapters.

FUND EVALUATION

Before we examine the use of exchange-traded funds in detail, there is at least one more area where ETF investors need expert advice and support, and that is in the evaluation of competitive exchange-traded fund offerings. Even the rare investor who can handle all the asset allocation, risk management, and tax issues raised here needs help in choosing from the growing number of seemingly similar exchange-traded funds and in evaluating the offerings of various fund management firms.

As this is written, none of the traditional mutual fund services offers a comprehensive ETF evaluation process and/or rating service. In part, this lack of coverage results from the fact that the products are relatively new and different in some important respects from the traditional fund products the advisory firms have dealt with in the past.

Some features of ETFs are relatively easy to evaluate, and others are much more difficult. While we will have much more to say on this issue in later chapters, let's spend a few paragraphs on it now. Our principal purpose here is to illustrate the importance of a comprehensive fund evaluation and—as in our prior examples—the need for expert assistance in this process. The key to a useful and successful fund service will be the service's ability to answer the questions we raise here, while making the output of their evaluation system user-friendly. Investors should not need to think about each of these issues in detail every time they want to initiate a transaction in an exchange-traded fund. The investor may not go through this detailed analysis on a specific fund, but he needs assurance that someone who understands the issues has done the analysis and produced accurate comparative evaluations of the funds considered for investment.

For the long-term taxable investor, the easiest feature to quantify and, in some respects, the most basic characteristic that every "open-end" exchange-traded equity fund should have, is tax efficiency. For fiscal years ending in 2000 or after, no "open-end" exchange-traded fund that holds stakes primarily in U.S.-based common stocks should have to make a material, taxable capital gains distribution. For complex reasons, certain funds specializing in foreign securities might have small capital gains distributions that will be difficult to offset or avoid. Likewise, most fixed-income ETFs will probably distribute some capital gains during a period of interest rate declines. With these exceptions, taxable capital gains distributions in 2000 or later years, should be readily avoidable unless there is a major change in ETF tax treatment.

Index efficiency, or the "fund-friendliness" of the index underlying an "open-end" exchange-traded fund, is probably a greater distinction across funds than tax efficiency and relatively easy to understand. Although we will be discussing this issue at length in Chapter 6, a fund-friendly index will go a long way toward reducing the fund's transaction costs associated with changes in the index composition and increasing the fund's operating efficiency. Some of this may be readily apparent from the fund's financial statements, but other aspects of index efficiency may be more difficult to evaluate. Generally, a fund-friendly index will not serve as a standard performance benchmark. Rather, it will be devised and maintained for the primary purpose of building a fund around it. Other things equal, the efficiency of any fund will benefit from derivatives on the index and on the fund. A variety of derivatives ranging from futures through options on the funds should be available.

The fact that a fund's underlying index is licensed from a well-known index publisher or, alternatively, from some other index developer is not important. For a variety of reasons, the issuer of the fund may have felt a particular index was uniquely useful in achieving the investment objectives sought for the fund. In some cases, indexes have been modified to meet important criteria for fund-friendliness. The degree of investor familiarity with a standard index could be a reason to license such an index rather than create a new fund index if the index brand brings in assets and helps spread the fund's fixed costs over a larger asset base. On the other hand, we will see that the embedded transaction costs in funds based on some well-known indexes make funds using these indexes relatively unattractive.

Another obvious criterion for evaluation of a fund is its lack of correlation and corresponding risk offset when used with other investments, including other ETFs that an investor might hold. For example, a fixed-income fund, a foreign equity fund, or a real estate investment trust (REIT) fund might provide useful diversification for a portfolio that is invested primarily in large capitalization domestic equities, whether the equities are held directly or through another "open-end" exchange-traded fund. One basic piece of information we would expect an advisory service to provide would be a table of correlations between and among the various indexes used as the basis for "open-end" exchange-traded funds.[15]

The very specific characteristics discussed so far can go a long way toward the selection of one fund over another. Beyond risk characteristics and economic efficiency, the evaluation of an "open-end" exchange-traded fund becomes significantly more difficult. The investor may need help from a fund evaluator to understand the market environment where a particular fund might perform particularly well or badly and how a fund may fit into an investor's risk-reward trade-off objectives and traditional investment strategies.

A host of other fund features are amenable to quantitative or qualitative evaluation using some traditional investment tools and some tools that are purpose-built to use the data provided by ETFs. Applying new tools to more extensive data will help to answer questions few have thought to ask about conventional funds because there was no hope of getting a useful answer.

We should be able to get answers about:

Manager quality
• Tax efficiency
• Trading costs
• Stock selection (active funds)

Market quality
• Trading spreads
• Market depth

Total expenses—not just the reported expense ratio
• Trading costs
• Tax efficiency
• Index efficiency

In this brief introduction, we have touched on at least three topics where an investor in exchange-traded funds should consider obtaining some expert assistance: asset allocation and risk management, taxation and financial planning, and fund selection and evaluation. We will examine these and other investor needs in greater depth at appropriate points in our examination of exchange-traded funds and how investors can use them effectively. We will return to a discussion of sources of advice and sources of additional ETF information in Chapter 9 and in the Appendix.

ENDNOTES

1. For an outstanding perspective on this revolution, see Young and Theys (1999).

2. The existing ETFs are index funds and, according to some mythologies, are unmanaged. While fund management techniques are not a principal topic of this book, the comparative performance of rival index funds offers ample evidence that an index fund manager makes important investment decisions. The value of a good manager is enormous, even at an index fund.

3. See Chapter 8 for more detail.

4. Useful citations are Markowitz (1991) and Sharpe (1992 and 1994), but good finance texts like Bodie, Kane, and Marcus (2001) benefit from the passage of time to reflect, clarify, and sometimes simplify the ideas. A very brief discussion of some of the important issues comes up later in this Introduction. One example that illustrates the potential usefulness of this work for the on-line trader is an implication of Markowitz's work on diversification. A diversified portfolio will have a less volatile return than the average stock in the portfolio, but stocks with many risk characteristics in common will not reduce portfolio volatility very much when they are combined. The trader may want volatility if she is buying options or if she is making a short-term trade in the stock and higher volatility increases the possible profit. A reduction in volatility would be desirable if she were selling options. Loeper (2001b) discusses diversification in the context of large positions in low-cost-basis assets. In all cases, knowing what to expect from the different

degrees of diversification that come automatically with each ETF should help an investor makes better decisions.

5. NASDAQ did not exist in anything like its current form in 1975. Adding NASDAQ volume would make the comparisons even more dramatic.

6. In addition to the market impact of a larger trade that moves the mid-point of the bid-asked spread, institutional investors obtained a wide range of services for their fixed commissions before 1975, and some of them receive similar services for "soft dollar commissions" today. The level and nature of the payments and services involved has changed too much to make the resulting transaction costs readily comparable. See Schwartz and Steil (2001) and Wagner (2001).

7. Readers interested in more information on this risk–compound return link should see Gastineau (1988) pp. 310–312, Kritzman (2000) pp. 65–75, and Michaud (1981) for progressively more technical discussions. Other useful volatility discussions are in Wilcox (2001) and Campbell, et al. (2001). The author wishes to thank Richard Michaud for producing the data used in Exhibit 1-3.

8. We ignore the highly attractive, but typically small, Roth IRA accounts in this example.

9. An investor who expects to leave an estate, particularly a taxable estate, will need to consider additional issues such as the opportunity to step up his heirs' tax basis in a low-cost equity position at his death and a variety of trust and insurance products that can help reduce taxes during the investor's lifetime and during the lifetimes of the heirs to the estate.

10. Many analyses of where various assets should be held assign nearly everything but tax-exempt bonds to tax-deferred accounts if they are available. These analyses assume capital gains are hard to defer in an actively managed account or even in an index mutual fund. We will learn in Chapter 4 that a patient investor might defer nearly all capital gains in an ETF.

11. Every investor should thoroughly understand the "magic" of compound interest in building assets. Excellent discussions of compound returns are available, in increasing order of complexity in Wagner and Winnikoff(2001); Bogle (1999), (2001a), and (2001b); and Kritzman (2000).

12. The on-and-off character of the recently enacted estate tax changes has led most estate planners to assume that the changes will expire as scheduled after 2011 and that estate planning will still be necessary.

13. Welch (2001), Gordon (2001), and Stein et al. (2000) do an excellent job of summarizing the options open to an investor whose portfolio is dominated by a large position that carries a tax penalty or other impediment to diversification.

14. We did not vary the fixed-income returns beyond the market volatility assumptions because fixed-income returns will certainly fluctuate within a narrower range and changing the equity return seemed the most realistic way to deal with possible variations.

15. Technically, the correlations should be based on the funds' net asset values rather than the indexes, especially if the indexes are not naturally regulated investment company (RIC) compliant. See Chapter 6 for a discussion of RIC compliance. No correlation tables are offered in this volume because correlations can change materially over time. An outdated table might give readers an inappropriate feeling of comfort.

Chapter 2

The History and Structure of ETFs—and Some Competitors

The phenomenal growth of exchange-traded funds (ETFs) is a frequent topic in the financial press. These funds, with assets more than doubling each year from 1995 through 2000, have been warmly embraced by most advocates of low-cost index funds. Vanguard, the leading advocate of index funds, has introduced an ETF share class and plans to add exchange-traded share classes to a number of additional domestic index funds. Most of the press coverage has correctly noted the major advantages of ETFs—low expense ratios, intra-day trading, and high tax efficiency with no material premiums or discounts to the funds' intra-day net asset value. However, there is a fair degree of misunderstanding about how ETFs work, why the expense ratios tend to be low, and how most of the funds manage to avoid significant capital gains distributions. This chapter and Chapters 3 and 4 attempt to answer these and other basic questions frequently asked by investors. In addition, we compare ETFs with other basket products that often compete with them.

A BRIEF HISTORY OF ETFS[1]

Exchange-traded funds, referred to by friends and foes alike as "ETFs," are outstanding examples of the evolution of new financial products. We begin by tracing the history of the ETFs' antecedents—the proto-products that led to the current generation of exchange-traded funds and set the stage for products yet to come.

Portfolio Trading
The basic idea of trading an entire portfolio in a single transaction did not originate with the TIPS or SPDRS, which are the earliest successful

examples of the modern portfolio-traded-as-a-share structure. The idea originated with what has come to be known as portfolio trading or program trading. In the late 1970s and early 1980s, program trading was the then revolutionary ability to trade an entire portfolio, often a portfolio consisting of all the S&P 500 stocks, with a single order placed at a major brokerage firm. Some modest advances in electronic order entry technology at the NYSE and the Amex and the availability of large-order desks at some major investment banking firms made these early portfolio or program trades possible. At about the same time, the introduction of S&P 500 index futures contracts at the Chicago Mercantile Exchange provided an arbitrage link between the futures contracts and the traded portfolios of stocks. It even became possible, in a trade called an exchange of futures for physicals (EFP), to exchange a stock portfolio position, long or short, for a stock index futures position, long or short. The effect of these developments was to make portfolio trading either in cash or futures markets an attractive activity for many trading desks and for many institutional investors.

As a logical consequence of these developments affecting large investors, there arose interest—one might even say insistent demand—for a readily tradable portfolio or basket product for smaller institutions and the individual investor. Before the introduction of "mini" contracts, futures contracts were relatively large in notional size. Even with "mini" contracts, the variation margin requirements for carrying a futures contract are cumbersome and relatively expensive for a small investor. Perhaps even more important, there are approximately ten times as many securities salespeople as futures salespeople. The need for a security, i.e., an SEC-regulated portfolio product, that could be used by individual investors was apparent. One of the first such products introduced were the Index Participation Shares, known as "IPS."

Index Participation Shares (IPS)

The Index Participation Shares were a relatively simple, totally synthetic, proxy for the S&P 500 Index. While IPS on other indexes were also available, S&P 500 IPS were the most active. They began trading on the American Stock Exchange and the Philadelphia Stock Exchange in 1989. IPS traded with a level of activity that showed significant public interest, in spite of a lawsuit by the Chicago Mercantile Exchange

(CME) and the Commodity Futures Trading Commission (CFTC), which charged that IPS were futures contracts. As futures contracts, they would be required by law to trade on a futures exchange regulated by the CFTC, not on a securities exchange. In spite of the cloud cast by this litigation, IPS volume and open interest began to grow.

The IPS were, candidly, much like a futures contract; but they were margined and collateralized like stocks. Like futures, there was a short for every long and a long for every short. IPS were carried and cleared by the Options Clearing Corporation, and they provided a return essentially identical to the long or short return on the underlying shares in the index with an appropriate quarterly credit for dividends on the long side and a debit for dividends on the short side.

Alas, success eluded the IPS. A federal court in Chicago found that the IPS were indeed illegal futures contracts and had to be traded on a futures exchange if they were traded at all. The stock exchanges began to close down IPS trading and investors were required to liquidate their IPS positions in an orderly manner.

While a number of efforts to find a replacement product for IPS that would pass muster as a security were underway in the United States, another effort achieved success first in Toronto. There, the TIPs (*Toronto* Stock Exchange *I*ndex *P*articipation*s*) were introduced.

Toronto Stock Exchange Index Participations (TIPs)

TIPs were a warehouse receipt-based instrument designed to track the TSE-35 index, and a later product tracked the TSE-100 index as well. The TSE-100 product was initially called HIPs. These products traded actively and attracted substantial investment from Canadians and from international indexing investors. TIPs were unique in their expense ratio. The ability of the trustee (State Street Bank) to loan out the stock in the TIPs portfolio and frequent demand for stock loans on shares of large companies in Canada led to what was, in effect, a negative expense ratio at times.

The TIPs were a victim of their own success. They proved costly for the Exchange and for some of its members who were unable to recover their costs from investors. Early in 2000, the Toronto Stock Exchange decided to get out of the portfolio share business, and TIPs positions were liquidated or rolled into a Barclays

Global Investors (BGI) 60 stock index share at the option of the TIPs holder. The BGI fund was relatively low cost, but not as low cost as the TIPs, so a large fraction of the TIPs shares were liquidated.

While the TIPs were flourishing in Toronto, two other portfolio share products were under development in the United States: Supershares and SPDRs.

Supershares

Supershares were a product of Leland, O'Brien, Rubinstein Associates (LOR) and, in the post-1987 market crash environment, were often referred to by skeptics as being "from the folks who brought you portfolio insurance." Supershares were a complex product using both a trust and a mutual fund structure—one inside the other. Supershares were a high-cost product, particularly after a fee was extracted to compensate the creators and sponsors. The complexity of the product, which permitted division of the Supershares into a variety of components, some with option characteristics, made sales presentations long and confusing for many customers. The Supershares never traded actively, and the trust was eventually liquidated.

Standard & Poor's Depository Receipts (SPDRS)

SPDRS (pronounced "spiders") were developed by the American Stock Exchange approximately in parallel with Supershares, although their introduction was deferred until after the Supershares were offered.[2] SPDRs are the shares of a unit trust that holds an S&P 500 portfolio that, unlike the portfolios of most U.S. unit trusts, can be changed as the index changes. The reason for the selection of the unit trust structure was the Amex's concern for simplicity and costs. A mutual fund must pay the costs of a board of directors, even if the fund is very small. The Amex was uncertain of the demand for SPDRs and did not want to build a more costly infrastructure than was necessary. While SPDRs are the essence of simplicity relative to Supershares, they are more complex than TIPs and IPS, and the education process has been a long one. SPDRs traded reasonably well on the Amex in their earlier years, but only in the late 1990s did SPDRs asset growth become truly exponential. As investors began to look past the somewhat esoteric in-kind share creation and redemption process (used by market makers and large investors to acquire and redeem SPDRs in large blocks) and focused on the investment characteristics and tax efficiency of the individual SPDRs shares.

Today, the S&P 500 SPDRs have more assets than any other index fund except the Vanguard 500 mutual fund. The SPDRs account for more than one-third of ETF assets in the United States. Interestingly, however, from 70 to 90% of traditional U.S. index fund money goes into S&P 500 portfolios. Clearly, the interest in ETFs based on indexes other than the S&P 500 suggests that there is more to exchange-traded funds than an alternative to conventional index funds.[3]

World Equity Benchmark Shares (WEBS)— Renamed iShares MSCI Series

The WEBS, originally developed by Morgan Stanley, are important for two reasons. First, they are foreign index funds. More precisely, they are U.S.-based funds holding stocks issued by non–U.S.-based firms. Second, they were among the earliest exchange-traded index products to use a mutual fund as opposed to a unit trust structure. The mutual fund structure has more investment flexibility, and there are some other differences in dividend reinvestment and stock lending, but most of these differences are in the process of being eliminated. We would expect most new funds to use the mutual fund structure, but competitors' whispers that the SPDRs and other ETFs structured as unit trusts suffer from an evil affliction called "dividend drag" are gross exaggerations. The subtle and relatively unimportant differences between the unit trust and mutual fund ETF structures are a topic we will return to later in this chapter.

A product similar to WEBS was introduced on the NYSE at about the same time WEBS appeared on the Amex. For a variety of reasons (the most important of which were structural flaws in the product), these "Country Baskets" failed and the trust was liquidated.

In addition to WEBS, a variety of additional ETF products are now available. The Mid-Cap SPDRs (a unit trust run by the Bank of New York) actually came before WEBS, and the DIAMONDS (a unit trust based on the Dow Jones Industrial Average and run by State Street Bank) and the NASDAQ 100 (a unit trust run by the Bank of New York) were introduced later. The Select Sector

SPDRs used a mutual fund structure similar to the WEBS and were introduced in late 1998. Of these products, the NASDAQ 100 and the Sector SPDRs deserve a closer look.

NASDAQ 100 Index Tracking Stock—The QQQs

In spite of the name, the NASDAQ 100 Trust, sponsored by NASDAQ, is not a tracking stock as the term is generally used in the United States—and, from a strictly technical point of view, it's not even a stock. The basic unit of trading, however, is a "share," and the NASDAQ 100 Trust, as a unit trust, is more like the original SPDR than most of the other currently traded ETFs. The reason for focusing on the NASDAQ 100 Trust is its spectacular success, partly as a result of a sound marketing effort by NASDAQ, but primarily because of the spectacular performance—until March, 2000—of stocks listed on the NASDAQ market. The NASDAQ 100, perhaps more than any of the other ETF products, illustrates the variety of applications for, and reasons for investment in, exchange-traded funds. The NASDAQ 100 Shares serve as a volatile trading vehicle on both the long and short side of the market and as a proxy for the technology sector. Heavy trading volume and narrow bid-asked spreads for small orders attracted both large and small traders and the growth in volume attracted more traders, leading to even more volume.

Sector SPDRs

The Sector SPDRs, developed by Merrill Lynch, provide another interesting perspective on the ETF world. Although each stock in the S&P 500 is assigned to a Sector SPDR, the balance of investor interest has been very different from sector capitalization weights. Investor interest has been greatest in the Technology Sector SPDR, followed at a considerable distance by the Financial Sector SPDR and at a great distance by all the other sectors. These sector funds have served, at least initially, primarily as a mechanism for expressing a strongly held view about a particular segment of the market. In part because their relatively low share prices increase transaction costs for many investors, Sector SPDRs have not yet caught on in a major way as the basis for weighting a portfolio more heavily in sectors favored from a fundamental perspective or less heavily if the sector is relatively unattractive. The very slow start of the iShares Dow Jones sector funds suggests a need for more information, education and appropriate allocation tools to help individual investors and their advisors to develop interest in sector funds.

BGI iShares Funds

Barclays Global Investors, a major institutional index portfolio manager, launched iShares in a bid to develop a retail branded family of financial products. The extremely low expense ratio on the S&P 500 component of the iShares offering and the former WEBS for which BGI has served as investment advisor since inception get special attention. By early October 2001, BGI accounted for more than 73% of the funds and only about 18% of U.S. ETF assets. Most of the money was in funds with expense ratios of 20 basis points or less.

State Street Global Advisors streetTRACKS Funds

The original 500 SPDRs and the DIAMONDS were developed cooperatively by the AMEX, outside counsel, and State Street; and the Sector SPDRs were developed with important participation by Merrill Lynch. The streetTRACKS Funds represent State Street's first solo ETF effort in the United States. BGI's strategy of cornering many branded benchmark index licenses left State Street with an unusual collection of indexes as the basis for its funds. All in all, State Street's U.S. effort has been mildly disappointing, but they have done much better in the launch of the Hong Kong TraHKers Fund and other funds for investors outside the United States.

Nuveen Investments Fixed-Income Funds and Selected Equity Index Funds

The focus of Nuveen's initial effort in index ETFs has been on the development and licensing of fund-friendly indexes as templates for its proposed index fund products. Nuveen attempts to develop funds that meet specific investor needs rather than launch a fund simply because an index happens to be available. Nuveen was the first advisor to file an exemptive request with the SEC to launch fixed-income index funds.[4]

ETFs AND OTHER TRADABLE BASKET PRODUCTS

While most readers think of the fund products described above as ETFs, various financial instruments, each referred to by some of its advocates as an exchange-traded fund, are designed to meet specific portfolio investment needs. In many cases, the needs met are practically identical; in other cases, they are quite different. In spite of some confusion about what the term ETF includes, most observers agree that a range of exchange-traded portfolio basket products compete for investors' dollars.

Our purpose in this section is to introduce the major categories of financial instruments which sometimes have been called "ETFs" or which compete with ETFs. We will appraise the features of each. Our objective is to provide a relatively straightforward comparison of features. The purpose of the comparison is not to suggest that one structure is always superior or that the emphasis should always be on competition between the products. In fact, Folio customers have been important users of the fund-type ETFs described in the previous section and of HOLDRs, which are described below.

Closed-End Funds

Nuveen Investments began using the term "exchange-traded funds" for its closed-end municipal bond funds traded on the New York and American Stock Exchanges in the very early 1990s, several years before the first SPDRs began trading on the American Stock Exchange. The use of the name "exchange-traded funds" was selected to emphasize the fact that someone buying and selling these municipal bond fund shares enjoyed the investor protections afforded by investment company (fund) regulation and by the auction market on a major securities exchange. Interestingly, the intra-day trading convenience and trading cost reduction of the pooled portfolio structure and exchange trading for these closed-end funds was similar in many respects to the contribution of the pooled portfolio structure and exchange trading to the newer "open" exchange-traded funds, originating with the TIPs in Canada and the SPDRs in the United States.

Both these types of exchange-traded funds provide an efficient means to assemble and trade a portfolio of securities—in the case of the closed-end funds, recent offerings have been primarily municipal bond portfolios; in the case of the "open" ETFs, they have been primarily stock portfolios. Typically, both these vehicles are able to trade the components of their portfolios at narrower spreads and manage these portfolios at lower cost than an individual, an institutional manager of separate accounts or the manager of a conventional "open-end" mutual fund could manage such portfolios. Limited liquidity in the municipal bond markets makes it especially difficult to manage a municipal bond portfolio with as high a degree of efficiency in an "open-end" portfolio structure as in a closed-end fund. Creation and redemption in-kind—in some respects the defining characteristic of "open" ETFs—is not yet practical in U.S. municipal bond markets.

Given the diversity and relative illiquidity of most individual municipal bond positions, the closed-end fund structure seems to be the most efficient choice for that market today. The relative increase in liquidity for the fund shares and the reduction in portfolio transaction costs available in a well-managed, closed-end municipal bond fund usually more than compensate for the occasional discount from net asset value associated with the fixed capitalization of a closed-end fund. Depending on an investor's objectives, the liquidity and cost advantages of the closed-end municipal bond fund may be as important as the cost and liquidity advantages of the newer "open" ETFs.

"Open" Exchange-Traded Funds

The SEC requires that references to what we are calling "open" exchange-traded funds as open-end funds be made only in the context of a comparison with conventional open-end investment companies (mutual funds). We are about to make such a comparison, so we will now drop the quotes around *open*, and fully qualify the limits of openness in such funds. Shares in what we have been calling open ETFs can be issued and redeemed directly by the fund at their net asset value (NAV) only in creation unit aggregations, typically 50,000 fund shares or multiples of 50,000 shares. The shareholder who wants to buy or sell fewer than 50,000 shares may only buy and sell smaller lots on the secondary market at their current market price. The secondary market participant is dependent on competition among the exchange specialist, other market makers, and arbitrageurs to keep the market price of the shares very near the intra-day value of the fund portfolio. The effectiveness of market forces in promoting tight bid-asked spreads and fair pricing is discussed at length in Chapter 8. To anticipate the conclusion of that discussion, open ETF shares have consistently traded very, very close to the value of the underlying portfolio in a contemporaneously priced market.

Before we move beyond the issue of share creation and redeemability to compare these new funds with conventional mutual funds in more detail, it is worth noting that the first open exchange-traded funds were not mutual funds. They were, as noted in the previous section, unit investment trusts (UITs) selected by the AMEX for simplicity and cost-saving reasons. The AMEX was concerned that the new funds might turn out to be very small, leaving the Exchange with the expenses of compensating a board of directors in perpetuity. In fact, the portfolios of the unit trust-based products have grown quite large. At the end of December, 2000, the 500 SPDR would have been ranked 21st in size among mutual funds, just behind Janus Twenty and ahead of AimValue. The NASDAQ 100 Trust would have ranked 23rd, ahead of Vanguard Windsor.

The differences between the SPDRs and NASDAQ 100 UIT structure and the open-end investment company structure used for most of the newer ETFs are not important to most investors in an equity index fund. Some providers of open ETFs structured as management investment companies have criticized the older UIT structures because dividends from their portfolio stocks cannot be equitized, i.e., reinvested in portfolio shares. The dividends must be retained as cash and invested, in effect, in money market instruments until the dividend payment is made.[5] Furthermore, securities in the UIT portfolios cannot be lent out to obtain securities lending income to help offset portfolio expenses. The impact of these differences is not material under most circumstances, but State Street Bank, trustee of the 500 SPDR and the DIAMONDS, has asked the Securities and Exchange Commission to permit a change in the rules of the trust to permit equitization of dividends and securities lending. There is every reason to believe that this application will be approved in time, making the equity index UIT ETFs and the investment company ETFs functionally equivalent for all practical purposes.[6] The UIT structure and the investment company structure share a broad range of similar characteristics, most of which are advantages relative to the traditional open-end mutual fund structure.

For the typical retail or even institutional investor, purchasing and selling ETF shares is the essence of simplicity. The trading rules and practices are those of the stock market. ETF shares are purchased and sold in the secondary market, much like stocks or shares of closed-end funds, rather than being purchased *from* the fund and resold *to* the fund.

Because they are traded like stocks, shares of ETFs can be purchased or sold any time during the trading day, unlike shares of most conventional mutual funds, which are sold only at the 4:00 p.m. net asset value (NAV) as determined by the fund and applied to all orders received since the prior day's share-trading deadline. While the opportunities for intra-day trading may not be important to every investor, they certainly have appeal to many investors during a period when there is concern about being able to get out of a position before the market close when prices are volatile.

Primary market transactions in ETF shares, that is, trades when shares are bought or redeemed with the fund itself as a party to the trade, consist of in-kind creations and redemptions in large size. For example, the SPDR and NASDAQ 100 creation aggregations are 50,000 fund shares, and creation/redemption occurs only in multiples of 50,000 shares. There have been a number of occasions when creation and redemption of fund shares has resulted in asset flows of $1 billion dollars or more in or out of the SPDR or the NASDAQ 100 Trust in a single day. Exchange specialists, market makers, and arbitrageurs buy ETF shares from the fund by depositing a stock portfolio and a cash-balancing component that essentially match the fund in content and are equal in value to 50,000 ETF shares on the day the fund issues the shares. The same large market participants redeem fund shares by tendering them to the fund in 50,000 share multiples and receiving a stock portfolio plus or minus balancing cash equivalent in value to the 50,000 ETF shares redeemed. The discipline of possible creation and redemption at each day's market-closing NAV is a critical factor in the maintenance of fund shares at a price very, very close to the value of the fund's underlying portfolio, not just at the close of trading but intra-day. A proxy for intra-day net asset value per share is continuously disseminated for each ETF throughout the trading day to help investors check the reasonableness of bids and offers on the market.[7]

An extremely important feature of the creation and, more particularly, the redemption process is that redemption-in-kind does more than provide an arbitrage mechanism to ensure a market price quite close to net asset value. Redemption-in-kind also reduces the fund's transaction costs slightly and enhances the tax efficiency of the fund. While a conventional mutual fund can require shareholders to take a redemption payment in-kind rather than in cash for large redemptions, most funds are reluctant to do this, and most shareholders have fund positions considerably smaller than the $250,000 minimum usually required for redemption-in-kind. As a consequence, most redemptions of conventional mutual fund shares are for cash, meaning that an equity fund faced with significant shareholder redemptions is required to sell shares of portfolio stocks, frequently stocks that have appreciated from their original cost. When gains taken to obtain cash for redemptions are added to gains realized on merger stocks that are removed from the index for a premium over the fund's purchase price, many conventional index funds distribute substantial capital gains to their shareholders, even though the continuing shareholders who pay taxes on these distributions have made no transactions, and the fund, looked at from a longer perspective, has been a net buyer of most or all of its index's component securities.

The in-kind redemption process for exchange-traded funds enhances tax efficiency in a simple way. Low-cost shares of each stock in the portfolio are delivered against requests from shareholders redeeming in multiples of 50,000 fund shares. The shares of stock in each company remaining in the portfolio have a relatively higher cost basis, which means that acquired companies generate smaller or no gains when they leave the index and are sold for cash by the fund. In contrast, a conventional fund would tend to sell its highest-cost stocks first, leaving it vulnerable to substantial capital gains realizations when a portfolio company is acquired at a premium and exits the index and the fund.

One further feature of the existing exchange-traded funds requires an explanation. It causes a degree of misunderstanding and seems to create an expectation that all ETFs will be extremely low-cost funds. First, the existing ETFs are all index funds. Index funds generally have lower management fees than actively managed funds, whatever their share structure. Second, ETFs enjoy somewhat lower operating costs than their conventional fund counterparts. The principal reasons for lower costs are (1) the opportunity to have a somewhat larger fund because of the popularity of the exchange-traded fund structure, (2) slightly lower transaction costs due to in-kind deposits from, and payments to, buyers and redeemers in the primary market and, most importantly, (3) the elimination of the transfer agency function— that is, the elimination of shareholder accounting—at the fund level.

As all U.S. ETFs are "book entry only" securities, an exchange-traded fund in the United States has one registered shareholder: the Depository Trust Company (DTC). If you want a share certificate for a SPDR or QQQ position, you are out of luck. Certificates are not available. The only certificate is held by the Depository Trust Company, and the number of shares represented by that certificate is "marked to market" for increases and decreases in shares as creations and redemptions occur.

Shareholder accounting for ETFs is maintained at the investor's brokerage firm, rather than at the fund. This creates no problems for the shareholder, although it does have some significance for the distribution of exchange-traded funds. One of the traditional functions of the mutual fund transfer agent is to keep track of the salesperson responsible for the placement of a particular fund position, so that any ongoing payments based on 12b-1 fees or other marketing charges can be made to the credit of the appropriate salesperson. There is no way for the issuer of an ETF to keep track of salespeople because these fund positions do not carry the recordkeeping information needed to use the DTC Fund/SERV process. They are, in a word, just like shares of a stock—and a stock with no certificates at that. The elimination of the individual shareholder transfer agency function reduces operating costs by a minimum of five basis points and probably by much more in many cases. ETF expenses tend to reflect the cost savings on this function.

The trading price of an exchange-traded fund share will be subject to a bid-asked spread in the secondary market (although these are very narrow on most products) and a brokerage commission. A simple breakeven analysis divides the round-trip trading costs by the daily difference in operating expenses. Anyone planning to retain a reasonably large fund position for more than a short period of time and/or anyone who values the intra-day purchase and sale features of the exchange-traded funds will find the combination of the lower expense ratio and greater flexibility make the ETF share more attractive than a conventional mutual fund share.

Powerful advantages notwithstanding, there are a few disadvantages in the exchange-traded fund format for some investors. An investor cannot be certain of his or her ability to buy or sell shares at a price no worse than net asset value without incurring some part or all of a trading spread and a commission. It is the trading spread in the secondary market which pays the costs of insulating the ongoing shareholder from the cost of in-and-out transactions by active traders. These transaction costs in open-market ETF trades mean that, even with lower fund expenses, certain small investors will not find ETFs as economical as traditional funds if they are in the habit of making periodic small investments. Since most conventional mutual funds take steps to refuse investments from in-and-out traders if they trade in and out too frequently, the transaction costs associated with ETFs are simply a more equitable allocation of these costs among various fund shareholders. A long-term investor, particularly a taxable long-term investor, will benefit greatly from the exchange-traded fund structure because in the long run that investor should enjoy lower fund expenses and a higher after-tax return than he would find in an otherwise comparable conventional index fund. This allocation of costs and benefits is ironic given the only significant criticism that has been leveled at exchange-traded funds, i.e., that they encourage active trading. In fact, the long-term taxable investor enjoys the greatest benefits from the ETF structure. However, as our discussion of ETF trading and trading costs in Chapter 8 will show, the incidence of trading costs, appropriately, moves from the fund and from ongoing shareholders to the active trader. Even so, the ETF structure has probably reduced the active trader's costs, given the obstacles and special redemption fees these traders often incur when they use conventional funds.

As noted earlier, all current open exchange-traded funds are equity index funds. As time goes by, there will be a wider variety of funds available. The introduction of fixed-income index funds, enhanced index funds, and ultimately actively managed funds seems inevitable. It is in the advance from simple indexation with full replication of the index in the portfolio to more complex funds that the investment management company (mutual fund) structure shows its greatest advantages over the open UIT structure. The latter structure does not provide a mechanism for anything beyond full replication of an index. The open-end management investment company structure permits a portfolio to differ from the structure of an index fairly easily. The UIT structure provides for replication of an index with limited variations based on rounding share positions and limited timing adjustments of index replicating transactions by advancing or deferring them for a few days. As in most evolutionary developments, whether in biology or finance, there is more than one way to accomplish an objective.

Alternative portfolio or basket structures differ from both the UIT and the exchange-traded investment management company. These other structures have their own unique features. Foremost among these are *HOL*ding company *D*epository *R*eceipts (HOLDRs), a structure pioneered by Merrill-Lynch, and Folios, which have been introduced by a number of firms that would otherwise be characterized primarily as deep discount brokers. Both HOLDRs and Folios are unmanaged baskets of securities that may have an initial structure based on an index, a theme, or just a diversification policy.

Holding Company Depository Receipts

HOLDRs use a grantor trust structure, which makes them similar to the open ETFs discussed above, in that additional HOLDRs shares can be created and existing HOLDRs can be redeemed. The creation unit aggregation for the open ETF management company structures is typically 50,000 fund shares, and the minimum trading unit on the secondary market is a single fund share. In contrast, the creation unit *and* the minimum trading unit in HOLDRs is generally 100 shares. Most brokerage firms will not deal in fractional shares or odd lots of HOLDRs.[8] An investor can buy and sell HOLDRs in the secondary market, or an existing HOLDRs position can be redeemed (exchanged for its specific underlying stocks). A new HOLDRs position can be created by simply depositing the stocks behind the 100-share HOLDRs unit with the custodian bank. (The original stock basket underlying a 100-share HOLDRs unit will always consist of whole shares of the component stocks. In the event of a merger affecting one of the companies, any cash proceeds will be distributed. The surviving company's shares will usually be retained in the HOLDRs basket.) The creation/redemption fee for HOLDRs will generally be roughly similar in *relative* magnitude to the comparable fee on investment company ETFs and the pricing principles and arbitrage pricing constraints operate in a similar way. To the extent that one of the stocks in a HOLDRs basket performs poorly and the investor wants to use the loss on that stock to offset gains elsewhere, the HOLDRs can be taken apart and reassembled without affecting the tax status of any shares not sold. The ability to realize a loss on an individual position may give the HOLDRs structure a slight tax advantage over the investment company–based ETFs in some circumstances. On the other hand, unlike the redemption-in-kind of the shares of an open ETF, the HOLDRs structure does not permit elimination of a low-cost position in the HOLDRs portfolio without realization of the gain by the investor. This important tax feature of an in-kind redemption of shares in a regulated investment company will be examined in greater detail in Chapter 4.

An investor who maintains an account at Merrill-Lynch will probably be able to obtain good tax reporting for HOLDRs positions. An investor transferring an account or carrying a HOLDRs position elsewhere may find tax preparation cumbersome and time-consuming.

The first HOLDRs were based on the split-up of Telebras into 12 separate companies in mid-1998. They were designed to provide a single vehicle to absorb the split-off companies, much as earlier unit trusts were designed to absorb the component pieces of AT&T at the time of the court-mandated divestiture of the regional operating companies. The Telebras HOLDRs traded an average of over 700,000 shares per day in the first half of 2001. Subsequent HOLDRs baskets were created initially out of 20 securities in each of a number of relatively narrowly defined industries and, more recently, out of a larger number of companies with various investment characteristics.

The principal disadvantages of HOLDRs are that they lack the indefinite life of an investment company and there is no provision for adding positions to offset attrition through acquisitions of basket components by other companies. No HOLDRs component that disappears in a cash merger can be replaced in the HOLDRs basket. There is a provision in some of the HOLDRs trusts that, once the number of stocks represented in the HOLDRs portfolio drops below a certain level, the trust will be dissolved and the remaining shares will be delivered to the holders of HOLDRs in proportion to their ownership. The thematic nature of many of the HOLDRs baskets reflects this relatively temporary structure, though the Telebras HOLDRs and many of the recent broadly diversified portfolios have a longer-term orientation.

The HOLDRs share one very important characteristic with the index ETFs: It is frequently less costly to trade the basket in the form of HOLDRs than it is to trade the individual shares, particularly for a small- to mid-sized investor who might be trading odd lots in many of the basket components if HOLDRs or ETFs were unavailable.

HOLDRs also feature a variation on a front-end load in their initial public offering (IPO). Once the HOLDRs are trading in the secondary market, additional HOLDRs can be created and redeemed at relatively low cost. The IPO structure may turn out to be an important feature of HOLDRs. If HOLDRs can continue to be launched in environments less favorable to the IPO structure, they may have a lasting role in the financial engineer's repertoire of financial instruments.

Folios

In contrast to the other ETF variations and competitors described here, Folios are not standardized products nor are they investment companies. They are baskets of stocks that can be modified one position at a time or traded in a single transaction through brokerage firms. The firms that advocate and provide Folio baskets for trading do provide semi-standardized baskets—in some cases based on indexes and in other cases based on a simple diversification rule. In practice, however, each investor's implementation of the Folio basket may be slightly different.

An investor may have $20,000 to invest. Upon examination of the group of "prefabricated" Folios suggested by the firm she trades with, she may decide she likes a specific basket of 40 stocks. The investor can choose how many shares of each stock she would like to buy or she can request a customized basket prepared by the firm and giving her an "appropriate" number of whole and sometimes fractional shares of each stock in the selected basket. She can modify the basket immediately—or later—until she finds a mix that matches her needs and inclinations.

Because Folio baskets will not be standardized, Folios cannot be traded like fund shares or like HOLDRs. Each of the stocks in a Folio will trade separately. The Folio firm can provide low-cost commissions and even the opportunity to execute trades against its other customer trades at selected times during the day. However, if the basket does not trade as a standardized basket, the investor will miss some of the transaction cost advantages that traders in standardized basket shares often enjoy.

A tax advantage of Folios over investment companies in certain circumstances is similar to a tax feature of HOLDRs. An investor can sell one position out of a Folio to take a loss and use that loss to offset gains obtained elsewhere—outside the Folio basket. In contrast, a fund taxed as a regulated investment company cannot pass losses through to shareholders. If the fund experiences large losses, an investor can take a loss on the fund shares by selling the share position; but losses on an individual portfolio component are not available to the investor who continues to hold the shares as a passthrough. In a reasonably bullish market environment, the ability of the UIT or management company ETF to modify its portfolio with creations and redemptions without taxable gain realizations will probably be more important to an individual investor than the ability to take specific losses in either HOLDRs or Folios. Other market environments may make the selected loss realization opportunity of the HOLDRs or Folios more valuable.

Folios, like HOLDRs, can be difficult from a tax accounting perspective, although all the Folio providers offer a service whereby careful entry of the cost of each position delivered into the account and automatic entry of positions purchased and sold in the account can be translated into a relatively simple schedule of gains and losses, suitable for attachment to the investor's tax return. An important competitive advantage of FOLIO*fn*, compared to some other purveyors of basket products, is the combination of its ability to provide and carry fractional share positions and a portfolio management and reporting system designed for use by independent advisors working with investors.

Folios have been criticized for the tendency of their advocates to minimize the true costs of acquiring and holding a Folio basket. While the promoters of Folios provide tools for measuring diversification effects of changes in the portfolio to realize losses or to make a change in the composition of the basket, the Folio baskets lack the inherent discipline of a product that is modified in response to a change in an index or in response to a decision by a portfolio manager. Investment managers and index publishers make mistakes and bad decisions, but they are unlikely to let a portfolio drift from neglect, as could easily happen with an unsupervised Folio basket. We expect Folios to become primarily a vehicle for advisors working with clients rather than a service for the on-line trader who trades his own account. Folios will use ETFs like stocks in the construction of Folio accounts.

In contrast to the ETFs' fund structure, there is no "tax-realization-free" mechanism for reducing the impact of a very successful position in either HOLDRs or Folios. In the regulated investment company structures (exchange-traded unit trusts or funds), tax rules would limit the size of any single stock to 25% of the assets of the fund under most circumstances. Reductions in the commitment to a particular position in a regulated investment company with redemptions-in-kind might be obtainable without realization of taxable gains. This would not be possible for very successful positions underlying HOLDRs or for components of a Folio. Basket mechanisms that do not offer a way to reduce a large, successful position without capital gains realization force the investor to choose between tax deferral and diversification.

In the long run, it seems likely that Folios are more likely to be co-opted by specialized investment managers than they are to succeed in the format in which they were first introduced. Without an increase in fees charged to the individual customer or substantial income from sale of their investors' order flow, it seems unlikely that the retail, discount brokerage Folio service is an economically viable business model. Nonetheless, the Folio structure and flexibility is intriguing. While the initial product probably tried to take some aspects of do-it-yourself portfolio management too far, Folios can be an excellent vehicle for an advisor serving individual investors.

A SIDE-BY-SIDE COMPARISON OF TRADABLE BASKET PRODUCTS[9]

The accompanying table, Exhibit 2-1, provides an eclectic comparison of open exchange-traded funds to the other basket products we have discussed. Most of the items on this comparison table are relatively straightforward and readily understandable from the previous text, but several items do require some discussion. First, these comparisons are based on the current product offerings in each category. At present, all open ETFs and open UITs are based on indexes. The lack of active management is virtually inherent in the open UIT, but there is reason to believe that open ETFs will be able to serve as the vehicle for enhanced index funds and actively managed funds in the future. Active management is also compatible with the closed-end funds, but not with the HOLDRs. Actively managed Folios become the equivalent of separate accounts, something very different from all the other basket products.

In assigning tax-efficiency ratings, we have placed significantly greater value on the redemption-in-kind feature of the open ETFs and open UITs than on the separable loss feature available in Folios with no particular change and in HOLDRs through the exchange of the HOLDR for the basket of underlying securities followed by realization of the loss, re-establishment of the position after the wash sale period is past, and reconstitution of the HOLDR—a relatively complex and non-user-friendly process.

Closed-end funds are rated higher than conventional mutual funds on tax-efficiency because they are characterized by a closed portfolio and do not face the forced realization of gains which can come about through cash redemptions in an open-end mutual fund.

Exhibit 2-1: Basket Product Comparisons

Feature/Product Structure	Open ETFs	Open UITs	Conventional Mutual Funds	Closed ETFs	HOLDRs	Folios
Creation of Shares—primary market	In-kind deposit	In-kind deposit	Cash deposit with fund	IPO	IPO/in-kind deposit	NA
Purchase of Shares—secondary market	Open market purchase	Open market purchase	NA	Open market purchase	Open market purchase	Open market purchase
Sale of Shares—secondary market	Open market sale	Open market sale	NA	Open market sale	Open market sale	Open market sale
Redemption of Shares—primary market	In-kind redemption	In-kind redemption	Cash redemption	NA	In-kind redemption	NA
Underlying portfolio structure (available today)	Index	Index	Index or managed	Managed	Preset basket	Investor's choice
Tax structure	RIC	RIC	RIC	RIC	Structure is tax transparent	No structure
Tax-efficiency factors	Redemption in-kind	Redemption in-kind	Cash redemption	Cash redemption	Separable losses	Separable losses
Investor tax-efficiency rating	1	1	5	4	3	2
Effect of structure on shareholder's trading cost	Usually reduces	Usually reduces	Usually reduces	Usually reduces	Usually reduces	No effect except discount brokerage
Investor's Trading cost rating	1	1	2	1	1	3
Shareholder attention required	Minimal dividend reinvestment	Minimal dividend reinvestment	Minimal dividend reinvestment	Minimal dividend reinvestment	Dividend reinvestment principal reinvestment tax loss sales and replacements significant	Dividend reinvestment principal reinvestment tax loss sales and replacements significant

Ratings 1 = best, 5 = worst.

The investor's trading cost ratings are based on the advantages associated with trading a basket at the share level versus transacting separately in all the securities making up the basket. All of the standardized ETFs are ranked highly because trading in the composite share should be more efficient than trading in the underlying positions separately. It is certainly possible to differentiate among individual products in terms of the cost of trading the product or trading the underlying securities separately, but the difference is more related to the nature of the underlying market and the quality of the market in the basket product than it is on anything systematically related to the product structure. The conventional mutual funds are rated slightly below the exchange-traded products other than the unstructured Folios on the assumption that, on average, a redemption charge or other obstacle to short-term trading will increase an investor's costs of trading.[10] Folios are rated lowest simply because they do not provide any of the advantages associated with trading the other products as portfolios or baskets. Even when the transactions in a Folio are aggregated, each stock is traded separately. None of the Folio providers have reached a size that permits them to match and offset many customer orders to eliminate the bid-asked spread.

The topic that probably requires the most consideration for long-term investors is the shareholder attention required to use each product effectively. Any basket or portfolio product will typically be less risky than a random collection of a few of its component securities, and any basket product will provide at least a degree of diversification, though some of the more specialized HOLDRs baskets or, for that matter, sector funds provide only minimal internal diversification. Nonetheless, these basket products are generally designed to require minimal shareholder attention from day to day and even from year to year. Most, for example, provide either automatic dividend reinvestment or let an investor make a variety of arrangements for automatic reinvestment of the dividends with the brokerage firm holding the account.

HOLDRs and Folios require somewhat greater investor (or manager) attention than the conventional fund or exchange-traded fund products for at least two reasons: First, to the extent that any of the companies in the HOLDRs or Folios are taken over in a cash acquisition, the shares will automatically be turned into cash and the shareholder will have to deal with reinvestment of the principal. Also, both these less structured products provide for their variety of tax efficiency by permitting tax loss sales of individual securities. Folios, which are marketed principally as a way to take advantage of the automatic diversification a portfolio of stocks provides, require some kind of replacement or re-balancing activity to maintain a useful degree of diversification. With the other products, either a portfolio manager or the process for weighting or re-weighting the index and insuring regulated investment company diversification compliance in the fund will retain a minimal level of diversification without action by the investor or an advisor employed to manage the investor's position.

Importantly—and this is a topic we will return to—few, if any, of today's basket products in their elementary form are appropriate as an individual's entire investment position for the investor's entire life span. Most investors would benefit in terms of an improvement in their risk-reward trade-off by having at least some fixed-income positions in their portfolio, for example. Furthermore, most investors' total portfolios require a degree of attention and intervention which relatively few individual investors are in a position to provide. An investor who does not earn his livelihood as a financial advisor or a financial planner (or even one who does) could probably benefit from independent and objective advice in the construction of an overall investment plan.

Dividend Reinvestment Plans for ETF Shares

Some of the earliest ETFs permitted investors to reinvest dividends automatically in additional whole ETF shares if their brokers supported the DTC dividend reinvestment service. Some brokers may offer similar dividend reinvestment into whole or fractional shares for all dividend-paying shares.

Dividend reinvestment has not been widely used by ETF shareholders. Most investors view ETFs as more like stocks than like traditional mutual fund shares. Investors seem to expect cash dividends to be swept into their brokerage account's money market fund to be ready for their next portfolio transaction or for use in adjusting asset allocation.

ENDNOTES

1. For an expanded version of the material discussed in this section, see Gastineau (2001).

2. The elaborate structure of the Supershares helped clear the way for the SPDRs and later ETFs.

3. For specific analysis of the 500 SPDRs see Elton, et al. (forthcoming).

4. For a slightly different perspective of the ETF landscape with more data on individual funds, see Fredman (2001a).

5. Actually, the trustee uses the cash and credits the Trust's expense account with the equivalent of interest.

6. The Bank of New York will undoubtedly file a similar application for the Mid-Cap SPDRs and NASDAQ 100 Trust when approval of the State Street filing nears.

7. As described in more detail in Chapter 8, this proxy value does not have the status of a formal NAV calculation.

8. DTC does not transfer fractional shares or fractions of the basic trading unit of a security which is 100 shares in the case of the HOLDRs. However, some firms use trading and accounting systems that accommodate the New York Stock Exchange's Monthly Investment Plan (MIP). MIP was designed to let investors buy odd lots and fractional shares as a start in owning their share of America. Firms that can accommodate fractional share positions (including Folios) see the ability to handle fractional shares as a competitive advantage.

9. For a slightly different but useful perspective, see Fredman (2001b).

10. An investor can do an in-and-out trade in some conventional mutual funds with almost no transaction cost, but many funds will probably not accept a repeat order from that investor.

Chapter 3

The Regulatory Structure and Mechanics of the Open ETF

This chapter opens with a discussion of the "secret" behind the low expense ratio of ETFs: the absence of shareholder accounting at the fund level. Other sections cover the regulatory framework within which the open ETF operates, introduce the transaction and tax cost allocation functions of the in-kind fund share creation and redemption process and the arbitrage pricing mechanism which prevents meaningful premium or discount pricing of fund shares. Fund share creation and redemption will come up again when we look at tax efficiency in Chapter 4 and arbitrage pricing issues appear again in the discussion of trading in Chapter 8.[1]

NO SHAREHOLDER ACCOUNTING AT THE FUND LEVEL

An open ETF has one registered shareholder for the fund's internal record-keeping purposes: the Depository Trust Company. Brokerage firms and banks that have accounts with DTC provide shareholder accounting to the beneficial owners of ETF shares. One important implication of this structure is that, except for the relatively modest cost of mailing periodic fund reports to beneficial shareholders, variable fund expenses are small and they are primarily a function of the trustee/custodian charge for holding assets rather than a function of the number of shareholders. The firms which carry the shareholder accounts combine the shareholder accounting associated with ETF positions with other services they provide their clients, and these firms are compensated for their services by other fees or by sales commissions. The result is an overall cost reduction for the investor. Most of this cost reduction is reflected in the lower expense ratios of ETFs.

REGULATION—THE INVESTMENT COMPANY ACT OF 1940 AND OTHER SECURITIES LAWS AND REGULATIONS AFFECTING THE GROWTH OF ETFs[2]

The Investment Company Act of 1940

The Investment Company Act of 1940 is unusual among United States securities laws in that it lists specific requirements or prohibitions rather than stressing full disclosure—the focus of much other U.S. securities regulation. Enactment of what is familiarly called the "40 Act" was preceded by extensive Congressional hearings that uncovered an extensive range of management and marketing abuses in the investment company industry in the 1920s and 1930s. Congress concluded that disclosure was not an adequate remedy or deterrent for the abuses uncovered. Consequently, the focus of the 40 Act is on direct regulation, on requirements and prohibitions more akin to the prescriptive and proscriptive legal system of Continental Europe than to the Anglo-Saxon legal system which underlies much of U.S. securities law. The 40 Act is based explicitly on the overriding principle that investment advisors are fiduciaries, and that they must bear specific responsibilities.[3]

Among the provisions of the 40 Act are a number of structural and operating requirements for investment companies that are not consistent with ETF operations. Fortunately, Congress provided the Securities and Exchange Commission (the "SEC" or the "Commission") with blanket authority to grant exemptions from the prescriptions and proscriptions of the 40 Act. The specific language in Section 6(c) of the Act provides, "The Commission by rules and regulations upon its own motion, or by order upon application, may conditionally or unconditionally exempt any person, security, or transaction, or any class or classes of persons, securities, or transactions, from any provision or provisions of this [Act] or of any rule or regulation thereunder, if and to the extent that such exemption is necessary or appropriate in the public interest and consistent with the protection of investors and the purposes fairly intended by the policy and provisions of this [Act]."[4]

It would be difficult to draft language giving the SEC broader exemptive power than it has under Section 6(c), but exemptions are not automatic, nor are they granted casually. One consequence of the necessity of getting ETFs approved through the exemptive process has been considerable delay between the time a request for exemption is filed and the time the needed exemptions are granted. The development and proliferation of ETFs has been significantly— some would say severely—constrained by the process of obtaining exemptions for each issuer and each category of funds. It is reasonable to expect that the process will be streamlined somewhat in the months and years ahead, but it is likely to be some time before a new issuer will be able to bring out a new ETF of a previously exempted type without an exemptive filing, and even longer before an established ETF issuer will be able to bring out a new type of ETF without specific exemptive relief from the Commission.[5]

The exemption process is agonizingly slow, but it does seem to work. The 40 Act has been amended modestly on several occasions, most extensively in 1980. The amendments have affected other structures and businesses, but little has changed in the sections of the original legislation that govern regulation of management investment companies (mutual funds) in the more than 60 years since the legislation was enacted. In its enforcement of the original legislation, the SEC has gradually shifted its emphasis in the direction of disclosure and away from the requirements and prohibitions embedded in the original legislation. The shift has been slow and it is unlikely to accelerate dramatically. Proposals to amend the 40 Act are infrequent and there does not seem to be any enthusiasm for a significant rewrite of the Act.[6] Changes will probably continue to be made through the exemption process, and they are unlikely to be rapid.

Exemptions from the Investment Company Act of 1940 Necessary to Permit Issuance of Open ETFs

The 40 Act requirements and prohibitions are quite specific. As a consequence, an open ETF, whether organized as a management investment company (a mutual fund–type structure) or as a unit investment trust, needs a large number of exemptions from securities legislation to create and redeem shares in-kind and only in large blocks and to permit shares to be traded at market prices on an organized securities market. In addition to the general exemptions that we will describe in some detail here, individual ETFs may require additional specific exemptions which are not obvious to the fund investor. Some of these additional requirements are exemptions granted to the issuer, to the listing exchange, to other markets trading the shares, or to specific broker-dealers who act as specialists and market makers. Some of these requirements are so specialized that they are not spelled out here.[7]

The key initial exemptions granted to all open ETFs were first granted to the Supershares (described in Chapter 2) and have been granted to the issuer or sponsor of every open ETF launched since the Supershares. These exemptions:

- permit ETFs to redeem shares only in creation unit aggregations;
    The significance of this exemption is that the individual ETF shares are *not* redeemable securities and are not bought back by the fund at their daily net asset value.

- permit shares to trade throughout the trading day at prices other than the net asset value next determined by the fund;
    The significance of this exemption is simply to permit prices of individual shares to be determined by market forces rather than by the net asset value calculation at the close of trading each day.

- and permit affiliates to deposit portfolio securities with the investment company and to receive them from the investment company in the creation or redemption of fund shares.
    This exemption provides relief from the self-dealing provisions of the 40 Act in recognition of the transparency of in-kind creation and redemption that is available to all sizable market participants.

In addition to these three major exemptions which every open ETF must have to operate, various other exemptions are required either by the ETF and its sponsor or by the markets where the ETFs trade. Specifically, the UIT structures (SPDRs, MidCap SPDRs, DIA-MONDS, and the NASDAQ 100 Trust) have received exemptions permitting some expenses normally paid by the sponsor to be borne by the trust, exempting the sponsor from the $100,000 initial capital requirement and permitting additional transactions with affiliates beyond the deposit and receipt of portfolio securities in the creation and redemption process. Other ETFs have applied for, and in some cases received, additional exemptions, including:

- exemption from the prospectus delivery requirement for certain secondary market transactions;

  The UIT structures and Vanguard's VIPERS share class have the prospectus delivery exemption for secondary market transactions. They must provide a product description, however; and they must provide a prospectus upon request.

- permission to delay redemption beyond the statutory seven calendar days under certain circumstances;

  This exemption is necessary to facilitate operation of some funds that hold non-U.S. stocks that trade in primary markets with holidays and clearance and settlement cycles different from those in the United States.

- permission to issue an exchange-traded share class as part of a multi-class share structure;

  The Vanguard VIPERS were the first shares of this type.

- permission to make certain exchanges with shareholders or other ETFs;

- permission for a fund-of-funds structure; and

- other relief from the conflict of interest provisions of Section 17 of the 40 Act if the relationships among the fund and its participants and service providers require such relief to operate without violation of the statute.

  This relief would be needed if the Adviser was affiliated with the Trustee.

Exemptions from the Securities and Exchange Act of 1934[8]

When the issuer of an ETF is in the later stages of its exemptive relief application, the market or markets which plan to trade the shares will be applying for their own exemptive relief. In a few cases, these exemptions have become automatic or embedded in exchange rules. But in other cases, they are still granted individually to each fund.

The specific 34 Act exemptions include:

- relief from the up-tick rule for short sales of ETFs;

  The up-tick rule requires that a short sale of a stock may not be executed unless it is done at a price higher than the last sale at a different price. While this rule is widely considered by market participants and regulators alike to be archaic, it remains on the books and an exemption is required to permit the sale of ETF shares on a downtick or zero minus tick. The specific grounds for granting such exemptions for ETFs is that the presumed ability of a "bear raider" to drive the price of a given stock down through a succession of short sales at progressively lower prices does not apply to ETF shares because they are based on baskets of securities and, as a practical matter, it would be impossible for the largest trader to profit by trying to drive the price of the basket down to push a single stock price down.[9]

- relief from rules which otherwise restrict the ability of broker-dealers and others to bid for, purchase, redeem, or engage in other secondary market transactions for ETF units, shares, and portfolio securities during a distribution or tender offer for portfolio securities;

  Since both the distribution and the continual offer to repurchase fund shares in exchange for portfolio securities are ongoing, exemption from these provisions is necessary for normal market operations.

- permission to the ETF to redeem units and shares in creation unit size during the continuous offering of units and shares;

- permitting broker-dealers and others to deposit portfolio securities and to receive portfolio securities without providing their customers with a statement of the number, identity, and price of each individual portfolio security;

- permit margining of ETF shares without the 30-day waiting period after issuance which applies to conventional mutual funds under most circumstances; and

• provide exemption from the 10% holder reporting requirements. This provision is important because the specialist and some market makers as well as individual investors may find from time to time that, as a result of creations on their part and/or redemptions on the part of others, they are holders of more than 10% of the fund shares outstanding. In fact, it is probably a fair statement that in most of the existing ETFs, the specialist's position will normally be in excess of 10% of the ETF shares outstanding. Many of the shares held by the specialist will be on loan to investors who have borrowed them for any of a variety of reasons (including selling the ETF shares short as part of an investment strategy), but the constructive owner of the shares will still be the exchange specialist responsible for maintaining a fair and orderly market in the shares.

Exemptions for Actively Managed and Other New ETF Categories

As new types of ETFs are developed, the exemptive orders permitting them will probably not look very different from the exemptive orders already granted to the first few "generations" of equity-indexed ETFs. The fund descriptions will change and the conditions imposed on the exemption may change—probably growing more complicated; but the structural framework should be very similar for some time to come. Eventually, departures from the current fund creation and redemption structure to accommodate radically different types of actively managed funds holding new classes of securities or operating in new ways may necessitate new exemptions; but such changes are at least a few years in the future.

The long interval between an issuer's filing for exemptive relief and publication of the exemptive order in the Federal Register is likely to get longer unless the Commission changes its procedures. High turnover in Commission staff positions, combined with the complexities of ETF structures and regulatory issues, suggest that the lag between the first exemptive request filing and issuance of the first ETF shares under the exemptive order is likely to get longer as funds become more complicated and their investment policies become more flexible. Shortening the interval will require a change of focus from the Commission. This change can take one of several paths. The Commission can routinely grant the types of exemptive relief it has granted in the past and turn its attention to the suitability of new fund features. This change has the desirable effect of freeing resources from repetition of a thoroughly examined and vetted structure and procedure. It also settles and sets aside some of the more complex features of ETFs, permitting new applications to describe and analyze the similarities and differences of new fund proposals. The lives of a large number of trees could be saved as well.

There seems little reason to fear that simplification of the exemptive side of the regulatory process will imperil investors. The success of the ETF structure in the marketplace has stimulated a number of related innovations that have attempted to create new structures or modify existing structures to incorporate some of the investment flexibility and cost-saving features of the initial equity index ETFs. Some examples include:

- intra-day pricing of conventional funds (Rydex);[10]
- ETF share classes of conventional funds (Vanguard's VIPERS);
- intra-day trading of new portfolio products (HOLDRs, Folios); and
- reduced expenses for larger fund accounts to reflect the relatively fixed, per-account cost of shareholder accounting (Vanguard's Admiral share classes).

One suspects that the intensely competitive nature of the investment management industry will lead competitors to point out any real— and many imaginary—problems with any future ETF innovation.[11]

CREATION AND REDEMPTION IN-KIND

Creation and redemption in-kind is an essential feature of all existing ETFs, whether they are organized as special-purpose unit investment trusts or as management investment companies. Creation and redemption in-kind is actually a very simple process. It puzzles many users of ETFs, not because of its complexity, but simply because it is different from some of the procedures used by conventional funds.

What Is In-Kind Creation and Redemption, and Why Was It Done This Way?

Nathan Most, the principal developer of the original SPDR at the American Stock Exchange, has a background in commodities. Partly as a result of this background, he envisioned the SPDR as a warehouse receipt-based product. The idea was that broker-dealers or large investors would deposit baskets of stock with the trustee and receive warehouse receipts (fund shares) in return. If they decided at some point in the future that they no longer wanted fund shares, they could exchange the fund shares for the underlying basket of portfolio securities. If the index on which the fund was based changed its composition in the meantime, the basket the investors would receive in the redemption would change from the basket they had deposited; but it would change according to the index (or fund prospectus) rules.

The creation and redemption process in use by all existing ETFs is simply an implementation of this modified warehouse receipt concept. A careful reading of Part B of any of the UIT ETFs or of the Statement of Additional Information (SAI) for any of the management investment company ETFs will spell out the detailed creation and redemption process that is designed to assure that an investor can create as many additional shares of an ETF as he or she desires by depositing multiple creation baskets of stock with the trustee and can redeem as many such baskets as the investor can assemble standard aggregations of fund shares to cover. All creation and redemption transactions occur at net asset value with the portfolio securities and the fund shares priced on a consistent basis. There is a flat transaction fee for both creations and redemptions. This fee of a few hundred to a few thousand dollars per transaction is largely a function of the number of different securities in the fund portfolio. The flat fee will permit the creator or redeemer to create or redeem an unlimited number of creation unit aggregations on any given business day for a fixed charge per transaction.[12]

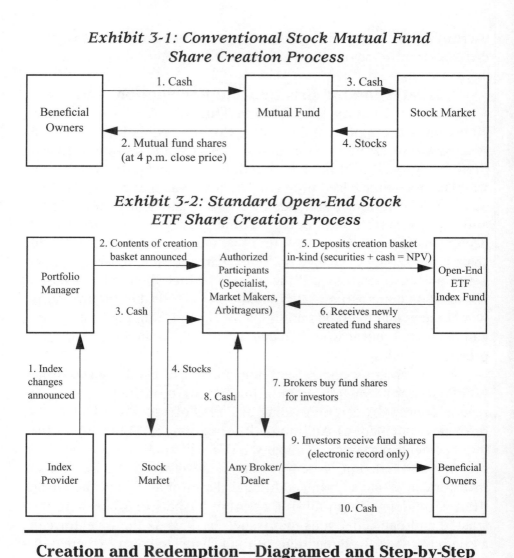

Exhibit 3-1: Conventional Stock Mutual Fund Share Creation Process

Exhibit 3-2: Standard Open-End Stock ETF Share Creation Process

Creation and Redemption—Diagramed and Step-by-Step

Exhibit 3-1 illustrates the conventional stock mutual fund creation (purchase) process, in which the purchaser of fund shares deals directly with the fund, pays cash and receives fund shares at the 4:00 p.m. net asset value price calculation. The fund purchases portfolio stocks in the open market for cash, frequently in a market-on-close transaction on the day the new shares are issued.

Exhibit 3-2 shows the standard open-end stock ETF share creation process, which is somewhat more complex because of the role of the index which underlies all existing ETFs. In this case, Authorized Participants deposit securities and a balancing amount in cash equal to the net asset value of the requisite number of fund shares (Step 5) and receive newly created fund shares (Step 6). These shares, in turn, are sold by the Authorized Participants through any broker or dealer (Step 7) to beneficial owners (Step 9), who pay cash (Step 10) to the broker-dealer, who, in turn, pays cash (Step 8) to the Authorized Participant, who is usually the specialist, a market maker, or an arbitrageur.

Exhibit 3-3 shows the conventional stock mutual fund redemption process which is identical to the purchase process in reverse in that the owner of the fund shares tenders shares to the fund at the next 4:00 p.m. net asset value calculation and receives cash in return. The fund usually will sell stocks in the open market for enough cash to pay the redeeming shareholder. A significant difference between conventional funds and ETFs in both the creation and redemption process is that the conventional fund will usually make an open market stock transaction in each case. In other words, the conventional fund buys and sells portfolio securities as opposed to exchanging them in-kind for fund shares.

Exhibit 3-4 shows the redemption process in an open ETF. As with the redemption of shares by the conventional fund, this is the reverse of the ETF creation process—fund shares are being tendered to the fund (Step 6) in exchange for a basket of portfolio securities from the fund (Step 7). Authorized Participants engage in cash transactions (Steps 4 and 5) with any broker-dealer. That broker-dealer, in turn, trades with (or on behalf of) its customers (Steps 2 and 3). The fund, as in the creation, trades primarily in-kind.

Exhibit 3-3: Conventional Stock Mutual Fund Share Redemption Process

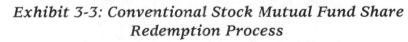
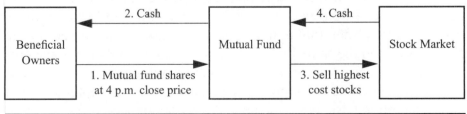

Exhibit 3-4: Standard Open-End Stock ETF Share Redemption Process

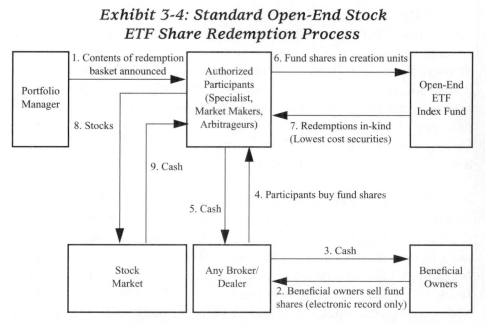

Exhibit 3-5: Standard Index ETF End-of-Day Time Line

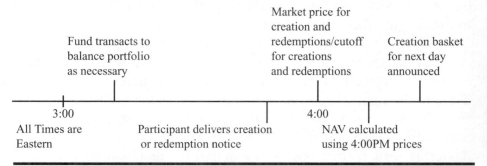

Exhibit 3-5 shows the standard equity index ETF end-of-day time-line. As late in the day as shortly after 3:00 p.m., the fund transacts to balance its portfolio in any way that might be necessary. Before 4:00 p.m., an Authorized Participant delivers a creation or redemption notice, and at 4:00 p.m., the cutoff for creations and redemptions occurs. Shortly after 4:00 p.m., the net asset value is calculated for the fund shares and the same prices are used to value the shares in the creation and redemption baskets. The cash-balancing amount is calculated and credited to the appropriate party. After the close, the creation and redemption baskets for the next day are announced.

Exhibit 3-6 shows what happens on days when there is a change in the index. In Step 1, the index change effective at the end of Day Two is announced by the index provider. The creation and redemption basket which is generated after the market close—in this case, at about 6:00 p.m. on Day One—will reflect the index change in the contents of the creation and redemption baskets. At the start of Day Two, the fund holdings do not yet reflect changes in the index. Note that in this case, the fund owns 2,000 shares of Security XYZ, and in order to conform with the index at the close, the fund needs to hold 1,000 shares of Security C instead of the 2,000 shares of XYZ. During the day on Day Two, the portfolio manager will sell 2,000 shares of XYZ and buy 1,000 shares of Security C. The portfolio manager will make these trades without regard to any creations and redemptions because the creation and redemption baskets *do not include any shares of XYZ*. They include Security C. So, in order to be able to meet redemptions or to be certain that the portfolio has the proper number of shares in Security C at the close, any creations and redemptions will both include Security C on that day.

Because, in this example, the fund portfolio and the creation basket are different, using the intra-day value of the creation basket as a proxy for the intra-day price movement of the fund may not be satisfactory. As a result of this difference between the fund and the creation basket composition, many index funds are moving away from the earlier practice of using the creation basket to calculate the intra-day pricing proxy. They increasingly use a basket based on the actual portfolio of the fund to calculate this intra-day proxy when the creation/redemption basket anticipates an index/portfolio change.

In any event, in this particular case, a participant requests fund shares in exchange for a creation basket before 4:00 p.m. on Day Two. The creation basket, which contains 100 shares of Security C, will be tendered in exchange for fund shares. The revised fund holdings after the deposit of the additional creation unit will reflect the creation, and the fund holdings will be in proportion to the index in the creation basket, as stated in Step 1. Since no change in the index is scheduled for Day Three, the creation basket for Day Three based on the revised index fund holdings is identical to that on Day Two and is published on Day Two at approximately 6:00 p.m.

Exhibit 3-6: Standard Open-End ETF—Simplified Example of Daily Processes When an Index Changes

1. Index change effective end of Day 2 announced by index provider. Creation basket generated based on revised index. (Day 1—6:00 PM)

Index/Creation Basket

Security A	Security B	Security C
100 shares	70 shares	100 Shares

2. Start-of-day fund holdings do not yet reflect changes in index. (Day 2—8:00 AM)

Fund Holdings

Security A	Security B	Security XYZ
1000 shares	700 shares	2000 shares

3. Fund portfolio manager trades so fund holdings reflect revised index. (Day 2—before 4:00 PM)

Sell	*Buy*
Security XYZ	Security C
2000 Shares	1000 Shares

4. Participant requests fund shares in exchange for a creation basket (Day 2—before 4:00 PM)

Creation Basket Effective on Day 2

Security A	Security B	Security C
100 shares	70 shares	100 shares

5. Revised fund holdings reflect creations and today's trades. (Day 2—after 4:00 PM)

Fund Holdings

Security A	Security B	Security C
1100 shares	770 shares	1100 Shares

6. No change in index scheduled for Day 3. Creation basket for Day 3 based on revised index/ fund holdings (Day 2—6:00 PM)

Index/Creation Basket

Security A	Security B	Security C
100 shares	70 shares	100 Shares

What Is the Reason for Doing Creations and Redemptions In-Kind?

Conventional mutual funds have widely varying policies on how they offer their shares to the public and on how they redeem them. The most common practice among no-load mutual funds is simply to offer shares to investors at net asset value as next calculated after the buyer's payment is received by the fund company. The fund company will usually require at least a few hours' notice of the purchase and can invest the payments in new shares without obvious transaction costs.[13] Conventional funds often redeem shares at net asset value even if the redemption request comes in only a few days or weeks after the purchase order was received.

The conventional fund will often have to sell shares to cover a redemption. While, again, it is often possible to sell the shares without a readily measurable cost to be borne by the ongoing shareholders of the fund, a significant number of such transactions over time is likely to have some cost to ongoing shareholders. To protect long-term shareholders, an increasing number of fund companies have been instituting redemption fees. These redemption fees may range up to 1% of the value of the redeemed shares in the case of a fund that holds small capitalization or other high-transaction-cost securities, and even higher in some funds that attempt to protect ongoing shareholders from realization of taxes triggered by the sale of low-basis stock for cash to meet redemptions. The purpose of these redemption fees is to discourage in-and-out trading. In some cases the fees permit ongoing fund shareholders to "profit" from the entry and exit of short-term traders. The problem with setting such a fee level is that, in relatively quiet markets, the cost to the fund to transact may be significantly less than the redemption fee it charges in-and-out traders. In highly volatile and unsettled markets, the cost of transacting may be much greater than the redemption fee. It is impossible to set a fixed rate which is fair to all parties because the costs are not identical in all markets or at all times.

One key feature of the in-kind creation and redemption process with its fixed administrative transaction fee is that the transaction fee is designed to cover the cost of setting up and running the creation and redemption process as well as the cost of the paperwork for a specific transaction. The transaction costs associated with assembling the creation basket for deposit in exchange for fund shares or of taking the redemption basket of portfolio securities and selling it in the marketplace will be borne by the Authorized Participant—the specialist, market maker, or other broker-dealer who facilitates the creation and redemption process. The Authorized Participant may recover its costs for the creation and redemption process from its market-making activities. The bid-asked spread in the secondary market for the fund shares will reflect those costs. Whatever the costs are, *they are not borne by the ongoing shareholders of the fund*. In short, then, the original purpose and the compelling case for in-kind creation and redemption is protection of ongoing shareholders from essentially *all* of the impact from entry and exit of short-term shareholders.

Future ETFs will develop variations on the in-kind creation and redemption process. For a variety of reasons, certain funds will provide for partial cash-in-lieu payments on some creations or redemptions. In the simplest case, this may be because a broker-dealer cannot trade in a specific security as a result of its investment banking activities or because its own shares are part of a portfolio. The broker-dealer will request a custom basket and pay cash plus any costs associated with the purchase or sale of the affected shares by the custodian of the fund or by the fund portfolio manager. By such means, the protection of ongoing shareholders from the costs of in-and-out transactions by other shareholders will be preserved, and an Authorized Participant will be able to create and redeem without transacting in its own shares or the shares of a banking client.

In the case of redemptions, an additional reason for providing cash in lieu of certain securities might be the desire of the fund portfolio manager to realize a loss in the fund on certain securities. In this case, the redemption basket will not reflect the presence of these securities, although their presence will be taken into account by any market maker for purposes of creating hedging portfolios or by anyone calculating an intra-day fund share value.

The original purpose of the in-kind creation and redemption process was simply to allocate transaction costs in an appropriate way.[14] But, as we will see in the discussion of tax efficiency in Chapter 4, in-kind redemption has a serendipitous tax advantage for some ongoing shareholders. Assume that an in-and-out trader bought 100 shares of the fund at $9 per share and sold them after a few days at $10 for a total profit of $100. Also, assume that 100 fund shares is the size of the in-kind creation unit. In a conventional mutual fund transaction, the trader had a short-term capital gain of $100 *and* the fund could sell (for cash) the same stocks it purchased when the trader bought fund shares—for a $100 short-term gain in the fund. The *total gain* on the transaction was $100, but the trader would pay taxes on that gain and, other things equal, the fund would distribute an identical taxable gain to its ongoing shareholders. The gain would be, in effect, taxed twice. The trader would pay a tax on the gain from sale of his fund shares and the ongoing shareholders of the fund would pay tax on a gain from a trade in portfolio shares that they did not make and that did not add to the net asset value of any of *their* fund shares.[15]

Fortunately, the treatment of this transaction is different if the creations and redemptions are in-kind. With a redemption in-kind, the fund does not experience a taxable gain, so there is no $100 gain distributed to fund shareholders who did not benefit from that gain. The in-and-out fund shareholder, appropriately, pays tax on a short-term gain. Selling portfolio securities for cash to cover redemptions can hurt ongoing shareholders in a conventional fund even more than this example suggests if a fund faces heavy cash redemptions when it has a great deal of low-cost-basis stock. The point to be made here is that the ETF in-kind redemption structure helps overcome some of the odd inequities of mutual fund taxation.

What About Creation and Redemption with Actively Managed Funds?

We expect the dominant method of creation and redemption of shares in actively managed equity funds to be nearly identical to the creation and redemption process in index funds. That is, we expect actively managed funds to grow and shrink predominantly through creation and redemption in-kind. If a relatively freeform (as opposed to a distinctly ETF-oriented) active management process is achieved, a fund manager will operate more or less as he or she does today in an actively managed conventional fund, and there may be

greater variation in the way the fund creation and redemption process works.

There are enough reasons to retain the in-kind process to
believe that it will continue to be the dominant mechanism, certainly for the Self-Indexing Fund, which we expect to be one of the
first types of actively managed funds and even for the broad range of
more freeform actively managed funds which will probably be
introduced within a few years. There is an extensive discussion of
these two possible types of actively managed ETFs in Chapter 7.

INTRA-DAY PRICING, TRADING, AND THE
ROLE OF THE ARBITRAGEUR

Each open ETF, its listing exchange, or some other organization dis-
seminates an up-to-date proxy for the market value of the assets
behind each fund share. For existing funds, an updated share value
of the portfolio is calculated every 15 seconds throughout the normal trading day. The procedure in the early days of ETFs was to
base the intra-day price calculation on the creation basket, which, in
most cases, is essentially identical in composition to the redemption
basket—and to the fund portfolio. If the fund is an index fund and
the number of companies in the index is quite large, this usually
works out reasonably well. However, funds based on indexes with
small numbers of stocks like the DIAMONDS (30 stocks) have to
provide intra-day values based on the actual portfolio while their
creation basket reflects the updated index as of the close of trading
on the day for which the basket is issued.[16]

The creation and redemption process is conditioned by arbitrage relationships. *This does not mean that creation and redemption
is generally motivated by arbitrage.* As described in more detail in
Chapter 8, the primary motivation for creation and redemption is
inventory management by the specialist and market makers in the
fund shares. Arbitrage profits, when they are available, are typically
very small relative to the money at stake in the trading process. Market making profits, particularly in an actively traded ETF share, can
be much greater than arbitrage profits. Arbitrage-constrained intra-

day pricing and trading simply assures reasonable spreads for all market participants and fair pricing. As we will see in Chapter 8's discussion of premiums and discounts, material premiums and discounts are prevented by the presence of potential arbitrage between the ETF shares and the underlying creation and redemption baskets.

CONCLUSION

This chapter has introduced the nuts and bolts of ETFs. We will revisit the transaction cost and taxation issues in subsequent chapters. The creation and redemption process will come up regularly, not only in connection with trading, transaction costs and taxes, but in the development of new ETF variations.

ENDNOTES

1. Different and useful perspectives on some topics in this chapter are offered in Elton, et al. (forthcoming) and Fredman (2001a).

2. This section draws heavily on Moriarty (2001) and Frankel (1978, 2000).

3. Frankel (1978), page 25.

4. Frankel (1978), page 93.

5. Frankel (1978), page 94.

6. Gramm (2001). This press release summarizes the Senate Banking Committee's legislative agenda for the 107th Congress. Gramm promises a "top-to-bottom review of U.S. securities laws," but, implicitly, seems satisfied with the 40 Act. There is no mention of specific changes proposed for fund regulation.

7. See Moriarty (2001) for more details.

8. Based primarily on Moriarty (2001)

9. All existing funds have obtained the relief as of the end of 2001, but an investor might take the precaution of checking on the up-tick exemption of new funds.

10. Periodic intra-day pricing has been available on some Fidelity sector funds for sometime.

11. The SEC's appropriate rejection of a proposal that Folios should be subject to 40 Act regulation comes to mind.

12. Barclays Global Investors launched their first domestic funds with a per-creation-unit transaction fee. Objections by specialists and market makers soon forced them to adopt the flat "all you can eat" fee structure. The original SPDRs also had a higher and more complex transaction fee structure that generally charged more for redemptions than creations. This was changed to flat and equal fees for creation and redemption in the mid-1990s.

13. A large fund can often find brokers that will take orders for the day as market-on-close (MOC) orders and guarantee a fill at the close or better without charging a commission. From the fund's perspective, this appears to be a free transaction. The apparent cost of any market impact from the MOC order is borne by entering or exiting shareholders. Unfortunately, measuring market impact costs is not quite that simple and this approach does not work for all stocks and all funds.

14. The creators of ETFs also expected to reduce the fund's overall transaction costs. Any such reductions have been modest in the aggregate.

15. A taxable gain calculation technique called equalization is used by many fund companies to protect ongoing shareholders from some of the tax impact of share redemptions. It would be difficult to combine equalization and redemption in-kind unless a fund had both conventional and ETF share classes, like the Vanguard VIPERS. See the text box on equalization on page 97.

16. In an ideal world, all of today's index ETFs should post creation and redemption baskets that reflect index changes as of the day's market close. The intra-day portfolio value calculation should be based on the day's opening portfolio.

Chapter 4

Distinctive Characteristics of Exchange-Traded Funds: Transactions, Shareholder Protection, Payment for Value Added, Fund Evaluation, and Taxation

T he purpose of this chapter is to summarize, in one place, the key distinguishing features of open exchange-traded funds. While most of the features highlighted here are discussed elsewhere in the book, these features are approached from a different perspective in other chapters. It seems appropriate to list and analyze the key features and their interaction in one location. In doing so, we begin with a section on the disadvantages—or at least the frequently cited disadvantages—of ETFs.

PRESUMED DISADVANTAGES OF ETFS

The Small, Periodic Share Purchaser

The most frequently cited disadvantage of the open ETF is its higher cost to the small investor who makes small, periodic—say, weekly or monthly—purchases of fund shares. Indeed, it is clear that an investor who maintains a brokerage account that requires payment of a transaction charge on each small, periodic investment in a fund is at a disadvantage relative to an investor who buys shares in a conventional no-load fund that offers shares at net asset value in whatever transaction size the investor chooses and in whole or fractional shares. Brokers carrying ETFs in commission-only accounts cannot offer a comparable service at a profit.[1] To stay in business, these brokers charge a fee or commission to trade ETF shares, just as they charge to trade shares of stock.

What we need in looking at this example of an ETF "disadvantage" is an appropriate perspective. An investor who is going to invest a few hundred or a few thousand dollars at a time in an ETF account is, in fact, paying a price for the small ETF position that covers the costs of taking that position. It should be encouraging to other, larger investors in the ETF that, in contrast to all the shareholders in a conventional fund, other ETF shareholders are not subsidizing the small, periodic ETF buyer. The conventional fund that accommodates small shareholders by accepting very small, periodic payments and processing them at no extra charge to the small investors is doing its larger shareholders a disservice. In fact, many conventional funds charge variable expense ratios depending on account size and charge annual account maintenance fees for smaller accounts. For example, Vanguard has begun offering Admiral Class shares with lower expense ratios to its larger investors in recognition of the lower cost—as a percent of assets—of carrying their accounts. Just as appropriately, Vanguard charges an annual account maintenance fee for certain small accounts. Non-profit TIAA-CREF recently raised its minimum for regular fund accounts to $1,500 from $250 and the minimum additional investment to $50 from $15. It will still open an account for as little as $50 if the investor makes minimum $50 monthly payments.

The reason the small, periodic investor incurs proportionately higher costs for his transactions is that his transactions are costly relative to the size of his account. The brokerage firm that handles ETF transaction charges accordingly. A conventional mutual fund that accepts small, periodic deposits without charging extra is, in effect, charging the cost of these transactions to its other shareholders to subsidize the service extended to the small investor. The investor seeing a separate transaction charge for each trade as a major disadvantage of ETFs should ask, "Who, if not me, should be paying the costs of these transactions?"

Stimulation of Excessive Trading

With respect to the use of ETFs by active traders—some with small accounts, others with large ones—in the secondary market for ETFs, there is occasional criticism that the mere existence of ETFs encourages a high level of trading activity. While we deal with this subject at greater length in Chapter 8, it seems appropriate to note here that the decision to trade or not to trade is a personal decision which each investor makes. It seems inappropriate that others should try to make that decision for him.

Transparency Cost in Actively Managed ETFs

A future possible ETF disadvantage has emerged in some discussions of actively managed ETFs. Some investors and fund managers argue that there will be a transparency cost or loss of information value by the holder and manager of an actively managed ETF. This transparency cost arises because there will inevitably be a greater degree of portfolio transparency in an actively managed ETF than in a conventional actively managed fund. In fact, greater transparency and a corresponding loss in the value of information will be facts of life for *some* actively managed ETFs.

Some additional information on the character of the portfolio held by an actively managed ETF will have to be revealed to specialists and market makers (and consequently to all interested investors) to encourage dealers to trade in the shares. The SEC is virtually certain to insist that a proxy for the intra-day value be disseminated during the trading day for the first actively managed funds. The share value changes reflected in this intra-day information will provide astute analysts with a great deal of information about the content of the portfolio. Future funds may provide less portfolio and pricing information than we have described here, but the level of disclosure required of actively managed ETFs will probably always be closer to that required of today's equity index ETFs than to that required of today's conventional active funds.

It is difficult to think of many cases today or in the recent past when a high level of secrecy as to the recent contents of a mutual fund portfolio has been necessary to protect actively managed fund shareholders from predatory traders who would front-run an active portfolio manager's purchases and sales.[2] It is hard to develop a credible argument that there should be no more knowledge of a fund's holdings than the information provided today by most conventional mutual fund managers. In most cases, a great deal more information could be made public without harm to the fund's shareholders. The SEC seems inclined to require increased disclosure by conventional funds and will soon face decisions on disclosure requirements for actively managed ETFs. We discuss this topic at greater length in Chapter 7 and conclude that *the market itself can and should determine the appropriate level of portfolio disclosure.*

In summary, for most investors, the suggested disadvantages of ETFs merely reflect an equitable distribution of costs and ongoing shareholder protection from in-and-out trading.

We turn now to the clear advantages of ETFs.

INTRA-DAY TRADING

A large fraction of the investors who use exchange-traded funds place a value on intra-day trading *solely* because it gives them the opportunity to liquidate their position any time of day in an adverse market environment. Even if *buying* shares in a conventional mutual fund at the 4:00 p.m. net asset value is acceptable to investors, many of them like the idea that with ETFs they do not have to *sell* at the price determined at the close. A smaller group values the ability to use the wide range of types of orders available for the execution of an order in a common stock.

More sophisticated investors who have no intention of selling shares in a tumbling market or with complex orders embrace the ETF mechanism because it offers *a fairer allocation of trading costs* than does the conventional mutual fund structure. To the extent that an investor holds shares in a conventional fund for the long run and the fund does not charge a premium over net asset value to new shareholders or a redemption fee, the chances are that the longer-term holders of the fund subsidize in-and-out traders. The ETF structure simply and fairly allocates the cost of trading to those who trade. Of course, intra-day trading also makes arbitrage pricing (which eliminates material premiums and discounts) and other important features of ETFs possible. This issue is described more thoroughly in Chapter 8, but remember—the fact that investors have the ability to trade actively does not mean they will do it.

PROTECTION OF ONGOING SHAREHOLDERS

For products that are used by many online traders and which almost invariably dominate the most actively traded share list on the American Stock Exchange, exchange-traded funds do an inspiring job of protecting ongoing shareholders from inappropriate trading costs, most of which are generated by active traders. The way the ETF structure protects ongoing shareholders from the trading costs and tax costs generated by active traders has been discussed both in the previous section and in the previous chapter, and it will come up again in other contexts. The fact that there are minimal shareholder costs at the fund level is the best indication that the costs paid by the fund are common costs attributable to all holders of the fund and that no shareholder subsidizes any other shareholder.

FLEXIBILITY IN EXPENSE MANAGEMENT AND PAYMENT FOR VALUE ADDED

As discussed in Chapter 1, we believe that most investors need some degree of advice and support in their investment program. Exchange-traded funds provide an unprecedented degree of flexibility in deciding how much advice and support an investor wants to purchase. In contrast to many actively managed conventional funds with built-in sales loads, the operating cost of all existing open ETFs is essentially the cost of running the fund.

When they are offered, actively managed open ETFs will almost certainly be of at least two types. One type will carry a sales or service fee to cover the cost of advice and support from an experienced advisor. The other type will be "no load" like the existing index funds, but even these no-load funds will be supported by many advisors, as the existing index ETFs have been. Wrap accounts (where the investor pays a fee covering advice and the commission cost of secondary market transactions) will be used to package different levels of investor support and to mix index and active ETF positions in a supervised account. Open ETFs seem to be accelerating the trend away from the fee-for-service (brokerage commission) model toward the relationship or comprehensive service model where an investor pays an asset-based fee for access to a range of information and support. This change is not necessarily good for all investors, but it does encourage dialogues between an investor and one or more advisors about fees and service arrangements.

A NEW FUND ANALYSIS AND EVALUATION MODEL

Another desirable feature of the open ETF is that a more complete, up-to-date picture of the fund will provide more information for fund analysts and fund evaluation services. Even an individual investor with relatively little investment experience can project a picture of a transparent portfolio's investment characteristics: What will cause it to go up? What will cause it to go down? How will it react relative to other funds with similar or slightly different features? Because their portfolios are an open book, the existing open ETFs can be subjected to many new kinds of analysis by ETF specialty analysts. Traditional fund analysis often focuses on the sensitivity of fund share price behavior to a variety of economic and financial market phenomena. ETFs lend themselves to such analysis—and much more. ETFs can be the subject of intense analysis of such things as the efficiency with which the manager or advisor trades the fund, the inherent efficiency or inefficiency of the fund's underlying index (if it is an index fund), or the relative performance of the stocks an active manager buys and those she sells. It is useful to look at some examples of new approaches to fund evaluation and comparisons.

Manager quality is extremely important. Even in managing an index fund, there are important differences in performance based on the way the manager uses the flexibility available to time the changes that must be made in the portfolio. One good general clue to manager quality is the fund's tax efficiency. An equity ETF which is not managed in a tax-efficient manner is probably not managed in a cost-efficient manner. Over time, the better fund advisory services will develop measures of management quality. Among these measures will be fund trading costs, embedded index trading costs and comparisons of the performance of an active manager's purchases with the performance of the stocks she sells—after the latter leave the portfolio.[3] A well-managed equity index ETF will match or beat its template index before fund expenses, and a good active manager will generally add value when she trades.

Another clue to manager quality and overall attractiveness of an ETF may be its use by fund-of-funds managers and managers specializing in creating tax-managed asset allocation portfolios based on ETFs.[4] While some of these "fund-picking" managers may be using some or all funds which are affiliated with their own organizations, it should be possible to examine the portfolios of fund of funds managers who do not have affiliated funds or who use both affiliated and unaffiliated funds. Some choices may be dictated by availability and by business arrangements, but selection of a fund by a fund-of-funds manager may be a favorable indication of fund quality. An evaluation service should be helpful in determining that the fund-of-funds manager's economics of holding a fund are essentially the same as an individual investor's economics.

The quality of the trading market in the ETF shares is also an important fund evaluation tool. While trading volume itself may not be a good indicator, to the extent that an investor focuses on trading volume, it should be on dollar volume, not share volume. A well-structured fund will have a high share price, typically something in the vicinity of $100 a share at the time of launch. A slightly lower share price may be due to a market decline in the market sector represented in the fund, but a much lower share price probably reflects poor product design. The iShares MSCI family (formerly WEBS), for example, were initially launched as low-priced shares. In part, because of their low prices, but also because the underlying markets are often not open during U.S. market hours, the spreads on the iShares MSCI funds are generally wider—on a percentage basis—than those of other exchange-traded funds.

In the final analysis, fund market quality is a function of the markets made by the specialist and market makers in the fund, and the quality of the underlying market in the securities held by the fund. It is worth noting that the advisor of an exchange-traded fund chooses the specialist. Consequently, the specialist choice is partly a reflection of the advisor's ability. We would expect a fund evaluation service to analyze the quality of the markets in a fund's shares in a number of ways. Some of these measures of market quality are discussed at length in Chapter 8.

The relationship of the fund share trading spread and the spreads in the underlying market for the stock basket should also be compared to the daily movement or variability of the underlying index, and the size of the underlying market. A fund based on large capitalization stocks, for example, which has a daily movement typical of a sector index based on large capitalization stocks should enjoy a relatively narrow spread, and feature a large average bid and offer size. The bid and offer size indicates the ease with which an investor could take or sell a large position. In this respect, the fund's spread alone is often misleading. Ordinarily, a specialist in a large cap exchange-traded fund will be prepared to make a market in substantial size: 100,000 to 1 million shares on each side of a narrow spread in the United States. In the case of a large-cap domestic stock index with an active futures contract, a small bid or offer is usually indicative of a retail order inside the specialist's market. The specialist is required to display this retail order, and, while it may give the small investor an opportunity to trade inside the ordinary trading spread, a high frequency of small orders and fluctuations in the spread may indicate that the specialist is not making a tight market for large traders.

ETF expenses are relatively low because there is no shareholder record-keeping at the fund level, because existing ETFs are index funds, and because the level of the expense ratio is a matter of public focus. Expense analysis may start with the expense ratio, but it should not end there. Transaction costs for index portfolio modifications and transitions are a much larger cost for most ETFs than the costs traditionally included in the expense ratio. Plexus Group and other transaction-cost-analysis organizations have databases that permit comprehensive transaction cost analysis. These databases were not developed primarily from index fund transactions, but they may be adaptable to index modification transaction cost analysis with some manageable assumptions.

The absence of good data on index portfolio modification transaction costs has masked the effect of inefficient indexes used as the basis for funds. Most index rules permit any manager to be certain of tracking the index by matching all fund trades to the rules. The index rules may cause the fund to experience substantial trading costs that are embedded in the index. We will illustrate this feature of the S&P 500 and the Russell 2000 in Exhibit 6-5.

If an index fund lags the performance of its index, the lag reflects on the skills of the portfolio manager unless there is an obvious problem with the index. If the fund beats the index, the result is probably due in part to a good portfolio manager. A good manager may take advantage of an index with large embedded transaction costs. We will return to these issues in Chapter 6. In the meantime, it is useful to keep in mind that both the choice of the index and the choice of the manager are the responsibility of the fund advisor (or the UIT sponsor).

Some parts of the exchange-traded fund market, most obviously the market for S&P 500–based exchange-traded funds, are extraordinarily competitive. With expense ratios occasionally under 10 basis points and bid-asked spreads often at 10–20 basis points for large size, it is useful to put these numbers in perspective in evaluating S&P 500 ETFs relative to others. With a $100 share price, a basis point is a penny a year in terms of differences in the expense ratio, and 10 basis points is 10 cents a year. If market quality and trading volume are comparable, the most reasonable basis for comparison of S&P 500 ETFs is how well or poorly they have performed relative to the index after expenses. In evaluating other large-cap ETFs relative to the S&P 500, the investor needs to examine not only the differences in cost and price, but the differences in diversification and other difficult-to-measure embedded transaction costs as well as the simple expense ratio and the trading spread. We will address these issues and try to put a framework around them. It may be several years before comparisons between real ETFs of the type illustrated in Exhibit 6-5 are routinely available, but such comparisons are inevitable.

The growing transparency of fund construction, transaction costs, and portfolio management efficiency will shift some of the burden of practical ETF analysis and product support from traditional fund services to brokerage/investment banking firms with their depth of information on and familiarity with trading and portfolio execution costs. The traditional fund services do not yet have a full appreciation of the differences between conventional funds and ETFs. It may take them a while to catch up. On the other hand, the fund services may find they are selling more of their research and data through "new" channels: smaller brokerage firms and online brokerage firms. Regardless of the changes in fund service marketing programs, the relative growth in importance of the major investment firm research analyst in fund evaluation will increase the availability of ETF information and support for many investors.

TAXATION OF ETFs: SUBCHAPTER M AND REGULATED INVESTMENT COMPANY (RIC) REQUIREMENTS[5]

This section summarizes and attempts to explain the important provisions for taxation of regulated investment companies under Subchapter M of the Internal Revenue Code as those provisions apply to open ETFs in the United States, based on the law in effect when this was written. We also consider taxation of investment company distributions in the hands of their shareholders. The standard disclaimer that the author is not in the business of offering tax advice is fully applicable. If we know that a particular provision or position is controversial, we will try to describe the nature of the controversy, but every investor should obtain tax advice from his or her personal tax advisor. In contrast to the other sections in this chapter that summarize specific ETF advantages, this section is the principal discussion of investment company and fund shareholder taxation in the book. The emphasis is heavily on U.S. taxation, with an occasional comment on fund and fund shareholder taxation in other countries.

Tax Passthrough Principles

In most developed countries and many less developed countries, the general principle of an investment company as a passthrough vehicle for tax purposes has been adopted. This does not mean that the holder of investment company shares will always be as well off as the investor who holds a similar basket of shares directly in a separate personal account. As we review the provisions of the U.S. Tax Code for regulated investment companies, some disadvantages of regulated investment company taxation will appear, as will some distinct advantages. While it is by no means equally attractive to every kind of investor in a U.S.-based fund, U.S. investment company tax law is close to tax neutral on balance, in contrast to some other countries (Japan, for example) where the investment company form is appreciably disadvantaged.[6] Some non-U.S. investors may be able to defer or even avoid taxes if they own shares in an investment company that does not pass through distributions of investment income and capital gains to shareholders.[7]

Passthrough Positives

In general, a U.S. investment company will pass through most kinds of income to its shareholders without a significant change in their character or tax timing impact. For example, dividend and interest income, net of fund expenses, is passed through as income dividends and generally taxed to the shareholder in the calendar year the income was received by the fund. If a fund has generated net long-term capital gains through the sale of shares held for more than a year, they are passed through to shareholders as long-term capital gains. Interestingly, these gains are passed through as long-term capital gains regardless of the investor's holding period in the fund shares. In other words, a capital gains distribution paid near year end will be a long-term capital gain to the shareholder even if her shares were purchased in September or October—or even later. The reason for tax treatment that ignores the investor's actual holding period appears to be that, with capital gains distributions made each year by many funds, it would be very difficult for a new shareholder to avoid having less than a one-year holding period before a (long-term) capital gains distribution was made. The United States taxes these capital gains distributions at the investor's long-term capital gains rate and increases the investor's basis in the fund shares by any amount of the reinvested capital gains distribution. A capital gains tax will not be imposed on the same gain a second time when the investor sells the fund shares.[8]

Passthrough Obstacles and Constraints

There are a number of obstacles to full passthrough of income and avoidance of taxation at the fund level. The obstacles to full passthrough of income usually result in the character of the income being changed in the process of distribution. For example, a regulated investment company does not distribute short-term capital gains in the character of short-term capital gains. Any net short-term capital gains realized by the fund which are not offset by short- or long-term capital losses at the fund level will be treated as being paid out as part of the fund's income distribution by its shareholders. The fund's financial reports will state that the distribution is from short-term capital gains but a shareholder cannot use this distribution to offset other capital losses. To the extent that an investor is only casually monitoring the performance of an index fund, it may appear from the size of the income distribution that the fund has done unusually well. Careful attention must be paid to the content of the income distribution and to any slippage of the net asset value of the fund behind the performance of the index or other benchmark. Published fund analyses will usually provide help with these evaluations.

In addition to short-term capital gains being treated as ordinary investment income, the composition of a fund portfolio can be an obstacle to tax-free passthrough to the fund shareholder. For example, unless the fund meets the diversification requirements for a regulated investment company ("RIC"), the fund does not qualify for passthrough and taxes must be paid at the fund level[9] as well as by the shareholder when a distribution is ultimately made. The diversification requirements are relatively simple. With the exception of the U.S. government, (1) no issuer can account for more than 25% of the total assets of the fund, and (2) the combined issuers each accounting for more than 5% of the total assets of the fund cannot exceed 50% of assets at the end of each quarter of the fund's fiscal year. What this means is that a fund can have positions from two corporate issuers, each of which constitutes just less than 25% of the fund's assets, with the remainder invested in positions, each of which constitutes less than 5% of the assets of the fund. Treasury securities are exempt from these diversification requirements, so all the assets of a fund can be invested in Treasuries.

In a few cases, there is a portfolio *concentration* requirement that must be met to keep the character of a distribution intact for tax purposes. For example, if a fund holds tax-exempt securities (municipal bonds), these securities must account for more than half the total assets of the fund at the end of each quarter of the fund's fiscal year or the income loses its tax-exempt character when income dividends are paid to shareholders. If eligible municipal bonds are more than half the fund's assets, all tax-exempt income earned by the fund is passed through as tax-exempt income when distributed to shareholders.

Another possible passthrough obstacle occurs when a fund holds foreign equity securities which are subject to withholding at the source by the host government of a company. Unless at least half the total assets of the fund are invested in foreign securities at the end of the fund's fiscal year, any withholding tax is simply deducted as an expense of the fund. If foreign securities are more than half the assets of the fund, then the fund can pass these withholding tax payments through to shareholders either as a deduction or as a potentially more valuable credit against the shareholder's U.S. income taxes.

The above provisions make it attractive to have municipal bonds as the predominant securities in municipal bond funds and foreign securities as the predominant securities in funds holding foreign equity securities. The recent fashion for global ETFs has resulted in the creation of a number of tax-inefficient funds, as described in somewhat more detail in Chapter 6.

Another passthrough variant, at least under some circumstances, is the separation of fund and shareholder tax bases. The fund has its own basis in each of the positions it holds. Collectively, the fund's basis in its portfolio may be above or below the current market price of each portfolio security. It is determined by the price which the fund paid or, in the case of an in-kind creation, it is usually the price of the shares at the market close on the day the shares were deposited in the fund. If an 80% holder of the fund's shares deposits portfolio securities which had a basis to the holder that was different from the market close on the day of deposit, the fund inherits any lower basis. All ETFs take steps to avoid such problems by requiring proof and/or certification that an 80% holder is depositing shares with a contemporary cost basis.[10]

One significance of the separation of fund and shareholder tax bases is that an in-kind redeeming shareholder pays any taxes based on the shareholder's basis in the fund shares, not on the fund's basis in the portfolio shares tendered to the shareholder in redemption of fund shares. This separation of basis is an important feature behind the tax efficiency of ETFs and will be discussed in more detail below.

In contrast to shares sold at a loss in an individual's separate account, net capital losses on portfolio shares sold by a fund cannot be passed through and deducted from capital gains the investor might realize outside the fund. These losses in the fund must be off-set against the fund's own capital gains, with any resulting net gains being distributed to shareholders. Any net capital losses can be carried forward for up to eight years and used to offset the fund's capital gains in the future. However, if an investor has suffered serious short-term capital losses on the shares of a fund, the best way to realize those losses quickly and as short-term losses is to sell the fund shares and realize the loss in that manner. The U.S. Internal Revenue Code (or Tax Code) provides that if a shareholder redeems or exchanges shares of a fund held for six months or less, any loss realized will be first offset against any long-term capital gain distribution received on those shares. Any remaining portion will be considered a short-term capital loss.[11] In contrast to an investor who holds the same individual security positions in a separate brokerage account, it is not possible for the fund to selectively harvest losses and pass them through to shareholders to offset gains obtained elsewhere. This feature is one of the most widely criticized provisions in U.S. investment company taxation.

RICs and the Mechanics of Shareholder Taxation

Taxation of regulated investment companies in the United States is certainly not symmetric. There are some advantages to this taxation and some disadvantages. Among the advantages are the previously noted fact that long-term gains retain their character when distributed as such, even if the shareholder has not held the fund shares for the usually required year-and-a-day holding period for long-term capital gains treatment.

Another advantage is that, in contrast to a separate account where investment management fees are not deductible unless they and other miscellaneous deductions exceed 2% of adjusted gross income,[12] fund expenses and fees are deducted from a fund's investment income before a distribution is made—making them, in effect, fully deductible from the investor's ordinary income before the calculation of taxes in most cases. This is unlikely to be a material advantage unless the fees and expenses of the fund are quite high, but it is certainly better than the treatment of fees in a separate account.[13]

Redemptions in-kind, even if the shares of portfolio securities paid out in the redemption have a very low-cost basis to the fund, do not create a realized gain at the fund level, nor do they result in a taxable capital gains distribution at year end. This long-time provision of the Tax Code was designed to permit a fund's advisor to distribute low-cost positions in-kind to departing shareholders to protect remaining shareholders from being stuck with large and inappropriate tax bills from gains on shares sold to meet redemptions.

Occasionally, conventional mutual funds redeem their shares in-kind.[14] All ETFs now trading redeem most fund shares in-kind under ordinary circumstances. To the extent that it redeems its lowest-cost positions first, in-kind redemption enables an ETF to defer taxation and be even more tax-efficient than a conventional index fund based on the same underlying index. This tax feature is an advantage to a very long-term holder, as we will see, but it has little or no significance for someone who is a shareholder of the fund for less than, say, five years.

One more, usually minor, advantage of RIC long-term gains distribution rules is that the capital gains distribution year ends in October. Fund portfolio gains realized in November and December will be deferred to the investor's next tax year.

Other Tax Features of Regulated Investment Companies

Probably the most frequent complaint about regulated investment company taxation is that the shareholder has no control of the character and timing of taxable distributions. Any distribution of realized capital gains is not linked to the shareholder's own transaction timing. Gains are realized within the portfolio of a conventional fund on a schedule determined by arrivals and departures of investors or modifications of the portfolio by a portfolio manager (or the rules of an index). The shareholder who buys the shares and is hit with a sizeable capital gains distribution has done nothing which would appear to "merit" taxation on that distribution. Even more objectionable than a distribution shortly after a fund purchase is a distribution at the end of a bad performance year for the fund. The RIC structure makes these events relatively common for the shareholders of conventional funds.

Another disadvantage of RIC taxation is that new holders, particularly new holders of a conventional mutual fund, may participate in the fund's low basis in its securities in a way that may accelerate taxation of their gains from investment in the fund. If the fund is unable to take advantage of opportunities to redeem in-kind, it may eventually realize and distribute much larger long-term capital gains than an investor's own basis in the fund shares warrants.

Finally, possible problems associated with wash sales deserve some attention. A wash sale occurs when, within 30 days (before or after) of the realization of a loss, an investor acquires securities substantially identical to the securities that were sold at a loss. In the event of a wash sale, the loss is not immediately recognized, but is added to the basis of the purchased securities and recognized when those securities are sold.

Wash sales occurring at two levels may affect an ETF shareholder. Within the fund, the portfolio manager may realize a loss on a security by selling shares of portfolio stocks for cash. If a creation transaction occurs within a period beginning 30 days before and ending 30 days after the realization of this loss, and shares of the same portfolio stocks are deposited as part of the creation, the loss may be disallowed (deferred) as a wash sale. Different tax advisors take different positions on the deductibility of these losses. Some tax advisors hold that such transactions in a fund are not wash sales and that the losses are immediately deductible and/or characterizable as losses. Other advisors take the position that the deposit of shares of the same stock in a creation makes the sale a wash sale. There is currently no definitive answer on this issue.

Another place where wash sales may enter the picture is if an investor has a significant loss in the shares of a fund due to an unfavorable market environment for the securities in the underlying portfolio. The investor can realize this loss simply by selling the fund shares. The question is: Does the purchase within 30 days of a different fund using a similar investment approach—perhaps even based on the same underlying index—trigger the wash sale rule? Many observers argue that buying a different fund is enough to avoid the effect of the wash sale rule, but there is no unanimity that buying another fund based on the same index will not force deferral of the loss. The reader should check with a personal tax advisor to get appropriate comfort before making a similar fund purchase within 30 days before or after realizing a loss on the sale of fund shares.

Investment company taxation in the United States as implemented through Subchapter M is a mixed bag—not always disadvantageous and not always favorable. On balance, the tax treatment is relatively fair for ETFs if a fund's portfolio manager understands fund taxation thoroughly and avoids the pitfalls. Significant potential tax advantages are usually attributed to the redemption in-kind feature which permits the portfolio manager to eliminate low-cost basis positions from the fund in a redemption without realizing a taxable gain while realizing losses through cash sales. This feature is of value only to very long-term holders of the fund. Deferring long-term capital gains for, say, three years is not of enormous value to a taxable shareholder. Deferring long-term gains for twenty years or more can be of great value. Unfortunately, very few shareholders in any fund stay for twenty years. When advisors or writers of articles on funds discuss ETFs, they frequently refer to them as more tax-efficient than conventional funds. What they are talking about in nearly every case is this ability to defer taxation on long-term portfolio gains. It is important that all ETF users understand exactly what this feature can do for them—and what it cannot do. If it is important to them, they should avoid funds that do not deliver this kind of tax efficiency.

What We Mean When We Talk About Fund Tax Efficiency

One of the most significant features of an investment fund from the viewpoint of the taxpaying *long-term* investor is the fund's tax efficiency. The ideal tax-efficient investment will earn a high return, but very little of the return will come from ordinary (dividend or interest) income each year. Furthermore, the fund will distribute very little in the form of taxable capital gains. Most of the fund's total return will be in the form of unrealized capital gains. The capital gains will continue to accrue year after year; but, because they are not realized, the investor does not pay tax on them unless and until the investment in the fund is liquidated.

Mutual funds and other pooled portfolios vary greatly in their tax efficiency.[15] In general, funds managed by an active manager will realize more taxable capital gains than equally successful index funds where the only absolutely necessary turnover occurs as a result of changes in the index. Even conventional index funds vary considerably in tax efficiency, based in part on the stability of the index composition and in part on changes in the size of the fund.

An open exchange-traded fund may offer its shareholders the possibility of tax treatment that is substantially different from that offered by a traditional mutual fund. Other things equal, re-balancing a fund to adjust for changes in an actively managed portfolio or changes in the composition of the underlying index will have the same tax effect in the open exchange-traded fund as in the traditional mutual fund. Essentially, the fund will buy new stock, sell the old stock and, perhaps, adjust weightings in the rest of the portfolio. This basic procedure will be followed in some form whether the portfolio is an index portfolio or an actively managed portfolio.

From a tax perspective, the significant difference between the two fund types is in the process by which fund shares are redeemed. Unlike a traditional mutual fund that will ordinarily sell stocks inside the fund and pay cash to a fund shareholder who is redeeming shares, the redemption mechanism for the exchange-traded fund is usually "in kind." The fund delivers portfolio stocks, in kind, to a redeeming dealer that has turned in shares of the fund for this exchange. This is not a taxable transaction from the point of view of the fund, so *there is no realization of taxable gain or loss inside the fund*. Occasionally, a conventional fund—particularly a non-index fund—will deliver stock in kind to a large redeeming shareholder. However, opportunities to redeem fund shares by delivering portfolio stock in kind are limited in most conventional funds. Usually, a traditional mutual fund will experience a tax event from selling shares when holders of a significant number of shares redeem their positions.[16]

The in-kind redemption process for exchange-traded funds can enhance tax efficiency in an additional way. Low-cost shares of stocks in the portfolio can be delivered against redemption requests. In contrast to a conventional fund, which will tend to sell its highest, cost stocks first—leaving it vulnerable to substantial capital gains realizations when, for example, a portfolio company is acquired by another firm at a premium price and the stock exits the fund—the lowest-cost shares of any stock held by the ETF are tendered first to redeeming shareholders. The shares remaining in the portfolio have a relatively higher cost basis, which means that stocks generate smaller gains when they leave the index—and the fund.

One other point about in-kind redemption occasionally causes confusion. The redeeming shareholder does not acquire the fund's cost basis in the stocks delivered in a redemption. The fund's basis is the fund's basis and the shareholder's basis is the shareholder's basis. There is no necessary or usual link between the two. In other words, a redeeming shareholder pays capital gains taxes on gains over the shareholder's cost basis in the fund shares, not over the fund's basis in the portfolio basket that the fund tenders the shareholder upon redemption.

There is no unequivocal statement we can make as to the net tax impact on a traditional mutual fund from the purchase and sale of fund shares by investors over a period of time. The stock market has generally risen over time, and many traditional funds have accumulated substantial unrealized capital gains. It is a safe generalization that the most likely impact of the ordinary cycle of fund share purchases and redemptions by shareholders will be to generate taxable capital gains distributions for a traditional mutual fund. Under this assumption, these gains generally will be in excess of the taxable capital gains that are generated by changes in the portfolio of a similarly managed or indexed ETF that redeems in-kind. Thus, the redemption of exchange-traded funds in kind will make them more tax-efficient investments under most circumstances because more of the capital gains taxes will be deferred until an investor sells the fund shares.

In several circumstances, the deferral of capital gains can mean that tax never has to be paid, even if the shares are ultimately sold. These circumstances include the step-up of basis at death of a taxpayer and the gift of an appreciated asset to a qualified charity.[17] Under current U.S. tax law, capital gains that are unrealized at the date of death of a natural person are never subject to a capital gains tax. Generally, the market value of the investment on the date of death and not the cost is included in the decedent's gross estate for estate tax purposes. The decedent's heirs use this stepped-up basis of the assets used in the estate tax calculation as their tax basis. This Tax Code provision offers a substantial incentive for many taxpayers to defer capital gains for as long as they live. Unless the tax-efficient fund is held for life, efficiency means only deferral, not avoidance of the capital gains tax. In fact, if the shares are sold during the holder's lifetime, the government may collect more tax from gains in a tax-efficient fund than it collects from gains in an ordinary fund because the assets stay invested longer and, other things equal, build greater capital gains.

There is another side to this picture. Today's tax rate on capital gains may be replaced with a higher rate in the future. Also, the recent tax law changes that promise to eliminate the estate tax in 2010 (and bring it back in 2011) could be revised and/or the basis step-up provision could be eliminated permanently. Generally, however, the typical investor will be better off with tax deferral—even with the threat of legislative changes.

A taxpayer who gives a share of stock or a share of a fund to a qualified charity will be able to deduct nearly all of the value of the gift from his personal income tax return in the year of the gift without paying the capital gains tax on the unrealized gain. Conventional mutual fund shares are rarely the basis of such gifts because funds are required to distribute realized gains each year. There is less unrealized gain in the fund, making capital gains tax avoidance through contributions less valuable than it would be if capital gains were largely or entirely deferred for many years.

Tax Equalization and Exchange-Traded Funds

Conventional mutual funds that have experienced periods of net redemption during a fiscal year may use special allocation rules to protect ongoing shareholders from having to pay a disproportionate share of the taxes due on the fund's income and/or capital gains. The concept behind these allocation rules, which are called equalization, is authorized in the Tax Code, but the procedures used vary from fund to fund.

Equalization may be used for ordinary income by some ETFs. In theory, a portion of the fund's undistributed investment income is attributed to the redeemed shares rather than held for the next distribution to ongoing shareholders. The net asset value of the ongoing shares is unaffected, but the taxable income distribution to shareholders staying in the fund may be reduced.

Equalization applied to capital gains in a conventional mutual fund may protect ongoing shareholders from some of the gains realization effects of stock sales necessitated by the departure of redeeming shareholders. Equalization essentially allocates some realized gains to the redeeming shareholders. An ETF can avoid some gains distributions for its ongoing shareholders by allocating low-cost basis shares to redemption baskets, making capital gains equalization unnecessary and inappropriate for most ETFs.

The only significant question about using equalization for capital gains in an ETF occurs when the fund has both conventional and exchange-traded (redeemed-in-kind) shares. In this case, some equalization in connection with redemption of the conventional shares could be justified. How, if at all, to use equalization should be addressed by each fund's tax advisors.

Tax Efficiency of Conventional Mutual Funds, Exchange-Traded Funds, and Portfolio Baskets

Advocates of conventional mutual funds, exchange-traded funds, and separate stock portfolios (including HOLDRs and Folios) have engaged in extensive discussions about the relative tax efficiency of their respective approaches to equity portfolio management. The purpose of this sub-section is to codify appropriate information for investors who may be justifiably confused by what they have been hearing or reading from diverse sources. While we have attempted to summarize our conclusions on the relative tax efficiency of the three portfolio structures in Exhibit 4-1, the answer to the question, "Which way of holding a portfolio of common stocks offers the greatest tax efficiency?" is still, of course, "It depends on investment results."

Discussing the principal tax issues as we work down the table in Exhibit 4-1, our objective is to help investors understand what tax features are most important as the first step in making an informed choice, given their personal circumstances. In many instances, the appropriate choice will depend on holdings (or gains and losses) outside the fund or basket under consideration. As with any tax issue, investors should consult their personal tax advisors. We offer this material only to help investors approach the tax issues of interest to them, not as tax advice.

Exhibit 4-1: Factors Affecting Tax Efficiency of Mutual Funds, ETFs, and Separate Accounts (HOLDRs, Folios, etc.)

	Mutual Funds	Exchange-Traded Funds	Separate Accounts (HOLDRs, Folios, etc.)
Deductibility of investment management expenses	+	+	–
Passthrough of losses	–	–	+
Passthrough of STG (in character)	–	–	+
Deferral of STG	–	+	–
Deferral of LTG (with changing portfolio)	o	+	o
Step-up of basis at death	o	+	+
Appreciated shares for charitable gifts	–	o	+
Tax impact of stocks acquired for cash in mergers	–	+	–
Successful portfolio—little turnover	o	+	o
Successful portfolio—high turnover	–	+	–
Mediocre portfolio	o	o	+
Capital gain/loss accounting	+	+	check with advisor

Key:

+   Best
o   Okay
–   Worst
STG   Short-term capital gains
LTG   Long-term capital gains

Deductibility of Investment Management Expenses

As suggested by the +'s in the fund columns of Exhibit 4-1, any investment management expenses incurred by the fund are deductible from the fund's income before anything is distributed to shareholders. This expense deductibility holds for both conventional mutual funds and exchange-traded funds. An investor who pays any investment advisory expenses such as a wrap fee which covers advice as well as replaces stock trading commissions in connection with HOLDRs or Folios will not be able to deduct those expenses for tax purposes unless they and other miscellaneous itemized deductions exceed 2% of the investor's adjusted gross income. The magnitude of the amounts involved is relatively easy to estimate, but it is probably not large enough to be a material consideration for most investors if the only funds used are low-cost index ETFs. On the other hand, higher fees embedded in actively managed ETFs or conventional funds may be tax-advantaged relative to a separate, non-deductible or less deductible, advisory fee.

Passthrough of Losses

Here, the separate portfolio investor is at an advantage over the investor who purchases shares in a fund. If some of the stocks in the underlying portfolio go up and some go down, the mutual fund and exchange-traded fund cannot pass net losses through to the shareholder. In contrast, the separate account, HOLDRs, and Folio/basket product shareholder owns each of the securities in the basket product, and can (perhaps with effort and some modest expense in the case of the HOLDRs) decompose the portfolio, take losses on positions that have experienced losses, and let gains run. Of course, the funds' losses cannot be passed through to the shareholder for offset against gains on positions outside the portfolio. The only way to take a capital loss on a fund is to sell the fund shares.

Passthrough of Short-Term Gains with Character Retained

In the taxation of regulated investment companies, any net short-term gains are reported and taxed as ordinary income as opposed to short-term gains in the fund investor's tax returns. An investor with realized or unrealized long-term or short-term capital losses in other investments would be unable to offset short-term capital gains from distributions made by a fund against capital losses outside the fund. The investor in HOLDRs, Folios, or other separate stock basket products could reflect realized short-term stock gains on his tax return and offset them with capital losses realized from another source. Short-term capital gains are unlikely to be a material issue for most equity funds. Unless a fund manager is making extensive use of initial public offerings (new issues) to spike performance or assumes most fund shareholders do not benefit from the lower tax rate on long-term capital gains, realized net short-term gains in an equity fund that is more than a year old are improbable, unless the fund is an index fund based on an index that is very fund-unfriendly.[18]

Deferral of Short-Term Gains

Whenever deferral of a portfolio capital gain (short-term or long-term) is desired, the ETFs stand out relative to both conventional mutual funds and the separate portfolio products for the simple reason that an astute ETF portfolio manager should be able to redeem out enough of the portfolio's net capital gains so that the *value* of gains can be retained, untaxed, in the fund even if the portfolio is changed. Barring the presence of offsetting losses, holders of a conventional mutual fund or a separate portfolio product will be taxed at their full marginal ordinary income tax rate on any short-term capital gains. Holders of mutual fund shares will not be able to offset the short-term gain with capital losses outside the fund because the short-term gain will be taxed as an ordinary income dividend. Again, net realized short-term gains should be rare in most equity fund portfolios.

Deferral of Long-Term Capital Gains

Each of these vehicles should be able to defer long-term gains—as long as there are no changes made in the portfolio. If changes are made and resulting realized long-term gains are likely to be material, the ETF once again stands out as the vehicle of choice. The investor who owns any other non-fund portfolio products may be able to offset long-term gains with losses on other components of the portfolio or other positions outside the portfolio, but this process offers less flexibility than the ETF which defers the gains but permits a very wide range of changes in the portfolio—including complete portfolio turnover without realization of taxable gains at the extreme.

Step-up of Cost Basis of Stocks at Death as a Meaningful Feature of the Portfolio Structure[19]

Here both the ETF and the separate stock portfolio products can shine. Other things equal, the very long-term holder of an ETF should have most of a lifetime's return in the form of unrealized capital gains. With astute management, the holder of a separate stock portfolio might approach this ideal, but rating the separate portfolio as equal to the ETF may be a bit generous. Under the assumption that the investor has held a number of stocks for most of the period from initiation of the position until death, the heirs of the holder of the conventional mutual fund are unlikely to avoid as much capital gains tax as ETF or separate portfolio investors because more capital gains will have been realized, distributed, and taxed over time in the conventional fund.

Appreciated Shares Usable for Charitable Gifts

Here the separate portfolio products triumph. With individual stock positions which can be separated, the one with the greatest appreciation—i.e., the one with the lowest relative cost basis—can be donated to charity to maximize the deductible donation without paying capital gains tax on the gain. In the case of the ETF, the stock positions are combined or averaged so the appreciation of the fund shares will be approximately the average capital gain return on the portfolio as opposed to the separate account portfolio where the most appreciated security would be the one chosen for a charitable deduction. With a conventional mutual fund, more capital gains likely will have been realized so that some of the appreciation of the shares will have been taxed previously. Over time, the tax basis on conventional fund shares may be increased by reinvestment of realized gains, making the conventional fund shares poor candidates for in-kind charitable contributions.

Tax Impact of Low-Basis Stock Acquired by Another Company for Cash

Here the dominant portfolio format is the exchange-traded fund under the assumption that the portfolio manager will be able to redeem out the appreciated stock in-kind. If the stock is redeemed out in-kind rather than sold, no gain is realized at the fund level and, thus, nothing is distributed to shareholders and taxed. In contrast, of course, the conventional mutual fund and the separate portfolio product would have experienced taxable capital gains with fewer opportunities to shelter or defer them.

Making a Choice

Let's look at three market scenarios in an attempt to determine the environment where each of the portfolio structures does best:

Highly Successful Portfolio—Relatively Little Turnover

Here, all the portfolios do well because there is no need to shelter or go to extraordinary lengths to defer gains. ETFs should do slightly better because they may be able to shelter all net capital gains from taxes.

Highly Successful Portfolio—High Turnover

In this case, the ETF shines because of the ETF portfolio manager's ability to redeem out many of the gains in securities the manager of an active fund wants to unload or, in the case of an index fund, has to sell to continue to track the index. Unloading a successful position in either a conventional mutual fund or a separate portfolio would usually give rise to a capital gains tax.

Mediocre Portfolio Performance

In this case, neither the ETF nor the mutual fund portfolio is likely to do quite as well as the portfolio of separate securities. Taxes are of limited importance under these circumstances because any net gains are modest. The ability to realize losses on unsuccessful positions may, under these conditions, be more valuable when the positions are held in a separate account. With a separate account, losses can be realized to offset any gains both in the portfolio under discussion and in other positions that the investor holds.

Consolidated Accounting of Gains and Losses

The rankings on this topic can be very important if the portfolio is traded actively. In both the mutual fund and the exchange-traded fund, all of the accounting information an individual needs to complete a tax return is provided by the fund. In the case of the basket products, there may be a question mark. To the extent that the investor is an active trader, it can be extremely important that the broker or advisor provide a schedule of gains and losses. The schedule of gains and losses should be comprehensive—i.e., if the investor deposits securities with the firm rather than using cash to buy all new positions there, the consolidated accounting of gains and losses should include all positions.

Ordinarily, a brokerage statement will provide adequate detail on such things as dividends and interest received and interest expense; but an investor who is an active trader may have to devote considerable time to preparation of a schedule of realized gains and losses. Every investor should ask about consolidated reporting of gains and loses for tax accounting. At present, Folio accounts usually have access to a capital gain and loss schedule, but many users of HOLDRs do not receive this service.

Even a cursory examination of the table suggests that the ETF dominates the conventional mutual fund under essentially all the conditions discussed. The decision is more complicated when comparing an ETF with HOLDRs, Folios, or baskets where each position can be treated as a separate position as opposed to a component of a portfolio inside a regulated investment company. Here, too, however, some generalizations are possible. To the extent the period in which the portfolio or fund is held is a period characterized by poor or mediocre returns, it might be that the basket product—HOLDRs, Folios, etc.—would be more attractive because of the ability to separate out and take losses. Of course, to the extent a portfolio has capital losses, such losses do not have a great deal of value for most investors unless they can be offset against gains elsewhere in the same tax year, or on a carry-back or carry-forward basis.

If an investor does not have a reservoir of unrealized gains outside the portfolio under discussion or if the return from the portfolio is quite high and the investor experiences a high rate of portfolio turnover, then the ETF is a conspicuously superior choice from a tax-efficiency perspective.

Outlook for Changes in Investment Company Taxation

In mid-2000, Representative Saxton (R-NJ) introduced a bill[20] which would defer or eliminate taxation on capital gains distributions on mutual funds to the extent of $3,000 for an individual and $6,000 for a married couple. The bill did not pass in 2000 and its provisions were not part of the major tax cut package in 2001. It is hard to assess the probability of such a feature being part of future tax legislation, but it is probably no more than an outside possibility.[21]

A frequent topic raised by tax pessimists is the possibility that deferral of gains through redemption of fund shares in-kind might be eliminated. Complete elimination would require legislation because the provision is part of the Tax Code. An interpretation or IRS ruling which might require a redeeming fund to deliver shares at, say, the average cost of the shares held in each security in the fund is possible; but it would seem to run counter to the intent of Congress in deciding to include this provision in the Tax Code.

We are not aware of any specific effort to change the tax treatment of investment company redemptions in-kind. Given the public enthusiasm for tax efficiency combined with the very, very small number of investors who actually benefit materially from it, there is little reason for even the most aggressive tax hawk to champion a change in this provision. Many investors would be angered and the additional tax revenue would be negligible.[22] From a tax policy perspective, the best change in mutual fund taxation would be to eliminate all taxes on capital gains reinvested in funds until the shareholder liquidates some or all of the fund position.

Another tax issue which comes up frequently is the diversification requirement for a regulated investment company because it is a tax requirement rather than an investment company requirement.[23] Many portfolio managers would prefer to be able to use whatever distribution of holdings they chose or whatever distribution is dictated by the composition of an index. There seems little likelihood that Congress will revise the RIC diversification requirements anytime soon. Many Congresspersons are fully aware of the risk reduction advantages of diversification and they are unlikely to go out of their way to let investors reduce their level of diversification.

ENDNOTES

1. Deliva (2001) provides a framework for evaluating the disadvantage of the small, periodic purchaser—at least on a pre-tax basis. While we might quarrel gently with a few of Deliva's calculations, a letter from Brad Zigler of BGI in a subsequent issue of the same journal—Zigler (2001)—can only with charity be described as disingenuous. Among other things, Zigler lists low-cost transaction techniques that would not be available to most small, periodic ETF share buyers. It seems more appropriate to simply acknowledge that the ETF trading system is not designed for the small, periodic share purchaser unless a brokerage firm decides it wants to serve this market pro bono.

2. It is much easier to make a case that index fund investors are disadvantaged by traders who exploit index changes. We will begin to examine that issue in Chapter 6.

3. Zweig (2001) does this kind of analysis in a very basic way when he castigates the S&P Index Committee for the results of the changes the Committee has made in the S&P 500.

4. We expect fund-of-funds applications to grow, as described in Chapter 7.

5. This section and other tax observations rely heavily on Hervey (1999), which is generally considered the bible of investment company taxation in the United States. The term Regulated Investment Company (RIC) and the diversification rules associated with it are tax related. A Registered Investment Company is registered with the SEC, but it may or may not meet the RIC requirements for passthrough treatment of earnings.

6. In Japan, unrealized capital gains are taxed at the fund level, essentially making it impossible for a fund shareholder to obtain as good a return from the fund as he would from holding the same portfolio in a separate account. See Goetzmann, et al. (2001). There are indications that this may be changing, directly or indirectly, for smaller Japanese investors. A recent tax proposal made in concert

with the issuance of the first ETFs in Japan would tax small holdings in funds approximately to the same extent as holdings in individual stocks.

7. This usually occurs when a fund is domiciled in a tax jurisdiction which does not tax income or capital gains received by an investment company and the investor resides in the same jurisdiction or another jurisdiction that taxes only distributions—which the investment company does not make.

8. This tax treatment is not ideal for every shareholder. An investor with a short-term loss in the fund shares might be better off selling the shares before the capital gains distribution is made to keep the entire loss short-term and to take it earlier.

9. Just like a regular corporation.

10. Each ETF has provisions in its participation agreements to assure that its basis in any shares acquired is the basis at the close of the market on the day the shares were deposited.

11. Sec. 852(b)(4)(A).

12. Many investors face additional obstacles in claiming these deductions.

13. Unless the advisor of the fund has made a firm commitment to cap certain expenses, the investor cannot limit expenses in the fund, whereas the investor might have some control of expenses in a separate account. This is a minor qualification of the statement in the text.

14. Conventional funds may require a departing shareholder redeeming more than $250,000 worth of fund shares to take a redemption in-kind.

15. Dickson and Shoven (1993) show that a fund's after-tax ranking can change dramatically from its pre-tax ranking.

16. Conventional funds have another tool, called equalization, which offers some protection from capital gains distributions caused by the sale of appreciated securities to meet a redemption. Equalization, generally less effective than redemption in-kind, is described in a text box on page 97.

17. The step-up of basis at death is currently scheduled to expire in 2010 and to be reinstated in 2011.

18. See Chapter 6.

19. As noted in note 15, step-up of cost basis at death is scheduled to disappear in 2010 and, like most changes made by the 2001 tax law, it is scheduled to be reinstated in 2011.

20. H.R. 4723, June 22, 2000.

21. See Saxton (2000).

22. In fact, if any change occurs, the pressure seems to be for elimination of the tax on distributed capital gains. See, for example, Currier (2001).

23. Most funds undertake in their prospectuses to qualify as regulated investment companies, making qualification an SEC issue.

Chapter 5

ETF Applications for Investors and Investment Advisors

E TF enthusiasts are hard to subdue once they start listing the applications and advantages of their favorite investment instrument. While we will not dispute the proposition that ETFs are the best investment idea to come along in at least a generation, it is appropriate to conduct any discussion of ETF applications with a degree of balance. Cost comparisons with other ways of achieving a similar risk/return result are not consistent across all ETFs and pertinent competitive products or across time. In general, index ETF holding and trading costs have been falling more rapidly than futures and stock basket costs. The introduction of single-stock futures (SSF) contracts on ETFs will drive ETF trading costs lower and will introduce the ETF SSF contract as a competitor to the ETF itself in many applications. In other applications, ETFs and their SSFs will be elegantly complementary. Of equal importance, ETF SSF contracts will be major competitors for cash-settled stock index futures contracts.[1]

We do not hold out this discussion of ETF applications as exhaustive. It is clear that the range of applications is increasing steadily. All we hope to do is provide some illustrations and a frame of reference for present and prospective ETF users. Readers should ask their ETF advisors for up-to-date material on currently attractive applications and on types of applications that are of particular personal interest. Our discussion is necessarily more general than a reader will need for a specific implementation. Effective use of ETFs will come naturally to investors who recognize the fund as a portfolio, not just of stocks, but of risks and rewards. It is a package that needs to be analyzed for its contribution to an investment program and evaluated for its efficiency.

AN ETF AS A PORTFOLIO

In using an ETF in constructing a portfolio, it is important to keep in mind that an ETF is already a portfolio. It may represent a large number of stocks or a relatively small number of stocks. In the latter case, it usually will be a small component of an investment program with important differences in how it might be used. In the former, it might represent a sizeable fraction of the diversified portfolio an investor might need. One key feature which many index ETFs now have and some actively managed ETFs may have is that the *portfolio basket trades as a unit*. What we mean by this is that the fund and/or the basket of underlying stocks may trade at lower cost than the individual shares might trade as an "anonymous" or unbundled group because the fund (or its index or basket) is a standardized trading instrument. A standardized basket will be cheaper to trade as a fund share or even as a basket of portfolio shares underlying a fund than as a portfolio of unrelated stocks—in part because an investor is buying a larger amount of a single "stock" and the trading, clearance, and settlement is essentially the trading, clearance, and settlement of a single security rather than however many stocks are represented in the index and in the fund. If the basket is particularly popular, it may be cheaper to trade than the median or average component share even before the trading cost reduction from incorporating a portfolio into a single share is taken into account. Relatively few index or fund baskets will achieve this level of investor acceptance.

The evaluation of a particular ETF should proceed first on the basis of the usefulness of this particular cut of the total market in conjunction with other positions an investor holds or its usefulness in isolation, and secondarily, on the economic attractiveness of this way to own this cut of the market. The decision as to the appropriate way to own a particular cut of the market will ordinarily turn on the relative attractiveness of a specific application of the basket product, defined relative to a derivative such as an index futures contract or a single-stock futures contract physically settled into the fund itself. Each of these alternative ways of taking a position in a specific basket has its own characteristics and its own usefulness to a wide range of investors.

COST-SAVING APPLICATIONS

Temporary or Incremental Equitization of Cash

There are many reasons why an investor or an investment advisor acting on behalf of an investor might want to use an ETF or a related derivative to implement a temporary or incremental (i.e., on the margin of a portfolio) equitization of cash.

Temporary Investments

To take a simple example, an investor might open an account with an advisor and the advisor might feel the most effective way to manage the account is to put the cash immediately into a broad market index fund. The investment advisor then might gradually liquidate the fund shares and put the proceeds into specific investments selected for the client on the basis of their attraction and availability at various times. The position is held in the fund shares temporarily while a more complex strategy is gradually implemented. It is held because the advisor deems the fund's equity exposure a more appropriate (better risk/return) investment than a money market fund.

Choosing an ETF for temporary equitization of the cash may be simply a decision to use an instrument with a lower trading cost than some other portfolio instrument. ETFs are difficult to beat on the trading cost side. In fact, the only close competitor to ETFs and their baskets usually will be futures contracts, and traditional cash-settled stock index futures contracts offer far less variety than ETFs as partial portfolio building blocks. ETFs have no particular personality or uniqueness relative to other ways of incorporating an index or portfolio exposure into an aggregate portfolio or broad investment plan. Regulatory issues frequently affect the choice of an ETF or a future, but the dominant consideration for large accounts is usually cost.

In contrast to futures, which provide the exposure of an equity basket without the cash commitment or with the cash commitment (including interest and dividends) handled separately, the ETF incorporates both cash and basket characteristics in a single unit. Some money managers use ETFs as portfolio components to provide a known portfolio exposure at low cost. A number of standard ETFs may be combined into a complete investment program, or one or more

ETFs may be combined with an actively managed segment. The whole package may be offered at a single fee or separate fees may be charged for the ETF portion and the actively managed portion—the latter fee, of course, being higher than the fee for the ETF portion. If the positions are combined, the entire fee usually will be essentially an average of the low fee that would have been charged for putting the ETF piece(s) together and a higher fee for the actively managed portion.

Customization

The low expense ratio of any index ETF combined with an additional fee for putting several ETFs together can provide a fairly high degree of customization and appropriate asset allocation for a modest cost and with a modest level of service from the manager. The combination can be attractive to all parties even if the level of customization is limited.

Integrating Diverse Family Accounts

A number of advisors have used ETFs as implementation vehicles for some or all of the small accounts that proliferate in any family group with significant assets. It is not at all unusual for two or three generations of a single family to have dozens of accounts. Custodial accounts, conventional IRAs, Roth IRAs, trusts of various sizes and with diverse objectives, and small, medium, and large personal accounts seem to proliferate in families that accumulate wealth. The investment manager who handles the family's "serious" pools of capital is frequently expected to help with this mélange of accounts. Each account does not need a distinct philosophy or complex investment plan. From the family perspective, they all can be integrated into the overall investment objective. Each needs only enough attention to see that it is appropriately and fully invested in securities or portfolios that recognize its unique characteristics (including tax features) in a general way. The accounts also need to be integrated, using standard software, with the other family accounts and examined, say, once each year to ascertain that each is fulfilling its role.

The manager of the family's major accounts finds it difficult to avoid taking responsibility for these smaller accounts. To the extent that ETFs can be an appropriate vehicle for integrating them into the family asset allocation plan without a great deal of extra work and at a lower cost than conventional mutual funds, this comprehensive account management process can be useful to the family and to the advisor rather than becoming an annoyance to all.

Short Selling and Market-Neutral Strategies

An important application for many ETFs has been their ability to serve as a vehicle for short selling. The typical common stock has a short interest of 1% to 2% of its capitalization. Short interests in ETFs typically run 10 to 20 times higher. So far, all ETFs may be sold short without an up-tick because they are basket securities. They can be borrowed at relatively modest cost and their status as securities has led to applications that replace short futures contract positions. The advent of single-stock futures early in 2002 may take over a large part of this short selling role and reduce the costs of taking a short or short equivalent position even further. The introduction of single-stock futures may at first reduce the magnitude of long positions in funds that are hedged into cash equivalents before the fund shares are loaned out to facilitate short sales.[2] In the intermediate and longer term, the existence of single-stock futures contracts will almost certainly reduce fund transaction costs and increase the role of ETFs and their derivatives in portfolio and risk management applications.[3]

ETFs may be an important factor in the implementation of part or all of a market-neutral strategy. A portfolio manager who wishes to buy certain market segments and sell others short so that the overall position of a portfolio is neutral *relative to the overall market* but reflects important views on the relative attractiveness of various sectors, segments, styles, etc. will find ETFs and, soon, their associated single-stock futures contracts made to order for this implementation. The cost of transacting will be quite low relative to the use of conventional short sales in baskets of stock, and the results of this strategy should quite clearly reflect the astuteness of the manager's investment judgment—or any lack of such astuteness—without the cost penalty such strategies often faced before these new instruments became available.

An alternative market-neutral strategy might involve the purchase of specific securities *from* a market segment, sector, style, etc., and the short sale of an ETF (or its single-stock futures contract) representing that segment, sector, or style in the *aggregate*. The purpose of the overall position would be to reflect the manager's judgment in making stock selections that will outperform some comparable index or basket. Again, to the extent that the portfolio manager's selections are appropriate, the costs of implementing this strategy will be significantly lower than long and short positions in individual stocks and baskets with all of the stock lending and borrowing costs that the typical long and short technique implies. The cost savings might make a strategy which would not otherwise be economically feasible, viable, and attractive—if the portfolio manager's skill is as great as he believes it to be.

Tax Management

An important feature of any ETF application for a taxable account or series of related accounts should be tax management. This statement is true even if some of the accounts in a group are tax-deferred pension and profit-sharing accounts or special-purpose trusts. A great deal has been said and written about the tax efficiency of ETFs,[4] and while many ETF applications do not take advantage of (or need) this tax efficiency, an astute asset allocation program for an individual or a family will be sensitive to the tax treatment of various portfolio components.

Planned Loss Harvesting

An advisor's notion of tax management may be as simple as taking positions in a variety of sector funds which, in aggregate, provide approximately the same market exposure as a broad market index or a large-cap actively managed fund. If some of the component funds do particularly poorly the first year or so that the portfolio is in place, the advisor will realize losses for use against gains on this portfolio or elsewhere on the taxpayer's tax return. The object is to reduce tax payments and increase investment flexibility, perhaps by using such losses to offset a locked-in capital gain without payment of tax. The proceeds from the sale of the position with the previously locked-in gain can be used to improve the investor's overall level of diversification.

Integration of Taxable and Retirement Accounts

In its highest form, a tax management program will take into account tax-deferred retirement plans such as the investor's self-directed 401(k) or an IRA or Keogh account as well as fully taxable personal accounts. The decision as to where specific types of assets should be held— between the tax-deferred retirement plan and the taxable personal account—has received a great deal of attention from tax planners over the years. For many investors, where to put specific investments is an easy decision because there is not much choice—the asset classes have to go where the assets are. Most investors' assets that can be managed or allocated are predominantly tax-deferred or predominantly taxable. Moderate net worth investors generally have substantial tax-deferred accounts but small taxable portfolios. As net worth climbs, tax-deferred asset growth is increasingly restricted and asset growth comes in taxable accounts. Most investors, appropriately, put as much in tax-deferred accounts as possible because the assets working for an investor shrink when taxes are paid. When reasonably attractive tax-deferral opportunities are exhausted, income taxes are paid and most incremental cash flow goes into taxable investment accounts until assets reach the level where complex estate management trusts become appropriate. Obviously, the tax issues are complex, and we are not trying to deal with all of them. What we hope to establish is that ETF tax characteristics should often change some allocation and location decisions.

Most investors and advisors start with the presumption that any taxable bonds should be held in a tax-deferred retirement plan and equities, particularly equities without high dividend payouts, should be held in taxable personal accounts. Actually, most comprehensive tax-managed accounts are handled very differently. Some taxable debt is held in the tax-deferred retirement accounts. However, to the extent it is appropriate to hold substantial equities, a common conclusion has been that equities should be held first in the tax-deferred accounts and tax-exempt debt should be held in taxable personal accounts. The notion that equities held in separate accounts and via mutual funds should not be held in taxable accounts until space in tax-deferred accounts is filled, is contrary to most intuition. Nonetheless, holding equities, particularly funds in tax-deferred accounts, is based on generally sound analysis when the funds are conventional mutual funds and separate stock positions are subject to an average holding period of no more than a few years. The rationale for keeping conventional equity mutual funds and separate stock positions in tax-deferred accounts has been the frequency and magnitude of fund capital gains distributions on the one hand and turnover in fund and separate account equity holdings on the other hand. If an investor were capable of making a long-term commitment to a particular fund and the fund itself were able to avoid capital gains distributions, the appropriate allocation strategy would change. Indeed, with ETFs, virtually complete avoidance of capital gains realization should be possible for an astute portfolio/tax manager. The perennial mantra of many astute advisors is "hold your winners," and the ETF that avoids cap gains distributions makes such a mantra more compelling in a taxable account. Exhibit 1-5 and the accompanying text illustrate the compound return effect of deferred capital gains taxes in taxable equity accounts.

A well-run, high-return, equity ETF, designed to be used by long-term taxable investors in their personal (taxable) accounts, should not make material capital gains distributions. Most ETFs are managed for a variety of types of investors. They are not ordinarily authorized to take extraordinary, and sometimes not even moderately, costly steps to avoid capital gains distributions; so an occasional cap gains distribution may occur. Such an isolated distribution is unlikely to be large and distributions are unlikely to be frequent in any well-managed equity ETF. If the owner of the account can avoid temptations to sell the appreciated ETF shares, the ETF's natural avoidance of capital gains distributions should make equity ETFs look better in taxable personal accounts where they can grow indefinitely with taxes deferred.

There are a number of long-term tax advantages to the placement of equity positions in taxable accounts. First, when assets are needed to support expenditures, any taxes paid from the sale of appreciated ETF shares *will be taxed at the lower capital gains rate and only on the amount of any gains*. The capital gains tax rate has changed frequently over the years, but it has consistently been below the tax rate on ordinary income, which rate must be paid on the *total amount of any distributions from a tax-deferred retirement account*. Second, appreciated ETF shares, like appreciated single-stock positions, are attractive candidates for charitable gifts in that the appreciation will escape the capital gains tax and the deduction will be almost equal to the market value of the security if the shares are given as a donation. A third advantage of holding equity in a personal account is that if appreciated shares are held until the death of the original owner, heirs receive them with a stepped-up cost basis. If the same shares had been held in a tax-deferred retirement account, the account would not only be part of the estate for tax purposes (a characteristic it would share with the personal account), but all the assets of the retirement account would be subject to tax at ordinary income rates when they were distributed. Many investors with estates subject to the maximum estate tax rate have found it attractive to make 401(k), IRA, and Keogh accounts the subject of charitable bequests when there is no surviving spouse to receive them.[5]

Basic Tax Planning with ETFs

In contrast to virtually all conventional mutual funds, and to a greater extent even than typical individual stock portfolios, the distributions from an equity ETF will typically be modest.[6] The equity ETF can and should be an extraordinarily tax-efficient position, and a successful ETF can be held as readily in an individual taxable account as in a retirement account if the investor can resist the urge to sell the shares. Selling the shares, of course, triggers capital gains taxes on a profitable position and places a serious dent in the rationale for this kind of tax planning. The investor who can follow this buy-and-hold strategy should be extremely well rewarded, but the typical transaction-oriented behavior of even conventional mutual fund shareholders holds out little hope that this will be as popular a strategy as it should be. If an investor plans an aggressive ETF trading program, it makes much more sense to make the trades in a tax-deferred retirement plan. The inherent tax efficiency of the ETF will not add value in a taxable trading account.

DIVERSIFICATION AND
ASSET ALLOCATION APPLICATIONS

Most investment advisors who use conventional mutual funds and/or ETFs in the development of investment programs are keenly aware of the effects of diversification. They know that diversification can be increased by adding additional ETFs representing different markets, market segments, styles, etc. It is a relatively simple matter to measure the degree of overlap in composition between any two funds and, correspondingly, to measure the improvement in diversification from adding additional funds to an investor's holdings. With ETFs, it is possible to add additional markets and exposures that would not be economically interesting if the investor were dealing with individual stocks. For example, foreign country funds, fixed-income funds, real estate investment trusts, and low-correlation sectors not represented in some broad market indexes come to mind in this context.[7] The temptation is great to obtain diversification by investing in a relatively small number of highly diversified funds, but from the viewpoint of tax and operating efficiency, *a single fund can be too diversified.*

One tax advantage of getting diversification from a number of separate funds rather than a single broadly diversified fund is that one or more of a group of funds may decline in value while the others rise. The funds that decline can be sold to realize losses that can provide protection from taxes in a re-balancing or offset taxable gains from a large, low-cost stock position that might be reduced and the assets reallocated to increase diversification. If the investor bought a single broadly diversified fund, the available losses would probably be smaller and it would be harder to achieve as much ultimate diversification without paying more in taxes.

Clearance and Settlement Issues

To the extent that broad-based index funds are available with very low expense ratios, simply buying and holding them can be an attractive strategy, though more attention should be paid to the fund-friendliness of the index underlying such a fund than most investors realize. We expect increasingly sophisticated analyses of index fund transaction and settlement costs to show great divergence in fund efficiency among broad market indexes. Also, there are cases where broad diversification is inappropriate and uneconomical. For example, clearance and settlement regimes in various parts of the world are not consistent, and the gap between trade date and settlement date in different markets varies greatly. For these and other reasons, multi-country ETFs may be awkward structures and may face hidden costs associated with clearance and settlement and with inefficiencies in the market-making process. Authorized Participants who are involved in the creation and redemption of fund shares may be faced with unusual costs in assembling and disassembling creation and redemption baskets. The costs market makers *and the fund itself* face in a complex clearing and settlement environment affect the bid-asked spread on the fund shares and may be reflected in hidden transaction costs inside the fund. None of these costs shows up in the fund expense ratio; yet, in total, they will often dwarf the expense ratio.

It appears that some clearance and settlement inconsistencies are in the process of being ironed out within the European Monetary Union where great effort is being made to harmonize clearance and settlement with participation by the United States' Depository Trust and Clearing Corporation. Nonetheless, there are still substantial obstacles to incorporation of a large number of markets in a single fund, and tax and settlement abominations such as global sector funds and large-cap global funds are inappropriate and costly vehicles.

Tax-Inefficient Diversification

A feature which an investor should always avoid is a tax-inefficient mix of assets in a single fund or from several funds filtered through a fund-of-funds vehicle. Two examples come to mind: First, to the extent that a global equity fund receives dividends from companies domiciled outside the United States, any withholding tax levied on those dividends can be passed through to the fund shareholders as a tax credit, applicable against U.S. taxes on dividends *only if more than 50% of the assets of the fund are in foreign securities*. If less than 50% of the assets are in foreign securities, the withholding tax is still a deduction from the fund's investment income; but a deduction is usually worth a great deal less than a tax credit, and foreign dividends in developed countries are frequently considerably higher than dividend rates have been in the United States in recent years. The adverse tax effect of this inappropriate asset mix is material in some existing global ETFs.

Another example of tax-inefficient diversification is an inappropriate mixture of fixed-income instruments in a fund. Many states do not allow passthrough treatment of Treasury interest as exempt from state taxes unless Treasury interest accounts for more than a certain fraction of the income distribution of the fund. More significantly for a wider range of investors, unless tax-exempt bonds account for more than half the assets of a fund, their interest loses its tax-exempt character when paid out as an income distribution by a regulated investment company. This can have a very dramatic effect on the tax treatment of distributions from such funds.

These and other, generally less significant features of regulated investment tax treatment are often ignored or given short shrift by product developers who like the idea, for example, of a fund based on a "global" index. The fact that the index is totally inappropriate as the basis for a fund—both because of the passthrough feature of the withholding tax and the complications associated with multiple clearance and settlement regimes—is ignored. An inferior product is the result.

In connection with the fund structure theme, great care needs to be taken in fund-of-funds products and in any fund that incorporates stocks from varied clearance and settlement regimes. Global sector funds may not be of widespread investor interest, but investors would probably find them more attractive as conventional mutual funds where the clearance and settlement process is more easily handled and some tax inefficiencies might be alleviated by a fund structure designed for tax-deferred retirement accounts. Clearance and settlement times eventually may be unified on a global basis, but it seems clear that this is unlikely to happen soon. ETF enthusiasts must learn the limitations as well as the strengths of this investment company structure. ETFs work best when some of the avoidable obstacles and costs are avoided. Certain markets or securities combinations are best handled by conventional funds or with ETFs covering separate markets.

Diversification is a highly desirable objective; but, in many cases, the diversification is best obtained by holding a number of separate funds, each designed to take advantage of its own efficiencies in clearance, settlement, and tax treatment—rather than holding a single all-purpose fund. Increased efficiency in cross-border clearance and settlement will make diversification with a single fund more practical, but the advantage of separate funds will remain for taxable accounts.

Asset Allocation—Fixed-Income

Equity investors tend to diversify by adding more equities that they hope or believe will have low correlations with the equities they already hold. Sometimes this works, but even cross-border equity correlations have shown a distressing tendency to rise during periods of market weakness. A better idea might be to add some fixed-income exposure first. The first fixed-income ETFs will offer a range of consistent U.S. Government debt maturities (one, two, five, and 10 years). They will trade and settle like other U.S. ETFs, and in appropriate quantities they should enhance the risk/reward features of many equity portfolios. Other fixed-income funds with different characteristics will be available in the future.

The issue of trading costs outside the fund expense ratio is usually a greater problem in fixed-income funds than in equity funds. Trading costs are lowest on Treasuries and other government securities, intermediate on investment-grade corporates, and relatively high on issues rated below investment grade. Trading costs also tend to rise on debt that has been outstanding for longer than six to twelve months. In fixed-income markets around the world, settlement times are usually shorter than in equity markets. Differences in settlement times will probably not be a significant incremental cost element in any fixed-income or balanced ETFs that may come along.[8]

COMPLETION FUNDS AND BASKETS

For a variety of reasons, investors in ETFs based in the United States and abroad will find it desirable to purchase ETFs based on indexes which are compatible with the tax regime applicable to the fund. In the United States, this is the regulated investment company (RIC) diversification requirements, and in most European and a few Asian countries, the diversification requirements are often based on the undertaking for collective investment in transferable securities (UCITS), which is the standard implemented by the European Union. The diversification rules for UCITS differ somewhat from those for RICs.[9]

Under UCITS, positions in securities of a single issuer of corporate securities cannot represent more than 10% of the assets of the fund, and with respect to 40% of the fund's assets, no issuer can account for more than 5% of net assets. The treatment of sovereign debt is slightly less flexible than in the United States, in that sovereign debt must be divided into a number of different issues even if most or all of it comes from the same issuer. Given the RIC and UCITS constraints, a fund which is RIC- or UCITS-compliant will sometimes not be based on an index that accurately reflects the capitalization or float weightings in the country, industry, or other universe from which the stocks in the index are selected. Usually, any variation in index weight from cap or float weight will result in the truncation of some of the larger positions in an index, and an investor may wish to supplement a position in the fund shares with separate positions in some of the large, highly liquid stocks that cannot be fully accommodated in a fund that is RIC- or UCITS-compliant. Ordinarily, the fund or index provider will publish information on such truncation on a website, or it can be obtained through other means. The truncated position which will usually consist of a few highly liquid large-cap stocks can be added easily to a portfolio alongside the fund position, if strict capitalization or float weighting is desired.

A variant on ordinary completion baskets may be special baskets that include short positions or derivatives designed to help investors deal with the shift to float weighting on international indexes by mid-2002. This shift will affect the performance of all or nearly all international portfolios, indexed or not. The rapid move to acceptance of float weighting combined with deferred implementation of the new weights in some indexes creates opportunities for early adoption through purchase of float-weighted funds.

As discussed at some length in Chapter 6, a good general rule is to avoid funds based on an index that is not RIC- or UCITS-compliant, whichever is appropriate for the investor's particular tax regime. An increasing number of indexes are designed to be both RIC- *and* UCITS-compliant so that funds based on the same index can be offered in both the United States and the European Union Experience to date suggests that the difficulty of explaining substantial tracking error to investors who buy a fund based on an index that the investment manager cannot effectively replicate in the fund portfolio causes more trouble than the index is worth. For example, to the extent that the specialist and market makers charged with maintaining an orderly market in the stock are not aware of exactly how the advisor is dealing with this inability to replicate the index, trading spreads tend to be wider and funds tend to be smaller. A smaller fund means fewer fund assets and higher operating costs.

TRADING APPLICATIONS

Trading in an attempt to add value by capturing an opportunity will always be of interest to some users of a product as easy and inexpensive to trade as most ETFs. The reason for using ETFs rather than single stocks include the lower market impact component of their trading costs and their built-in exposure to a sector, a style, the broad domestic market in some size range, or a foreign market. They are often easier, cheaper, and maybe even less risky to trade than a few selected stocks that might be chosen to implement a similar trading idea. The idea can be to increase or reduce exposure along some line. It can be very short-term, even a day-trading idea. Assuming that ETFs will usually be the preferred vehicle for such trades, the investor's most important task is to choose the right fund to implement the idea most effectively. Some funds will respond more predictably to a correctly developed trading idea than others. For example, existing style funds are not very "style-pure" by most standards. Similarly, technology sector funds do not provide identical mixes and exposures. Comparing the price response and the other characteristics of various funds will continue to be a fertile ground for fund analyst activity.

Trading is not the heavy commission generation activity that it was prior to the elimination of fixed commissions in 1975. Discount and deep-discount brokers have cut commissions to nominal levels. To the extent an active trader needs information support from a broker, fee accounts such as the so-called wrap account cover charges for execution and various kinds of investor support with a single, asset-based fee. The fee-for-service (brokerage commission) business model will continue to be replaced by the single all-inclusive fee model. This change in the method of payment and continuing reductions in bid-asked spreads and in the market impact of ETF trades will stimulate further growth in trading ETFs and their derivatives. ETF trading issues are discussed at greater length in Chapter 8.

CONCLUSION

There are and will continue to be a growing variety of ETF applications. Many new applications will be similar to some of those described here. Some will be radically new. All will be developed by the analysts, investors, and investment advisors who are using exchange-traded funds. Probably the best sources of new applications will be the reports published by analysts at major brokerage/ investment banking firms. They and the advisors and clients for whom their reports are prepared are continually looking for new applications, and their reports introduce and describe these applications regularly. Major new applications will generally be picked up and discussed by one or more segments of the financial press. Some of the observations in this chapter should help the reader evaluate proposed applications with an appropriately critical eye.

ENDNOTES

1. Single-stock futures contracts on ETF shares will not be available before the spring of 2002.

2. A dealer, typically the specialist or an active market maker in the specific ETF, will buy shares in the ETF, hedge the fund's market risk with some combination of futures, options, and common stocks, and then loan the ETF shares to a short seller for a share of the interest credit from the cash generated by the short sale. This is a low-risk but satisfactory return business. It has the added benefit of providing an additional point of contact with active traders in the ETF and increases the lender's chances of seeing the borrower's order flow in the ETF. The purchase of the loaned ETF shares increases the fund size even if the shares are hedged. If the loaned shares are replaced by single-stock futures, these shares will not be needed and the fund size

may shrink temporarily. In the long run, the reduction in trading and hedging costs should stimulate growth in ETF shares outstanding.

3. See the text box on single-stock futures, pp. 249-251.

4. Including a substantial part of Chapter 4.

5. The distribution of investment structures and asset classes between tax-deferred retirement accounts and taxable accounts has received a great deal of attention including a classic article by the late Fischer Black (1980) and an extraordinary paper by Jeffrey and Arnott (1993). Most of the articles make the sadly realistic assumptions that investors cannot resist the urge to trade or cannot find a fund that can avoid material capital gains distributions. A patient investor with a well-run equity ETF should put it in her personal account and take a cold shower at the onset of any temptation to sell. For a comprehensive discussion of the issues, see Arnott, et al. (2001), Arnott and Ryan (2001), Bernstein Research (2000), Brenner (1998), Charron (1999), Clash (1996), Dickson (2000), Dickson and Shoven (1994), Jeffrey (2001), Poterba (1998), (2000), Price (1996), Shoven and Sialm (1998), Stein (1999), Stein and Narasimhan (1999), Stein, et al. (2000), and Tergesen (2001).

6. Any dividends realized on the portfolio will be reduced by the expenses of the fund, making the average dividend less than the average dividend on a typical common stock. As noted throughout the text, a well-managed equity ETF should not make material capital gains distributions.

7. Standard & Poor's, the holdout among publishers of U.S. indexes, has now declared real estate investment trusts to be eligible for its broad market indexes. See Rattray (2001).

8. It may be difficult to achieve high tax efficiency in a fixed-income fund, in the sense we have described tax efficiency in equity funds. When interest rates are declining, most sales of bonds or notes from a portfolio will result in small capital gains. Avoiding these gains

entirely would probably increase the fund's transaction costs. A better strategy might be to try to obtain long-term capital gains for distribution. See Davidson (1999).

9. The RIC requirements are discussed in detail in Chapter 6.

Chapter 6

Equity Index ETFs–
A Long Way to Go

Since its introduction about thirty years ago, indexation of stock portfolios has had a profound effect on equity markets and equity investment strategies in most of the world's market economies. The impact of stock portfolio indexation has been greatest in the United States.[1] The notion of using a stock market index as the pattern for a stock portfolio seems simple, obvious, and even compelling to many investors today. Index investors are indebted to a generation of academics, investment managers, and index developers, most of whom are still active and still promoting the virtues of indexing. With profound respect for the rich heritage of indexing, this chapter addresses what has become the weak link in portfolio indexation: the structure of common stock benchmark indexes and the way they are used as templates for index funds. The indexes in use today have served relatively well in the past, and their developers have contributed significantly to the growth of indexing, but there are signs of strain.

Most of the major U.S. equity benchmark indexes have been licensed as templates for the creation of the new kind of indexed investment company which is the subject of this book. While actively managed ETFs are on many drawing boards, all existing ETFs are index funds. This proliferation of index funds has led some casual observers to suggest that opportunities for significant product line extensions with new exchange-traded index funds will be severely limited.

We strongly disagree with any notion that the current range of indexed equity ETF products exhausts the possibilities. In addition to opportunities to create "enhanced" equity index fund products, some fixed-income index funds, and non-indexed or actively managed funds, there are still many new indexed ETF opportunities in equity markets. In fact, the focus on well-known benchmark indexes as the basis for exchange-traded funds seems profoundly misplaced. Many popular indexes simply do not work very well as the basis for an index fund. A new type of index, which we call a fund-friendly index, is a better template for index fund construction than most popular benchmarks. Furthermore, we will argue that *pre-implementation publication of fund index changes is contrary to the interest of fund shareholders.*[2]

BRANDED INDEX FUNDS— THEIR SUCCESSES AND FAILURES

One of the controversies in ETF development and growth is the significance of branded or "name" indexes in the success of related index ETFs based on these indexes. Obviously, a variety of things affect the success of any product or service, and an index brand name is only one of many features relevant to the success of any given ETF. Clearly, many of the issuers of ETFs have felt that branding was important. The American Stock Exchange felt that the Standard & Poor's 500 was the appropriate index for the first ETF: the S&P 500 SPDR. The Amex also paid substantial fees for the right to use the Dow Jones Industrial Average as the basis for the DIAMONDS ETF. Barclay's Global Investors took the branding issue to an entirely new level by attempting to offer a broad menu of index funds based on indexes from Standard & Poor's, Dow Jones, the Frank Russell Company, NASDAQ, Cohen and Steers, Goldman Sachs, and Morgan Stanley Capital International (MSCI). NASDAQ feels that the NASDAQ name was an important feature in the success of the NASDAQ 100 Trust, though others argue that a comparable index that performed as well as the NASDAQ 100 in the first year after the fund's launch would have attracted a comparable pool of assets even if the fund name had been the Goofus Index Trust.

A look at the assets of existing ETFs suggests that the only real candidates for a strong brand value claim are the S&P 500 and the NASDAQ 100. The Dow Jones Industrials and the Standard &

Poor's MidCap have attracted significantly more assets than the other branded indexes, but this can be attributed at least in part to a combination of their somewhat earlier starts than other funds and relatively good performance in parts of the 2000–early 2001 market environment.

Many who assign value to the S&P 500 brand name argue that the role of the S&P 500 in indexation is attributable to that index's selection by early indexers, especially Vanguard, as the most suitable broad market index available at that time. This historic role in index funds, combined with the introduction of S&P 500 index futures in the early 1980s and the use of S&P 500 portfolios as the basis for early program trading, have led to standardization on the S&P 500 index portfolio and reduced costs of trading this particular basket. Interestingly, the S&P 500 has obtained a much smaller ETF market share than it holds in U.S. indexed portfolios in the aggregate. The rapid growth of the NASDAQ 100 Trust suggests that index performance may be as important as brand name in investor selection of ETFs. There is also evidence that the size of the market represented by the index and that market's popularity with U.S. investors have affected the level of assets committed to ETFs based on an index. For example, large-cap indexes have been more popular than small-cap indexes, and the relative sizes of the iShares MSCI series country funds have broadly reflected their respective country market capitalizations.

Stock indexes have often been developed for a single purpose and then used for a wide range of applications. Some of these additional uses have been appropriate to the characteristics of the index and some have not. The widespread use of benchmark and performance measurement indexes as templates for index funds was rarely questioned before the development of the open-end exchange-traded index fund. Managers of conventional index funds have generally tolerated problems of index unsuitability in stoic silence. However, the market impact of some recent changes in the S&P 500 index and the development of exchange-traded index funds have combined to highlight some of the weaknesses of popular indexes in fund portfolio applications. The intra-day liquidity and in-kind creation and redemption of exchange-traded index fund shares focuses attention on features any fund-friendly index should have. Among other features, a fund-friendly index should facilitate regulated investment company (RIC) compliance, minimize portfolio turnover, be rules based, make investment sense, and promote tax-efficient investing. Some of these features can be obtained by simple rules of index construction, but there is room for "art" as well as "science" in the construction of fund-friendly indexes.

As the balance of this chapter indicates, there is a revolution under way in index development and index fund management. We would expect future successful index ETFs to be based on indexes developed specifically to serve as templates for ETFs rather than on indexes selected on the basis of their brand name or benchmark status. Once regulators come to appreciate that certain features of the current index publication process are dysfunctional from the perspective of fund shareholders, we expect the way fund indexes are published and index funds are managed to change significantly. Most importantly, we expect benchmark indexes to lose market share as fund templates.

STOCK INDEX CHARACTERISTICS AND FUND APPLICATIONS

A Brief History of Stock Indexes

To understand the genesis of the fund-friendly index, it is useful to look at the evolution of stock indexes over the years. Some popular indexes, such as the Dow Jones Industrials and various market composite indexes, were created simply as indicators of what a market has done or is doing on any given day. In contrast to the era when the Dow Industrials were the principal gauge of "the market," comparisons of the Dow with the S&P 500 and the NASDAQ Composite are now offered routinely to illustrate divergent performance in various segments of the stock market. Benchmark and performance measurement indexes such as the S&P 500, the Russell 3000, and the Wilshire 5000 are designed and used foremost as a basis for comparison of risk and return in an actual portfolio with the standard or benchmark.

Exhibit 6-1: The Evolution of Stock Indexes

Type of Index	Well-Known Examples	First Index Published
Market Indicator	Dow Jones Industrial Average, New York Stock Exchange Composite, NASDAQ Composite	1896
"Investable" Benchmark Indexes	S&P 500, MSCI, Salomon Smith Barney, FTSE country and regional indexes	1957
Performance Measurement Indexes	Wilshire 5000, Russell 1000 and 2000, Style Splits, Dow Jones U.S. Sector Indexes	1975
Fund-Friendly Indexes	Select Sector (SPDR) Indexes, NASDAQ 100 (modified)	1998

None of the indexes mentioned so far was originally *created* with the idea that a fund portfolio replicating the structure and rules of the index would be a popular investment. These indexes were developed to serve as market indicators and/or as a standard for comparison with actual portfolios managed by active portfolio managers. The Dow Jones Industrials and the S&P 500 predate all serious efforts to construct an index portfolio as an investment fund vehicle. The more recently developed benchmarks are generally based on a broader cut of the relevant equity market or on smaller stocks. However, 2,000, 3,000 or "5,000" U.S. stocks can create an unwieldy index fund portfolio — especially for an exchange-traded fund that creates and redeems fund shares with in-kind deposits and withdrawals of baskets of its component stocks.[3] Furthermore, the timing and magnitude of stock additions, deletions, and re-balancings often cause costly turnover and tax inefficiency in a fund.

Exhibit 6-1 lists the major index types and the date the first index in that category was introduced in the United States.

With the exception of the original Dow Jones Industrial Average (characteristics and origin discussed below) and the Nikkei Average in Japan (which was patterned after the Dow Jones Industrial Average), most popular indexes are capitalization weighted. Adjustments for float and regulatory diversification requirements for funds aside, cap weighting is certainly the norm for broad-based indexes.

It is tempting to attribute the widespread adoption of cap weighting to the Capital Asset Pricing Model's (CAPM's) stress on the optimality of the market portfolio in an efficient market, but the

S&P 500 predates nearly all CAPM work, and several other cap-weighted indexes were developed before CAPM was well articulated. A simpler explanation for cap weighting is the wide divergence in company market values and the link between capitalization and liquidity. The first attempt to create an index fund (by some CAPM pioneers) used an equal-dollar-weighted approach. The indexing pioneers learned quickly what traders have known for years: Liquidity is highly correlated with market capitalization.[4] With the capitalization of the largest company in most broad indexes at 50 to 500 times or more the capitalization of the smallest company, equal weighting and price weighting are hard to justify and rarely capture the structure of real portfolios which, in the aggregate, must be approximately cap weighted. Whether CAPM or the hard realities of portfolio assembly and disassembly are the cause, cap weighting—with deviations for float and diversification requirements—is the gold standard for index construction.

Fund-friendly indexes tend toward cap weighting for essentially the same reasons that benchmark indexes do:

(1) Fund performance is measured against cap-weighted benchmark indexes and other portfolios which are inevitably cap weighted in the aggregate.

(2) Practically, a large index fund will find it much more difficult to trade as much of its smallest-cap stock as its largest-cap stock without sharply increased transaction costs on smaller stocks.[5]

If both benchmark and fund-friendly indexes tend to be cap weighted, what is the reason for developing a new type of index? What distinguishes the new indexes from existing indexes? Why are the new indexes better for funds and, more importantly, for fund shareholders? The answer to all of these questions, briefly, is that fund-friendly indexes take into account the structural requirements of funds, the economics of trading, the investment objectives of funds, and the presence of other investors in the marketplace. The contrast with benchmark indexes is simply that benchmarks have not been developed with fund applications in mind. A benchmark index is not designed to create specific problems for a fund. The problem is one of neglect of fund requirements, not malice. The balance of this chapter develops and illustrates these points and provides examples of fund-friendly index construction.

There are a few broad generalizations and some specific rules for fund-friendly indexes, but there is room for creativity in solving problems whether the index fund is a broad-based large-cap fund, a small-cap fund, a style fund, or a fund designed to capture outperformance from an unusual source. Each reader will apply personal evaluation standards to the fund-friendly index approach. We suggest two closely related standards that might be on every reader's list:

1. Would I prefer to have my money invested in a fund using (a) the fund-friendly index or (b) the closest conventional benchmark index as a template?

2. Would I expect a fund-friendly index fund to outperform a fund based on an otherwise similar index constructed on typical benchmark index rules?

Such questions will be increasingly pertinent as new fund-friendly indexes are introduced. The 1998 introduction of the first deliberately constructed fund-friendly indexes has drawn a favorable response from investors, judging by the growth of the NASDAQ 100 and Sector SPDR funds using those indexes.[6]

Index Rules

Most indexes have rules for modifications and updates to keep the indexes effective at their designated task. The sometimes elaborate rules usually call for modifications based on periodic re-examinations of market capitalizations and other characteristics of companies in a designated stock universe or on some corporate actions. The time at which the index will be modified is typically known in advance and may represent a compromise on the part of the index developer in weighting the conflicting needs of various index users. Index rules generally require membership changes (deletions and/or additions) whenever certain corporate actions, such as mergers, bankruptcies, etc., eliminate an index component or when the market value of a company's capitalization goes outside an absolute or relative range or is outside that range on a specified re-balancing date. Some benchmark indexes like the S&P 500, Mid Cap, and Small Cap Indexes will re-balance all positions whenever there is a membership change. In fact, a merger that eliminates a company from the S&P 500 may lead to promotions from and to the two S&P smaller-capitalization U.S. indexes and require re-balancings in all three indexes. As we will see, the rules tend to be different for fund-friendly indexes to reduce portfolio turnover.

A number of index publishers have special-purpose advisory groups or committees that "manage" or "oversee" benchmark indexes in some way. These committees may have authority to intervene only in rare circumstances or they may actively select the stocks for the index. The most powerful and free-ranging of these groups is the S&P Index Committee. Our discussion of this committee in a later section will stress some of the problems for funds that come with deliberate deviations from rules-based index construction, particularly when the index change is widely known before a fund can act on it.

Using Indexes as Fund Templates
Index Economics
The economics of producing and maintaining a benchmark index can be quite different from the economics of producing and maintaining a fund-friendly index. The licensors of indexes typically earn their revenues from third-party license fees based on intellectual property claims. These claims are usually based more on the trademarked company/index name than on index methodology or association of an index with a particular market or subset of the market. It is relatively easy to trademark a name. However, most ways to construct an index that can be clearly explained to a prospective user may not be unique enough to patent.[7] In the context of intellectual property claims, the use of a committee rather than fixed index rules suggests periodic proprietary intellectual input. Even though that input may not be constructive as far as the index user is

concerned, it may seem to support the legal position behind the licensing process.

The revenues associated with a fund-friendly index are as thoroughly based on intellectual property (trademark) claims as revenues from a benchmark index, but the focus of a fund-friendly index will be more on earnings from licensing a successful fund and its derivatives than on revenue from publishing and performance measurement applications. Only with the introduction of ETFs have license fees from funds become an important source of income for benchmark publishers.[8]

Index Branding and Fund Sales

There is often a premium on consistency of construction for a family of benchmark indexes. Similarity to other index family members may promote adoption of newer indexes as benchmarks for relevant markets because users are familiar with an index publisher's product style. In contrast, while a "hot" index universe designation (e.g., technology in 1998 and 1999) may help attract investors, there is no evidence that the index name or brand, per se, has obvious marketing appeal for exchange-traded funds.

Perhaps the best illustration of investors' indifference to an index's benchmark status is the growth in ETFs that are *not* based on widely known benchmark indexes. Exhibit 6-2 shows the inception date and total assets of all the open-end exchange-traded funds listed in the United States as of year end 2000. Total equity portfolio indexation is 70%–90% based on the S&P 500 in the United States. The indexes that have succeeded in the ETF market are much more diverse.

The S&P 500 SPDR, the first of the open-end exchange-traded funds, now has an expense ratio of only 0.12%. This expense ratio makes the SPDR one of the world's lowest-cost funds of any kind available to the individual investor. Nonetheless, the SPDR accounted for less than half the total market value of U.S. open-end exchange-traded fund shares outstanding, and all funds based on benchmark indexes accounted for less than two-thirds of ETF assets at the end of 2000. A surprising fraction of the assets in open-end exchange-traded funds are based on indexes that are not designed like standard benchmarks.[9]

Exhibit 6-2: Open-End Exchange-Traded Funds (ETFs) as of December 31, 2000
Benchmark Indexes

Fund	Index Tracked	Inception Date	Net Assets
SPDR Trust	S&P 500	1/29/93	$25,484,026,750
MidCap SPDR Trust	S&P 400	5/4/95	$3,946,980,960
DJIA DIAMONDS Trust	Dow Jones Industrial Average	1/20/98	$2,431,899,840
streetTRACKS DJ Global Titans	Dow Jones Global Titans Index	9/29/00	$30,796,000
iShares MSCI Australia	MSCI Australia	3/18/96	$58,838,000
iShares MSCI-Austria	MSCI Austria	3/18/96	$10,822,000
iShares MSCI Belgium	MSCI Belgium	3/18/96	$11,589,600
iShares MSCI Brazil	MSCI Brazil	7/14/00	$15,561,000
iShares MSCI Canada	MSCI Canada	3/18/96	$17,342,000
iShares MSCI EMU	MSCI EMU	7/14/00	$40,381,000
iShares MSCI France	MSCI France	3/18/96	$94,454,850
iShares MSCI Germany	MSCI Germany	3/18/96	$164,995,640
iShares MSCI Hong Kong	MSCI Hong Kong	3/18/96	$70,451,740
iShares MSCI Italy	MSCI Italy	3/18/96	$54,192,000
iShares MSCI Japan	MSCI Japan	3/18/96	$648,941,150
iShares MSCI Malaysia	MSCI Malaysia	3/18/96	$88,452,000
iShares MSCI Mexico	MSCI Mexico	3/18/96	$31,027,000
iShares MSCI Netherlands	MSCI Netherlands	3/18/96	$39,088,980
iShares MSCI Singapore	MSCI Singapore	3/18/96	$69,133,000
iShares MSCI South Korea	MSCI South Korea	5/12/00	$16,173,000
iShares MSCI Spain	MSCI Spain	3/18/96	$40,365,000
iShares MSCI Sweden	MSCI Sweden	3/18/96	$24,678,000
iShares MSCI Switzerland	MSCI Switzerland	3/18/96	$50,896,960
iShares MSCI Taiwan	MSCI Taiwan	6/23/00	$70,959,500
iShares MSCI United Kingdom	MSCI United Kingdom	3/18/96	$179,817,980
iShares DJ US Basic Materials	Dow Jones US Basic Materials Sector	6/16/00	$9,632,500
iShares DJ US Chemicals	Dow Jones US Chemical Index	6/16/00	$17,088,000
iShares DJ US Consumer Cyclical	Dow Jones US Consumer Cyclical	6/16/00	$13,840,000
iShares DJ US Energy	Dow Jones US Energy Sector	6/16/00	$40,980,000
iShares DJ US Financial	Dow Jones US Financial Sector	6/16/00	$21,755,000
iShares DJ US Financial Services	Dow Jones US Financial Services	6/16/00	$24,625,000
iShares DJ US Healthcare	Dow Jones US Healthcare Sector	6/16/00	$57,416,000
iShares DJ US Industrial	Dow Jones US Industrial Sector	6/16/00	$22,572,000
iShares DJ US Internet	Dow Jones US Internet Index	5/19/00	$18,540,000
iShares DJ US Consumer Non-cyclical	Dow Jones US Non-cyclical Sector	6/16/00	$15,099,000
iShares DJ US Real Estate	Dow Jones US Real Estate Index	6/16/00	$34,101,000
iShares DJ US Technology	Dow Jones US Technology Sector	5/19/00	$111,945,000
iShares DJ US Telecommunications	Dow Jones US Telecommunications	5/26/00	$44,631,500
iShares DJ US Total Market	Dow Jones US Total Market	6/16/00	$36,858,000
iShares DJ US Utilities	Dow Jones US Utilities Sector	6/16/00	$35,560,000
iShares Russell 1000	Russell 1000 Index	5/19/00	$238,204,000
iShares Russell 1000 Growth	Russell 1000 Growth Index	5/26/00	$106,491,000
iShares Russell 1000 Value	Russell 1000 Value Index	5/26/00	$152,719,500
iShares Russell 2000	Russell 2000 Index	5/26/00	$394,625,000
iShares Russell 2000 Growth	Russell 2000 Growth Index	5/26/00	$16,057,500

Exhibit 6-2 (Continued)

Fund	Index Tracked	Inception Date	Net Assets
iShares Russell 2000 Value	Russell 2000 Value Index	5/26/00	$162,134,000
iShares Russell 3000	Russell 3000 Index	5/26/00	$312,481,000
iShares Russell 3000 Growth	Russell 3000 Growth Index	5/26/00	$25,625,000
iShares Russell 3000 Value	Russell 3000 Value Index	5/26/00	$125,334,000
iShares S&P 500	S&P 500	5/19/00	$2,319,408,000
iShares S&P 500/BARRA Growth	S&P 500/BARRA Growth	5/26/00	$130,492,000
iShares S&P 500/BARRA Value	S&P 500/BARRA Value	5/26/00	$229,068,000
iShares S&P Europe 350 Index	S&P Europe 350 Index	7/28/00	$86,549,000
iShares S&P MidCap 400	S&P MidCap 400 Index	5/26/00	$216,552,000
iShares S&P MidCap 400/BARRA Growth	S&P MidCap 400/BARRA Growth	7/28/00	$92,925,000
iShares S&P MidCap 400/BARRA Value	S&P MidCap 400/BARRA Value	7/28/00	$42,685,000
iShares S&P SmallCap 600	S&P SmallCap 600 Index	5/26/00	$125,143,000
iShares S&P SmallCap 600/BARRA Growth	S&P SmallCap 600/BARRA Growth	7/28/00	$31,288,000
iShares S&P SmallCap 600/BARRA Value	S&P SmallCap 600/BARRA Value	7/28/00	$38,390,000
iShares S&P/TSE 60	S&P/TSE 60 Index	6/16/00	$8,065,500
iShares S&P 100 Index Fund	S&P 100 Index	10/27/00	$182,002,000
iShares S&P Global 100 Index Fund	S&P Global 100 Index	12/5/00	$118,524,000
TOTAL:			$39,351,269,450

Non-Benchmark/Fund-Friendly Indexes

Fund	Index Tracked	Inception Date	Net Assets
NASDAQ 100 Trust	NASDAQ-100 Index	3/10/99	$23,574,696,000
The Basic Industries Select Sector SPDR Fund	Basic Industries Select Index	12/22/98	$78,219,500
The Consumer Services Select Sector SPDR Fund	Consumer Services Select Index	12/22/98	$77,862,000
The Consumer Staples Select Sector SPDR Fund	Consumer Staples Select Index	12/22/98	$205,632,000
The Cyclical/Transportation Select Sector SPDR Fund	Cyclical/Transportation Select Index	12/22/98	$67,734,000
The Energy Select Sector SPDR Fund	Energy Select Index	12/22/98	$262,912,000
The Financial Select Sector SPDR Fund	Financial Select Index	12/22/98	$504,479,500
The Industrial Select Sector SPDR Fund	Industrial Select Index	12/22/98	$53,210,000
The Technology Select Sector SPDR Fund	Technology Select Index	12/22/98	$1,068,694,000
The Utilities Select Sector SPDR Fund	Utilities Select Index	12/22/98	$72,842,000
streetTRACKS DJ US Large Cap Growth	Dow Jones Large Cap Growth	9/29/00	$28,804,000
streetTRACKS DJ US Large Cap Value	Dow Jones Large Cap Value	9/29/00	$54,620,000
streetTRACKS DJ US Small Cap Growth	Dow Jones Small Cap Growth	9/29/00	$16,076,000
streetTRACKS DJ US Small Cap Value	Dow Jones Small Cap Value	9/29/00	$23,812,000
streetTRACKS Morgan Stanley High Tech	Morgan Stanley High Tech 35	9/29/00	$60,543,000
streetTRACKS Morgan Stanley Internet	Morgan Stanley Internet	9/29/00	$35,737,500
FORTUNE 500	FORTUNE 500 Index	10/10/00	$92,430,000
FORTUNE e-50	FORTUNE e-50 Index	10/10/00	$49,760,000
TOTAL:			$26,328,063,500
GRAND TOTAL:			$65,679,332,950

Source: Amex/Bloomberg

The NASDAQ 100 Trust, which initially attracted assets primarily on the basis of the NASDAQ's technology stock performance, is based on an index that some investors may confuse with the widely cited NASDAQ Composite benchmark index. The NASDAQ 100 has been the basis of limited futures and index options trading for a number of years, but it was not a widely followed index before NASDAQ modified its cap weighting to make it compliant with the diversification requirements for a regulated investment company (RIC) just before the launch of the NASDAQ 100 Trust. (The RIC diversification requirements will be discussed in detail in the next section.)

The Select Sector Spiders are based on sector indexes carved out of the S&P 500, but these sector indexes are *not* standard S&P benchmarks. The assignment of stocks to a sector is done by the Merrill Lynch Research Department, not by the S&P Index Committee and not based on the S&P industry or sector classification system. The Merrill Lynch Research Department should be able to do the sector allocation as well as S&P, but the fact remains that these funds are not based on S&P's sector benchmark indexes.[10] Furthermore, some of the stock capitalization weightings are modified to make the Sector SPDR *indexes* RIC compliant.

As a final note on the value of index family branding in fund promotion, investor comments often demonstrate that many of the very retail investors who might be attracted to a branded index fund do not even realize that SPDR's name is derived from "S&P." As mutual fund research services and leading brokerage firms increase their ETF research coverage, fund family or index provider branding is likely to become even less important *relative to the features of an individual fund*. In contrast to conventional mutual funds, ETFs lack the switch privileges and statement consolidation features that encourage an investor to choose a new fund from a fund family where he already has an account. This structural independence of other fund family members further reduces the impact of family branding.[11]

Exhibit 6-3 summarizes some of the general characteristics of fund-friendly indexes and serves as a point of reference for the balance of this chapter.

Exhibit 6-3: Some Desirable Characteristics for Fund-Friendly Indexes

1. Meet RIC requirements for a U.S. fund or UCITS requirements for a fund distributed outside the U.S. at low cost either (1) naturally, (2) by special weighting rules, (3) with custom structured instruments, or (4) by representative sampling. (1) and (2) are vastly preferable to (3) and (4).

2. Re-balancing and replacement rules minimize portfolio turnover.

3. If the index or a related index does not include large-cap companies in its universe, the index and the fund retain exposure to the best performing companies in some way.*

4. Style indexes (growth/value) should not cover all the companies in the corresponding broad market aggregate index because many companies are not distinctly growth or value.

5. This index creates a fund that makes investment sense and appeals to investors.

6. The resulting fund has multiple uses and useful derivatives.

7. The index is rules based. A backup decision-making entity is only used for emergencies not anticipated by the rules.

8. The fund is inherently tax efficient.
   a. Low turnover, but some stocks will be completely removed from the index each year.
   b. No loss of foreign withholding tax credit or other passthrough benefits due to structure or portfolio composition.

9. Index license fees are modest relative to benchmark index licensing fees unless the licensed name or other features promise to bring in enough assets to lower total fund costs.

10. The index fund structure must recognize the limited integration of clearance, settlement, and custody systems across international borders. Improvements are underway, but multi-country funds can be costly to manage in the open-end ETF format.

Issues:

Handling of float: Float is rarely an issue for a fund-friendly index that is designed for a single fund. It can be very important if an index is designed for use by a number of funds. A minimum capitalization percentage requirement on float or a delay on IPO entry into an index past the lockup period is okay, but staged additions to weighting as float increases should be avoided.

Modularity: It is harder to create and redeem in kind if the index has a large number of issues, so funds of funds can be useful in creation and redemption of funds with a large number of issues.

* For example, a conventional small-cap index might be linked to or, even better for some investors, combined with a larger-cap index in a single fund to preserve exposure to successful companies. Alternatively, the index could retain companies that may otherwise "graduate" out of the index as they grow. Retaining these companies would let the fund capture the impact of large gains.

SHORTCOMINGS OF BENCHMARK INDEXES AND STRENGTHS OF FUND-FRIENDLY INDEXES FOR USE IN FUNDS

Weighting

In contrast to most benchmark and performance measurement indexes, *fund-friendly indexes are designed to serve efficiently as templates for fund portfolios*. While the weightings of both these types of indexes are usually, although not always, based on a capitalization weighting, the weighting of a fund-friendly equity index should be modified to accommodate the requirements for pass-through treatment of dividends and long-term capital gains by a regulated investment company (RIC), the tax structure used by most U.S.-based funds, and/or by the undertaking for collective investment in transferable securities (UCITS), the diversification standard adopted by the European Union and several countries in Asia.

Specifically, in order for a fund to be "RIC qualified," its portfolio—and usually the index that is being used to create the portfolio—will take regulated investment company diversification requirements into account. These diversification requirements are relatively simple. The securities of any issuer other than the U.S. government cannot account for more than 25% of the assets of the fund. Furthermore, with respect to the smallest companies together constituting 50% of fund assets, no issuer other than the U.S. government can account for more than 5% of fund assets. To meet the UCITS requirements, no corporate issuer's securities can account for more than 10% of an equity fund portfolio and, with respect to the smallest companies together constituting 40% of assets, no corporate issuer can account for more than 5% of fund assets. Sovereign debt can exceed these limits, but it must be in the form of multiple debt issues.

To put the RIC requirements in perspective, Exhibit 6-4 shows that the minimum requirements for a fully invested common stock portfolio would be at least 13 companies if the weights were controlled very precisely. Since the diversification test is applied to a fund portfolio quarterly, any sensible index portfolio strategy will use appreciably more than 13 companies. A UCITS-compliant portfolio would have at least 15 corporate positions, and a portfolio compliant with both RIC *and* UCITS diversification standards would have at least 16 positions.

Exhibit 6-4: Fund Diversification Requirements
Minimum Common Stock Diversification Requirements for a Regulated Investment Company (RIC)

Position	1	24.9%
Position	2	24.9%
Position	3	4.9%
Position	4	4.9%
Position	5	4.9%
Position	6	4.9%
Position	7	4.9%
Position	8	4.9%
Position	9	4.9%
Position	10	4.9%
Position	11	4.9%
Position	12	4.9%
Position	13	1.2%
		100.0%

Minimum Common Stock Diversification Requirements for an Undertaking for Collective Investment in Transferable Securities (UCITS)

Position	1	9.9%
Position	2	9.9%
Position	3	9.9%
Position	4	9.9%
Position	5	9.9%
Position	6	9.9%
Position	7	4.9%
Position	8	4.9%
Position	9	4.9%
Position	10	4.9%
Position	11	4.9%
Position	12	4.9%
Position	13	4.9%
Position	14	4.9%
Position	15	1.4%
		100.0%

Exhibit 6-4 (Continued)
Minimum Common Stock Diversification Requirements for Both RIC and UCITS

Position	1	9.9%
Position	2	9.9%
Position	3	9.9%
Position	4	9.9%
Position	5	9.9%
Position	6	4.9%
Position	7	4.9%
Position	8	4.9%
Position	9	4.9%
Position	10	4.9%
Position	11	4.9%
Position	12	4.9%
Position	13	4.9%
Position	14	4.9%
Position	15	4.9%
Position	16	1.5%
		100.0%

Some ETFs are based on indexes that are not inherently RIC- or UCITS-compliant. The fund advisor may find rather quickly that changing the index template is easier than creating and explaining a portfolio that does not match (track) the index. Barclays Global Investors (BGI), for example, has indicated that they have actively considered adoption of "special" Morgan Stanley Capital International (MSCI) RIC-compliant country indexes for countries where the standard MSCI index is not naturally RIC-compliant.[12] This change would eliminate one source of confusion over World Equity Benchmark Shares (WEBS)—now iShares MSCI Series—and their "tracking error" relative to some of the benchmark MSCI country indexes. Most of the apparent tracking error is due to efforts to qualify the funds as RICs, not to a failure of the fund management process.

It is not always necessary to modify the index to combine RIC or UCITS compliance with close index tracking and efficient fund operation. Derivative instruments, including a special type of repurchase agreement or swap, are available to bring the fund composition into RIC compliance while the fund performance pattern approaches the performance of the unmodified index very closely. For domestic funds, RIC compliance usually can be accomplished with such derivatives. The drawbacks in using these derivatives to combine RIC compliance with close tracking of a non-compliant index are the hidden costs and the counterparty credit risk associated with the derivative position. Also, if the derivative position is not managed and renewed carefully and consistently, it can cause, rather than cure, tracking error. We do not know of any ETFs that use these derivatives, probably because their managers prefer to avoid having to explain using them.

ETF managers faced with indexes that are not naturally RIC- or UCITS-compliant use two very distinct approaches to portfolio construction. Some, like Sector SPDRs, the NASDAQ 100, and the Morgan Stanley High Tech and Internet funds, structure or restructure the index to ensure RIC compliance. Others, like the iShares MSCI Series and other iShares Series like the Dow Jones Sector Indexes, use a technique usually called "representative sampling" to approximate the performance of a non-compliant index with a RIC-compliant portfolio. Briefly, representative sampling involves techniques as diverse as using other oil stocks in place of Exxon Mobil to keep individual positions below 25%, 10% or 5% of the fund or using futures or other derivative contracts. Some U.S. portfolios are somewhat arbitrarily changed by reducing a position that exceeds a RIC limit just before a RIC compliance testing date.[13]

The case for using a RIC- or UCITS-compliant index as the portfolio template for an index fund and replicating it accurately is compelling. Tracking error should be minimal with an index replicating policy. Aside from protecting investors from surprises, close tracking protects the exchange specialist and other market makers from losses caused by failure of the portfolio to match the index. If these market makers lose money, their bid-asked spreads will be wider—to the detriment of investors.[14] An ETF manager could reveal the contents of a "representative sampling" portfolio to the market makers only if the same information was available to everyone in the market. This would be like creating a second "inside" index. Modifying the index itself to make it compliant is far simpler.

Representative sampling is a legitimate management technique for a fund based on an index that has more than a few hundred

underlying securities—and that is naturally RIC- or UCITS-compliant. A fund does not need to own all of the index's approximately
2000 components to track the Russell 2000 very closely. On the
other hand, representative sampling is not an appropriate technique
and it should be avoided by managers when the index consists of
fewer than 100 equity securities and the index could be modified for
diversification compliance as easily as the fund. Funds based on
such indexes should also be avoided by investors. It is easier for an
investor or a research analyst to evaluate the fund manager's performance if the index and the fund portfolio have the same composition.
Any fund tracking error relative to an index with fewer than 100
issues should be a function of disclosed expenses or the result of a
deliberate decision by the manager to deviate from the index, not an
almost random event caused by inconsistency of the underlying
index structure with tax or regulatory diversification requirements.

Diversification compliance is not the only reason to modify
weightings of a benchmark index. An index designed to be used as a
fund template can embody rules or a structure selected to remove
obstacles to good investment performance. As we examine differences
in the ways different types of fund-friendly indexes handle weighting,
turnover, and membership issues, remember that the purpose of a fund-
friendly index is to create an attractive (to investors) and successful (in
terms of cost and performance relative to appropriate benchmarks)
fund. A benchmark index exists principally to evaluate the success of
actively managed portfolios. These are very different purposes.

Float Adjustments

Some fund-friendly indexes can serve as performance benchmarks
just as benchmark indexes can be the basis for a fund, but a fund-
friendly index that does not adjust for float may be a doubtful benchmark. A benchmark index will usually adjust capitalization weightings for differences in float or set a minimum float requirement so
that users tracking a popular benchmark will not exhaust the float
and distort the valuation of an illiquid stock. Such adjustments are
less necessary for a fund-friendly index so long as the index is not
being marketed to multiple fund managers who will create funds that
compete for a limited float. If a stock is an appropriate holding, it can

be a component of a single fund on the basis of its role in the economy or the total size of its capitalization, but an index publisher that wants to license multiple users will usually feel the need to focus more on liquidity and share availability. That publisher will tend to make float adjustments.[15] With the MSCI reconstitution, scheduled for completion in mid-2002, all major benchmark indexes except the S&P U.S. indexes will be float-weighted. Many of the market-roiling changes in the S&P 500 index discussed later in this chapter were exacerbated by the need to transact in stocks with limited floats.[16]

Portfolio Turnover

In contrast to some benchmark indexes with complex committee functions, fund-friendly indexes will usually rely heavily on rule-based modifications. Of course, there is usually a designated individual or organization authorized to deal with highly unusual situations not contemplated in the rules of an index; but, by definition and in fact, these are rare events. The modifications, re-weightings, and re-balancings of fund-friendly indexes are designed and timed to minimize market and tax impact to the greatest extent possible. In this context, fund disclosure documents generally grant portfolio managers flexibility to make the portfolio change before or after the index change to minimize market disruption, tax liabilities, and the fund's transaction costs. If the indexing process changes, as we propose below, the cost of these portfolio changes will be further reduced.

The user of a fund-friendly index will find that the circumstances which lead to elimination or replacement of a position are not greatly different from the rules for some benchmark indexes, but there will usually be fewer arbitrary changes and more thought given to the timing and market impact of changes in the fund-friendly index and its associated portfolio. A benchmark index (e.g., the S&P 500) may call for elimination of a position involved in a merger when it stops trading, and for complete re-balancing of the index when a company leaves and a new company is added. A fund-friendly index may drop a company after a definitive merger agreement is reached and all known obstacles to the merger are cleared, giving the fund manager more flexibility in eliminating the position and more time to make the change with minimal impact. In a fund-friendly index, a replacement company or companies may come in at the weight of the company that was dropped if the companies are close enough in size, eliminating the need for a fund to transact in all the stocks in the index when it re-balances. Fund-friendly index re-balancing is more frequently a quarterly or annual event—typically quarterly in a small-cap or volatile-sector index and annually in a large-cap fund. When complete re-balancing is not contemporary with each relevant corporate action, the index composition will deviate slightly from cap or float weighting until the next re-balancing. Ordinarily, these deviations will be small. They may not be acceptable to all investors accustomed to precise S&P 500 re-balancing rules, but they are almost certainly cost-effective. The trade-off is between the cost of re-balancing and a random theoretical benchmark tracking difference which can add to or detract from performance. Both numbers are likely to be small under most circumstances. Because of the certainty of the cost reduction element, there should be a small performance gain, on average, from less frequent rebalancing.

Problems with Particular Indexes as Templates for Funds
The Dow Jones Industrial Average
The Dow Jones Industrial Average (DJIA) is a price-weighted index based on the stocks of 30 large corporations. The DJIA was devised more than a hundred years ago to serve simply as a market indicator—its change from the previous close, measured in index points, is still the standard answer to the question "How's the market today?" Mechanical calculators were rare and extremely primitive in 1896, so the calculation method had to be simple. Likewise, there was no systematic reporting of changes in corporate capitalizations before the securities legislation of the 1930s, so a cap-weighted index would not have been possible even if the computational barriers could have been overcome.

No one would create an index like the Dow Jones Industrial Average today to serve either as a benchmark or as the basis for a fund. Even before J.P. Morgan (JPM) shares went up on the rumors/announcement that JPM, one of the smaller companies in the Dow, would merge with the much larger Chase Manhattan Bank, J.P. Morgan was by far the most heavily weighted component of the Dow (about 9%) on the basis of its high share price. The erratic timing of stock splits and the small number of issues in the Dow (30) under-mines any notion that this price-weighted index should be an index fund template. Even with cap weighting, a 30-stock index is too small to represent even the large-cap segment of the U.S. stock market.

The Dow Jones Industrial Average is a historic icon. Although it remains the principal basis on which U.S. and global investors describe the U.S. market's day-to-day or hour-by-hour behavior, for most other purposes it is obsolete. Its limited suitability for pur-poses beyond its original indicator function is reflected in the fact that, despite substantial, well-directed advertising and promotion and, in part, because of mediocre performance of the index in the early years of the fund, the DIAMONDS ETF based on the Dow Jones Industrial Average has not been as successful as the frequency of references to the DJIA suggest it might have been.

The Dow Jones Index Group, with funding from licenses on the DJIA, has done an excellent job of bringing up-to-date index techniques to most of its recently created indexes. Some of the newer Dow Jones benchmark indexes are more fund-friendly than the products of some major competitors.

The Standard & Poor's 500 Index

After some experimentation with the entire NYSE stock list, the first successful U.S. index funds were based on the Standard & Poor's 500 stock index.[17] The most important reasons behind the choice of the S&P 500 were that the index was capitalization weighted and that it was linked to a set of stock price data developed in the 1950s which covered a period going back to 1926. The index was not entirely con-sistent over the 1926–1957 period and it did not cover a 500-stock universe for the entire period. Nonetheless, by 1957, when the S&P 500 was introduced, it seemed appropriate to use 500 stocks. *Fortune* had come out with the popular "Fortune 500" in 1956, and by 1957 it was easy enough to provide daily pricing data on a 500-stock index.

The S&P 500 is the index used most widely today as the bench-mark for U.S. stock index fund portfolios, yet about 4% of its member-ship by weight consists of non-U.S.-based stocks.[18] The after-tax return effect due to the loss of any withholding tax credit on foreign shares by taxable U.S. shareholders of index funds based on the S&P 500 is probably in the vicinity of a single basis point per year, but this characteristic represents the sort of inefficiency that can occur when an index fund uses a benchmark index.[19] S&P Index Committee members have stated that some foreign stocks are essentially grandfathered into the S&P 500 for the rest of their corporate lives. Nonetheless, an astute index fund manager who is not required to own all 500 stocks might consider looking for a reason to exclude Royal Dutch and Unilever from his own S&P 500 index fund. The S&P Index Committee's decision to remove Chrysler from the S&P 500 when it merged with Daimler Benz in 1998 surprised and annoyed many S&P 500 index fund managers. S&P had been vague enough about its plans to keep Chrysler in the S&P 500 to lead many managers to believe it would stay. Daimler Chrysler's removal from the index led to some large taxable capital gains distributions from S&P 500 funds. It also indicated the S&P Index Committee's sensitivity to the presence of foreign stocks in the index.

About 140 of the S&P 500 stocks had capitalizations of less than $5 billion at the end of 2000. More than 100 of these companies would have been excluded from the index at that time if membership had been based strictly on market value. These smaller companies tend to be relative failures rather than emerging growth companies. They were added when their capitalizations were relatively, if not absolutely, larger, and they remain in the index because the S&P Index Committee is reluctant to remove companies unless they are in conspicuous financial trouble or they "disappear" in an acquisition. Collectively these smaller companies are, like the foreign stocks in the index, candidates to underperform the index over a period of 5–10 years because indexers that do not have to match the index exactly realize that a number of these companies will be eliminated from the index when the S&P Index Committee wants to add a new company. When these companies are dropped from the index and begin to be sold from indexed portfolios, their share prices usually fall even further.[20] S&P removed more of these fading stocks in the fourth quarter of 2000 than ever before, but there is no clear evidence that these recent changes indicate a change in policy.[21]

Some of the shortcomings of the S&P 500 as the basis for an index fund arise from its great popularity for that purpose. The S&P Committee's decisions to add some companies to the index only after they became large enough to be among the largest 100 stocks illustrates the problems that stem from this popularity. America On Line (AOL), Yahoo (YHOO), and JDS Uniphase (JDSU) were added to the index in December 1998, December 1999, and July 2000, respectively. The additions of YHOO and JDSU, in particular, forced indexers to sell billions of dollars worth of shares in all their other index holdings to make room for the new companies. Large net sales of 500 stocks (including the very small-capitalization stocks YHOO and JDSU replaced) put downward pressure on the index on the days of change. The S&P 500 contains most large-cap U.S. stocks, so the adverse *relative* impact of each single event on the investors in these index funds was partly temporary. As we will see shortly, however, these events, including the re-balancing effects, have a greater impact on index fund transaction costs than most investors realize. If these companies had been added on the basis of capitalization, they would have joined the index earlier and the fund turnover and market turmoil associated with their addition would have been largely avoided. Index—and fund—performance would also have been enhanced.

Many managers try to replicate the S&P 500 index rules exactly when they adjust positions in their S&P 500 index fund portfolios, but a number of index fund managers attempt to improve their results relative to the index by modifying the timing of their transactions to take advantage of low-risk opportunities to enhance return by making an index membership or weighting change in their fund before or after the time the change is made in the index.[22] The increasingly disruptive crush of less venturesome S&P 500 index fund managers making portfolio changes at the market closing price on the effective date of an index change has provided opportunities for flexible managers to improve results by stepping back from the market when everyone else is adjusting their index funds. Picking up a few basis points on the S&P 500 by skillful timing of portfolio adjustments has become the leading sport of astute index fund managers.[23] Good index fund management is not a "passive" activity.

The success of the S&P 500 as a template for large-capitalization U.S. stock index funds may be either self-perpetuating or self-defeating. The existence of so many large S&P 500 indexed portfolios makes it cheaper to trade S&P 500 portfolio baskets as a unit than, say, a dartboard 500 or a Russell 1000 portfolio.[24] Furthermore, the competition among multiple offerings of S&P 500 ETFs will keep readily visible fund expenses low. Several things seem capable of shaking the S&P 500's hold on large U.S. index portfolios:

- Continuation of market-roiling trading activity accompanying changes to the index by the S&P Index Committee as described above may result in more decisions by indexers to stray from S&P's "rules" or from the index itself.

- Continued improvements in portfolio trading techniques and overall market liquidity may make it almost as easy and cheap to trade 500 or more individually selected stocks as 500 in a standardized basket.

- The possibility that an objective, float-weighted index comprised of an all-U.S. portfolio of the largest 500 or so companies would be recognized as superior to the S&P 500. This new index would already have the next large stock (like AOL, YHOO, or JDSU) to be added to the S&P 500. Of less importance, it would not suffer from S&P 500 eliminations. It would be easy and inexpensive to create and use an all-U.S., top 500 stock, fund-friendly index as the basis for what are now S&P 500 index funds.

- The possibility that continued aggressive moves like the McGraw-Hill lawsuit against Vanguard over the latter's plan to introduce ETF share classes of its S&P index funds may alienate a number of S&P index licensees (McGraw-Hill is Standard & Poor's corporate parent).[25]

The methods of the S&P Index Committee appear to be antithetical to the core principle of the portfolio indexation philosophy: Objectivity. The S&P committee uses its own vague criteria to determine what stocks are to be added to the index—and when. Except for departures from mergers or bankruptcies, elimination of a company from the S&P 500 is at the whim of the com-

mittee. **Additions of large companies like AOL, YHOO, and JDSU occur when the committee decides to include them, not because they are, suddenly and objectively, the largest eligible companies. This is precisely the kind of investment decision-making that indexing is supposed to avoid. Instead of avoiding it, much of the investment management industry has implicitly delegated portfolio management decisions to the S&P Index Committee.**[26]

Global Benchmark Index Competition and Implications for Index Funds

By the late 1980s, Morgan Stanley Capital International (MSCI) nearly owned the benchmark index market for stock markets outside the United States. Except for the United Kingdom, where the predecessor of the current FTSE index family had a strong benchmark position among U.K. money managers, MSCI dominated the country benchmark indexes, and its Europe, Australasia, Far East (EAFE) multinational index was the composite benchmark for Eastern Hemisphere equity investments by U.S. investment managers.

The early MSCI indexes covered large companies, but market liquidity was improving for smaller stocks around the world, and the FTSE/Goldman Sachs Group and Salomon Brothers stepped up the pace of innovation in global benchmark indexing with expanded company coverage. After a few benchmark index adoptions were lost to the innovators, MSCI improved and broadened its indexes and largely reestablished its grip on the non-U.S. benchmark index market. The current FTSE focus is still on benchmark indexes. The former Salomon Smith Barney (SSB) index group, whose product is now called Citigroup Global Equity Indexes, develops custom benchmark and fund-friendly indexes. Citigroup's benchmark indexes addressed a number of the failings of other index providers early in the game. The Citigroup indices are all-inclusive and have consistently been float-weighted.

In the late 1990s, the three long-time competitors in the global benchmark index market were joined by Dow-Jones Global Indexes, with their focus on standard benchmarks plus custom index construction and maintenance, and by Standard & Poor's, which has stressed index co-sponsorships with established stock exchanges in Toronto, Tokyo, Sydney, and other locations.

Ten years ago, the smart money would have been on S&P's strategy of exchange alliances, with its opportunities for trading futures and other index instruments.[27] Today, the probable outcome is less clear. The company coverage in S&P's non-U.S. indexes is far less extensive and less consistent in different countries than any of its competitors, and the relative importance of alliances with local stock exchanges has declined. A long global bear market might reduce interest in smaller companies; but growing relative interest in very large companies is probably S&P's only hope for global index dominance. If Dow Jones continues to spend money on index development after the proceeds from its initial lucrative DJIA fund and derivatives license agreements are exhausted, it will probably have an advantage over MSCI because the latter's investment bank affiliation is an issue for some benchmark users. Dow Jones' move to float weighting has stimulated the FTSE group and MSCI to move in that same direction. Although MSCI has lost some clients, they have handled the move to float weighting effectively; and there is little reason to believe the net competitive impact of the move to float weighting will be meaningful. An important wild card in the contest is the improvement in data quality and availability, which increases the opportunities and cuts the costs for smaller competitors. Finally, if the full power of Citigroup gets behind the high-quality former Salomon Smith Barney indexes, the entire playing field may change.[28]

A Darwinian might predict a proliferation of new index genera and species, followed by some painful extinctions. To the extent that the future holds a greater role for fund-friendly indexes and a reduced role for benchmark indexes as fund templates, the roles of at least some of the traditional index publishers will decline.

DEVELOPMENT AND CHARACTERISTICS OF FUND-FRIENDLY INDEXES

The Short History of Deliberately Fund-Friendly Indexes

As suggested in the earlier brief discussion of non-benchmark indexes underlying exchange-traded funds, the history of fund-friendly indexes is very short. Early index fund managers were looking exclusively for broad-based indexes to replicate, so RIC compliance was rarely a problem. Early fund index license fees, like early index funds, were small, making customization of indexes for funds impractical.[29] Index rules were designed for benchmarking and performance measurement applications, not fund efficiency. Only when the NASDAQ 100 Index was modified for RIC compliance and the Sector SPDRs were designed around new RIC-compliant indexes, were fund-friendly indexes deliberately created for the first time. The relatively high license fees demanded by the traditional index licensors have been a major incentive for exchange-traded fund managers to demand more fund-friendly index structures and to consider new index providers who offer a less well-known index brand but a more appealing index structure as a fund template. More fund-friendly indexes are being created to meet ETF requirements. The need for fund-friendly index features is clearer and more important to ETF managers than to conventional index fund managers; but the latter are beginning to realize that their shareholders also can benefit from better (more fund-friendly) indexes.[30] Although the history of fund-friendly indexes is extremely brief, the advantages of and requirements for fund-friendly indexes are increasingly clear.

Advantages of Fund-Friendly Indexes

The advantages of fund-friendly indexes are relatively easy to articulate and the indexes themselves are only slightly more difficult to create than traditional benchmark indexes. The advantages of the fund-friendly indexes generally include:

- Natural RIC (and often UCITS) compliance or, less desirably, availability of low-cost synthetics to make the fund compliant.
- Reduced turnover and re-balancing as aids in fund transaction cost control
- License fees that reflect the investment characteristics of the index, not its benchmark "fame"
- Investment common sense
- Inherent fund tax efficiency

Not every index needs to have a special feature or rule to achieve each of these advantages and, as the reader might suspect, "investment common sense" is something of a catch-all that has different implications for different kinds of portfolios. An examination of Exhibit 6-3 and a careful reading of the remainder of this chapter should clarify the advantages of keeping the requirements of the fund and its investors in mind when specifying index characteristics. It should also further clarify what makes fund-friendly indexes different from the traditional benchmarks. In the interest of managing reader expectations, however, it is important to note that there is no universal formula for a fund-friendly index. Developing an appropriate index requires a constructive state of mind and a willingness to question traditional index structures.

Performance Measurement—Objective Tests of a Fund-Friendly Index and Its Fund[31]

An index fund's operating performance should be evaluated by comparison with the performance of its index, whether that index is a traditional benchmark index or an index designed for fund operating and tax efficiency. It is also appropriate that the index fund's performance be compared to the performance of a benchmark index that covers approximately the same stock universe as the fund's template index. An even better and more comprehensive evaluation will include a comparison of tax and operating efficiency and tracking error relative to the template index with similar measures for any index funds based on the standard benchmark. Of course, a five-basis-point improvement in operating or tax efficiency relative to the fund's index is meaningless if the fund is based on a fund-friendly index that systematically lags the standard benchmark.[32] Long-term comparisons of operating efficiency and performance that favor a fund constructed on a fund-friendly index will be necessary to establish the principle. In time, fund data and evaluation services and fund analysts will develop a variety of ways to appraise funds relative to their own indexes *and* relative to standard benchmarks. These fund efficiency tests will certainly measure transaction costs, particularly market impact. Other variables measured will include index/portfolio turnover and frequency of diversification re-balances. At present, there are no consensus standards for measuring the effect of many of the index inefficiencies that affect index fund performance; but developing suitable and widely accepted standards for the cost burden of both index and actively managed funds should not be difficult.

When an accepted performance measurement framework measures the fund efficiency of indexes, managers using fund-friendly indexes will be evaluated on the basis of how well their fund tracks its index, and how fund performance compares to broadly similar funds based on benchmark indexes. Obviously, there is a random element (noise) in such comparisons; but the reader will soon understand why a fund manager and fund investors might accept some randomness with confidence that the probabilities of improved performance are comfortably on their side over a period of a year or two.

In Exhibit 6-5, we attempt to compare hypothetical relative cost efficiencies of two pairs of funds. One fund in each pair is based on a benchmark index and the other on a fund-friendly index designed specifically to replace the benchmark in fund applications. The first comparison, of the S&P 500 to the Fund-Friendly "500," assumes that the Fund-Friendly "500" has enough companies to cover 85% of the U.S. market as measured by capitalization of all U.S. companies with a market value over $100 million. This will be, coincidentally, about 500 companies. It is worth noting that the S&P 500 includes only about 75% of U.S. companies by capitalization. The new index would be float-weighted with annual re-balancing and various rules designed to reduce turnover. The second comparison pits the Russell 2000 against a Complementary Small Cap Fund-Friendly index, which includes the remainder of the U.S. corporate market cap from the largest U.S. company not included in the Fund-Friendly 500 down to the $100 million capitalization level. The two fund-friendly indexes would cover all U.S. publicly traded companies with capitalizations over $100 million, or more than 99% of total U.S. equity market capitalization.

Exhibit 6-5: Hypothetical Annual Index Fund Cost Comparisons—Benchmark vs. Fund-Friendly Indexes (All Numbers Are Basis Points)

Fund Cost Element	Index			
	S&P 500	Fund-Friendly "500"	Russell 2000	Complementary Small Cap
Fund Expense Ratio	10	20	25	30
Fund Transaction Costs Annually (Index Efficiency)	50–100	Less than 25	200–300***	Less than 100
Index Membership Effect*	?	?	?	?
Value Added by Fund Manager**	?	?	?	?
Range of Determinable Cost Elements	60–110	Less than 45	225–325	Less than 130
Cost of Trading Fund Shares	10	20	20	30

* Historically, there has been a positive effect on the performance of stocks when they join the S&P 500 and, based on activity connected with the annual reconstitution, when they join the Russell 2000. There also has been an ongoing S&P membership effect, probably as a result of the growth in indexing. If the arguments we make here have any impact, the S&P 500 membership effect should be a historic artifact.

** Aggressive index fund managers have traditionally added value by trading at a different time than the official moment of index change. By doing so, they have recovered part of the annual transaction costs. Based on the performance of Vanguard and others, the best managers seem to have recovered 10%–20% of the transaction costs in the S&P 500 and as much as one-third of the Russell 2000 transaction costs.[33] This transaction cost recovery relative to the formal index value is not a zero-sum game. More managers should be able to beat the benchmark index (before expenses) than underperform the index. This opportunity to recapture transaction costs will largely disappear when fund-friendly indexes are adopted.

*** Part of the evidence for the extremely high re-balancing cost of the Russell 2000 is the finding by Julian (2001) that the stocks which graduated from the Russell 2000 to the Russell 1000 in 1990 had a return of 15.6% through the end of 2000 versus the 11.8% return on the Russell 2000. It is not possible to divide this outperformance between the superior performance of the stocks that "graduated" from the 2000 to the 1000 that year and the transaction costs associated with the annual reconstitution; but there is widespread agreement that the annual cost of the reconstitution has been rising as use of the Russell 2000 as a small-cap fund template has grown.

A quick glance at Exhibit 6-5 shows that the benchmark index funds have two advantages over the fund-friendly index funds. The expected fund expense ratios are lower and the cost of trading the fund shares (which is in large measure a function of the standardization and acceptance of the portfolios) is presumed initially to be lower for the benchmark index funds than for the fund-friendly index funds. Focusing on the large-cap funds, the expense

ratio on the S&P 500 fund is assumed to be 10 basis points (reflecting the expense ratio of 9.45 basis points on the iShares S&P 500
Fund) whereas the Fund-Friendly "500" is assumed, at least initially, to be a smaller fund. With fewer assets to spread expenses
over, we assume an expense ratio of 20 basis points. It might be
realistic to assume that the manager of the new fund would match
the expense ratio on the S&P 500, but the manager might decide to
stake its case for the new fund on *performance after expenses*.

The cost of trading in or out of an S&P 500 standardized basket in the form of fund shares is now generally around 10 basis
points. Although the Fund-Friendly "500" should track the S&P 500
very closely most of the time, we still assume that the cost of trading
these shares—until the new basket becomes widely accepted—will be
about 20 basis points. Fund and basket cost differences are unlikely to
be materially larger than Exhibit 6-5 indicates because of the inevitable close correlation of the two indexes and the larger average size of
the significantly weighted companies in the Fund-Friendly indexes.

Certain other effects, such as any index membership performance effect and the value added by a fund manager in timing transactions differently from those required in the index rules, we treat as
unknowns. We could argue that these unknowns could affect the contest either way, but the net impact is likely to be very small.

The remaining difference between the two indexes in each
index pair is in the expected transaction costs inside the fund that
are associated with index changes and re-balancing trades. In the
case of the benchmarks, the 50–100-basis-point estimate for the
S&P 500 and the 200–300-basis-point estimate for the Russell 2000
are rough estimates for annual transaction costs for funds based on
these indexes. Trading costs inside S&P 500 portfolios probably
exceeded 100 basis points in 1999 and ran closer to or even below a
50-basis-point rate for the first 9 months of 2001. The transaction
costs on average may be higher than the estimates simply because
most index managers underestimate the importance of market
impact *on both sides* of an index fund reconstitution. In the case of a
new company being added to the S&P, the market impact on the
stock of the new index member is obvious. Less clear, but often
quite important, is the market impact on the other side from transac-

tions in the stock being removed from the index and 499 other stocks whose relative weight is changed. The transactions on both pieces of the trade are done at a time and in an environment where they represent one-way transactions. That is, there is no obvious party interested in trading in the other direction and providing natural liquidity. Greater market impact is likely in a one-way transaction than in a randomly timed transaction. These are one-way transactions because many investors are using the same indexes in the same way—everyone wants to buy or everyone wants to sell.

The very low transaction cost estimates for the two fund-friendly indexes reflect the fact that these new indexes are designed to minimize transactions at all times and to offset as many transaction costs as possible with trading between the two complementary fund portfolios at the annual fund re-balancing. The tendency of an S&P fund to engage in a large number of relatively small re-balancing transactions (but one-way transactions) over the course of a year causes transaction costs to build up rather than be largely offset in an annual re-balancing between complementary funds. In the case of the Russell 2000, the greater (relative to capitalization) popularity of the Russell 2000 than the Russell 1000 means that the market impact of transactions in re-balancing the Russell 2000 is much greater than in its complementary large-cap index, the Russell 1000. In contrast to the Complementary Small Cap Index, the Russell 2000 is a middle-range index in the sense that it gains and loses some sizable companies not only at the top, but at the bottom. Rather than being representative of a capitalization range or percentage of the market capitalization, it accepts a fixed number of companies each summer. This structure leads to a 25 to 30% annual turnover at re-balancing. Because of the relative weighting disparity in the use of the Russell 1000 and the Russell 2000 in indexed portfolios, this turnover is reflected in the 200–300-basis-point estimate of embedded annual transaction costs for the Russell 2000.

The fund-friendly indexes are fully complementary. The Fund-Friendly "500" would cover the largest 85% of the capitalization range, and the Complementary Small Cap index would cover most of the remainder. At the bottom of the small-cap index, the impact of interaction with companies moving up from the below-

$100 million capitalization range or down into it would be relatively modest, and—with a buffer capitalization range between the small-cap and large-cap indexes, turnover would be well below the annual two-way migration between the Russell 1000 and the Russell 2000. If a fund issuer was responsible for large-cap and small-cap funds with proportionate capitalizations, or if the overall adoption of the two indexes was approximately proportional to their capitalization weights, the market impact of the re-balancing transactions involving switches between large cap and small cap would be negligible on the combined funds—perhaps even less than the estimates in Exhibit 6-5. Even if the adoptions were not ideally weighted at 85% and 15%, it would be a long time before market impact costs approached recent levels for the S&P 500 and the Russell 2000. Given the cost-saving opportunities which development of such indexes appears to offer, product developments along this line seem inevitable.

One even more interesting new approach to indexing which should revolutionize the management, cost, and effectiveness of index funds will be discussed in connection with an application of the Self-Indexing Fund described in Chapter 7, but it seems appropriate to introduce the concept here.

The dominant portion of the transaction costs that S&P 500 and Russell 2000 index funds experience is due to the fact that these funds have so much company whenever they need to transact. From the time index funds were introduced until a few years ago, market impact costs from index modifications were a non-issue for index fund managers. The success of indexing and, the consequent growth in the size and impact of index modification trades is the direct cause of the growing magnitude of these portfolio modification transaction costs. The recent S&P 500 index changes discussed above demonstrate clearly that only one change other than the end of growth in equity fund indexation will keep the benchmark index fund internal portfolio transaction costs illustrated in Exhibit 6-5 from continuing to grow. The necessary change is in the way index changes are made and revealed. An index fund manager not only needs to adopt a fund-friendly index, she needs an index that has modification rules that are *as independent as possible from the rules used by other indexers operating in the same general market space (e.g., large cap, small cap, sector, or style).* We will elaborate on this point in the next chapter in connection with a suggestion for a new operating format for index funds, and we will also return to it in Chapter 9 in connection with a brief discussion of the perennial struggle between index fund managers and active managers for the high ground on fund performance and value added.

Application of Fund-Friendly Index Principles to Some Specialized Funds

Small-Cap Index Funds

Benchmark indexes generally—and appropriately—emphasize faithful representation of the universe which the index covers or draws from. The Russell indexes, for example, re-balance to full and precise coverage of their universes once a year. As a template for index fund management, this works reasonably well with a large-cap index, but it tends to remove the best performers from a small-cap index. Most small-cap indexes lose their largest and most successful holdings into a larger-cap index from the same index family with periodic re-balancing. A stock can be promoted out of the small-cap index just as the stock is getting started and the stocks "demoted" from a larger-cap index are often less desirable (as reflected in their recent poor performance) than the stocks promoted out of the small-cap index. This is a particular problem for an index fund investor if different members of an index family (1) are used more or less widely for different capitalization ranges (like the Russell indexes) or (2) if the investor's commitment to small cap and large-cap positions are not weighted by total market capitalization—perhaps with a float adjustment. Fund-friendly index modification rules can at least mitigate this problem even if points (1) and (2) apply—as they do in many instances.

The increased use of the Russell 2000 as a basis for small-cap index portfolio construction apparently has encouraged Russell to re-evaluate the rules for the index because of complaints about market disruption from the drastic annual re-balancing. No changes have yet been announced. While awaiting possible changes from Russell, a fund-friendly index that plans on periodic re-balancing might try to benefit from the Russell re-balancing rather than adopt the Russell rules.

A stand-alone, small-cap, fund-friendly index can be designed to keep high performance stocks in the index—and in the fund based on that index—as long as they meet earnings or other performance requirements. As John Bogle has said, "You don't need to structure an index so that it throws out a stock when it gets too big."[34] Fund-friendly indexes can be designed to help implement a sensible, hopefully money-making, investment position, not just to reflect consistency of coverage. Consistency of composition and coverage are, appropriately, the hallmarks of benchmark and performance measurement indexes.

Style Indexes and Funds

Standard & Poor's and Russell feel an obligation to make their style-split indexes additive to their capitalization range aggregate benchmarks. To put it another way, if you weight the S&P 500 or Russell 1000 growth and value indexes (or weight funds replicating the style indexes) appropriately, you will get an index (or fund) that replicates the corresponding S&P 500 or Russell 1000 aggregate benchmark index (or fund). The apparent reason for this assignment of *all* stocks to either the growth side or the value side of the ledger (or, in the case of Russell, sometimes partly to each side) is the benchmark index publisher's traditional commitment to consistent or comprehensive coverage.

Many stocks lack distinctive growth or value characteristics. Nonetheless, stocks that are neither distinctly growth nor distinctly value are assigned to fit a capitalization split requirement (S&P), or a single non-growth, non-value stock is divided between growth and value indexes in an attempt to neutralize its impact (Russell). The result of these procedures is growth and value benchmark indexes that differ less than most investors' concept of the typical difference between growth and value stocks. An active growth or value manager would rarely come as close to the S&P 500 or Russell 1000 aggregate index composition as each firm's respective growth and value indexes come to the combined index. A typical active growth (value) manager who might be evaluated by comparisons with these growth (value) benchmarks will not consider a number of the stocks in the benchmark style split to be growth (value) stocks. A significant fraction of all stocks rarely appear in any sentient manager's growth *or* value portfolio, but they are all in one or the other or both of the S&P and Russell style benchmarks. It should not be surprising that, since 1979, the S&P/Barra and Russell style indexes have given *opposite* style performance indications an average of 2.5 months out of each year.[35]

Obviously, one difference between style benchmark and style fund-friendly indexes will be that *complementary fund-friendly style indexes will not include all the stocks in the aggregate index* used as a reference universe to develop the growth/value split. Classifying every stock as growth or value may make sense to a compulsive benchmarker, but it does not meet an investor's or fund manager's needs.[36] Stimulated, in part, by the introduction of style-split ETFs, we expect renewed interest and activity in the quest for appropriate ways to categorize stocks as growth or value—or "other."[37] The introduction of ETFs may even lead to more sensible S&P and Russell style benchmarks, if fund success by indexes with less comprehensive style coverage leads those index publishers to reformulate their approach.

Sector and Industry Indexes and Funds
Sector or industry indexes for funds will not usually be as different from benchmark sector indexes as style fund-friendly indexes will differ from style benchmark indexes. Nonetheless, sector and industry index funds often have multiple uses, and a particular sector fund-friendly index may represent a compromise between ideal benchmark features and ideal fund features. If the sector or industry indexes are designed to add up to full coverage of a broad market benchmark for comparison and systematic asset allocation purposes, the trade-offs may require careful handling. As with style categorizations, sector ETFs and their indexes will stimulate analysis and bring out new approaches.

Some generalizations about sector and industry indexes are useful to illustrate some of the issues raised by sector or industry index funds. An internet index, whether comprehensive or covering only an internet segment (B2B, B2C, infrastructure, etc.), would not be a component of an aggregate benchmark index. The internet cuts across a number of traditional industries, even if we segment it. While categorizations may change over decades, it is premature to restructure traditional sectors to pull out internet links. The same principle applies to many other investment themes like home computing, personal fitness, and lifestyle changes which affect companies in a number of more traditional sectors. A technology index can be a component of a broad market index (most cap-weighted and broadly defined ETF technology indexes) or it can be strictly a special-purpose index—fund-friendly or not—with no pretensions as a component of an aggregate benchmark (the Morgan Stanley High Tech Index). Indexes for most components of a fund-of-sector-funds product can be consistent with cap-weighting requirements if the sectors are large enough. However, simultaneous adherence to cap weighting and RIC or UCITS compliance requires special treatment if the aggregate index is to be split into very many sectors. The largest-cap stocks in any market dominate their sectors, and the dominance is most pronounced when the sectors are narrowly defined.

We expect that all successful sector fund indexes will be designed to be "naturally" RIC- and/or UCITS-compliant for a number of reasons:

- Diversification-compliant sector indexes have the collateral benefit of being less dominated by the largest companies in the sector because the positions in these large companies have to be reduced, sometimes greatly, relative to a pure cap-weighted index, to make the fund RIC-compliant. A sector index fund with a 50% position in General Electric or a 35% position in Exxon Mobil leaves little room for smaller company impact.
- A sector fund based on a diversification-compliant index should not have to explain a significant tracking error relative to its index, unless there is a truly substantive problem that merits explanation.
- A fund based on a diversification-compliant index should not need to use derivatives to ensure tracking.
- If the sector funds are made compliant by reducing the weight of the largest-cap stocks while smaller positions are kept pro-

portional to their cap weights, the resulting funds will be usable by investors who want *either* diversification within the sector or precise cap weighting. The latter group of investors need only add a few separate stock positions in the largest component companies to achieve pure cap-weighting either at the sector level or at the aggregate broad-market index level by combining sector funds and a completion basket to track a broad market index. These adjustments, combining ETFs and individual stocks, could easily be done and monitored for a match with an aggregate index in a Folio-type account. The resulting multi-instrument position would usually provide more opportunities for tax loss harvesting than a single broad-market index fund in (at least) the early years of its use in a taxable account.

Historically, index creators have not committed many resources to assigning companies to appropriate industries and sectors. Mergers across traditional industry or sector lines have not made this task any easier. There are four or five classification systems in use by index publishers. Few independent analysts will agree completely with any of these classification systems, but the process is certainly getting more attention than it received just a few years ago.

We expect any successful industry or sector classification system to be based on the North American Industry Classification System (NAICS, pronounced "nakes"), which was developed cooperatively by Canada, Mexico, and the United States to replace the outdated SIC codes in the collection of economic data and dissemination of statistics.[38] Securities analysts will be using this data for a wide range of purposes like they used the SIC categories before NAICS. NAICS will underlie any successful sector or industry index structure. Most applications of NAICS of interest to financial analysts should have been in place by the end of 2001. Despite the name, the system is not uniquely linked to North America and can be adopted elsewhere without losing any usefulness or generality. One innovation of the system is greater attention to service industries. Classification of diversified companies into a sector or industry category will retain elements of art. Consequently, sector and industry categorization will continue to be one of the few areas where an index committee can make a consistently useful contribution. As in the case of style indexes, the growth of ETFs should stimulate new approaches and new attention to sector indexes and sector funds.

Special-Purpose Index Funds

Size, style, and sector or industry do not exhaust the ways an index can be characterized. Under some circumstances a theme index which crosses industries like internet or wireless telephony can be the basis for an index fund if there is an appropriate index selection agent. Similarly, published stock lists like the *Wired* (magazine) index, the Value Line Stocks Rated 1 for Timeliness list, or an index based on an investment bank's purchase or "selected" list can be attractive theme indexes. These latter indexes convert an established stock selection process into an index which serves as the template for a portfolio. The resulting indexes are at least as objective as the DIAMONDS based on the Dow Jones Industrial Average and the SPDRs based on the S&P 500. Neither of the latter indexes are based on criteria more objective than the examples above and stock selection for both is managed by committees.

Broad-Market Indexes

Setting aside some unusual issues which arise when a broad-market index is created out of sector indexes, the principal problem in making a broad-market index fund-friendly is re-balancing. The two extreme solutions to re-balancing are well illustrated by S&P and Russell. S&P essentially re-balances every time their rules or the S&P Index Committee dictate a capitalization change or a membership change. This is less disruptive than it sounds, but it is more costly (in terms of transaction costs) than most S&P index users realize, as noted earlier in the chapter. The changes are relatively small for most positions on most occasions, and computers do the myriad calculations needed to develop buy and sell lists with ease; but all S&P indexers are trying to make the same portfolio changes at about the same time. The lack of two-way order flow increases transaction costs. Furthermore, the assets indexed to the S&P 500 have reached a size where the market impact of S&P re-balancing is nearly always material. At the other end of the spectrum Russell re-balancings are exciting annual affairs. Membership changes, particularly in the Russell 2000, make the re-balancing a major trading frenzy.[39]

The boundary between two different size segments could be managed with a buffer of a percentage point or two of capitalization weight that would have to be crossed before a stock would move up to the larger-cap index or down to the smaller-cap index. A buffer range of 84–86% of capitalization coverage would be appropriate for the complementary fund-friendly indexes of Exhibit 6-5.

Turnover

Fund-friendly indexes will generally attempt to minimize index changes that require portfolio turnover. In non-replication applications of benchmark indexes there is no obvious penalty associated with instability in the composition of the index. The user of the index as a benchmark is not obligated to transact when the index changes. An index fund, however, can experience a great deal of turnover from these benchmark index changes. The S&P 500 index rules call for re-weighting the positions in the portfolio for changes in shares outstanding each quarter *and whenever there is a change in the index membership*. In contrast, large-cap fund-friendly indexes should require a full-scale re-weighting no more frequently than once a year. A change in membership during the year may not require re-weighting of other companies because a new company or companies may come in at, say, the weight of the departing company under some circumstances. The reduction in portfolio turnover may save transaction costs and may lower tax bills for the owners of the fund shares. Users of a benchmark index as a benchmark for an active portfolio may be indifferent to the frequency of re-balancing, but it matters greatly to the index fund manager—and to the index fund investor.

IGNORING FUND-FRIENDLY INDEX PRINCIPLES— GLOBAL EQUITY INDEX FUNDS

Global equity index funds, i.e., funds holding stocks from both U.S. and foreign markets, have been rare in the United States. There are at least two reasons for this scarcity. First, most Americans have shown only modest interest in having a personal portfolio of both U.S. and non-U.S. equities with weightings determined by an index publisher. Anyone who is interested in foreign stock funds usually buys one or more specialized non-U.S. stock funds to supplement U.S. holdings in a desired proportion to domestic holdings. Second, a single fund holding both U.S. and foreign stocks is not tax-efficient for a taxable U.S. investor unless *more than half the fund's assets are foreign securities*. Unless most of its investment is in foreign securities, a fund cannot pass foreign withholding *tax credits* to its shareholders to offset U.S. taxes on the net dividends. If the fund invests less than half its assets in foreign securities, the foreign withholding taxes are a much less valuable tax *deduction* inside the fund.

As if to provide classic examples of tax-inefficient indexes developed for fund use, three recently published large-cap global indexes and index-based fund products based on at least two of the indexes seem to ignore this feature of the U.S. Tax Code. The three indexes in question are the Dow Jones Global Titans (50 stocks), the S&P 100 Global Index (100 stocks), and the FTSE Global 100 Index (100 stocks). The offering of fund products based on two of these indexes suggests that not everyone is up to date on fund-friendly indexes.[40]

Interestingly, Merrill Lynch has introduced a global basket product in its HOLDRs series called "Market 2000+" that avoids this tax *faux pas*. HOLDRs are not investment companies; hence, the withholding tax credit is passed through separately with respect to each foreign stock (ADR) position.[41]

The introduction of global sector ETFs by several issuers starting in mid-2001 provides a further example of insensitivity to the characteristics an ETF must have to achieve reasonable economic efficiency. Evidence has been accumulating at least since the adoption of the Euro by most of Continental Europe that international or global sector diversification was becoming at least as useful and perhaps more useful than country diversification.[42] If funds reflecting this idea are designed for U.S. investors, it might be possible to leave out U.S. stocks in a sector and just make the funds international (non-U.S.) sector funds. Unfortunately, even this less-than-satisfactory modification does not fully reflect the current operating economics of ETFs. A conventional fund manager can deal with global markets because she is buying and selling securities for cash. There are currency, clearance, and settlement issues; but they can be approached one stock at a time using well-established procedures, and everything does not have to be done at once. When a dealer is creating or redeeming shares in a multinational ETF, he is exchanging fund shares for a basket of portfolio shares that may trade and settle under five, 10, or even more different clearance and custody regimes. Ideally, everything should come together at once. The reality is often ragged and ugly with various pieces of the puzzle missing for days or even weeks. The result is usually an increase in portfolio costs that are not reflected in the expense ratio, but that, nonetheless, cost the fund money in terms of net asset value. It was no accident that the original WEBS were single-country funds. Multinational ETFs will become increasingly manageable with time, but an investor cannot assume that all the costs of someone's experiment in complex ETF construction will be reflected in the fund's expense ratio. Many of the costs may appear only as a reduction in fund performance or in a much wider bid-asked spread that replicates the costs and risks faced by the dealers who create and redeem the shares. Until 2003 or so, multinational ETFs should be approached with skepticism. By that time there is hope for better clearance and settlement integration.

CONCLUSION

The dramatic growth of both conventional index funds and, more recently, exchange-traded index funds has focused investment manager attention on the characteristics of stock indexes that make them desirable or undesirable templates for construction of an index fund portfolio. While there are some modest differences in the index structure a conventional fund manager might choose relative to the needs of a manager of an exchange-traded index fund, there are definite principles that nearly all index fund managers are looking for. Among other features, these include facilitation of regulated investment company (RIC) and undertaking for collective investment in transferable securities (UCITS) compliance, minimum portfolio turnover, clear and usually definitive index rules, tax efficiency, and a coherent investment theme that has appeal to institutional and/or retail investors.

Using examples of benchmark indexes which do not serve the needs of investment managers or the ultimate investor when used as a fund template, we have examined changes in index construction and maintenance techniques which should have the effect of improving an index's usefulness in the management of a portfolio. The fund-friendly approach to index construction and maintenance should increase the likelihood that the resulting fund will track its template index more closely. The fund based on such an index also may have a better chance of matching or surpassing the performance of a standard benchmark index covering a similar investment universe.

No claim is made that this chapter provides definitive answers to all issues concerning fund-friendly indexes. It seems clear that thoughtful index construction is a topic which will be of increasing interest and concern as indexing in general—and exchange-traded index funds in particular—continue to grow.

ENDNOTES

1. Morgenson (1997) quotes unnamed sources at Standard & Poor's as estimating that about 8% of U.S. stocks are held in indexed portfolios, presumably as of the end of 1996. We have seen and heard much higher estimates. For example, Bernstein (1992) uses a 30% figure for institutional portfolios. The difference is probably due largely to the degree of commitment fund managers have to following the index. S&P is probably looking at committed index trackers. Many of the institutions Bernstein refers to are apparently more relaxed about the process. The committed enthusiasts are the ones who move markets. Allowing for the continuing high popularity of indexing since 1996, a figure of 10% seems both reasonable and conservative for the percentage of the capitalization of an S&P 500 stock held in committed S&P 500 indexed portfolios.

2. The index and index fund principles discussed in this chapter were developed primarily for equity index funds. Some of these principles are applicable to specific fixed-income index funds.

3. The quotation marks around "5000" stress that the Wilshire 5000's objective of covering the entire U.S. equity market makes the actual number of index members open-ended.

4. The early attempt at indexation using an equal dollar-weighted index of all NYSE listed stocks was undertaken by Wells Fargo Bank, a distant corporate ancestor of the present-day Barclays Global Investors. Execution was described as "a nightmare." See Bernstein (1992), p. 247 or Bogle (1999), p. 114 for a description of this incident. Neither of these discussions of this first attempt describes the process of using equal dollar weighting very clearly. Achieving and then maintaining such a weighting structure is much more complicated than capitalization weighting. Even with today's computer-assisted trading, equal dollar index funds are very rare. This experience helped set the tone for subsequent preferences for cap-weighted indexes. In the early 1970s, the S&P 500 was the leading cap-weighted index based primarily on U.S. stocks, hence its widespread adoption for large-cap U.S. stock index funds.

5. If the Vanguard 500 fund were equally weighted in all S&P 500 companies, it would be the largest stockholder in a number of S&P 500 companies. It would have had effective control of such well-known "fallen angels" as Owens Corning, Bethlehem Steel, W.R. Grace, and Polaroid until these stocks were demoted to the S&P Small Cap Index as part of a late 2000 index cleanup by S&P. In the change, S&P removed seven fallen angels with total capitalizations of about $2.5 billion from the S&P 500 and replaced them with companies from other indexes in its family with total capitalizations over $58 billion. The changes were made over two trading days and required re-balancing transactions in all 1,500 components in three S&P indexes on each day.

6. The NASDAQ 100 Index had been around for a number of years, but it was modified as described below just before the NASDAQ 100 Trust was launched.

7. A patent has been issued for the weighting scheme used in the NASDAQ 100 Trust, but the weighting scheme sacrifices simplicity for no obvious purpose. This patented index construction method is highly unlikely to be used by any index creator that has to pay a patent license fee.

8. For an important example, see the discussion in endnote 29.

9. A large number of the ETFs based on benchmark indexes have been introduced since the end of the first quarter of 2000. Most of these funds have attracted few assets. The DIAMONDS fund (based on the Dow Jones Industrial Average) is listed with the benchmarks in Exhibit 6-2, but its index structure is very different from the other benchmarks.

10. Recently, S&P announced that its industry and sector assignments would be based on the Global Industry Classification System (GICS), developed jointly by S&P and MSCI. State Street announced that the Sector SPDR stock assignment process would not change.

11. For reasons unrelated to their names or the names of their fund issuers, the complementary index funds illustrated in Exhibit 6-5 and described later in this chapter might stimulate use of each other.

12. Remarks of Lee Kranefuss of BGI at a Salomon Smith Barney fund conference at the Plaza Hotel, March 28, 2000. Nothing of the sort has happened as of this writing. We suspect nothing happened because MSCI sees its indexes as consistently constructed benchmarks, and BGI's brand consciousness makes them reluctant to describe the underlying indexes for the funds as custom indexes developed to serve as the template for a more efficient, but non-benchmark index fund.

13. Whereas the RIC diversification rules specify quarterly compliance, UCITS rules require that a portfolio be brought into compliance within a few days anytime a position exceeds the 10% limit.

14. Fund sponsors also prefer tight bid-asked spreads because tight spreads encourage new investors to buy shares in the fund.

15. One could argue from CAPM assumptions that total capitalization weighting is more appropriate for each investor than float-adjusted weighting. This argument suggests ignoring float in a moderate-sized fund that is the only fund using an index. A popular benchmark index or a multi-use index almost *has* to consider float because *all* its users cannot ignore this limitation on liquidity.

16. Interestingly, as astute an observer as *The Economist* (2001) mistakenly thinks S&P has switched fully to float weighting. We do not expect S&P to adopt float weighting in the United States. The tax penalty and transaction costs in S&P portfolios would be staggering. We do expect some portfolios to switch to more fund-friendly indexes from concern about such a possibility.

17. See note 4 supra.

18. A recent investment quiz in *Money* (Updegrave 2000) included the following question:

> "Standard & Poor's 500-stock index contains:
> a. The 500 U.S. stocks with the highest market values;
> b. The 500 top-performing stocks in the U.S.;
> c. The 500 stocks that Standard & Poor's index committee believes should be in the index."

Clearly, the casual reader is expected to choose (a). The quiz has not been given systematically to determine what fraction of *Money*'s readers know the correct answer. It is easy to see how someone could get the impression that the S&P 500 consisted of the 500 largest companies in the United States. This notion has even slipped past the usually perceptive proofreaders at the *Wall Street Journal* (Abreast of the Market, September 5, 2000).

19. A RIC cannot pass the tax credit for foreign dividend withholding taxes through to its shareholders unless more than half the fund's assets are foreign securities. This point is developed at some-

what greater length later in the text. Not all of the "foreign" stocks in the S&P 500 are subject to dividend withholding taxes by their country of domicile. If a company's foreign domicile is only nominal, it should be considered domestic for investment purposes.

20. These companies cannot gain from the positive S&P 500 membership effect because they are already members of the index. They can be hurt by ejection. Because they are so small relative to some of the larger foreign stocks like Royal Dutch and Unilever, the loss to a portfolio from any one of these stocks being removed from the index is unlikely to be material. Clifford (2000) provides an interesting commentary on the jetsam of the S&P 500 and its fate. Plexus Group (2001) finds little effect on the prices of stocks recently dropped from the S&P 500.

21. Garnick, et al. (2001) and note 5 supra. See also comments by the chairman of the S&P Index Committee quoted in Zweig (2001).

22. Trades anticipating S&P index changes start even before the change is announced. This anticipation makes estimation of fund portfolio modification transaction costs very difficult.

23. Cramer (2000) and Serwer (2000) describe attempts to profit from S&P 500 index changes.

24. It is important to distinguish between a portfolio trade in which a fund buys or sells the entire index basket and a portfolio modification trade when the basket is changed. The former costs little and the latter costs a lot, at least in terms of the stocks most affected. The fact that *all* trades are one-way trades when they involve an index change increases trading costs *within* the fund. This point is discussed at greater length later in this chapter and in Chapter 8.

25. The major issues in this litigation were well summarized in Lucchetti and Lauricello (2001). The broader importance of the litigation stems from the probability that a U.S.-based index fund will find it impossible to compete for taxable shareholders without an exchange-traded share class to improve the fund's overall tax effi-

ciency. An ETF share class will also attract assets which will help spread expenses over a larger asset base.

26. Readers who want to balance the viewpoint on the S&P Index Committee expressed here should read Blitzer (2000). Blitzer is chairman of the Committee. The title of his article is a riff on Brendan Gill's *Here at The New Yorker*. Some additional examples of the Committee's activities are highlighted in Bary (1998, 1999), and Cushing and Madhavan (2000). For other specific and implied critiques of the S&P 500 and the Committee, see Morgenson (1997) and Carty (1999 a and b). Zweig (2001) makes the point that the S&P Index Committee has shown extraordinarily poor timing in its selection of S&P 500 stocks to add and delete over the past 10 years. There is no question that this conclusion is correct and that the reason is the Committee's *ad hoc* process. Zweig seems almost to suggest that the Committee leave the index alone. Our partial remedy would be to define the index as the 500 largest U.S. stocks or as a percentage of market capitalization and modify the membership annually on that basis.

27. See Gastineau (1994).

28. For more comparative information on global index families, see Schoenfeld, et al., (2000).

29. The trial court decision, Hellerstein (2001), in the McGraw-Hill vs. Vanguard litigation (U.S. District Court, Southern District of New York, 00 Civ. 4247 (AKH)) on introduction of exchange-traded share classes, indicates that the license fee Vanguard pays S&P is capped at $5,000 per year. This figure is more correctly stated as $50,000 per year in Lucchetti and Lauricello (2001). In contrast, the more recently negotiated uncapped index license fee for the 500 SPDRs is generally estimated to be approaching $10,000,000 per year.

30. Although the issue is well beyond the scope of this book, with the exception of their lack of concern over RIC or UCITS diversification requirements and tax efficiency, pension and endowment accounts should be as interested as investment companies in the fund-friendliness of the indexes underlying their indexed portfolios. Specifically,

they should be as interested as anyone in reducing the impact of the transaction costs incurred in implementing index changes.

31. The material in this section will be part of a forthcoming article in the *Journal of Portfolio Management.*

32. This statement implicitly assumes that the benchmark is close enough to RIC compliance and the fund-friendly index is close enough to the benchmark that close tracking is a reasonable expectation. Such an assumption is not reasonable on many sector indexes, but it should work for capitalization range indexes.

33. See Bogle (1999). p. 134.

34. Teitelbaum (2000). Julian (2001) is an interesting study of the honors graduates of the Russell 2000 that were promoted to the Russell 1000. They have continued to outperform the Russell 2000 and most other indexes as well. Part of their long-term outperformance of the Russell 2000 is probably due to the latter's high transaction cost of re-balancing.

35. See Kim, et al. (2001).

36. The Dow Jones US Value and Growth Indexes, patterned after indexes originally developed by State Street, depart slightly from the all-inclusiveness of the S&P and Russell style benchmarks. Unfortunately, the difference is not great enough. The Dow Jones Large Cap Value and Growth Indexes, in particular, are too inclusive. Over 95% of the capitalization weight in this size category is shoehorned into either value or growth, leaving less than 5% of cap weight in a neutral zone. The mid-cap and small-cap versions of the Dow Jones Value and Growth Indexes include about 80% of the eligible capitalization, intuitively a more reasonable proportion. The index rules offer no explanation for their provision that any company accounting for more than 0.5% of the capitalization weight in its size category *must* be assigned to either value or growth. This rather arbitrary index percentage cap rule requires the larger companies in an index to be allocated to either value or growth *even if the analytical rules consign them to "neutral."* This rule affects the

large-cap indexes far more than the mid-cap or small-cap indexes. The greater diversification of the typical large-cap company suggests that a large-cap company might be slightly *more likely* than a small company to fall *between* value and growth in the absence of this rule. Apparently, the lack of analyst coverage of smaller companies and the consequent shortage of earnings estimates causes the higher neutral percentages for the smaller companies.

37. One fund manager has taken the notion of excluding non-growth/non-value stocks from the style indexes a step further by dividing the remaining growth and value stocks into stable or variable categories with distinctive characteristics. See Jankovskis (2000).

38. For more information, start with www.census.gov/epcd/www/pdf/naicsdat.pdf. See also Klieson (2001).

39. The 2001 re-balancing was rendered more difficult by a NASDAQ breakdown, but the problem is perennial. It will continue to worsen unless (a) the Russell 1000 gains massive market share from the S&P 500 or (b) indexers abandon the Russell 2000 because of high transaction costs.

40. The Global Titans Fund at least uses ADRs, sidestepping major clearance and settlement problems.

41. Some HOLDRs shareholders will have to tabulate the tax credits on each dividend paying ADR in the Market 2000+ basket or obtain the details from the HOLDRs website. At this time, HOLDRs do not offer every shareholder consolidated portfolio and tax reporting that is as convenient as reporting by a fund.

42. See Baca, Garbe, and Weiss (2000) and Cavaglia, Brightman, and Aked (2000). The same information is presented in a more user-friendly way in Updegrave (2001). Other key work on foreign diversification and cross border risk is in Schoenfeld (2000), Barnes, et al. (2001), and Hopkins and Miller (2001). Barnes, et al. and Hopkins and Miller suggest it is too soon to abandon country diversification completely for industry diversification.

Chapter 7

New Generations of ETFs

There have been a large number of discussions in the press and at industry conferences about the nature of future ETFs. Most of the attention has centered on (1) the applicability of the ETF structure to fixed-income funds and (2) the possibility of actively managed ETFs. This chapter will explore these and other important milestones in ETF development.

A brief discussion of fixed-income ETFs starts this chapter, followed by a discussion of enhanced index funds and quantitative strategies that could be accommodated in the current equity index ETF format. Building on Chapter 6's discussion of the problems index funds are encountering as indexing absorbs a growing fraction of the available shares of major index member stocks, we suggest a way to reduce transaction costs and correspondingly improve index fund returns. This new approach to indexing also shows promise as the best initial format for actively managed ETFs. The balance of the chapter examines various shapes actively managed ETFs might take and more complex forms of active ETFs.

Most of the published discussions of actively managed ETFs have been relatively superficial in their treatment of the opportunities and obstacles to be encountered in the development of active ETFs. This chapter's discussion of several ways of handling actively managed funds should fill in the gaps and help the reader develop a greater understanding of the important features of existing ETFs that will be used in the same way or in modified form in new types of ETFs.

ETFS BASED ON FIXED-INCOME SECURITIES

The principal obstacle to successful and widely diversified fixed-income ETFs is limited liquidity and relatively high transaction costs in most fixed-income markets. With the exception of the active U.S. Treasury and Agency debt markets, (1) the cost of dealer intermediation between buyers and sellers of debt securities and (2) the tendency of corporate and municipal bonds and notes to disappear from dealer's and traders' inventories into investors' portfolios within months of their initial issue, increase transaction costs and limit the liquidity of mature paper. In contrast, generally higher and less certain equity returns and the "perpetual" life of a common stock have made investors less sensitive to stock transaction costs and more willing to spread such costs (mentally) over a higher expected return and a longer holding period than they would use to judge the acceptability of the transaction costs of a fixed-income instrument, including a fixed-income fund.

Compounding the liquidity challenge of debt instruments is the large number of debt issues. Most corporations with traded stock have multiple debt issues outstanding, and many entities that do not issue common stock, such as government and quasi-government organizations, issue debt. In the U.S. municipal debt market alone, there are about six times as many distinct issuer, rate, and maturity combinations as there are publicly traded common stocks in the United States.[1] The dealers who trade these bonds build a spread into each trade to compensate them for the risk and carrying cost of holding slow-moving inventory. A market structure which funnels every trade through at least one dealer tends to build a spread into all trades, whether intermediation by a dealer is necessary or not in a specific case. Spreads on more actively traded debt instruments often subsidize the cost of trading less active paper. Efforts to build alternative markets that bypass dealers on heavily traded issues have not been very successful, but the prospect of competition from such markets has reduced spreads in the more active bonds and notes, increasing the range of instruments that may be suitable for use in fixed-income ETFs.

Most Treasury and benchmark Agency obligations and some larger and recently issued investment-grade corporate note issues meet the liquidity and transaction cost qualifications to be used in ETFs.[2] As trading costs per transaction and per dollar of assets continue what appears to be a long-term decline, the number and value of debt instruments that are "ETF eligible" will gradually increase.

In recent years, the issue of fixed-income market liquidity has been complicated by projections that U.S. government public debt will be retired within a few years. A skeptical study by economists at the Saint Louis Federal Reserve Bank,[3] passage of the 2001 tax legislation, and a slower rate of growth and productivity improvement in the U.S. economy have combined to reduce the frequency and intensity of such discussions and almost turn them around.[4] As this is written, the public debt implications of the terrorist attacks on the World Trade Center and the Pentagon have barely begun to be assessed. The now receding prospect of a smaller federal government debt "supply" had the effect of stimulating more standardized and, hence, more tradable debt issuance by Fannie Mae and Freddie Mac and by a number of large investment-grade corporate borrowers. These issuers' growing attention to the aftermarket trading of their debt is clearly in the process of extending the range of "ETF eligible" debt instruments. The greater liquidity of a standardized issue increases primary market demand for the initial and follow-up tranches of the issue and correspondingly reduces the issuer's cost of borrowing.

While some fixed-income ETFs may be based on traditional broad-market debt indexes, some of the issues raised in Chapter 6 about fund-friendly equity indexes apply equally to fixed-income ETF indexes. There is a very limited role for callable debt in general-purpose fixed-income ETFs. Callable debt generally becomes less marketable as the probability of a call increases. A fund with a large percentage of callable debt will face a large transaction-cost-based fund share trading spread when calls become likely. ETFs using securitized mortgage debt as part of their portfolio are possible, but their risk characteristics will have to be described carefully to potential users and the natural reduction of liquidity for these instruments as they approach effective maturity will have to be recognized in the product structure.

The first successful fixed-income funds will be sensitive to liquidity issues and the need to provide intra-day pricing for the index and the fund portfolio. These funds will be useful for a number of applications, but they will not have all features found in the full range of conventional fixed-income funds.

- Consistent maturity ranges will be used to provide investors with the equivalent of automatic rollover of the benchmark Treasury issue at a lower cost than investors could spend to do the rollover themselves.
- An on-the-run (OTR) Treasury index will be used because the on-the-run Treasury is the most liquid instrument in each maturity range and it is the benchmark used to price dollar-denominated notes or bonds of similar maturity.
- The funds will not use just the on-the-run issue in their portfolios because the OTR issue often trades "special" (at a slightly higher price and lower yield than other Treasuries in its maturity range) reflecting its liquidity and popularity. A security that trades special must be loaned to dealers to obtain the maximum return it can provide, but the SEC limits a fund's securities lending to one-third of the fund's gross assets. Consequently, a fund with all its assets in the premium-priced on-the-run issue would suffer a return penalty. Each ETF portfolio will have a number of different debt instruments in its portfolio at any time. Those instruments will replicate the benchmark's cash flows, not simply the benchmark instrument or instruments. The Canadian iUnits model, in which a single Canadian government note is wrapped into a fund, will not be attractive in the United States.
- Using primarily on-the-run and just off-the-run Treasuries and Agencies in the portfolio minimizes transaction costs both inside the fund and for the Authorized Participants (dealers) who create, redeem, and make markets in the fund shares.
- The fixed-income ETFs will settle on T+3 in the secondary market on the Exchange, providing an ideal fit with equity ETFs for transition and asset allocation applications. They will settle on T+1 in the primary market (transactions involving the fund), consistent with settlements in the underlying securities and futures markets. Clearly, the dealers who will be creating and redeeming the fund shares can manage the repos and reverse repos necessary to carry positions more efficiently than retail customers who simply want an "equitized" debt instrument. As equities eventually move to T+1

settlement in the secondary market, the fixed-income ETFs will accompany them to that settlement schedule.

• Unlike equity funds, no attempt will be made to eliminate capital gains distributions entirely. When rates are declining, most portfolio sales will result in small capital gains. Avoiding these gains entirely would probably increase the fund's trading costs significantly. A more feasible strategy is to attempt to obtain as much of the return as possible as long-term capital gain.[5]

Future fixed-income ETFs will modify some of these features as liquidity improves in more types of debt instruments. The future for fixed-income ETFs is bright, but the focus of most ETF product development will continue to be on equity or predominantly equity funds.

Issue Size—One Indicator of Liquidity in Fixed-Income and Equity Markets

Liquidity in a market depends on many things: market structure, trading volume, availability of price data, etc. One important determinant of liquidity is issue size. If an issue is very small, it is not likely to trade actively or at a low transaction cost. Here are some estimates of the average issue size outstanding in some important U.S. markets. The figures have been rounded to two significant digits to avoid the impression of high precision.

	Total Market Value (Billions)	Average Issue Size (Millions)
Common Stock	$12,000	$1,600
Treasury Debt	2,200	2,800
Corporate and Foreign Dollar-Denominated Debt	1,700	430
Tax-Exempt Debt	780	19

Source: Our calculation as of June 30, 2001, based on data published by Wilshire Associates and Lehman Brothers. The corporate and tax-exempt debt numbers exclude issues with less than one year to maturity and small issues (under $150 million for corporations, under $5 million for tax-exempts) that would not be usable in most institutional portfolios, let alone in an ETF.

ENHANCED INDEX FUNDS AND
QUANTITATIVE STRATEGIES FUNDS

These funds, which we will refer to collectively as "enhanced index funds" for simplicity, are based on security selection processes developed, tested, and run by quantitative research groups affiliated with or serving a fund's portfolio managers. The assumption behind these funds is that the manager will provide relatively comprehensive disclosure of the quantitative method used to manage the fund. Some managements may even choose to provide an explanation so comprehensive that it would permit anyone with appropriate computer skills and data access to replicate the technique the fund uses and determine in advance the changes to be made in the fund portfolio. Other managements will provide a more general description of the qualitative model and reveal specific transactions after they are made, probably using the procedure of the Self-Indexing Fund, described in a subsequent section of this chapter.

Like traditional equity index ETFs, the first of these enhanced index funds may reflect portfolio changes in their creation baskets. Since enhanced index funds are likely, at least initially, to be based on relatively large-capitalization stocks, and the funds will be small at the start, disclosure is unlikely to lead to much trading ahead of the fund. Most portfolio changes in these funds will be made at a time determined by the fund's staff, not by an index publisher. These funds are relatively independent of an indexer's rules, unlike the existing equity index ETFs, which modify their portfolios to match any index change made by the index publisher within a narrow time window. They will be subject to inquiries concerning the correspondence of their portfolios to their model.[6] Some of these funds can operate with a mandate little different from the mandate granted existing index funds. Others will prefer the index and portfolio disclosure flexibility advocated in later sections of this chapter.

The description of an index enhancement model in Exhibit 7-1 is near the middle of the complexity range for this kind of investment process. It illustrates an attempt to improve on a standard large-cap portfolio without taking a high degree of tracking error risk.

Exhibit 7-1: OakBrook Enhanced Index
Strategy Investment Process

The OakBrook Enhanced Index Strategy uses a quantitative process focusing on changes in investor expectations to select stocks from among those with the 1000 largest market capitalizations to overweight and underweight. The sizes of the individual over- and underweights are determined subject to a system of risk controls designed to keep portfolio characteristics and performance close to that of an index of the 1,000 largest companies. The entire process, from stock selection to generation of portfolio trades, is governed by proprietary computer programs developed by OakBrook Investments, LLC.

Our investment process begins with the division of our 1,000-stock universe into the style subgroups at the core of our system of risk controls. First, all utilities are identified and placed in a group of stocks to be held at portfolio weights exactly equal to their weights in the index. Our selection process has no insight into the behavior of stocks in this group. The remaining firms are divided into two groups, differentiated and commodity, based on each firm's standard industry classification. Differentiated firms are found in industries where firms have had success in differentiating their products, such as branded consumer products, pharmaceuticals, and computer software. Commodity firms are found in industries where firms produce standard products that vary little from supplier to supplier, such as oil or banking. The behavior of these two groups differs substantially as you move through the different phases of the market cycle. Our computer program then divides the set of differentiated stocks into subgroups on the basis of capitalization and volatility of past returns. Similar subgroups are constructed for commodity firms.

After completing construction of the style subgroups, the program applies a quantitative measure of changes in the range of investor expectations to rank firms within each subgroup. The ranking variable combines a number of technical variables, such as price volatility and trading volume, using a proprietary weighting system. Every firm identified as having a narrow but growing range of expectations will be overweighted in the Oak-Brook Enhanced Index portfolio. Firms associated with a wide but shrinking range of expectations will be underweighted in the OakBrook Enhanced Index portfolio.

In the next step of our investment process, a second computer program uses the overweight and underweight signals generated above to construct a model Enhanced Index portfolio that complies with our stringent risk controls. Risk controls are applied at three levels: style, sector, and individual stock.

At the style level, the model Enhanced Index portfolio's weights for each of the capitalization and volatility subgroups within the differentiated and commodity groups can differ from their weight in the index of the 1,000 largest companies by no more than 1%.

At the sector level, each of the stocks in the index is assigned to one of 11 sectors based on standard economic sector codes. Within the model Enhanced Index portfolio, none of the 11 sectors can be over- or underweighted by more than 5% of the portfolio value.

Exhibit 7-1 (Continued)

At the individual stock level, the amount a stock can be over- or underweighted is based on its capitalization. Stocks with an index weight below 1.50% can have their weight reduced to zero or doubled in the model Enhanced Index portfolio. The weights of larger-capitalization stocks may diverge from their index weights by no more than 1.50% of the portfolio's value. If we were to set the weight of these larger stocks to zero or double them, the excess return of the Fund would be determined mainly by our model's decisions on a few large-capitalization stocks.

The OakBrook Enhanced Index Strategy is re-balanced four times per year. During each re-balancing period, a third computer program compares the existing portfolio to the model portfolio generated by the process described above and then generates a set of trades which will transition the portfolio with minimal trading costs. These trades are then transferred to a broker and executed as market-on-close orders.

ARE THERE IRREDUCIBLE MINIMUM FEATURES AN EQUITY ETF MUST HAVE?

In thinking about the development of new kinds of equity ETFs in the context of the advantages of ETFs outlined in Chapter 4, several features seem inextricably bound to the concept of an exchange-traded fund. The first of these is intra-day trading. Discussions of new types of ETFs invariably (and reasonably) assume that intra-day trading will be a feature of all new ETFs. Likewise, the elimination of shareholder accounting at the fund level which helps to reduce the fund's expense ratio is also likely to be retained in new ETF variations. While existing funds generally lack payments for distribution (there have been small 12b-1 fees used to support marketing in a few cases, but the size and frequency of these payments has not been material), a range of new product structures with distribution fees certainly seems possible. The variety of sales compensation choices possible with conventional funds cannot be replicated with ETFs except in (1) an external wrapper, (2) a fee for management of a portfolio of funds, or (3) a fund-of-funds structure.

Most future ETFs that do carry a built-in distribution fee are likely to feature an ongoing annual payment to the advisor who places (sells) and supports the use of a fund by a client. This process will be comparable, in some respects, to the mutual fund supermarkets which have been popular in recent years, although higher distribution charges may be associated with some ETFs than the 35 to 50 basis points per year that have been associated with fund supermarkets. There have been a number of discussions of front-end load (IPO) sales of ETFs, and we would not be surprised to see a few IPO efforts along this line. Front-end loading, beyond a few possible exotic IPO launches similar to the process Merrill Lynch has used with HOLDRs, does not appear to be a promising distribution method for ETFs.

One of the most important features of ETFs is the protection of ongoing shareholders from the transaction and tax costs of investors entering and leaving the fund. This is accomplished through the creation and redemption process that is likely to remain at least partly in-kind, leaving ETF traders to pay approximately their own costs of fund entry and exit. There will be pressure to include less liquid positions in ETF portfolios. Hopefully, ETF managers will await the long promised increase in liquidity in fixed-income markets and work with OTC derivatives dealers to improve liquidity in a number of markets before they launch a fund that is prohibitively expensive to create and redeem or fails to protect ongoing shareholders from fund share trading costs. We believe that the liquidity of some currently illiquid instruments can be enhanced (at an acceptable cost) by a cooperative effort of fund managers, exchanges, and derivatives dealers. ETF issuers should be sure they have, in fact, achieved a workable combination of liquidity and low costs before launching a product—lest they achieve experimental results similar to those obtained by Dr. Frankenstein.

Another pair of equity index ETF characteristics—portfolio transparency and tight trading spreads—will be under pressure in certain actively managed funds. However, we would expect the most popular actively managed funds to achieve a very high degree of portfolio transparency and correspondingly tight trading spreads, probably *approaching* the transparency and trading spreads of existing equity index ETFs. We will discuss this important topic at length when we examine the possible mechanisms for, and the constraints on, actively managed ETFs.

We expect the intra-day valuation proxy, which has been distributed every 15 seconds during the trading day for index funds, will continue to be a feature of new funds. The standard for timeliness of updates may be extended to a minute or five minutes in some cases, but the 15-second standard is likely to be maintained for a while—if for no other reason than that investors and the SEC are used to it. Ultimately, issuers should be allowed to experiment with different valuation frequencies and investors and dealers—the groups affected—should decide what valuation frequency is acceptable.

The high degree of tax efficiency which has characterized the better-run equity index ETFs is likely to be a feature of the better-managed active equity funds.

Several of these features deserve a fresh look in the context of the structure of new ETFs.

Protection of Ongoing Shareholders from Costs Associated with Fund Share Trading

As long as creation and redemption are at least largely in-kind for standardized securities baskets and variable transaction charges are levied to take into account any growth in the cash portion of creation and redemption baskets, traders ultimately will pay the entry and exit costs of trading ETF shares. Fairness in transaction cost apportionment reaches much higher levels in the ETF than has ever been achieved in any other investment company structure. This feature will be an important factor in leading investors to choose ETFs whether or not they plan to use the most obvious feature of the ETF—the ability to trade intra-day.

Along with transaction cost protection of ongoing shareholders through in-kind creation and redemption baskets, a second key feature, portfolio transparency, is likely to be retained in most future ETFs.

Portfolio Transparency versus the Trading Spread— The Active Manager's Trade-Off

To the extent that the creation basket or some other readily available hedging basket does not constitute a valid hedging portfolio *through the current day's market close*, we expect the investment advisor of the fund, a service organization supported by the fund advisor, or the listing exchange to publish a suggested hedging portfolio with a known tracking error relative to the existing fund portfolio. This basket would serve as a basis for hedging transactions by the specialist and other market makers. The larger the tracking error for this hedging basket, and the greater any disparity between the hedging basket and the creation basket, the wider the trading spread that specialists and market makers will quote. There will be a very clear linkage between transparency and market quality in active ETFs. We will return to this issue when we discuss several different approaches to active ETF development.

Index Transparency— An Unnecessary Feature of Today's ETFs

With equity index ETFs, the public-at-large has been fully aware of any changes that must be made in an index ETF portfolio *before* the index change was implemented. This is not to say, of course, that the manager of the index ETF will always make the change at the close of trading on the day that the index changes. Even the "manager" of the original SPDR has always had considerably greater flexibility than an exact timing match of index and fund changes.[7] Within some period, usually beginning about a week before the date of the index change, the world-at-large knows that a change will be made in an index fund and that the change in the fund will be made either before, at, or after the market close when the index change becomes official. Astute index managers have frequently (in some cases, consistently) traded early or late to avoid the crush at the market close on the day the index itself changes; so there is nothing new in making the change at a time selected by the manager. However, whether the management of a fund is based on a set of index rules or on the stock picking judgment of a fund manager, *there is no reason why anyone other than the fund manager needs to know when the index change or fund change will be made or even that a change will be made. As long as the index is used for no purpose other than as a template for the fund or for certain index or fund derivatives, no one other than the fund manager needs to know about the index change until after the fund has traded.*

Indexing was developed to manage a fund passively—without the costs associated with stock-picking or active trading. The early indexers determined that the easiest way to do this was to track an index—to replicate the index in a portfolio. The index for a fund need not be constructed in a fishbowl and published before the fund acts. Publication of index changes before fund portfolio changes puts the fund and its shareholders at a disadvantage. The pioneers of indexing used benchmark indexes because they were available. They could be licensed cheaply. At the time indexing began, index funds were such a small factor in the market that no one thought about the market impact cost of making an index fund portfolio change when the index changed.

As we have noted, the benchmark indexes which underlay the first index funds and which still underlie most index ETFs were originally designed as something other than index fund templates. They were market indicators, benchmarks and performance measurement tools in their primary employment—and they brought in a little revenue from indexing licenses on the side. For those multipurpose indexes, there is and there should be no alternative to announcing any index changes outside market hours and changing the index in the pre-announced way on a pre-announced date at market closing prices. If, in the light of the evidence of unnecessary transaction costs in funds based on these indexes presented in Chapter 6, an advisor wants to base an index fund on one of these indexes and investors want to buy that fund, those parties should be permitted to do business as they have in the past. On the other hand, if more astute advisors and wiser investors want to use special fund indexes that have no primary benchmark or indicator or performance measurement responsibilities, they should, respectively, create and purchase index funds that announce index changes only *after* the fund has traded, knowing that these funds will enjoy lower portfolio modification transaction costs than the older index funds.

The principle of confidentiality of fund trading plans until after the trade is complete stands behind a new breed of index fund—and behind the fund structure that will probably support the first actively managed ETFs.

NEW AND IMPROVED INDEX FUNDS[8]

The characteristics of portfolio changes and transaction costs that define existing index ETFs are that before the index change date arrives, there is widespread knowledge that the fund will trade to match the index change. The index provider publishes essentially what the fund will have to buy and what it will have to sell. In other words, *knowledge of the pending index change belongs to the world, not exclusively to the fund.* Given the ubiquity of this knowledge, the creation basket for an index fund on the day the index is scheduled to change (at the close) should reflect the index changes which will occur at the close, and both creations and redemptions should be done in the "new" index portfolio rather than in that day's fund basket. This process gives creators and redeemers full knowledge of what they will face in terms of creation and redemption baskets on that day.[9]

When an actively managed fund trades to change the composition of its portfolio, the creation and redemption baskets on the day of that trade will not similarly reflect the contents of the portfolio after the change made that day. We expect the creation and redemption baskets and the intra-day proxy value of any actively managed fund to be based on the actual fund portfolio—that is, the portfolio *at the beginning of the day.* The difference in timing of disclosure of changes in the fund's portfolio should not matter to any of the legitimate actors on the ETF stage as long as market makers can protect themselves from losses stemming from changes in the fund portfolio. We believe the market makers can be fully protected. The only participants in today's markets who will be deprived of information they use today in a significant way will be traders who buy and sell near the date of an index change to benefit a non-index-fund account. This change in information dissemination seems totally appropriate. To appreciate the implications of the change, we need to step back and look at how actively managed funds and index funds operate today from a slightly different perspective than we have used before.

Today, active fund managers go to great lengths to keep their intentions and transactions confidential until long after a trade is executed. With the exception of some pressure to report the positions they have already taken quarterly rather than semiannually, no one argues that an active manager of a conventional mutual fund should have to disclose more about her trading activity. There is certainly no case for forcing an actively managed fund to announce its plans in advance. No one suggests the manager announce that she will buy one stock to replace another stock she is selling until after the trade has been completed. In contrast, the current rules of index investing require that the manager of a fund tracking an index not find out about a change in the index before the change is announced to the world. The more popular and widely used the index, the more other fund managers and scalpers will be trying to trade on the index change information at about the same time the index fund needs to trade The index fund is usually paying a license fee to the index publisher for index trademarks and information, but a trader with no link to the index can get the index change information at the same time as the fund manager, and the trader may act on it sooner. Such procedures may make sense if an index is used for many purposes; but there is no reason an ETF or any index fund must be based on a widely used index—if using that index for the fund hurts the fund's investors by increasing the fund's trading costs.

The higher transaction costs for funds based on the benchmark indexes in Exhibit 6-5 are largely due to the fact that other indexers and investors with no financial connection to the fund and often with no licensing connection to the index, all made similar portfolio changes at about the same time as the fund traded. Financial industry procedures and regulations on index change disclosure have unnecessarily and inappropriately required identical treatment and pre-announcement of index information—whether the index is a major benchmark or a custom index developed for a single fund. We are not contending that disclosure is inappropriate for major benchmark indexes. It is inappropriate, unnecessary, and undesirable for fund-specific indexes. If indexing had not started with benchmark indexes, publication of changes in the index used by a fund before the fund trades would never have been an issue—and trading costs in most index funds would be far lower than they are today.

Even if changes in major benchmark indexes have to cause trading frenzies, there is no reason less prominent, specialized fund indexes have to announce and implement their changes in the same manner. The shareholders of a fund based on a custom index do not need to know the precise index rules for handling a corporate action any more than shareholders in an actively-managed fund need to know (or get to know) exactly how their manager will react to an earnings report or a management change. If an index is designed to be fund-friendly—in this case, to reduce the fund's transaction costs—it could be very advantageous to the fund without any adverse effect on other parties with legitimate interests, to announce index changes only *after the change has been implemented by the fund*. We will see the implications of this change in index and index fund rules more clearly when we look at the Self-Indexing Fund.

THE SELF-INDEXING FUND[10]— DAILY PORTFOLIO DISCLOSURE

The Self-Indexing Fund manager creates a Self-Indexing Fund Index by purchasing an initial portfolio or by accepting an initial deposit meeting her specifications. The basis for the initial deposit and for subsequent changes in the fund may be a formally calculated but unpublished index or it can be a portfolio basket developed using *any* of the traditional techniques of portfolio managers or new techniques devised by the manager or by others. Even if the fund is based on an index designed by an entity other than the fund's advisor, the principal index of interest to investors in the fund and its derivatives will be the Self-Indexing Fund Index, which will track any index used in the fund's management very closely. *The template index will be of interest only to measure how closely the fund's manager tracks it.* The implementation in the Fund is what matters going forward. For this reason, and because the Self-Indexing Fund is also a suitable vehicle for an actively managed fund, subsequent references to an index are to the Self-Indexing Fund Index unless otherwise specified.

The Self-Indexing Fund portfolio is offered to investors in the form of ETF shares, and the initial and subsequent net asset values of the ETF shares are published as a Self-Indexing Fund Index, which can be used for most of the purposes any other security index is used for. The value of the Self-Indexing Fund Index is determined by changes in the NAV of the fund shares. The fund manager changes the composition of the fund index by selling some of the components of the portfolio and/or buying new components for the portfolio. The fund manager discloses the Self-Indexing Fund portfolio daily and posts a creation basket and a redemption basket for public dissemination *shortly after the market closes each business day.* The fund creates additional fund shares by issuing them in exchange for deposits of portfolio components in multiples of the daily creation basket and redeems fund shares by accepting multiples of a preset number of fund shares in exchange for portfolio components in the form of like multiples of the daily redemption basket. The creation and redemption process is quite similar to the like process for existing equity index ETFs. The principal difference is that the Authorized Participant (the market maker or investor who creates or redeems fund shares) must notify the fund's distributor of plans to create or redeem fund shares earlier in the trading day than is required for most equity index ETFs. The earlier notice permits the manager of the Self-Indexing Fund to defer selling stock she will need to deliver as part of the posted redemption basket and to sell incoming shares from creation baskets in order to rebalance the fund portfolio.

The fund management process makes changes in the raw index value, that is, in the per-share NAV. To state it another way, the daily net asset value of the fund is the closing index value. Intraday index calculations are identical to cap-weighted index calculations, and the weights are the portfolio weights used in the 4:00 p.m. NAV calculations. If the fund holds a cash balance or is leveraged, the index will include a cash component (which presumably earns interest) or will be leveraged. In short, *the index fully reflects the fund's investment characteristics.*

In contrast to the existing exchange-traded equity index funds that attempt to create a portfolio to track the performance of an underlying index to the greatest degree feasible, the Self-Indexing Fund can use active stock selection to create a portfolio that serves as the fund portfolio on an ongoing basis, but also is the heart of the index which the fund's positions and its daily net asset value calculations create. This fund-created index has the essential characteristics of the indexes used as templates or patterns to construct exchange-traded index funds. If the portfolio manager is attuned to the principles discussed in Chapter 6, the index will be inherently fund-friendly. In fact, the Self-Indexing Fund operates as index funds should always have operated.

The fund index can be used as a basis of comparison with other funds and their managers and with other indexes. It can serve as the basis of a family of derivatives which can be based either directly on the fund (physically settled) or on the index created by the fund (cash settled).[11] Through the creation of its index and disclosure of changes in the Self-Indexing Fund and/or Index, the Self-Indexing Fund will report its portfolio and/or index changes within a few hours after the market closes on each business day when a portfolio change occurs.

The Self-Indexing Fund is probably the simplest solution to the problem of creating an Actively Managed Exchange-Traded Fund that meets all the requirements and objections that regulators and industry observers have raised for Actively Managed Exchange-Traded Funds. Specifically, the Self-Indexing Fund offers the same kind of intra-day net asset value (NAV) proxy calculation that open-end exchange-traded index funds provide, and the Self-Indexing Fund's creation basket can serve as a hedging portfolio for the Self-Indexing Fund shares during the trading day. In these respects, the Self-Indexing Fund is designed to look and work as much like the current exchange-traded index funds as possible, while providing a vehicle for more efficient indexing and for active portfolio management.

The Self-Indexing Fund offers continuous opportunities for creation of additional shares and redemption of existing shares in Creation Unit Aggregations. The Creation Unit Aggregations will approximate the composition of the fund portfolio as of the opening of the market on the current day at least as closely as an index-replicating ETF's creation basket approximates the index used as the fund's template. The creation unit portfolio will consist of the stocks held by the Self-Indexing Fund in very close proportion to the holdings of the Self-Indexing Fund in each stock. For example, if the Self-Indexing Fund holds a 3.1% position in IBM, the Creation Unit will have about a 3.1% position in IBM. These stock baskets will be faithful copies of the fund portfolio.[12]

In the active Self-Indexing Fund, a fund manager rather than an index publisher creates the index by establishing a portfolio.

Whereas an index publisher might list and weight some stocks, price them at today's market close, and list a few index maintenance rules, the manager of the Self-Indexing Fund and the creator of the Self-Indexing Fund Index is first and foremost the manager of the fund. She thinks and acts in terms of the fund portfolio, and the index almost takes care of itself. The fund's updated portfolio is disclosed in full detail shortly after the market closes each business day. The fund's investment objective and the manager's style define the "index" rules. The fund will be created and redeemed in kind like existing open-end index ETFs, so it will not have to hold material cash reserves to cover redemptions.

We expect most managers of these Self-Indexing Funds to make occasional significant transactions (with no specific or standard frequency other than a frequency that reflects the manager's style) that will materially change the portfolio and, in consequence, change the index. There is nothing inherent in the portfolio management/index creation process that prevents the manager from making a sequence of gradual changes in the portfolio to move from one security to another over a period of days or weeks. Of course, the fact that portfolio changes will be known daily over that period encourages concentration of transactions on both the buy side and sell side on a relatively small number of days, with the transition from one position to another typically taking place on a single day, unless or until the Self-Indexing Fund becomes very large.

We would expect asset growth following a high degree of investment success (consistent top quartile performance) to place a limit on further growth of some actively managed Self-Indexing Funds by reducing their attractiveness to certain investors. To protect investors, the Self-Indexing Fund's directors may restrict future creations, possibly permitting the shares to go to a premium over NAV in the secondary market. Apart from continued secondary market trading in the ETF, this would be essentially what occurs when a conventional open-end fund restricts new purchases. There might be limited creations to replace shares redeemed and to help the specialist make an orderly market, but there would be no limitations on redemption other than the need to accumulate enough fund shares to make up a standardized fund share Creation Unit aggregation for redemption.

To understand the management and position disclosure process of the Self-Indexing Fund and the hedging information and choices available to market makers, it is necessary to understand the daily accounting process of a fund and calculation of the fund's daily NAV. The net asset value of most U.S. funds is calculated using closing market prices, which become available shortly after 4:00 p.m. Eastern time in U.S. markets. Because a portfolio manager may be trading up to and past the 4:00 p.m. nominal close of most equity markets, the manager (and more importantly the fund accountants) may not know until well after 4:00 p.m. exactly what positions have been purchased and what positions have been sold over the course of the trading day. The need to provide a net asset value calculation promptly for dissemination to the fund's investors through newspapers and various electronic media has necessitated adoption of a procedure whereby the fund portfolio, adjusted for the previous day's transactions and today's dividends, interest payments, certain accruals, and, when appropriate, corporate actions, is the basis for today's NAV calculations. *Transactions which have taken place on a given day,* e.g., the purchase of one stock and/or sale of another, *are not reflected in that day's closing NAV calculation.*

A fund manager who purchased Company A's stock ("stock A") today at an average price below the closing price of stock A and sold Company B's stock ("stock B") at an average price above the closing price of stock B will have added value to the fund and the NAV would be higher if these position changes were incorporated in the NAV calculation at 4:00 p.m. prices. Given the impracticality of including this information by 4:00 p.m. on the trade date, however, it is incorporated into the portfolio that will be used *for the following day's NAV calculation.*

Differences in the prices at which purchases and sales are made relative to the closing prices used in the NAV calculation are not a cause for concern. It would be very unusual for the NAV calculation for a reasonably diversified fund to be materially affected by the one-day delay in adjusting for these transactions. The effect of such transactions can be either positive or negative for the next day's NAV depending upon the prices at which the securities were purchased and sold and the closing prices for the respective securities used in the trade date NAV calculation. Nonetheless, the fact of this phenomenon and other considerations discussed below may lead the first Self-Index-ing Funds to attempt to execute most purchase and sale transactions using market-on-close orders. Market-on-close orders in both the secu-rity purchased and the security sold will lead to transactions in which the NAV will be unaffected by any disparity between the price at which a security position was eliminated or taken and the price used in the calculation of a NAV because the prices will be the same. As time goes by and portfolio managers and investors become increasingly comfort-able with the Self-Indexing Fund structure, most managers will be comfortable executing some transactions earlier in the trading day.

Exchange-traded funds have a well-established tradition of protecting ongoing shareholders from the effect of shareholders entering and leaving these funds. To maintain this important tradi-tion, all or nearly all purchases and sales of Self-Indexing Fund shares that involve a transaction with the fund may be in-kind cre-ation deposits and full or partially in-kind redemptions.

In contrast to some types of funds where extensive use of spe-cialized creation and redemption baskets may occur, most creations and redemptions of Self-Indexing Fund shares may be for standard, identical creation and redemption baskets. There is certainly room for exceptions, but they are not likely to be particularly important and will consist primarily of situations where a specific creating or redeeming dealer is not able to purchase or sell a specific security or where the portfolio manager elects to sell some portfolio shares the Self-Index-ing Fund is carrying at a loss for tax purposes rather than include them in the redemption basket. A dealer will be able to create or redeem as many Self-Indexing Fund shares as it wishes in exchange for each day's posted creation and redemption baskets. Subject only to the pos-sible (pre-announced) removal of some positions from the redemption basket, both of these baskets usually will reflect the exact contents of the portfolio at the start of the day. Some minor differences due to rounding may be present, but they will not have a material effect on the ability of the authorized participant to use the securities in the cre-ation basket as a hedging portfolio.[13] The Self-Indexing Fund man-ager may make changes in the portfolio through the sale of existing positions in market-on-close or earlier transactions and/or through custom baskets in a manner that, except for the tax effect, is functionally and economically equivalent to a market-on-close sale transaction. All creations and redemptions will be priced consistently with the fund's NAV calculated at 4:00 p.m. Eastern time. Subject to the possibility of limiting creations if the fund gets too large, the Authorized Participants will be able to create or redeem as many fund shares as they wish in the form of each day's posted creation and redemption baskets. There will be no restrictions on redemptions. Apart from rounding and the removal of some positions (for tax purposes) before the redemption basket is posted, these baskets will reflect nearly the exact contents of the portfolio at the start of the day.

The Self-Indexing Fund will routinely require dealers to provide notification of creation or redemption intentions by 3:00 p.m. Eastern time or a fixed period in advance of any deadline for entering market-on-close orders. Once the manager knows the net number of shares of a stock she will have to sell by the market close and can judge the approximate proceeds of such a sale, she can enter appropriate orders to eliminate a position and complete any other transactions needed to change the portfolio—and the index. To complete a change in a position, the manager must be prepared to sell shares in the stock to be eliminated from an incoming creation basket on the day that it is tendered and refrain from selling shares of that stock needed to fill pending redemption baskets. This relatively simple fine-tuning will essentially require that at least part of the trading be done at or very near the close of trading and after creation and redemption intentions are known. To the extent that a manager wishes the Self-Indexing Fund to stay fully invested, we expect that brokers will accept orders to sell a fixed number of shares of one stock and invest the proceeds in another stock or stocks to the nearest whole share per Creation Unit Aggregation at the closing price of all the stocks in the order. Brokers also routinely execute large market-on-close orders net (without commission) so the NAV will be unaffected by the carryover effect of trades executed at the close.

This brief description is not intended to provide an exhaustive discussion or description of the portfolio management process. Managers will have different ways of using the traditional in-kind creation/redemption process that has become a defining characteristic of most open-end exchange-traded funds. Similarly, managers will develop different mechanical ways of incorporating the effect of a day's creations and/or redemptions into their stock purchase and sale plans

As with any other fund, the portfolio will be managed for the benefit of the shareholders, not for the benefit of anyone who has purchased fund derivatives or who is using the fund (index) as a portfolio benchmark. Because any changes in the composition of the fund determine the course of the index, changes in the composition of the fund/index will be announced after the market close on any day when changes are made. An investor wishing to track the fund precisely may have to do so through ownership of fund shares. Although someone can easily compare the performance of another portfolio to the index, the only way to track it precisely will be by holding the fund shares, some of their derivatives, or cash settled derivatives based on the Self-Indexing Fund Index.

Interestingly, fund prospectuses usually note, in discussing the difference between the performance of a traditional index and an index fund, that the index bears no transaction costs and has no expenses, so the fund should not be expected to match it exactly. In the case of the Self-Indexing Fund Index, the index *does* reflect the transaction costs and operating expenses of the fund. Anyone wishing to replicate the fund's (index's) performance need only buy shares of the fund. If the shares are purchased in a creation transaction and redeemed in a redemption, the investor's performance should match the index precisely except for entering and leaving transaction costs.

Another note common in index fund documentation states that the provider of the index is under no obligation to consider the interests of the fund or the fund's shareholders in any decision it makes in the management of the index. The manager of the Self-Indexing Fund's foremost obligation is to fund shareholders. The Index, appropriately, comes *after* the Self-Indexing Fund in importance.

The Self-Indexing Fund Index might be a more meaningful benchmark in one respect than traditional benchmark indexes for the simple reason that no adjustments are needed to compare the index with another fund which is attempting to compete with the

Self-Indexing Fund. Adjustments for transaction costs and other expenses are not necessary. The manager of the Self-Indexing Fund may make a trade which an outside manager benchmarking against the Self-Indexing Fund Index could not precisely replicate because he would not know about it until after it had occurred, but the outside manager is presumably hired to compete with the Self-Indexing Fund, not to replicate it. If the client wanted to match the Self-Indexing Fund, he could have bought the fund rather than hire a competing manager.

The Self-Indexing Fund Index has a uniquely interesting family of derivatives. The principal option contract will be options on the fund shares—like the highly successful options on the NASDAQ 100 index shares, which are virtually certain to be the most active option contract traded anywhere for the year 2001. Cash-settled index options are not likely to be popular, particularly if share prices of individual funds are relatively high, minimizing the fund options' transaction costs. Futures contracts should be physically settled, if the apparent congressionally mandated rapprochement between the SEC and CFTC on the subject of single-stock futures leads to timely introduction of such a product. The most logical candidates for the first single-stock futures contracts are futures on exchange-traded fund shares. Self-Indexing Fund shares might even be the very first choice for such physical settlement, because they would track both index futures and physically settled futures very precisely.

These funds are not likely to be replacements for actively managed, broad-based, widely diversified funds. Apart from natural index fund applications, they are more likely to be specialty funds, perhaps managed by a skilled stock picker or a featured analyst who will select favored stocks for the portfolios, or a market strategist who might select sector funds and specialty funds in a fund-of-funds approach. Other applications might include theme funds providing a portfolio manager's perspective on specific investment concepts or recommended stocks of a firm's equity research department. As noted, the fund could be based on an index that did not publish its changes until after the fund had implemented them. A comparison of conventional index fund and index and active Self-Indexing Fund characteristics is summarized in Exhibit 7-2.

Exhibit 7-2: Comparison of Index ETFs and Self-Indexing Active ETF

Feature	Conventional Index ETF	Improved Index ETF	Self-Indexing Active ETF
Index	Typically standard benchmark	Fund-Friendly Index—Designed for fund use	Self-Indexing Fund Index
Source of index	Index publisher	Index publisher or fund staff	Self-Indexing Fund NAV
Public knowledge of portfolio change	Announcement of Index change	Announcement of portfolio/index change	Announcement of portfolio/index change
Time of public knowledge relative to trade	1 week before trade	2–3 hours after trade	2–3 hours after trade
Index economics for fund	Fund pays license fee directly or indirectly	Fund may pay or receive fees, depending on source of index	Fund receives license fees for derivative products
Portfolio calculation algorithm	Index change template	Index change template	Pattern chosen by manager/trader
Can others trade on information that fund is trading?	Yes	Rarely, if ever	Rarely, if ever
Can fund use other than market-on-close orders without concern for tracking error?	No	No, with respect to template index; Yes, with respect to fund index	Yes
Does manager control portfolio turnover?	No	No	Yes
Does manager control portfolio composition?	No	No	Yes

FULL ACTIVE MANAGEMENT—
DELAYED PORTFOLIO DISCLOSURE

The Self-Indexing Fund is a relatively simple, though significant, extension of the traditional index ETF. Its significance is that it recognizes the fund's "ownership" of rights to make changes in the fund/index before the change is made public. The self-indexing structure, nonetheless, protects specialists and market makers from the risk of mistracking the fund/index to the extent that they plan their hedging activities to be flat in terms of exposure to the fund/index each day at the 4:00 p.m. market close. It is quite possible that some specialists and market makers, recognizing the tendency of the market to snap back from the impact of transactions, will ignore the opportunity to hedge through the market close and simply accept that risk in market making on the expectation that on average they will be as well off with this overnight exposure as without it. With full active management, in contrast, we expect that there will be more limited disclosure of the portfolio composition from day to day. The amount and timing of portfolio disclosure may be determined by the SEC or it may be left to the issuer of an active ETF. We expect considerable debate on this issue, but this disclosure process does not seem to require tight regulation. As will be clear from subsequent paragraphs, market forces can dictate optimum regulation of portfolio disclosure.[14]

Clearly, in periodic fund shareholder reports, most of the positions passing through the portfolio will be revealed, albeit on a delayed basis. In a truly actively managed fund with turnover of as much as several hundred percent a year, the usefulness of even quarterly disclosure of the portfolio composition will be limited. The intra-day share value proxy calculation will continue to be disseminated, perhaps at the 15-second intervals used today, or perhaps at a frequency chosen by the fund issuer. Very frequent publication of valuations will provide interested parties with a great deal of contemporary portfolio content information because a series of valuations at close intervals will provide good indications of the change in prices of large positions. Frequent valuations can provide good indications of portfolio changes and even of the relative size of positions. Comparing the prior reported portfolio with contemporary changes in the value of the portfolio could tell a sophisticated quantitative analyst a great deal about the current portfolio and changes the portfolio manager has made since the last full portfolio publication.

To the extent that the actively managed fund has concentration in particular securities, industries, sectors, etc., the concentrations and changes in them will be relatively clear—unless the information is swept away in a very high turnover rate or disguised by very infrequent portfolio pricing. The fund might publish a suggested hedging basket of highly liquid positions with a disclosed historic tracking error to be used as the basis for hedging transactions by specialists and other market makers. This basket also will provide information on the character of the portfolio. The hedging basket will have to be changed each time there is a material change in the content of the portfolio, and the tracking error will be recalculated, providing useful information about portfolio content and portfolio changes. The precision of this information, however, will not even approximate the precision of information available for today's index ETFs or for the Self-Indexing Funds. Nonetheless, it is substantially more information than today's actively managed conventional mutual funds publish. The suggested minimum level of information will be enough to entice some dealers to make markets in these funds. The manager will have to decide on a trade-off between any fund performance cost of portfolio disclosure and the effect of reduced fund share liquidity and higher fund share bid-asked spreads on his present and prospective fund shareholders. The manager cannot treat the fund market makers any better than he treats anyone else with respect to portfolio disclosure and he has an incentive not to abuse the market makers, lest they stop making markets.

It will take time to get from the current equity index ETFs to this kind of full active management. The resulting funds will have more transparency than we have today with actively managed funds and less than we have with index ETFs. Given the nature of U.S. securities laws' dependence primarily on full disclosure and with necessary, but probably appropriate, deference to the prescriptive and proscriptive aspects of the Investment Company Act of 1940 as described in Chapter 3, the Securities and Exchange Commission should eventually become comfortable with some combination of (1) an increased interval between intra-day fund share value proxy calculations, (2) reduced disclosure of ETF portfolio composition relative to existing index ETFs, and (3) an undertaking by the active fund manager or a service provider to publish a hedging basket with a known and disclosed historic tracking error.

Barring a performance record good enough for regular and enthusiastic discussion by the press and at cocktail parties all over the world, an active manager using this limited disclosure technique is unlikely to raise as much money as a manager using the Self-Indexing Fund variation of active management because of the inevitably wider fund share trading spreads and the difficulty many shareholders will have getting comfortable with this unfamiliar and less transparent ETF structure. Regulators should come to realize that they do not need to control transparency. If regulations and enforcement can attack the occasional fraud and the somewhat more common misrepresentations that affect market fairness in various investment products, market makers and investors will determine the acceptable level of transparency as market makers set their spreads and investors decide they are comfortable enough with the portfolio information and the market maker's spread. In this case, as in most others, the market itself is the most effective and impartial regulator.[15]

FUNDS-OF-FUNDS—ETFS-OF-ETFS

Perhaps the ultimate implementation of the active ETF idea which we can visualize today is an ETF fund of ETFs. The top-level fund will be a carrier or umbrella fund which will have the unique characteristics of an active ETF and be able to hold ETFs which, in turn, bring some unique and extremely attractive characteristics to an ETF fund-of-funds.

The top-level or umbrella fund will be an actively managed fund in the same sense as the Self-Indexing Funds with changes in the shares held in its subsidiary funds (the umbrella fund's portfolio) revealed each day after the close. The umbrella fund might not be particularly large, but it would have a diversified portfolio of securities underlying its portfolio of funds and it might hold individual underlying securities to complement its fund holdings.

The umbrella fund would be charged with a specific investment objective. In some cases, it would implement an asset allocation strategy designed to appeal to a particular type of investor. It might be the instrument of a manager of managers. In one implementation, it might consist of life strategy funds—different in many respects from funds that go under that general name today.[16] The example of the life strategy funds of funds offers a useful explanation of how such funds might operate and what they might accomplish.

Life Strategy Funds

Vanguard has inaugurated four series funds which it calls Life Strategy Funds. These funds range in aggressiveness from "growth" through "income," with the distinction hinging on the amount of relative exposure to equities and intermediate-term bonds. These are conventional fund-of-funds products, and Vanguard implies a high degree of tax efficiency, even though neither the umbrella fund nor the component funds are open-end exchange-traded funds. Vanguard can probably employ in-kind redemptions within its fund family to qualify for some of the tax advantages which in-kind redemption ETFs will achieve, but it will be difficult to achieve full deferral of capital gains at the umbrella fund level with a conventional fund structure.

The Vanguard funds have two basic shortcomings.

First, the only change in asset allocation that will occur in a specific Vanguard Life Strategy Fund is related to the presence of an Asset Allocation Fund in the mix of funds used to create each of the series. This component fund has an increased equity exposure when a quantitative model suggests increased equity exposure and decreased equity exposure when the model urges caution. This is fine as long as it works well, but it is tactical asset allocation, not a life strategy.

Second, the notion that market risk exposure should change systematically over the lifetime of an investor is not implemented within these funds. Aside from any modest, almost random, market risk adjustment associated with the Asset Allocation Fund's changing allocations between equity and debt, there is no automatic, tax-efficient mechanism to decrease equity exposure and increase fixed-income exposure *as an investor ages*. An investor looking for this kind of risk modification pattern would have to sell off some of the original Life Strategy Fund series he had purchased and invest some of the proceeds in a separate fixed-income fund. There is nothing in the fund he initially bought that will accomplish this asset allocation shift to a less aggressive portfolio. [17]

To the extent that the initial Vanguard funds purchased are predominantly a package of aggressive equity funds that perform well, selling these fund shares and reinvesting in a fixed-income fund may lead to a very substantial tax liability. Furthermore, the dividends on an aggressive equity life strategy fund are not likely to be sufficient to enable an investor to use after tax income to buy a large position in higher-yield fixed-income securities as he approaches retirement. Assuming that an investor has accumulated most of the assets he wishes to invest early in life and invests them in this fund, the opportunity to make the necessary adjustment simply may not exist without paying a substantial capital gains tax.

With an asset allocation overlay exchange-traded fund as the upper level or umbrella vehicle of this kind of fund-of-funds, it should be possible to create life strategy funds that allocate assets among various sector or style funds as well as broad-based equity funds, and that switch in and out of the sector or style funds and gradually or abruptly invest more of the investor's assets in fixed-income securities at a designated future date. To illustrate how this might work, imagine a 20-year-old coming into a substantial amount of money and wanting to invest aggressively between his 20th and 65th birthdays. In approximately 45 years, the assets would be shifted from an aggressive growth orientation to a tax-free yield orientation. This investor would simply make a single investment in *one* life strategy fund and, in this case, about 45 years after his purchase, the composition of that fund's portfolio would change, *hopefully on a tax-free basis*, from aggressive growth to tax-free yield. A series of these funds—with the conversion from aggressive equity to fixed income occurring at, say, 5-year intervals over the next 50 years—would give an individual the ability to take a position with the degree of aggressiveness that suits today's situation and simultaneously select appropriate levels of investment aggressiveness as his retirement years approach. These life strategy funds would provide a unique opportunity for sector and style management as well as asset allocation within a limited range and an automatic, hopefully tax-free, adjustment to a different investment policy at a pre-chosen time.

Actually, it will be possible in a life strategy fund to provide a great many choices and a great deal of flexibility by having a variety of component funds and a variety of umbrella or wrapper funds which will implement the strategy shift by switching among component funds. Some of the wrapper funds could switch automatically to make the portfolio more conservative in the investor's later years or the switch could be contingent upon a variety of events such as the rate of growth in economic activity, the performance of the securities markets or, most importantly, the rate of inflation. The number of possible umbrella funds could be quite large and the investment strategies followed could be extremely varied. To the extent that an umbrella fund had relatively few shareholders, it might not be actively traded on the open market, but the mere fact that people's needs do change assures that there would be enough turnover to provide opportunities for trading out of positions and to make in-kind redemptions of low-basis positions, both in the component funds and in the umbrella strategy fund itself.

There need be no reason for concern about lack of liquidity in the umbrella funds because there would be intra-day pricing on the component funds and on each umbrella fund, so that the specialists/market makers responsible for maintaining a market could undertake to provide an extremely high degree of liquidity and narrow trading spreads without incurring significant unhedged risk for their own accounts. It has been difficult so far to persuade a large number of investors that inactively traded, exchange-traded funds have essentially as much liquidity as actively traded funds investing in the same underlying market. However, a commitment to this kind of liquidity in the life strategy fund may go a long way in that direction. A market-making commitment to a tight spread may be a necessity in marketing these funds.

An ideal implementation of the life strategy or life cycle fund-of-funds might provide a heavy but diversified exposure to domestic equities in the earlier years. At a predetermined time, which would be set at the time of launch for each umbrella life strategy fund, the fund would begin a gradual transition, lasting about three years, from an approximately 90% diversified equity exposure and 10% investment in taxable fixed-income securities to a 10%–20% diversified equity exposure with 50%–90% investment in tax-free municipals.[18] With a contingency overlay that would modify the conversion instructions in the event of a high rate of inflation or some other circumstances, the fund would not move entirely out of any category of equities or aggressive investments because even the highest-risk investment is not particularly risky when it is a small part of a portfolio of imperfectly correlated positions. The ability to continue to hold such positions would make the tax efficiency of the umbrella portfolio even easier to manage. Nonetheless, for most investors, there will come a time in their lives when a transition to a less risky strategy is appropriate. One way to deal with the uncertainty of when that time comes is to make the transition partly a function of domestic equity market behavior. In other words, if the stock market does as well as it did in the 1990's just before the transition is scheduled to begin, it might be appropriate to initiate the transition earlier. If the market performed poorly and stock valuations were modest relative to an average year, as in 1973 and 1974, then it would be appropriate to delay the transition to a lower-risk portfolio for a few years. The idea in both cases is that the probable utility of the investment would be increased by a change in the transition schedule.

Exhibit 7-3: Composition of a Life Cycle Fund— Inception to Maturity (%)

Investments—All Domestic

Years from Start of Fund	0	10	20	30	40	45
Large Cap—Indexed	45	45	45	45	45	8
Large Cap—Sector Allocation	15	15	15	15	15	
Small Cap	10	10	10	10	10	2
Debt/Equity Asset Allocation	20	20	20	20	20	
Taxable Fixed Income	10	10	10	10	10	
Tax Exempt Fixed Income	0	0	0	0	0	90
Total	100%	100%	100%	100%	100%	100%

Any international diversification should be obtained with a 10–25% position in one or more *separate*, predominantly non-U.S. funds. See the discussion of Global Equity Index Funds in Chapter 6.

The change in risk structure would be executed by a portfolio management structure that managed tax issues and portfolio changes simultaneously. Some of the more aggressive equity commitments such as small-cap stocks would be sharply reduced, though not eliminated entirely. Subject to the issues raised in the previous paragraph, the tax-free transition to a largely fixed-income portfolio could proceed as rapidly as the fund's ability to make the transition without incurring capital gains taxes would permit.

The shareholder's tax basis in the life strategy fund shares could be unaffected by the portfolio transition under current tax law. From a tax perspective, he should treat the fund shares as low-cost-basis shares which would be liquidated only as needed to maintain a satisfactory lifestyle as a supplement to the largely tax-free dividend the fund would be paying at that time. The fund shares would be available for such things as charitable donations, where the ability to take almost the full deduction for the contribution without paying tax on the gain has appreciable value. To the extent that fund shares do not have to be sold, the gain is deferred and the shareholder's heirs will receive a step-up of basis in the shares. The heirs might be able to sell the shares free of capital gains tax.[19]

Throughout the shareholder's life, any taxes paid should be essentially a function of the net yield. After fees, this will be nominal before retirement because there will be only small distributions until after the switch to tax-exempt bonds. Then, of course, the distributions will be tax advantaged. There is no reason to expect any material shareholder capital gains tax on appreciation in any of the equity funds—with the usual caveat about retaining the current tax treatment.

The flexibility granted the fund's directors and managers will have to be substantial, given the lifelong strategy embodied in the fund's objectives and the probability of substantial investment company law and tax law changes over a holding period that could be as long as, say, 80 years.

USING HEDGE FUND TECHNIQUES IN AN EXCHANGE-TRADED FUND[20]

As soon as a fund manager understands that actively managed equity exchange-traded funds should present no insurmountable challenges to the ETF structure used in the United States, a new question comes up: "Can we put an exchange-traded fund wrapper or structure around a traditional hedge fund?" While this is a reasonable next question, it is also a loaded question. Given the diversification requirements, leverage limitations, and incentive fee rules for investment companies in the United States, only a limited number of hedge fund techniques have been used in conventional investment companies (mutual funds). Nonetheless, purveyors of alternative investments have long been interested in using the mutual fund structure to package their products. Funds open up an entirely new market which might be reached through intermediaries that could and would assume the responsibility for meeting customer suitability and disclosure requirements.

There are at least two additional reasons to examine the hedge fund/ETF issue now. The first reason is the possibility of achieving a high degree of tax efficiency (capital gains tax deferral) in an exchange-traded fund. The second is the proposed launch, in December 2001, of single-stock futures (SSF) contracts in the United States.

The exact features and final rules for U.S. single stock futures contract markets are still unclear, but if physically settled SSFs with ETF shares as the underlying deliverable become available, the opportunities for a variety of hedge fund–type applications within ETFs will be very interesting. We believe physical settlement of SSFs into the underlying shares is critically important to the success of SSFs in U.S. equity markets. In this spirit, we examine the essential elements of an ETF and then turn to ways in which the new single-stock futures contracts and other instruments and strategies popular with hedge funds might be implemented inside an exchange-traded fund.

The Essential Characteristics of an Exchange-Traded Fund That Are Important to Hedge Fund Applications

Without a great deal of amplification or repetition of material covered elsewhere, there are several distinctive characteristics of the exchange-traded fund which have important implications for hedge fund applications.

The creation and redemption of ETF shares in large blocks and largely in-kind has a number of implications for the market in

ETFs. First, it does a remarkably fair job of allocating the costs of transactions among long-term shareholders and short-term traders in the fund's shares. A second feature of the creation and redemption process provides an opportunity to achieve a very high degree of tax efficiency (capital gains deferral) in the fund. Tax efficiency may not be inherently high in some hedge fund ETFs because any net short-term gains (a common component of some hedge fund returns) would be converted into ordinary income when distributed to the investor. On the other hand, most capital gains in an ETF might come to the shareholder in the form of gains to be deferred as long as the shareholder stayed in the fund. This result would not be possible in every hedge fund application, but it certainly merits study by anyone considering the ETF format.

A required characteristic of today's exchange-traded index fund is consistent and relatively prompt disclosure of portfolio content. This disclosure goes far beyond what hedge fund operators are used to telling their clients on a regular basis. Although a hedge fund operator may reveal transactions to performance evaluators, the information is only given with assurance that the information is to be used for no purpose other than for performance reporting and evaluation. In any hedge fund ETF, a high degree of disclosure—probably shortly after the end of trading on the day a portfolio change is implemented—will almost surely be required.

Unless an ETF is part of a hedge fund family, there should be little objection to revealing positions that provide details on the strategies implemented shortly after the trade is made. The major objection might turn on the potential embarrassment of the hedge fund operator when it became evident that there was little interest in the transactions he had made each day.

In contrast to most current ETFs, the hedge fund version will probably have a high management fee with no performance or incentive bonus. A high fixed fee may be a marketing obstacle, but the SEC requires that any incentive fee paid by a fund be symmetrical: the manager must pay the fund if performance lags the benchmark. Hedge fund operators accept fee structures with high water marks on performance fees, but the possibility of negative fees has not been popular, to say the least.

The hedge fund operator would have to provide a "plain English" explanation of the strategy or strategies that the fund would follow and a risk statement equaling or exceeding the most self-abasing risk statement yet provided by a hedge fund. The fund would request approval from the SEC for the full complement of securities and derivatives strategies permitted a registered investment company. The fund would want to be endowed with the ability to leverage its positions to the maximum permitted level for an SEC-registered fund.

New Tools Needed

Given the nature of the ETF creation and redemption process, the hedge fund operator might find it desirable to work with an OTC derivatives dealer to develop derivative contracts which would permit automatic initiation of a derivative position triggered by a fund share creation and cancellation of the derivative triggered by a fund share redemption. In other words, the deposit of a new creation unit would result in initiation of a related derivatives position under previously agreed terms and the cancellation of fund shares in redemption would lead to the termination of a similar derivatives position. This mechanism could enhance liquidity in a few interesting market sectors.

Usable Hedge Fund Strategies

Having set the stage with a statement of minimum structural requirements and a few brief observations on what might be approvable by U.S. regulators, there are a number of basic hedge fund strategies which could be used in such a fund. Using the Hedge-Fund.net strategy definitions, a number of strategies appear to use markets with enough liquidity to support an ETF structure.[21]

Aggressive Growth

As hedge funds that trade stocks aggressively and accept higher levels of risk in order to produce the highest possible returns, these funds often use leverage and trade options and futures. They generally are opportunistic. In most cases, liquidity will not be an issue until the fund becomes quite large.

Most Sector Funds

Here, the manager is primarily invested in securities revolving around a specific sector (energy, finance, healthcare, technology, etc.). As long as outsized positions in undersized companies are avoided, sector strategies will usually work in an investment company format.

Long Only (Leveraged)

These are similar to an equity mutual fund, except the manager can trade a variety of financial instruments and use leverage. The ETF version might use fewer unusual instruments and less leverage.

Long/Short Hedged

The manager buys securities he believes will go up in price and sells short securities he believes will decline in price. Managers may be either "net long" or "net short" and may change their "net" position frequently. For example, a manager may be 60% long and 100% short, giving him a market exposure of 40% net short. Extensive use of options and futures is common in traditional hedge funds but would be limited in the ETF versions.

Short-Term Trading

The manager focuses on short-duration, opportunistic trades. Sometimes this strategy will include day trading.

Risk/Merger Arbitrage

The manager invests in event-driven situations, such as leveraged buy-outs, mergers, and hostile takeovers. Managers often purchase stock in a firm being taken over, and sell short the stock of the acquiring company.

Some Options Strategies

In the investment company format, limitations on options use and leverage will increase use of stocks.

Limitations

Each strategy will be constrained by the investment company structure in several ways. There will be a limit on leverage. Some less liquid opportunities will have to be turned down. Derivatives use will be limited. A few specific examples will illustrate some of these constraints.

Long/Short Strategies

Long/short strategies—using common stocks, long and short positions in other ETFs, options, or single-stock futures—could be implemented relatively easily in an ETF format. The constraints on the use of options and futures in an investment company and probable constraints on the use of single-stock futures when the regulatory framework for those instruments is fully developed will limit leverage. Nonetheless, there should be enough opportunities when combined with long/short opportunities in stocks and other ETFs to provide some interesting positions. The investment company structure will be less flexible than the limited partnership or LLC structure often used by hedge funds; but the regulatory position of the fund manager and the tax treatment in the ETF will make up for these limitations in some cases. Assuming that single-stock futures are regulated as securities in the context of an investment company, their principal function will be to expand the opportunities to do long/short-type ETF strategies on an economical basis and to take positions in these instruments more efficiently and with less stringent restrictions on the amount of capital at risk than could be achieved in an options or futures position or even in a short position in an underlying share of stock or ETF.

Volatility Strategies

While restrictions on the use of options and futures in an investment company are fairly rigid, certain risk-offsetting positions are possible without too great a "capital" penalty. If these positions can be supplemented by single-stock futures contracts both on ordinary shares and ETF shares, a more extensive volatility arbitrage position might be taken. Availability of additional, related equity instruments in combination with certain positions in high-yield debt instruments might provide a more liquid and more diversified portfolio with well-controlled risk.

Sector Strategies

The advent of single-stock futures on specialized-sector ETFs will expand the range of applications feasible in a hedge fund ETF.

It is too soon to proclaim actively managed ETFs as the key to bringing hedge fund strategies, with their general absence of close correlation with traditional equity strategies, to the small investor. Nonetheless, the opportunities seem likely to broaden.

CONCLUSION

In this chapter, we have tried to imagine and illustrate a few of the places exchange-traded funds might go from here. We have no illusions that these speculations cover all or even most of the possibilities or even that each of our speculations will be feasible. Nonetheless, the opportunities that seem relatively clear and straightforward have great potential. The more esoteric possibilities of the life strategy funds require more faith and imagination, but readers might speculate for themselves what the future for ETFs will look like after the first actively managed funds have been in operation for a few years.

ENDNOTES

1. There were nearly 42,000 issues in the Lehman Municipal Aggregate at June 30, 2001.

2. Important exceptions are issues with embedded call or prepayment options that significantly affect their valuation and liquidity relative to many recent benchmark debt issues that do not have such embedded options.

3. See Kliesen and Thornton (2001).

4. See Stevenson (2001).

5. See Davidson (1999).

6. Like all other index funds, the enhanced index funds described here should be able to make changes in their portfolios before announcing the changes if their aggregate portfolio will track a public index closely both before and after the portfolio change.

7. See Part B of the SPDR Prospectus, the section headed "The Portfolio—Adjustments to the Portfolio."

8. Certain aspects of financial instruments described in this section are the subject of a U.S. patent application.

9. Interestingly, the intra-day value proxy (IDVP), the every-15-second calculation of approximate fund share value, has usually been based on the creation basket rather than on the actual fund portfolio. This can lead to tracking and hedging deviations on the date an index change occurs. It is also worth noting that many funds do not change their creation and redemption baskets until the day *after* the index change is effective. This is not an issue of consequence if the index change is minor; but for major index changes it can lead to unanticipated tracking error. One way to avoid this and still use the pre-index change creation and redemption baskets is to require creation and redemption commitments earlier in the day—as described in the next section for actively managed funds.

10. U.S. patent applied for.

11. There may be regulatory reluctance to embrace cash-settled derivatives on an index with changes that are not disclosed until after a fund which both creates the index and is based on it has transacted in its portfolio. This is not a major issue. There can be no such objection to derivatives that settle in the fund shares and they are likely to be the most popular derivatives anyway.

12. Whereas, the current index ETF's creation basket is designed to replicate the index as closely as possible and the fund weights may be modified from the creation basket weights to bring the fund even closer to the index, we would expect most active managers to manage their funds *as strict multiples of the creation basket*. The man-

ager would manage the creation basket, knowing that she would have no odd or fractional share positions to keep track of. If there were 10 shares of a stock in a creation basket and the fund had 90 creation units in the portfolio, the fund would have exactly 900 shares of the stock. In short, trading to make small portfolio adjustments to get the portfolio closer to the index will not be necessary.

13. If the fund manager manages the creation basket as described in the previous note, the creation basket plus or minus some cash will be a *perfect* hedge portfolio.

14. This discussion implicitly assumes that there is some interest in trading ahead of or close on the heels of a fund's manager. For some legendary managers, this is clearly a valid assumption. Even a mediocre manager who is trading large positions might be justifiably concerned about secrecy. However, the average fund manager with the average-sized actively managed fund will probably be embarrassed by the lack of interest in her trading activities.

15. One note of caution on actively managed ETFs is worth sounding. Whereas *all holders of shares in an index fund should benefit in one way or more from the addition of an exchange-traded share class* (e.g., Vanguard's VIPERS share class for its conventional index funds), it is not clear that every shareholder of an existing conventional actively managed fund will want the fund to add an ETF share class. Some additional portfolio information inevitably will have to be revealed to facilitate pricing and market making in actively managed ETFs. This additional disclosure could be contrary to the interests of non-taxable shareholders of an actively-managed fund who were concerned about this information being used to trade against the interests of fund shareholders. For this reason, any actively managed ETF will probably be a new fund with a single class of shareholders. The advisor of any actively managed fund adding an ETF share class would probably face litigation.

16. Variations on this theme are provided by a number of fund issuers. The Vanguard funds are described in the text. The Smith Barney Allocation Series and One Group offer a number of portfolios that

are variations on a standard asset allocation theme. WM Group offers five traditional asset allocation portfolios. Only Fidelity offers six funds designed to provide traditional asset allocation overlain by a feature that moves to a more conservative portfolio as the shareholder's expected retirement date approaches. None of these fund prospectuses suggests an opportunity to change allocations on a tax-free or tax-deferred basis. In fact, they seem designed more for IRAs and similar tax-deferred accounts than for taxable accounts. These funds were reviewed briefly in Damato (2001).

17. The importance of this risk transition was highlighted by Vanguard's founder in a recent speech. See Bogle (2001b).

18. This suggestion is based on the implicit assumption that it may be possible to use municipals in an open ETF. We are nowhere close to that degree of liquidity yet. A better strategy which would need some additional regulatory relief might be for the fund to buy closed-end municipal funds.

19. This paragraph's description of tax consequences assumes that any transition or estate transfer occurs after "expiration" of the provisions of the 2001 tax revisions. Opportunities to transfer the shares to a trust are outside the scope of this chapter.

20. This section originally appeared in a slightly different form in *Risk and Reward*.

21. See www.hedgefund.net.

Chapter 8

Trading ETF Shares Without Angst

At the most elementary level of analysis, the average buyer or seller of small quantities of ETF shares can usually enter a market or limit order through a broker with no more concern than should precede the entry of an order for an actively traded common stock. Most fund share orders are executed promptly and fairly in a highly liquid, highly transparent market; however, there are important differences between the market in ETF shares and the market in stocks. An investor who trades regularly or in large size in ETF shares should understand those differences.

THE UNIQUE MARKET STRUCTURE AND TRADING PATTERN OF EXCHANGE-TRADED FUND SHARES

A number of sell-side analysts have recently produced excellent analyses of market quality in exchange-traded fund shares. In most cases, they have correctly focused on the market in the stocks underlying the fund's portfolio and, secondarily, on the availability of the fund shares themselves and derivatives (especially stock index futures and options on the funds) as additional sources of liquidity. Several of these studies have supplemented their evaluations of liquidity within a relatively narrow range around the quoted bid-asked spread with a discussion of the liquidity available in the underlying market in the portfolio stocks. Our purpose in this section is to provide a schematic to illustrate the distinctive features of liquidity, share trading characteristics, and market depth in exchange-traded fund shares.

The diagram in Exhibit 8-1 shows a Japanese-style bid-and-offer arrangement for a hypothetical limit order book in an exchange-traded share selling for approximately $100 per share. The buyers' bids are to the left of the segmented line in the middle of the diagram; the sellers' offers are to the right. Bids are below the intra-day proxy value (IDPV), which is indicated at $100.02, with the total range of quotes the book can display running from $99.80 to $100.20 in two-cent intervals. There are three kinds of bids and/or offers illustrated in this diagram. The very different nature and source of these bids and offers is the essence of the unique market structure we want to illustrate.

Exhibit 8-1: Schematic of an ETF Limit Order Book

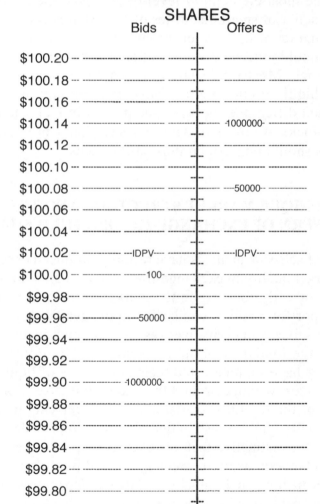

The smallest order on this limit order book is a retail bid for 100 shares at a price of $100.00, two cents per fund share below the IDPV of $100.02. The IDPV is, as the name implies, a proxy for the contemporary per-share value of the fund's portfolio. At three spaces ($0.06) below and three spaces above the IDPV are bids and offers for 50,000 shares. These quotes are the consensus of the specialist and market maker positions in the exchange crowd. They represent bids and offers that the specialist and market makers are making within the framework of the market with the expectation that they will be able to satisfy demand or absorb sales within their inventory of fund shares without having to create additional fund shares or redeem any excess shares to balance inventories.[1]

At three more spaces, i.e., another $0.06 per share, above and below the 50,000-share offers and bids are offers and bids for 1 million shares of the fund, valued at approximately $100 million. These bids and offers reflect what the specialists and market makers are prepared to bid and offer if they have to accumulate or lay off positions in the underlying stocks and create or redeem fund shares demanded of them in the case of their offer or sold to them in the case of their bid.

The significance of this bid-and-offer constellation is that the bid-asked spread is quite different depending upon the size in which one trades. A retail investor wishing to sell 100 shares and arriving in the market place at the appropriate second with a market order or a marketable limit order will be able to sell a 100-share position at $100 even, only two cents below the intra-day proxy value. Depending on the rules of the marketplace and the nature of the seller's order, an order to sell 10,000 shares might be executed at 99.96 cents, with the 100-share bid typically filled at the same price as the other 9,900 shares. In short, the bid for this seller was not $100.00, but $99.96 cents per share, or $0.06 below the IDPV. The other interesting part of this trade is that the limit order to buy 100 shares at $100 was filled at a better price. Price improvement more commonly has gone to users of market orders rather than users of limit orders, but this example does illustrate the almost random character of the exact execution price on certain small orders.[2] The spread illustrated is a tight spread by any standard, though it is not atypical of a large-cap exchange-traded index fund with a competitive specialist and market makers and active third market (off-exchange) trading.

The really unique feature of this diagram—and the unique liquidity of the market in exchange-traded fund shares—is that the liquidity of the market grows dramatically for larger transactions without a significant spread increase due to the way a portfolio trade disperses the market impact of a transaction over many stocks. The investor is quite literally buying or selling a substantial fraction of "the market" rather than the shares of a single company—an index basket rather than an isolated company share. The information reflected in an order is more likely to be meaningful when it is information on a particular company or that company's stock as opposed to information on the broad market or a market sector reflected in a portfolio of stocks. An investor wishing to buy or sell a few million shares of even a highly liquid security such as General Electric or Microsoft might expect a very large market impact from entering such an order. Furthermore, under some circumstances, the price impact on the stock might increase more than proportionately to any increase in the size of the block. In contrast, the investor seeking to take or lay off a very large position in an exchange-traded fund share usually will find that liquidity increases dramatically and the relative market impact of an order for more shares declines as the size of the order increases—within limits, of course. Market impact is absorbed readily over all the underlying securities in the index. Market makers are usually comfortable that they will not be hurt when they provide general market liquidity because there are a variety of hedging instruments they can use to offset broad-market or even some sector risks. In general, similar instruments are not as readily available to protect them from single-stock risk.

As Exhibit 8-1 illustrates, there are several distinct points at which liquidity increases. The first limited access to liquidity occurs in an execution against any small retail orders—a very, very limited source of liquidity. The next access to liquidity is in executions against specialist and market maker bids and offers grounded on the expectation that the market makers will be able to interact with a number of orders on both sides of the market before they will be obligated to go into the underlying market to create or redeem shares—accessing the liquidity in the underlying portfolio stocks directly—to rebalance inventories. The third level of liquidity, of course, is reached when creations or redemptions in size are required, and here the level of liquidity is a multiple of the level of liquidity one would find in a single stock because the order is not based on company-specific information and the demand for liquidity is spread over the individual markets in all the shares in the fund.

   An important point worth noting is that the large bids and offers based on creation and redemption of fund shares may be farther apart than we might expect based on the posted quotes in each of the underlying stocks in the portfolio. As we will see in a later section of this chapter, this "basket spread" is occasionally tighter than the fund share spread, *reflecting the costs and frictions of the creation/redemption process and, more importantly, the very frequent presence of retail quotes in stocks—like the 100-share bid in Exhibit 8-1*. The reason the larger trader faces a wider spread but can trade dramatically greater size is that the market in each of the separate stocks in the basket tends to look much like the posted fund share market in Exhibit 8-1 between $99.96 and $100.08: There are "retail" limit orders inside the specialist/market maker quotes that suggest illusory liquidity. In fact, the frequent quote changes in most ETF shares discourage limit orders. Consequently, a larger percentage of trades in most ETFs have the specialist or a market maker on the side of the market opposite a customer than in the market for an ordinary stock. Customer orders meet one another less frequently in fund share trades than in typical stock trades on an exchange. Just as the small 100-share limit order makes the fund share market look tighter than it really is for most participants, a relatively larger number of small limit orders in individual stocks often makes the basket spread look *much tighter than it is—for a large trade*. Once *all* the spreads in all relevant markets are adjusted for the small limit orders, there is a great deal of readily available liquidity for large trades, especially in the fund shares; but the spread for the large order is wider than it appears at first glance.

   The significance of this structure of bids and offers lies in its contrast to the more typical structure of the market in a single stock. If there are few public limit orders on a stock, liquidity may *decline* dramatically when an incoming order is presumed by the specialist and other market makers to be motivated by specific information about the stock. Such information can cause the stock to move up or down sharply in a short period of time. This is not a problem with fund shares because of the secondary liquidity in the market for the underlying stocks. There is no secondary reservoir of residual liquidity in single stocks comparable to what we see in funds. This market structure difference has important implications for trading strategy. In the case of a single security, an investor will frequently look for block indications which might suggest the presence of an investor with the opposite view on the stock. A large order on the other side of the market for a stock could provide liquidity and fulfillment of the trader's objective within a narrow range close to the current market price. An exchange-traded fund share investor could do approximately the same thing by working with the specialist or a market maker within the context of current values and with much less concern than the investor trading in a single stock might have for exhausting the supply available near current prices. An investor who, for some reason, wanted to buy or sell quickly would find it quite difficult to do a very large trade in a single stock without sending an implicit message that he had access to important information. An investor who wants to put a great deal of money to work or to eliminate a large position in an exchange-traded fund's shares can do so readily at a wider spread but with minimal market impact. The wider spread is the price for the convenience of immediate execution. The markets in fund shares tend to be more forgiving and accommodating than markets in individual stocks in this respect. Of course, an incorrect decision can inflict financial pain in either market.

Investors in fund shares are doing essentially the same thing that institutional investors have done for a number of years when they have executed portfolio trades. Like a fund share trade, a portfolio trade has less information content and, correspondingly, less market impact than a typical single-stock trade. An ETF share trade *is* a single-share variant of a portfolio trade.

Who Owns and Who Trades ETF Shares?

The title of this box is worded like two questions because there are two answers: The principal traders of ETFs own few shares relative to their trading activity.

ETF shares are DTC-eligible book-entry only securities without negotiable share certificates in circulation. Each ETF has a single shareholder—the Depository Trust Company (DTC), a subsidiary of the Depository Trust and Clearing Corporation (DTCC). Periodically, a fund issuer will learn the names and shareholdings of each of the DTC participants—largely banks and brokerage firms—that hold the fund's shares. These holders are identifiable as retail brokerage firms or bank trust departments, but a brokerage firm might clear and carry shares for a specialist, a market maker, or a hedge fund as well as its own retail accounts. A bank might carry positions for its personal trust accounts or act as a custodian for mutual funds, pension funds, or foreign banks and brokers. Thus, knowing the names of the DTC participants that hold an ETF's shares is not particularly useful information if you are trying to classify the fund's shareholders.

Institutional investors with more than $100 million under management are required to file quarterly 13-D or 13-F reports that list their holdings. These institutions account for all but a few percent of institutional equity holdings in the United States, and they consistently report that they are responsible for 30%–35% of the shares of the typical ETF, far less than their typical share of the average U.S.-domiciled common stock. These reports are the only reliable information regularly available on ETF share ownership.

> Speculating a bit, it seems likely that retail investors own most of the rest of the ETF shares outstanding. Brokerage firms and hedge funds (which are often organized as brokerage firms) are the largest traders of ETFs for market making, risk management, and other purposes.* Brokerage firms and hedge funds are responsible for most ETF trading volume, but they are not large and consistent holders of fund shares except in market making and share lending accommodation accounts.
>
> * To complicate the picture, a large hedge fund organized as a brokerage firm will usually report holdings as an institution. Furthermore, a wrap account managed by a reporting institution but domiciled at a brokerage firm would be reported by the institutional manager. As a final complication, if an institution loans 100,000 ETF shares to a short seller who sells them to a second institution, the 13-D and 13-F reports will show two institutional positions of 100,000 shares. Only one of those positions can show up as a holding by a DTC participant.

TRADING GUIDANCE FOR THE INDIVIDUAL INVESTOR

The prospectus, product description, and other sales literature for an exchange-traded fund mentions the creation and redemption of ETF shares in kind—and in large blocks. For the typical investor, this is information that should be comforting because it is responsible for some of the most important and desirable features of these funds, but this feature has little similarity to the process by which most investors buy or sell ETF shares. The party on the other side of most ETF trades an investor might make is a specialist or market maker or another investor, not the fund that issues the shares. We discussed the creation and redemption process in detail in Chapter 2. Our focus here is on trading tactics for the small to mid-sized investor—up to, say, 10,000 shares or $1,000,000 per trade.

Just Like a Stock

Mechanically, buying and selling an ETF share is just like buying and selling a share of stock. In fact, an investor can use essentially any type of order that is acceptable in stock trading to buy or sell ETF shares.

Like stocks, the minimum unit of purchase or sale is a single share and, like other exchange-traded shares, there is no odd lot differential—no extra charge per share—for trading less than a 100-share round lot.[3] ETF shares can be purchased through any broker-dealer that handles orders in common stocks. ETF commission schedules are usually identical to common stock commissions, margins are identical to common stock margins, and it is even possible to sell ETF shares short. In contrast to the rules for selling stocks short, there is no up-tick requirement for short sales. (Under up-tick rules, short sales of stocks are not permitted except at a price higher than the last previous trade at a different price.) The up-tick exemption is granted to each fund separately, so an investor should check that a new fund has this exemption.[4]

Placing an Order

While the exchange and most dealers that trade ETFs away from the exchange will accept a wide range of order types, most investors use either market orders or simple limit orders, depending on how anxious they are to get their order filled or how willing they are to accept the risk that the order will not be executed and the shares will move away from their price. Unless you are very patient or you are planning to buy or sell a large number of shares, you should be able to purchase or sell ETFs with a market order. An investor can examine pricing information for each ETF including a proxy for intra-day net asset value. This proxy value is not guaranteed to be 100% accurate, but it will usually reflect a value near the level where a trade can be executed.

You should expect the bid-asked spread on a broad-market, large-cap domestic U.S. ETF to be about 0.2% of the share price— about $0.20 on a $100 share—with the S&P 500 funds trading at a slightly tighter spread and most sector funds and smaller-cap funds trading at wider spreads. The spreads will widen during periods of market volatility and tighten when markets are stable. Similarly, the spread may be slightly wider if the fund shares do not trade actively.[5] Contrary to popular belief, however, an inactive ETF should not be materially harder to trade in either small or large size than an active ETF, and the spread should not be much greater. If the fund is inactive, however, direct contact with the specialist or a market maker is a good idea, especially if your order is larger than the size quoted.

In evaluating the bid-asked spread, an investor should be alert to the fact that the quoted bid-asked spread may reflect public orders as well as bids and offers posted by specialists and market makers on the exchange floor. If an investor sees a market at 100.00 bid–100.20 asked, either the bid or the offer may be from the floor or either side may reflect a customer order on the specialist's book. One way to tell is to check the size of the bid and offer. Ordinarily, a customer order at the same price as the specialist's bid or offer will be relatively small, and it will be added to the quantity in the specialist's quote. Here are some examples of quantities and educated guesses of the parties behind the quotes:

Bid–Asked:	$100.00–$100.20	$100.00–$100.15
Quantity:	500 × 500	500 × 10
Comment:	Specialist both sides	Specialist bid, Customer offer

Note that the quantities are expressed in round lots of 100 shares each, so 500 is 50,000 shares and 10 is 1,000 shares. Even if a public customer wants to trade only a small number of round lots, the specialist is required to show the customer bid or offer if it is the best bid or offer. Specialists and market makers are not, however, required to match the public order and increase the size at a price inside their market. The fact that a customer is offering to pay a little more or receive a little less than the specialist or market maker is quoting may mean that hitting a customer bid or lifting a customer offer is a way to trade inside the normal spread of the market. A public customer bid or offer may indeed represent such an opportunity, but it does not necessarily offer much of an advantage. If the market were, in fact, moving in the direction that would make the customer's bid or offer interesting, the specialist might find it desirable to transact with the customer's order, placing the specialist on both the bid and offer sides of the market for the next incoming order. On balance, it is not clear that the presence of a customer order inside the professional spread provides useful guidance for action by an investor. The only statement we can make with confidence about these customer limit orders is that the trader who wants to buy the quantity represented by a customer limit order (or less) may get a better execution if the order is routed to the primary market where the limit order is posted. If the order is directed to another market, it will not be able to interact with the customer limit order on the specialist's book.

If an investor is using a broker that enters orders on the exchange which is the primary market for the ETF, the investor might find it attractive to enter an order between the specialist's bid and offer—to become the customer order in the middle. This is probably not possible if the customer's orders are being executed off the primary or listing exchange because there may be little or no interaction with other customer orders. A retail investor who is not sure where an order is being sent will ordinarily get the best execution relative to an expected or mean price by entering a market order prior to the opening or, perhaps, a market-on-close order later in the day. If the posted quotes consistently show a tight spread and greater size than the customer's order, a market order is a reasonable choice with most market routing as long as the market shows no signs of stress. Market orders directed to the listing exchange during the trading session may be matched with market orders on the other side of the market that arrive at about the same time, giving both customers an opportunity for price improvement relative to the posted quotes. To complicate the picture further, some markets away from the primary listing exchange use a formula to improve executions on some small orders. The improvement is usually based on the size of contemporary bids and offers.[6]

At some risk of creating execution information overload, new SEC rules require publication of monthly reports that measure execution quality in a market, security by security. Brokers are also required to describe their order routing practices and to report quarterly any agreements on payments they receive in connection with the routing of customer order flow.

Some market data services provide additional information that can help an investor determine the direction the overall market or the portfolio represented in a particular ETF has been moving. It is usually possible to learn not only the spread in the market for the fund shares, but (on a per–fund share equivalent basis) what the bid and offer price is for the basket of securities used to create or redeem the fund shares. (This basket quote is described in more detail below.) Option quotations and futures prices also can provide

useful information to an investor who has the time and skill to analyze such information.

TRADING EXCHANGE-TRADED FUNDS WITHOUT ANGST OVER DISCOUNTS AND PREMIUMS

At the risk of eliminating all elements of suspense at the outset of
this section, we state that it is practically impossible for an open-
end exchange-traded fund investing in domestic securities to sell at
a material premium or discount unless the market structure has been
changed to impede free creation and redemption of shares under the
rules in the fund's prospectus. Our purpose in making this statement
up front is to encourage the reader to concentrate on how the markets for exchange-traded funds and their component securities work
and how arbitrage forces constrain or how inventory needs require
creation and redemption of fund shares to balance supply and
demand. Secondarily, the reader will want to understand that apparent premiums and discounts of a material magnitude are nearly
always the result of comparing non-contemporaneous prices or of
stressed markets.

We illustrate how the market makes ETF shares efficient substitutes for direct ownership of the securities in the ETF's portfolio.
An investor need not be concerned about the liquidity of an investment in an ETF as long as nothing interferes with the appropriate
functioning of the markets in the underlying securities and in the fund
shares. The investor does need to remember the misleading effect of
small retail orders on the true market for a sizable transaction in the
ETF and in a basket of its underlying stocks. After disposing of the
discount/premium issue, we will return to the trading discussion and
offer a few suggestions on choosing a fund that will trade efficiently.

Why Have ETF Price Premiums and Discounts Been an Issue?

The original S&P 500 SPDRs were proposed by the American Stock
Exchange and approved for issuance and trading by the Securities
and Exchange Commission based in part on the theoretical argument

that arbitrage would prevent the SPDR shares from trading at a material premium or discount to their contemporary net asset value.[7]

Evidence of efficient pricing in the *Toronto Stock Exchange Index Participation shares* (TIPs) that traded in Canada until recently might have been used to support this point, but we have been unable to find any evidence of TIPs premium/discount studies from the early 1990s. Lacking empirical studies, the proponents of SPDRs seem to have relied entirely on theoretical arbitrage arguments.

It is clear that by the standards usually applied to closed-end funds, any apparent premiums or discounts were very small from the earliest days of SPDRs trading. In an attempt to demonstrate consistency between net asset value and the closing market price for the SPDR shares or perhaps in response to an inquiry, subsequent applications to the SEC for other exchange-traded funds have included detailed summaries of daily comparisons between net asset values and closing market prices of the original SPDRs and other funds as continuing evidence of the efficiency of the arbitrage mechanism. These comparisons also found their way into prospectuses, annual reports, and analysts' ETF discussions as substantiation of the effectiveness of the arbitrage mechanism.

While they are questionable when applied to U.S. funds and portfolios, these daily NAV/closing price comparisons became seriously misleading when they were applied to World Equity Benchmark Shares (WEBS), subsequently renamed iShares MSCI series. These single-country funds are based on indexes of foreign stocks traded primarily on foreign markets. Trading hours in the foreign stock markets differ from trading hours in the United States—the market where the fund shares trade. There is no reason to expect the fund's NAV, which is based on currency-adjusted closing prices for the stocks *in their primary market,* to match the closing fund share price *in the United States*, many hours after the primary market for the stocks has closed. The U.S. closing prices for these funds are more likely to reflect expectations for tomorrow's opening in the primary market. Nonetheless, investors will see these comparisons because in an eleventh-hour objection to the proposed approval of an exemptive order to permit a new family of exchange-traded funds, a former Securities and Exchange Commission staff attorney requested more frequent and more prominent disclosure of such apparent premiums and discounts as evidence that pricing in ETFs is less efficient than the funds' advocates had claimed. This additional disclosure calls for comment because it perpetuates and legitimizes the misinformation provided in the original net asset value versus closing price comparisons. These comparisons not only fail to serve investors, they can be seriously misleading. Investors have every right to know about premiums and discounts, but the information provided should be accurate and useful. It will probably take a year or two to get better premium and discount data to all investors, but it is important to get the process underway.

In the next sub-section, we examine the inherent fallacy in the NAV versus closing price comparison—first for foreign and then for domestic stock ETFs traded during U.S. market hours. Fortunately, there is an appropriate way to measure any premiums and discounts *at the time an order is entered*. This process, as described below, should illustrate that material premiums and discounts are prevented by arbitrage forces as long as contemporaneous prices for fund shares and their underlying portfolio positions are available and there are no obstacles to the efficient working of the market in the ETFs and the underlying market in the stocks.

The Inherent Fallacy of a Daily Net Asset Value versus Closing Price Comparison

In the United States, the net asset value of most funds is calculated on the basis of prices gathered at approximately 4:00 p.m. Eastern time each day. These prices are collected by a variety of pricing services and checked carefully for errors. Since many securities do not trade frequently, techniques have been developed to price a security which has not traded at or very close to 4:00 p.m. Most securities are priced at their last sale, unless that sale occurred long before 4:00 p.m. or there is reason (such as a bid-asked range away from the last sale) to believe the earlier price is misleading. Funds are permitted to use an estimated fair value calculation if accurate, up-to-date price information on the underlying market is not readily available. One of the most important applications of fair value pricing enables directors of open-end mutual funds specializing in foreign securities to determine the fund's net asset value based on all available information when appropriate prices are believed to be very different at 4:00 p.m. Eastern time in the United States from what they were at the close of the primary market for the portfolio stocks in Europe or Asia.

Interestingly, a significant input to fair value estimates for foreign stock mutual funds is the price of exchange-traded fund shares from the same country or region. These fund share prices provide a *market* measurement of the likely change in value of an index based on equity securities in a particular country since the close of the primary market. Trading on the New York Stock Exchange in major securities that have their primary markets outside the United States has been another important source of such updated price information. These indicative prices help improve NAV calculations for conventional funds by providing prices that are set in an open market.

In contrast to conventional funds, the U.S.-based iShares MSCI Series NAVs and NAVs of other U.S.-based ETFs with foreign stocks in their portfolios are determined by the valuation of the underlying securities portfolio adjusted for changes in currency relationships since the close of the primary markets. This adjustment *does not* capture changes in the home currency valuation of the securities since the primary market close. This indicative optimized portfolio value (IOPV) or, as we prefer to call it for domestic funds, the intra-day proxy value (IDPV) is more misleading than it is useful as a proxy for the contemporaneous valuation (during U.S. trading hours) of a portfolio of foreign stocks. This calculation does not consider securities price changes that would have been apparent if the primary foreign market had been open during U.S. trading hours or if prices in the foreign portfolio stocks in other non-primary markets had been considered in the IOPV/IDPV or NAV calculation. Even if the NAV calculation incorporated non-primary market prices that might be available in U.S. trading hours, it is not clear that the calculation would be consistently improved. It seems likely that the NAVs on the iShares MSCI series would be closer to the fund shares' closing market value; but unless or until active, global 24-hour trading is an established fact in most stocks, the best estimate of the NAV of an ETF holding foreign stocks will be the contemporary market value of the ETF shares. Obviously, this begs the question of an NAV/market value comparison.[8]

A thorough understanding of the domestic portfolio ETF arbitrage process where more contemporaneous prices are available, will help clarify the problem and point to a resolution of the controversy and confusion. For domestic exchange-traded funds, i.e., on the funds holding domestic U.S. securities, there is one significant problem with the net asset value versus closing price comparison: The prices are often determined at different times. One problem is that the most active index ETFs are based on underlying stock indexes which also underlie stock index futures contracts, and both those futures contracts and shares of the ETFs trade after the close of the primary markets in the underlying stocks. There is a 15-minute time difference between the 4:00 p.m. stock prices which determine the fund net asset value and the 4:15 p.m. closing price for the exchange-traded fund shares and the stock index futures contracts.

A second problem is that, in the case of some new and relatively inactively traded ETFs, there may be no useful closing price for the fund share. The 4:00 p.m. NAV might be compared with a last sale price on the fund share that occurred at 11:00 a.m.[9]

Ordinarily, a comparison of a 4:00 p.m. NAV and a market price for the fund share that is captured 15 minutes later will not show much change, particularly when the fund share is actively traded. The difference in closing time for U.S. securities markets and the closing time for futures markets is widely known, and relatively little important corporate or other information that might impact stock prices is typically released during this period.[10] The significance of the difference between the timing of the net asset value calculation and the closing price of fund shares is, of course, that it is impossible to count on trading at or very close to the 4:15 p.m. price at 4:00 p.m. or vice versa. For most domestic funds, this is not a material issue. The point in spending time on it here is simply to illustrate that the comparison is inherently flawed. Fortunately, there is no need to focus on this comparison because there is a better way to make portfolio value and fund price comparisons *throughout the trading day*—comparisons that have more utility than a closing price comparison for the investor who wishes to be as certain as possible that the price paid for an exchange-traded fund share is very close to the contemporaneous value of the underlying portfolio during the trading day.

Useful data for evaluating the attractiveness of a purchase or sale or for measuring premiums or discounts is available in the form of a fund portfolio proxy calculation which we call the intra-day proxy value (IDPV) and which is usually based on valuing a stock basket and a cash component designed to reflect the contents of the fund portfolio. This valuation proxy goes by several names and is updated at 15-second intervals throughout the trading day, in most cases by the American Stock Exchange. For funds holding securities traded in U.S. markets during the U.S. trading day, IDPV calculations should provide a very close approximation of the contemporary value of the securities in the portfolio for comparison to the bids and offers available in the market for the fund shares. Since an investor will ordinarily buy at the asked price or sell at the bid posted by the fund's specialist and market makers, the investor's major concern should be that the IDPV fall between the bid and offer available on the exchange most of the time.[11] The 4:00 p.m. net asset value calculation is pertinent only to the Authorized Participants (APs). APs are specialists and market makers who create and redeem fund shares in creation unit aggregations to manage their inventories and, occasionally, to earn an arbitrage profit. The 4:00 p.m. NAV calculation is of limited interest even to APs because a change in the fund's net asset value will ordinarily be equally reflected in a change in the value of the securities they are depositing or redeeming.[12] What is relevant to the investor are the fund share bids and offers relative to a measure of the value of the fund portfolio, usually the intra-day proxy value.[13]

A Meaningful Comparison of Fund Share Values, Prices, and Quotes

To this point, our focus has been on an examination of what information is available on the pricing of ETF shares relative to the contemporary value of the fund portfolio. Approaching the problem from the other side is probably more useful: What information would we like to have to protect us from paying too much or selling too cheaply? Exhibit 8-2 is a sample page from a hypothetical website that will probably exist in the near future.[14]

Exhibit 8-2: Fund Pricing Table Layout
(all prices on fund share equivalent basis)

Fund Name	(1) SYM	(2) Basket Bid	(3) Fund Share Bid	(4) IDPV	(5) Fund Share Asked	(6) Basket Asked	(7) Spread as % Fund IDPV	(8) Check Dates
Sector SPDR Fin	XLF	29.17	29.16	29.20	29.31	29.23	0.5%	
iShares DJUS Fin Sec	IYF	85.97	85.94	86.09	86.31	86.16	0.4%	
iShares DJUS FServ	IYG	99.64	99.50	99.75	99.88	99.83	0.4%	

Such a website would provide enough information to help an investor determine that she is getting an appropriate price in any purchase or sale of exchange-traded fund shares with domestic U.S. portfolios. In a few cases, there may be additional information which the investor would want to obtain from other sources and indicators to alert the investor when more than usual care is necessary to check the information in the table against other sources. The table is designed to be as user-friendly as possible for the investor seeking to evaluate the economics of trading in a particular fund share. It facilitates pricing comparisons for a single fund and relative comparisons to competitive fund shares. A single example based on a snapshot of recent data is provided: a comparison of the Sector SPDR Finance Sector Fund and iShares funds based on the Dow Jones US Financial Sector and Financial Services Indexes.

The left-hand column is simply the fund name. Funds should be compared on the basis of fund type, putting comparable funds together in terms of their investment characteristics. Column (1) lists the trading symbol for the fund. Columns (2) through (6) present information on relevant bids and offers and intra-day value calculations for the specific fund share. Columns (2) through (6) are expressed in terms of the fund share price. Beginning at the left, column (2) is the index basket bid. This is simply the appropriately weighted per fund share bid for the stocks (and cash component) in the index portfolio used to calculate the IDPV. Column (3) is the fund share bid on the listing exchange limit order book. Column (4) is the intra-day proxy value (IDPV), which is generally the most current estimate of the value of the portfolio embodied in the fund shares, based on the most recent sale (or the mean of the bid and asked prices) of each stock in the portfolio. The next two columns to the right are, respectively, the fund share asked price and the index portfolio basket asked price—again, all on a per–fund share basis. The investor cannot be certain that all of the prices and quotes used in developing this information are absolutely contemporary and accurate, but bad prices and quotes tend to be corrected and replaced with new information relatively quickly. The fund share bid and offer may be closer together than the basket bid and offer, or they may be farther apart. Usually, however, there will not appear to be much of an arbitrage profit opportunity from the creation or redemption of fund shares. Creations and redemptions occur principally as a result of the specialist and other market makers managing their inventory of fund shares rather than because of arbitrage opportunities. To put the profit potentials for market making and arbitrage in perspective, a typical market maker might buy and sell the shares in a creation unit five or ten times between inventory adjustments with average trading profit ranging from a few pennies to a quarter of a point per share on each trading turn. An arbitrage profit of five cents per fund share would be rare in creation and redemption activity. If more specific evidence of the dominance of inventory management in the creation/redemption process is needed, consider that in 2001, there have been creations *and* redemptions in the NASDAQ 100 Trust on many business days. Quite often creations from one market maker take place on the same day another market maker is redeeming. Both these market makers expect to earn trading profits, but *they cannot both be earning arbitrage profits* on closing prices with these offsetting creations and redemptions.

Real arbitrage opportunities where the arbitrageur covers his costs and earns a trading profit are not common. Few investors are equipped to be active arbitrageurs and all readers are advised to seek much more comprehensive data than we describe here before they attempt to act as arbitrageurs.

If basket bids and offers are *inside* the bid and offer on the fund shares, this does not mean that there is a true arbitrage opportunity. There are several factors which affect fund and basket quote relationships. Other things equal, an index with an active futures contract is more likely to have fund shares with bids and offers close to or *outside* the basket bids and offers than a more specialized index with no futures. To oversimplify a bit, the presence of a futures contract generally reduces the effective spread on the basket. If the basket quote incorporates the effect of the futures market, the quote will be tighter. There will be frequent occasions for most funds when the fund share bid or offer will be outside the basket bid or offer, as in the example in Exhibit 8-2. If the basket quote is inside the fund quote on only one side, this may be an indication that a creation or redemption is likely, or that the prices may be changing. Basket quotes inside fund quotes on one or both sides may indicate simply that small limit orders inside the specialist's markets *on the stocks in the basket* make the basket spread look tighter. We will return to these issues in an attempt to resolve any remaining apparent spread paradoxes.

Most investors should use this information simply to satisfy themselves that the proxy value is usually between the fund share bid and the fund share offer. There are occasions when the proxy value may be outside the spread because prices are changing or due to errors in the data; but when the data is good and the pricing is contemporaneous, it is a reasonable expectation that the intra-day proxy value will fall between the fund share bid and the fund share offer most of the time.[15] When stock prices are changing, the investor will find it more useful to compare the basket quotes with the fund quotes because the last sale data often used to calculate the IDPV may lag the quotes that indicate where the next trade might occur.

Column (7) shows the fund share spread (i.e., the difference between the fund share bid price and the fund share offered price), divided by the proxy value and expressed as a percentage. This gives an investor data to make a rough estimate of the round-trip execution costs of trading in the fund shares. Very large transactions would be more likely to depend on some variation of the basket bid and asked prices because, ultimately, the very large investor will have to pay for the specialist or another market maker to go into the market and create additional shares or redeem shares, and at least part of the cost of those creation and/or redemption transactions will be included in the investor's cost of trading the shares. We will return to the relevant spread for a trade requiring a creation or redemption later in this chapter. A very small investor can ordinarily estimate the round-trip cost of trading by adding a figure for round-trip commissions to the quoted fund share spread.

Column (8) will provide a list of key check dates, to be provided in most cases by the issuers of the fund or the publishers of the underlying index. The purpose of these dates is that errors or inconsistencies in the proxy value calculation are usually due to one of a relatively small number of events that are not always accurately reflected in the proxy portfolio. The most important of these are an ex-distribution event affecting the fund NAV which is not fully or appropriately reflected in the calculation of the proxy value. Dates on which a distribution has been made or is expected would appear in this column. Another important cause of inaccurate portfolio information is a change in the index which is not reflected consistently in the data. Dates of known or expected index changes should be indicated in this column.

Several caveats are necessary. The bids and offers will generally come from the primary market for each security involved. Whether it involves the securities comprising the portfolio basket or the fund shares themselves, an investor's order may or may not be executed in the primary market. Because of the frequency of price and quote changes, especially for the fund shares, these prices provide only a frame of reference—but a very important frame of reference—for an execution in the primary market or away from that market.

We have two more items of unfinished business before we explore some of the implications of the information in Exhibit 8-2 for ETF trading and ETF selection. First, what about the funds with foreign stock portfolios? The absence of contemporary markets in all but the most actively traded foreign stocks during U.S. market hours, makes contemporary portfolio pricing nearly impossible. The problem is not premiums or discounts. It is the absence of enough usable data in a form consistent with the standard set by Exhibit 8-2. This does not mean all hope is lost. A study by analysts at Morgan Stanley has demonstrated that the price of the Japanese iShares MSCI Series reflects the same pricing information as other equity instruments based on Japanese stock prices and futures contracts that trade during U.S. market hours.[16]

Fund Share Price/Index Ratios*

We need to take a brief look at fund share price/index ratios. Fund share price/index ratios have something in common with premium/discount calculations based on NAVs and closing fund share prices: Both are fund pricing guides that should be abandoned.

It has been common practice since the introduction of the original SPDR in 1993 to begin trading in fund shares at a price which is a specified fraction or multiple of the value of the underlying index. For example, the S&P 500 SPDR NAV was originally set at one-tenth of the level of the S&P 500 Index. The problem with such a number is that investors take it as a received truth that the fund shares should always trade very close to this fraction of the index level. In making this assumption, they tend to forget that some funds will accumulate investment income and pay dividends at intervals. The appropriate share price to index ratio will change slightly from day to day to reflect these accumulations and payments. Less frequently, a fund's expenses may exceed its investment income, leading to a small but steady decline in the fund price relative to its index ratio. The NASDAQ 100 Trust is an example of an ETF with an expense ratio higher than the negligible dividend yield of its portfolio stocks. Of greater importance long term, if a fund makes capital gains distributions, the ratio relationship will be permanently changed. Last on the list, but potentially very important, is possible tracking error between the fund and the index. Investors should avoid reliance on ratios of initial fund share prices to index values because the relationship may change for any of these or other reasons. The IDPV is a much more useful fund pricing benchmark during trading hours.

* For a more extensive discussion, see Maier (2000).

As suggested earlier, the problem is not premiums or discounts. It is price discovery. For most ETFs based on domestic stocks, price discovery occurs in the U.S. stock market or, sometimes, the stock index futures market. For foreign markets, unless and until a different set of foreign stock ETFs comes along, the iShares MSCI Series are probably as good a price discovery vehicle for their markets as we have during U.S. market hours. Viewing these ETFs as price discovery instruments in off-market hours and comparing the funds' trading prices to other fragmentary price data is a more useful way to evaluate trading in these funds than reference to premiums or discounts relative to closing prices in the underlying portfolio's primary market.

OTHER TRADING ISSUES IN THE MARKETS FOR EXCHANGE-TRADED FUNDS[17]

An important characteristic of the market for any exchange-traded fund is that the fund share quotes are subject to change every time there is a change in the bid or offer for any of the underlying stocks in the index on which the ETF is based. Of course, *every* quote change in the underlying fund portfolio will not lead to a quote change in the market for the fund shares. Nonetheless, any ETF based on a broad-based index will experience more quote changes in its shares over the course of a trading session than all but the most active and volatile single stocks.

Measuring Market Depth

As described earlier in this chapter, a factor contributing to both the large number of changes in ETF bid and asked quotations *and to the tendency of the portfolio basket bid and offer to be inside the fund share bid and offer* is an SEC requirement that specialists expose public limit orders that improve upon the specialist's or floor "crowd's" market in a listed security. A NASDAQ market maker trading the ETF on an ECN is subject to the same rule for any public limit order. Public limit orders are much *less frequent* in exchange-traded funds than in most individual stocks. The market maker spreads in a fund share are usually narrow and deep (covering a large number of shares) on exchange-traded funds. The tight and deep markets plus very frequent quote changes in fund share markets encourage market orders. Investors have learned that limit orders for relatively small numbers of fund shares may have a less timely and direct connection to the market than larger orders, making their orders stale upon arrival in the market. Such delays, combined with more frequent quote changes, discourage limit orders on fund shares. Public limit orders are more common on the individual stocks in the basket, sometimes making the basket quote appear tighter than the fund share quote and tighter than it really is. The *in-depth* quote on the basket will usually be about as wide as or even wider than the fund share quote. The almost random presence of public limit orders—more common in stocks than in funds—means that the depth of the fund share market is nearly always greater than the apparent depth of the basket market and that the spread of the in-depth basket quote is usually wider than the basket quote suggests. An active futures market in the stock index underlying the fund may actually bring at least one side of the in-depth quote inside the fund share quote.

In evaluating any quotation, the investor should look at the size associated with the quote. If any customer order is at the same price level as the specialist's quote, the size of the bid or offer will be large to reflect the specialist's quote, often well in excess of 100,000 shares, or $10 million worth of securities if the share price is $100. If you ask, you may be able to do $50 or $100 million without much change in the quote. If a small bid or offer has improved upon the specialist's (crowd's) market, the size associated with a quote may be quite small, perhaps as small as 100 shares. Obviously, small public orders carry much less liquidity at the quote than a specialist's quotation for 100,000 shares or more.

Part of the significance of these disparities in quotation sizes is that the small investor might seem, at least at first glance, to have more opportunities to interact with other small investors without intermediation by a market maker. The ability to transact with such small investors will ordinarily be immaterial to the specialist or market maker or to an investor interested in taking a large position. The presence of small retail limit orders has been an occasional source of contention among market makers in rival markets on the one hand and large investors on the other. An investor seeing an attractive quote on a security he/she wants to trade is not pleased to find that the bid or offer is for a very small number of shares. The presence of these retail quotes is misleading to large investors who need to make a special inquiry to learn the price where they can trade in the size they need.

There are usually two price spreads which the large investor needs to think about One of these price spreads is the specialist's (crowd's) market, which will reflect prices at which a substantial block of fund shares can be traded without incurring the costs associated with a creation or redemption by the specialist or some other Authorized Participant. The other price spread of interest is the price at which a substantial number of new fund shares could be created or redeemed to cover the investor's requirements. Indications of these spreads can be obtained from the crowd by inquiry into fund share quotes for large orders. Most investors will find it difficult to analyze the basket quotes to determine the impact of small limit orders directly.

An investor who wants to accumulate a large stock position or feed a large stock position out gradually may leave the order with the specialist or someone else in the crowd to participate in some of the transactions with retail orders coming to the floor. Such an attempt to participate is a time-consuming strategy on a very large ETF order. In the final analysis, the investor must decide if he can be patient or if he must pay for immediacy and incur the cost of creation or redemption of fund shares.

Trading Activity of Fund Shares as a Measure of Liquidity
The appropriate measure of liquidity for any exchange-traded fund share for all but the smallest transactions should be the liquidity of the underlying market for the shares in the index/portfolio. If futures trading in the underlying index is active, the futures contract provides another source of liquidity which may be additive to the liquidity provided by the market in the underlying shares. Finally, to the extent that there is active trading in the fund shares themselves at the level of the NASDAQ 100 (QQQ) or the SPDR (SPY), active trading in the fund shares may add important liquidity. For the most part, however, the market in the fund shares themselves is a derivative market and few funds will achieve the absolute or relative trading volume of the QQQ or the SPY.

For most large investors, interaction with small limit orders is not likely to have much impact on the cost of trading in the sizes in which they prefer to trade. The presence of small retail orders generally will have the effect of making the average reported spread in an actively traded ETF appear to be narrower than it really is. Except for another small retail trader, the opportunity to interact with retail orders should make little difference in the liquidity or trading cost of two fund shares covering the same underlying market (say technology stocks or, as in Exhibit 8-2, financial stocks). Of course, if the trading volume is low in one fund because the index behind the fund is inefficient or ill-suited for use as a fund template, or because the specialist is not making an effective market, there can be significant liquidity and transaction cost penalties associated with taking and selling a position in that fund. This kind of illiquidity will be a problem both for the large investor and the small investor who relies on the liquidity of the specialist's market for later transactions to close out a position. To measure the quality of markets, one simple test is to examine the size of the specialist's market and the spread when no retail orders are present inside the market maker's spread, i.e., when the quote machine shows that the bid or offer is good for 25,000 to 100,000 shares or more on either side of the market on even the least actively traded fund share.

A series of comparisons across several funds that are otherwise comparable should provide an investor with information on the bid-asked spread as a percentage of the share price. This is probably a good indication of market quality for most exchange-traded funds without analysis beyond the resources of most investors. As time goes by, we expect to see a variety of services from both independent fund evaluators and brokerage and trading firms measuring the trading efficiency of various funds. Astute investors of all sizes should benefit from such analyses if they are done well.

Other Determinants of Liquidity
Derivatives
Many exchange-traded funds have options and related index futures contracts available. Today the futures contracts in the United States are on the underlying index, though regulatory changes may soon

permit single-stock futures contracts which will settle "physically" into the underlying fund shares. All of these instruments help improve the liquidity of the index as a basket of securities and, correspondingly, the fund based on the index basket.

Of far more value than index options are options on the fund shares themselves, and these have become increasingly popular. The NASDAQ 100 Trust options, for example, became the most active option contracts traded on the Amex in 2000 and have been the most active contracts on all U.S. option markets combined in 2001. While the contract is relatively small (the underlying is 100 shares of the QQQ fund), the number of QQQ option contracts greatly surpasses the notional equivalent volume in the regular and mini-NDX NASDAQ 100 Index option contracts.

Fund-Friendly Indexes

Other things equal, one of the most important yet subtle determinants of the cost of transacting in the shares of equity exchange-traded funds is the extent to which the fund's index is—naturally or by design—regulated investment company (RIC) compliant.[18] RIC compliance means that the diversification characteristics of the index (and the fund) are such that the fund meets the requirements for treatment as a regulated investment company for tax purposes. Funds based on stock indexes that are not RIC compliant often have to engage in unusual re-balancing transactions periodically or might enter into transactions in derivatives which expose the fund to a certain amount of credit risk—and have some extra cost.

In most cases, a fund based on a non-RIC-compliant stock index will experience more tracking error than a fund based on an index that meets the RIC diversification rules. The combination of periodic tracking deviations and the costs of special transactions to ensure RIC compliance on critical dates will cause specialists and other market makers to incur unusual and unexpected costs with a non-RIC-compliant index. Should the fund miss tracking the index by a material amount, the higher risks and costs associated with mistracking will have an effect on these market makers' enthusiasm for maintaining a tight bid-asked spread. Tracking losses commonly reduce a specialist's or market maker's profitability in trading the product. Consistent tracking gains increase the attractiveness of holding a market-making inventory in a specific fund share and can lead to tighter spreads.

Other features of the index such as its use of rules rather than committee decisions in the elimination and replacement of stocks and re-balancing the weights of various positions at frequent or infrequent intervals will have an effect on the transaction costs of managing the fund. Index rules that reduce frictional trading costs and other costs associated with re-balancing can help reduce the tracking risk which a market maker faces and tighten the spread the market maker is willing to provide. For anyone trading more than, say, $100,000 worth of a single fund, these features can have a greater effect on liquidity and the transaction costs associated with purchasing and selling the fund shares than the level of trading activity in the shares.

Trading Activity—Dollar Volume

Having a fund on the Amex Most Active List is excellent advertising for the fund issuer, but an astute investor will look closely at the factors discussed here and at the dollar volume of trading in the shares. A higher share price will frequently mean a lower bid-asked spread as a percentage of the size of the investment. Tightening the percentage spread on a higher-priced share, as a good specialist and market-making crowd will do, is usually more important in the long run than the number of shares traded. In fact, a more useful most-active list (which we would not be surprised to see someone publish regularly) would reflect the value of fund shares traded, not simply the number of shares. Most-active lists calculated on the value of shares traded are common outside the United States.

ETF DERIVATIVES AND ETFs INSTEAD OF DERIVATIVES

We have noted in earlier chapters that ETFs have at times served as substitutes for futures contracts. The development of a growing variety of index-based exchange-traded funds, increasing competition among specialists and market makers in their trading spreads, and the introduction of the Vanguard VIPERS should combine to accelerate this pattern. The widespread use of the NASDAQ 100 Trust as a substitute for futures suggests that there is ample room for continuation of this trend in other ETFs.

It is probably too early to draw many conclusions about the impact of ETF trading on derivatives markets in general, but a few comments on global trends seem in order, both with respect to products currently trading and additional products which are in various stages of development.

With relatively modest fanfare, the American Stock Exchange introduced options on the NASDAQ 100 index shares at the same time the fund shares began to trade. While the size of this contract is relatively small, reductions in transaction charges associated with option trading and increasing competition in options markets suggests that the small size of the contract is not a major obstacle. As noted earlier, the NASDAQ 100 fund options are now the most actively traded options in the United States. With options on the fund and the fund itself as the two leading ways to take a position in the NASDAQ 100 index, it is easy to see from the volume in both instruments how important fund derivatives and funds as substitutes for derivatives might be in the future. When all option minimum spreads drop to a penny, the NAS-DAQ 100 option volume may jump to a new volume level.

In a late-session move which received relatively little attention at the time, Congress passed the Commodity Futures Modernization Act in December 2000. This legislation renewed the Commodity Futures Trading Commission under the sunset provisions of the Commodity Exchange Act, and eliminated what has come to be known as the Shad-Johnson Amendment, which had prohibited the introduction of futures contracts on individual stocks in the United States.

Exactly how the joint or separate regulation of single-stock futures by the SEC and the CFTC will be implemented is impossible to say at this stage, but logical first candidates for single-stock futures would be futures contracts physically settled into fund shares. This would create a competitive market in an instrument with no cash value component and with slightly lower margin requirements (i.e., intermediate between futures margin requirements for hedged positions and common stock margin requirements).[19] These fund futures could go a long way to reduce the cost of implementation of many of the strategies covering long and short positions discussed in Chapter 5. The availability of physical as opposed to cash settlement should also substantially reduce frictional costs associated with determining a settlement price on cash-settled futures.

The combination of futures and options settling into the fund shares, perhaps on a coordinated expiration basis, should substantially enhance liquidity in all three markets—funds, futures, and options. The role of futures will be primarily to reduce transaction and holding costs with respect to a wide range of strategies which would otherwise call for a short position in the fund shares or a complex option position. There might temporarily be a reduction in the assets held in certain funds, particularly index funds, as shorts no longer dependably generate longs in the fund share positions themselves. In the long run, greater trading activity and the greater usefulness of the fund shares in a variety of risk management applications should enhance the growth of fund assets. While there is no question that the presence of short sellers has been a significant stimulant to the growth of the NASDAQ 100 Trust, the *relative* importance of short sellers (short interest as a percent of shares outstanding) has declined. At current short interest levels, "single stock" futures on the fund will not have a material impact on fund assets, but they should tighten the bid-asked spread on the fund shares even further.

With respect to options on index funds, intellectual property claims have generally prevented effective trading of options on multiple exchanges. Intellectual property claims can still be respected if multiple exchange trading of options on the same fund are licensed—as they are in the case of the NASDAQ 100 fund options.

Futures and options on actively managed exchange-traded funds are, in general, likely to be less popular and less actively traded than futures and options based on index funds. There may be, however, important exceptions to this generalization, and it will be interesting to watch developments. Of particular interest will be what we called in Chapter 7 the Self-Indexing Fund, where the fund price itself creates an index.

Single-Stock Futures (SSFs)—Their Significance for Exchange-Traded Funds

Early in 2002, a number of U.S. exchanges will begin trading a new hybrid product that is *both* a security and a futures contract. The most common name given this product is *single-stock futures (SSFs)*. Each contract will call for receipt or delivery at the contract's maturity of 100 shares of an underlying security— 100 ETF shares in the case we are interested in. SSFs will be carried in securities accounts and margined much like stock options.

Single-stock futures originated in Eastern Hemisphere markets, where common stock trading costs are usually higher than in the United States. Part of the success of financial futures contracts around the world has come from the fact that they are usually exempt from securities transfer taxes and they generally feature lower trading, clearance, settlement, and custody charges than are available in securities markets. Because the higher securities costs are usually associated with trading and holding securities, cash settlement has been the dominant way to handle a maturing financial futures contract, particularly in equity markets. In contrast to markets in other countries, commissions, fees, and taxes on U.S. securities settlements and holdings have declined to the point where they are similar to futures costs. While the cost rationale for cash settlement of futures transactions has largely disappeared in the United States, another issue concerning cash settlement has remained important. Many investors are not comfortable with the idea that their futures position will be closed out at an arbitrary time and at a cash price that is determined by a mechanism they are not totally convinced is immune to manipulation.

U.S. investor aversion to cash settlement is blamed for the decline in trading volume in index option contracts and lack of growth in most cash-settled financial futures.* In contrast, trading volume in physically settled common stock options has continued to grow. Options on ETF shares have been available for only a few years; but, thanks to the QQQ options volume, contract trading volume in ETF options is dramatically greater than volume in all cash-settled U.S. stock index options combined. When there is no significant cost penalty associated with physical settlement, it has become the preferred system in the United States. We expect all exchanges to adopt physical settlement for the new U.S. single-stock futures contracts.

The importance of single-stock futures on ETFs is that they will reduce the cost of selling ETFs short. In fact, reducing the cost of short selling should reduce the cost of trading ETFs for all market participants. The short interest in a U.S. common stock typically represents 1%–2% of the total shares the company has outstanding. In ETFs, it is common for the short interest to represent 10%–50% or more of the shares in the ETF.** Borrowing shares in an ETF to sell short is a relatively simple process, and such shares are nearly always available as an accommodation from specialists and market makers. There is a cost associated with borrowing shares, however. The borrowing cost can be avoided by an investor who, rather than sell short the shares in the ETF, sells a single-stock futures contract to be settled ultimately by delivery of the shares in the ETF.

* Ironically, cash settlement was considered extremely important in the early success of U.S. financial futures markets. See Miller (1986) for a brief but thorough explanation of this history. Gatoh (2001) illustrates some of the problems with cash settlement of a futures contract in the absence of a market-clearing transaction at the opening or at the close of a trading session—the equivalent of a Walrasian call market.

** There was a brief period early in the life of the QQQs when their short interest exceeded the number of shares outstanding. This is possible with linked lending of the same shares more than once and still happens occasionally with smaller ETFs. The short interest is published just after the middle of each month and, contrary to rumor, the growth in QQQ assets is not primarily related to short selling. The recent QQQ short interest has been near the 15%–20% level of the typical larger ETF.

In the current market environment, the specialist or the market maker who lends fund shares to a short seller will finance and carry a long position in the underlying ETF which is fully hedged with short positions in index futures contracts or short positions in the stocks that make up the ETF portfolios. The fund shares are then loaned to the short seller, who invests the proceeds of the short sale in money market instruments, sharing the proceeds of the money market investment with the lender of the ETF shares. There are a number of transactions and payments involved in this accommodation, making the cost associated with a short sale higher than the cost of simply selling the equivalent single-stock futures contract. The investors who are long and short the single-stock futures contract will find that they share an arbitrage spread versus the fund shares trade if a short sale is involved.

Every investor will not be indifferent between single-stock futures and a comparable ETF share position, but a number of investors will find them interchangeable. Consequently, the existence of ETF single-stock futures contracts will result in tighter trading spreads and higher volume for the ETF shares— as well as substantial trading volume in the SSF contracts.

Apart from the ETF application, it is difficult to predict the outlook for single-stock futures. However, this application alone—as ETF markets grow—is ample justification for the SSF product introduction.

DOES THE LIQUIDITY OF EXCHANGE-TRADED FUNDS ENCOURAGE EXCESSIVE TRADING?

Many of the traditional advocates of index funds have not embraced ETFs with enthusiasm. Their reticence usually comes from the belief that active trading of fund shares is inconsistent with the long-term investment focus of indexing. One of the classic arguments for indexing has been that index funds have an advantage over the average actively managed fund because index funds require less trading and portfolio turnover than an actively managed fund. Other things equal, transaction cost savings should help the average index fund outperform the average actively managed fund. If an investor trades the shares in the index fund as if they were shares of a stock, some or all of this expected transaction cost advantage will be lost.

A corollary of the put-it-away-in-a-low-turnover-index-fund thesis is that an investor should stay invested in the same securities for an indefinite period rather than switch from fund to fund or from stock to stock based on the investor's "view" of the market. In short, a buy-and-hold strategy will usually outperform an active trading strategy. Unless there are severe structural problems with the index as the template for a fund or the indexes underlying an investor's fund(s) do not provide adequate diversification, this is reasonable advice for most investors.[20]

One of the most vocal advocates of low turnover and indexing has been John Bogle, founder-chairman of Vanguard. While Mr. Bogle has sold indexing very effectively, he has been notably unsuccessful in selling the buy-and-hold strategy to many of Vanguard's shareholders. While Vanguard has not revealed specific figures for their combined funds, the average Vanguard equity fund shareholder appears to invest for a period only slightly longer than investors in other equity mutual funds.

The anonymity of securities market counterparties makes it difficult to estimate how long various groups of ETF investors hold their shares on average. (See text box on pages 225–226.) The limited data available suggests that broker-dealers, hedge funds, and, to a certain extent, small and mid-sized investment advisors use exchange-traded funds for equitization of cash and other relatively short-term applications. Major institutions are varied users of ETFs. Individual investors also hold the funds for widely varying periods, ranging from a day trade, where the shares are held for part of a trading day up to some very long-term holders who have been in from the beginning and show no signs of letting go. The fact that an investor *can* trade a position in an exchange-traded fund very frequently does not mean that a specific individual *will* trade frequently. Individuals in the aggregate are much longer-term holders of ETFs than, say, broker-dealers who (with hedge funds) account for most ETF trading volume. Even some of the longest-term ETF holders say that being able to sell shares any time during the day gives them a great deal of comfort even if they have no specific intention to use that ability anytime soon.

Setting aside the issue of excessive trading for a moment, exchange-traded funds have two important features that make them considerably "fairer" to investors than conventional index funds. First, without exception, all currently traded ETFs protect the ongoing shareholder from essentially all the costs associated with short-term shareholders moving in and out of the fund. This point was discussed in Chapter 4. In spite of Vanguard's best efforts, they cannot prevent an active trader from getting in and out of one of their conventional mutual funds—at the expense of longer-term shareholders—at least once. One of the features of Vanguard's new VIPERS ETFs is that ongoing fund shareholders are protected from *all* the costs of in-and-out trading by traders who use the VIPERS for a variety of short-term risk management and/or speculative trading activities. The VIPERS shareholders and shareholders who own conventional share classes of Vanguard's funds share this characteristic with all current ETF owners.

A second fairness feature of all currently traded ETFs is of at least equal importance to all an ETF's taxable shareholders. The in-kind redemption feature of ETFs and the same feature in the VIPERS ETF share class will improve the tax efficiency of the entire fund for all *taxable* shareholders. This tax efficiency is significant only in that it delays the taxation of a shareholder's capital gains until the fund shares are sold. This tax feature is of little or no use to a short-term trader, but when the combination of these features is added to the ability of the ETF holder to sell on an intra-day basis—whether he does that soon or years from now—it is clear that the ETF structure brings something important to a fund for every shareholder. Why, then, should the issue of an investor's opportunity to trade in and out of the fund be objectionable to the issuer of the fund? Recognizing fully the commitment which John Bogle and others have to both indexing and long-term investing, it is not appropriate that a feature which is very attractive to some shareholders and seen to be of some value by nearly all of a fund's shareholders should be rejected because short-term trading may not be in the best interests of shareholders.

The supporters of long-term investment in index funds argue in response to challenges to pure indexing that they are simply trying to protect the investor from himself. They argue that the online trader of ETFs or ordinary shares is unlikely to outwit the market in the long run—and will probably underperform the buy-and-hold investor. In response, we observe that the online trader of funds is probably better off than the online trader who trades individual stocks. Transactions costs—absolutely and relative to both the share price and the average daily price change—are usually lower on the fund shares. The issue, however, is not whether trading ETFs does less "harm" than trading stocks; the issue is freedom of choice.

Even if an active trader does not do as well as the average index fund, what about the satisfaction of learning about investing and markets? Who judges the value of another's satisfaction from engaging in these activities? One could argue at least as persuasively that the investor's protectors who believe that the costs of ETF trading are undesirable should be encouraged to argue for more efficient, more fund-friendly indexes as replacements for the benchmark indexes widely used for most index funds rather than arguing against trading fund shares. The critics might also be encouraged to look more carefully at the turnover in exchange-traded fund shares. The argument that the shares in a fund's capitalization turn over in a matter of days in the case of the NASDAQ 100 Fund and every few weeks in the case of the 500 SPDRs is not relevant to the experience of most small shareholders. Reported trading volume exaggerates the significance of turnover to these shareholders. For the most part, the active traders in these funds are not unsophisticated small investors who cannot afford the hypothesized costs and losses from active trading. Most large trades—the trades accounting for substantial volume—are made by broker-dealers and hedge funds that find these ETFs are often more cost-effective or convenient than futures transactions in hedging their broad-market risk—in the case of the SPDRs—and in managing technology stock exposure—in the case of the NASDAQ 100. These risk management applications help reduce transaction costs and improve liquidity for other investors.

Arguing from a utility or welfare perspective, economists have long maintained that the most effective markets are the most complete markets where the choices among close substitutes are most varied. Exchange-traded funds have lowered costs for many of the investors who use them and increased competition with and among conventional index funds. Reduced cost plus enhanced choice is a hard combination to fault. Trading and speculating may be a loser's game from the perspective of economic man, but it is not illegal or immoral and it can add to a trader's satisfaction by providing entertainment and mental stimulation.

As an employee of an issuer and manager of exchange-traded funds, I would far prefer that our shareholders buy ETF shares and hold them indefinitely. However, the "exchange-traded" feature is an important part of the product's success and it appeals to a wide range of investors. Far too much attention has been paid to investor behavior and to what increasingly seems to be an artificial distinction between actively managed funds and well-managed index funds, and far too little attention has been paid to measurable differences among the funds in each category. We cannot and should not attempt to "correct" investor behavior except by pointing out its consequences.

At the risk of compounding a heretical viewpoint, an investor who believes he or she can trade profitably, should *trade* ETFs in a tax-deferred retirement account (IRA or 401(k)) and *hold* ETFs—letting unrealized capital gains compound—in taxable personal accounts.

ENDNOTES

1. In a total market picture, particularly for a very active ETF like the NASDAQ 100 (QQQ) or SPDRs (SPY), there might be a variety of bids and offers on regional exchanges and electronic communications networks (ECNs). Some bids might be above some of the offers and, given the barriers to trading that separate some buyers from sellers who would hit their bid, it might be difficult at a given moment to say just where the spread is. This kind of confusion is

not a major problem for the market in most ETFs, and we will simplify this discussion from the picture created by a large number of small orders in a few of the very active ETFs.

2. Of course, the range in which the price of the small order can fall is very small.

3. HOLDRs (which have many trading characteristics in common with ETFs) ordinarily trade only in 100-share increments.

4. The investor and the firm entering an order to sell ETF shares short are responsible for borrowing shares to deliver to the buyer. The brokerage firm may be unwilling to handle a small short sale, but an investor should not accept a statement from a brokerage firm that fund shares cannot be borrowed. In virtually every case, the exchange specialist will make—or help arrange—a fund share loan.

5. Entry of a new market like the NYSE into trading QQQ, SPY, and the Dow Jones Industrial Average DIAMONDS (their symbol is DIA) may tighten the markets for a period of time, particularly for some small orders.

6. Securities firms are required to tell investors on their trade confirmation where a transaction was executed. This usually appears as a letter or number in a column headed "market" or "exchange." The key to the letter or number is usually on the back of the confirmation. If the trade is not executed on the primary market for the fund (where the shares are formally listed), an investor might monitor the relationship between the posted quote and the execution price.

7. Arbitrageurs buy and sell the same or similar items in different markets to profit from small price differences. The presence of arbitrageurs keeps such differences very small and, generally, relieves other investors from the need to worry about the efficiency of related market price relationships.

8. The reader might question the usefulness of the method of calculating NAV when the same sale prices used to calculate NAV are

used to price creation and redemption baskets exchanged for shares of the fund. Fortunately for both fund shareholders and fund pricing agents, the creation and redemption baskets are close replicas of the fund portfolio, making the exact transfer prices used to price creation and redemption baskets relative to the fund portfolio almost irrelevant.

9. Actually, if the last sale was below the closing bid, the closing bid is ordinarily used as the closing price. If the last sale was above the closing offer, the closing offer is used. If there is no meaningful last sale data, the closing price is usually taken as the mean of the closing bid and offer.

10. The reason for the difference in closing time in the regular session of the securities markets and closing time in the futures markets relates to a combination of an obsolete New York Stock Exchange rule and the relatively restrictive policy which most futures markets have taken to exchange for physical (EFP) transactions. In an EFP, a futures contract, long or short, is exchanged for a comparable position in a securities portfolio or for ETF shares. These low-cost EFP transactions have been popular with upstairs traders and ETF market makers. However, EFPs take volume off the floor of the futures exchange, so they have not been popular with futures exchange members. Until recently, futures exchange rules have been designed to place obstacles in the way of such trades. The New York Stock Exchange rule which restricted EFPs has been changed, and there is every indication that the futures exchanges will modify their rules as well. EFPs are likely to become more common, but we would not predict a change in the 15-minute time gap between securities and futures closing times in the near future.

11. The reason the fund share investor will usually buy at the offer and sell at the bid posted by the specialist and market makers is that relatively few public limit orders for fund shares are placed on the exchange limit order book. There are several reasons for the paucity of limit orders. First, the bid-asked spread in most fund share markets is relatively tight, reducing the incentive to use limit orders. Second, there are more quote changes in the average fund share than

in all but the most volatile stocks. The frequent quote changes make using and changing limit orders very cumbersome for most individual investors.

12. This statement is not fully applicable to some funds on days when an index change is scheduled to be made at the close.

13. This statement is based on the assumption that the IDPV is an accurate reflection of the contemporary value of the fund shares. It should be accurate on most occasions, but it can be based on inaccurate stock prices at times. Furthermore, every organization with a role in its calculation will disclaim any responsibility for the IDPV's accuracy. The reasons for these disclaimers include: (1) the inherent caution of legal advisors; (2) the multiple sources of data used in the calculations; and (3) the relative frequency of erroneous price and quote prints from the underlying markets. A wise investor will accept and use the data with appropriate caution.

14. Most or all of the individual data items in Exhibit 8-2 are available from market data vendors for most funds with domestic portfolios. Usually the information will not be organized as closely or consistently as Exhibit 8-2—hence the usefulness of a website display for cross-fund comparisons.

15. See McNally and Emanuel (2000). Their ongoing analysis found the intra-day proxy value fell within the fund share bid-asked spread 91% of the time. All listed domestic ETFs are included in the study. Increasingly competitive markets in some of the most active ETFs have narrowed spreads, often to a few pennies per share. With spreads this tight, the IDPV will be outside the spread more frequently.

16. Litt and Jhirad (2000).

17. This discussion is oriented primarily to ETFs holding domestic U.S. stocks, but many of the principles are equally applicable to funds holding foreign securities.

18. For ETFs traded outside the United States, natural or designed compliance with the Undertaking for Collective Investment in Transferable Securities (UCITS) diversification requirements is correspondingly important.

19. Single-stock futures will have margin requirements similar to options.

20. See Chapter 6's discussion of index construction issues.

Chapter 9

Developing an Investment Process Incorporating ETFs

I
n this chapter, we reprise a number of the structural issues and obstacles to investment success raised in Chapter 1 and touched on elsewhere in the text. We also describe the standard investment process practiced by experienced financial advisors around the world as they attempt to develop financial and investment plans for their clients and implement them in the form of specific portfolios. It will become clear within a few pages—if the reader retains any doubts—that this is not a work on how to get rich quickly; this book is about the sensible investment of serious money. Furthermore, the emphasis of this chapter is much less on clever ways of incorporating ETFs in an investment plan than it is on getting the overall process right. We are confident that readers of earlier chapters will be comfortable enough with ETFs that relating ETFs to the investment process will be a natural process. We will list a few rules of thumb for ETF selection and evaluation, taken largely from the discussions in earlier chapters.

As recently as a few years ago, quality customized investment advisory services now available to investors with $100,000 or less to invest would have been available only to investors with million-dollar portfolios. The same technological revolution which has reduced execution costs and made online stock trading feasible has automated many features of the investment advisory process.[1] An investor who made the decision to be his own advisor as recently as 12 months ago because he felt good-quality advisory help was not available at an affordable price should meet with representatives of several firms and re-evaluate the decision to go it alone in the light of improved service made possible by advisor training and new software. Improved training by colleges, graduate schools, securities firms, and advisor support and training organizations and the development of some remarkably sophisticated and user-friendly computer programs have improved and simplified many aspects of the investment advisory process.

Investment-oriented computer programs are usually developed first for the advisor market. Later, simplified—or at least more user-friendly—versions are offered to individual investors. We make a few suggestions on how to find out what technology is available to support the independent individual investor, but we caution that the best software for a particular purpose can change quickly. Consequently, the do-it-*all*-yourself approach will require a substantial time commitment from an investor to keep up with infrastructure alternatives as well as investment issues.

This chapter begins with thoughts on developing an appropriate and useful relationship with an advisor. Next comes a discussion of the investment process which the most effective advisors use and which do-it-yourself investors should also follow. The discussion of the investment process is followed by a few general suggestions on incorporating ETFs into a portfolio and a fresh look at the rivalry between index funds and actively managed funds. The chapter closes with a few generalizations from the author's personal experience that might help an investor improve her chances of investment success. While there are some important elements of "how to" in this chapter, there are relatively few absolutes, and the investor should generally feel free to reject suggestions that do not seem useful. If, after appropriate consideration, a suggestion or approach simply does not fit an investor's personal circumstances, the investor should be the final arbiter on what is or will be appropriate in a personal portfolio and, in the broader sense, a personal financial plan.

The role of this "advisory" chapter and the appropriate role of any advisor the investor might employ is to make suggestions, to highlight issues that advisors and investors have found important in the past, and to provide a framework for reaching the best investment policy and implementation decisions possible. There is important material here about ETFs, but the emphasis is on investment survival and success.

Exhibit 9-1: Sources of Help in the Investment Process

Name or Title of Individual	Firm Employing Him or Her	Possible Relative Strengths You Should Expect the Individuals to Have
Financial or Investment Consultant, Advisor, Broker	Investment banking firm/brokerage firm	Knowledge of market structure and procedures; access to useful investment information; experience in developing investment plans
Tax Accountant, CPA	Accounting firm or private practice	Tax and estate planning; ability to monitor investment results
Attorney	Law firm or private practice	Tax and estate planning
Financial Planner	National or local investment planning or consulting firm, investment banking firm, brokerage firm	Experience in developing financial plans; access to information on investment managers and funds; general knowledge of securities, tax, insurance, estate planning
Registered Investment Advisor	Investment advisory or money management firm	Experience and performance record in managing securities portfolios; general knowledge of securities and taxes

THE INVESTOR AND THE ADVISOR

Finding an Advisor

Exhibit 9-1 lists some of the occupational titles used by people who offer various kinds of investment advice and, in some cases, investment products and services. Exhibit 9-2 lists most of the "professional" designations which certain advisors are authorized to use on their business cards and in their presentations to prospective clients. In general, these designations are evidence of a specific type or level of training or experience which should prepare them to help investors in certain ways. No individual advisor can possibly provide the highest-quality advice along every dimension of a client's financial life. An expert in estates and trusts will often know little about investment policy and security selection. A specialist in tax avoidance may be of no help in finding an investment that will generate income or capital gains worth taxing. Advisors with complementary skills often work together to provide a wider range of services for their clients. Even if the appropriate combination is not available in a single organization, a helpful advisor in one field may provide referrals in others.

Exhibit 9-2: Credentials Offered by Investment Specialists

Abbreviated Designation	Full Name	Description
C.P.A.	Certified Public Accountant	Indicates experience with an accounting firm and success in passing licensing exams. Generally specialize in taxes when they deal with individual investors.
P.F.S.	Personal Financial Specialist	Indicates experience in financial planning, taxes; must be a C.P.A. and pass a six-hour exam.
C.F.A.	Chartered Financial Analyst	Indicates experience in securities analysis or related securities experience and success in passing three annual exams covering economics, financial accounting, portfolio management, securities analysis, and standards of conduct.
C.F.P.	Certified Financial Planner	Awarded based on completion of courses and examinations in personal financial and retirement planning and pledged acceptance of a code of ethical standards.
M.S.F.P.	Master of Science in Financial Planning	Indicates completion of a specialized syllabus in a college or university master's degree program. In addition to the degree requirements, the candidate must pass a certification examination given by the College for Financial Planning.
C.I.M.A.	Certified Investment Management Analyst	Indicates experience in the evaluation and selection of money managers; completion of a week-long course at Wharton Business School and a four-hour exam covering asset allocation, risk management, and the like; three years of related experience.
R.F.C.	Registered Financial Consultant	Indicates experience in financial planning; graduate degree in finance or business and four years of full-time experience in the financial industry required.
R.IA.	Registered Investment Adviser	Indicates experience in providing investment advice; disclosure documents must be filed with appropriate regulators.
C.L.U.	Chartered Life Underwriter	Indicates experience in life insurance underwriting; completion of eight courses and three years of insurance experience required.
Ch.F.C.	Chartered Financial Consultant	Indicates experience in financial planning and insurance; eight planning courses and three years' business experience required.
C.F.S.	Certified Fund Specialist	Indicates completion of most of the investment components of the C.F.P. program. Generally specialize in mutual funds, U.I.T.s, and annuities.
P.F.A.	Personal Financial Advisor	Similar to a C.F.P., usually charges fees only.

There are a large number of advisors out there. They do not hide from prospective clients. Every investor has acquaintances who will provide referrals to advisors they have found helpful. There is nothing wrong with accepting invitations to investment seminars from brokers and estate planners or taking adult education courses taught by advisors who teach those classes because they are looking for clients. For your own sake (as well as for the rest of us who like to eat dinner without interruptions), do not respond to telephone solicitations. Ask for hard copies of brochures and/or prospectuses by snail mail or electronic copies by e-mail.

Investors should not necessarily avoid an advisor with a good reputation if he lacks one of the qualifying designations listed in Exhibit 9-2, but these designations can provide some comfort if the advisor is not referred by a knowledgeable and trusted friend. By the time the reader has finished reading this chapter, she should have a reasonable idea of what topics or functions she needs help on and what skills an advisor should have to complement the investor's own skills. An investor who can acknowledge her own strengths and weaknesses should be able to articulate some useful thoughts about the knowledge base and personality type that would be most appropriate in her advisor. A review of the literature on advisor selection is outside this author's interest and expertise; but recognizing that the process is neither easy nor foolproof is an important first step. Many of the personal finance magazines regularly feature articles on advisor selection. Woolley (2001) and Brenner (2001) are excellent examples of advisor selection articles. Brenner (1997), Jaffe (1998), and other book-length treatments provide even more comprehensive guidance on advisor selection and use. Pachetti (2001) and Revell (2001) are interesting reading, but unless the celebrities and other case studies they describe reflect problems similar to your own, their applicability is limited. The lists of screened advisors in Phipps (2001) and Levy, et al. (2001) are the result of a journalistic approach that stops just short of "introducing" the investor and the advisor. Similar lists have been published in the past by *Barron's*, *Medical Economics,* and Bloomberg. If this screening process appeals to you, you may be able to find similar lists in future financial publications. The size of the net worth of the advisor's average client may intimidate some prospects.

Do not let the *process* intimidate you. You may not find a world-class advisor to help you with a $50,000 to $100,000 account, but you can find someone with some experience and a limited account base who will be pleased with the opportunity to work with you if you seem likely to accumulate assets and/or if you might make referrals to other attractive prospects.

Paying the Advisor

Good advice does not come cheap. Incomes of individuals in the financial services industry who provide investment advice and assistance are substantially higher than national-average personal incomes for all occupations. Most advisors expect to be well compensated for the time they spend with their clients because time and advice are what they sell. Some advisors are compensated solely by fees paid by the client, but most also obtain commissions or fees from the sale of products. Often, product-related income to the advisor is used to offset hourly or asset-based fees. The investor needs to know where the advisor's income is coming from. If a product carries a large payment to the advisor when the investor buys it or for several years in the future, that fact is worth knowing. Advisors want their clients to prosper, but conflicts of interest are common and the investor should learn where they are and evaluate their importance.

There are a variety of ways advisors are compensated by separate account money managers, by fund issuers, and by the creators and purveyors of other investment products. None of these compensation payments are or should be a secret to the investor. For the most part, they are revealed in prospectuses or other offering documents or in the ADV Part II statement of a registered investment advisor, all of which are available to any prospective client of the advisor upon request.[2]

A client who finds even the new "plain English" prospectuses to be heavy going might ask a prospective advisor for help in finding information on the fees built into the prices of products and services and for a rough estimate of any commissions the advisor's firm might receive as additional compensation. Any initial resistance to those requests for information should be followed by a frank discussion of the advisor's compensation. Assure the advisor

that you simply want to understand the economics of the relationship from the advisor's perspective and that you recognize the advisor needs to make a living.

If the advisor and the investor decide that they want to work
together, they need to reach an agreement on what and how the
advisor will be paid. While the investor has the right to know what
the advisor is earning on products, transactions, and services, nothing could be more unproductive than for an investor who wants the
time, attention, and assistance of the advisor on an extremely important part of her future financial security to drive so hard a bargain as
to damage the relationship with the advisor. Advisors are used to
meeting investors whose initial fee expectations are unrealistically
low, so you will not be surprising them. No investor should expect
to be able to engage a fully qualified advisor who does not have a
realistic expectation of earning *more than* $100 per hour (net of the
overhead of the advisor's firm, but before taxes) for the time committed to their relationship. Most advisors, particularly those in
major cities, will consider the $100 figure to be too low.

The investor should bear in mind that the gross revenue paid
in fees to an advisor who is employed by a financial services firm
must cover the firm's overhead (including compensation of support
personnel) and profit as well as the compensation of the individual
or individuals the investor deals with on a regular basis. Usually, the
advisor will receive less than half of the gross fees paid by the
investor. So for most advisors to net a minimum of $100 per hour,
gross fees will have to be over $200 per hour.

How the advisor is paid is sometimes as important as how
much he is paid. As noted in the tax discussion in Chapter 4, an
investor will often be better off from a tax perspective if the payment for the advisor's help is incorporated in the cost of a product.
In this way, the cost of paying the advisor will be deducted from
ordinary income or, at worst, from long-term capital gains before
the investor calculates his tax bill. If an investor pays the advisor a
management fee directly, the fee will not be deductible (will not
reduce taxes) unless the investor's miscellaneous deductions exceed
2% of gross income and are not adversely affected by tax law provisions that diminish the value of certain deductions for high-income

taxpayers. Since it is obviously better to pay a fee with pre-tax dollars than with after-tax dollars, the conflict-of-interest-free purity of a fee-only advisor relationship may not make good tax sense for an investor.

These figures and this process should not discourage you. You and an advisor can conspire to make very efficient use of her time. Several questionnaires can help investors get and organize information to evaluate an advisor.[3] The probabilities are high that your prospective advisor has filled out one of these questionnaires or a similar one for another prospect and will not have to spend time on yours if you offer to accept something similar. The advisor will respond by giving you a questionnaire. Take it seriously and answer it thoroughly, so the two of you can spend as much "face" time as possible on topics your respective questionnaires indicate are important to you and to your relationship with the advisor.

THE INVESTMENT PLANNING AND IMPLEMENTATION PROCESS FOR AN INDIVIDUAL INVESTOR

Exhibit 9-3 is based on two analyses and discussions of the investment process. Trone, Allbright, and Taylor (1996) set the standard in their formal discussion of the investment process in their book, *The Management of Investment Decisions* (McGraw-Hill). Their name for each step is indicated in bold on Exhibit 9-3 and in the sub-section headings in this section. Much of their discussion is designed to support the investment process at a pension fund or other institutional investment organization, but the process works equally well—usually with simplification—for an individual's investments. The portion of the label for each step in italics comes from Winks (2001), an article by an experienced senior brokerage executive who has given considerable thought to the investment process and how it should be practiced and has written extensively on the advisory process. The description of the process in each step is the present author's compilation and interpretation of the investment process discussion from both these sources.[4]

Exhibit 9-3: The Investment Planning and Implementation Process for an Individual Investor

Step 1. **Analysis**/*Asset Study*

Develop and evaluate a comprehensive list of assets and liabilities with clear descriptions of unusual items and cost basis information on all assets

Determine legal and regulatory constraints affecting restricted assets

Evaluate historic performance, expenses, risk, diversification

Develop income history, evaluate prospects and retirement plans

Examine tax returns

Search for non-earning assets

Step 2. **Optimize**/*Diversify/Strategic Asset Allocation*

Design an asset allocation that fits the investor's risk/return objectives

Part of the objective of this step is to improve the investor's understanding of diversification, risks, and returns and the mechanics of the transition to the new portfolio

Discuss costs, tax sensitivity, liquidity, and investment horizon

Risk tolerance, asset comfort, time horizon, and expected/needed returns from investments

> Risk impact—Financial engines or comparable software
>
> Asset classes—Employment and stock options may concentrate industry exposure, analyze visceral preferences
>
> Time horizon—Anticipate changes as retirement nears, plan a future time for reappraisals, longer time horizon usually means more equity
>
> Expected returns—What is realistic?

Step 3. **Formalize**/*Investment Policy Statement*

Establish a clear outline of who is responsible for each part of the plan

Output should be a formal investment plan linked to investment objectives and asset allocation

Define: Minimum level of cash reserves for emergencies

> Attitude toward taxes

Set re-balancing policy, define guidelines and allocation narrowly

Set securities and instruments guidelines, policy on manager qualifications

Set asset control procedures and responsibilities, performance criteria

The plan should be clear enough that another advisor could take over implementation if necessary

Exhibit 9-3 (Continued)

Step 4. **Implement**/*Manager (Fund) Search and Selection*
Selecting a fund is similar to selecting a manager—but not identical
> Managers operating through consultants usually respond to information requests
> Fund services often compile information that funds provide rather than insist on specific answers that investors want.

Selection procedure should be formalized and followed consistently
Avoid too many funds/managers for the assets available
Consider how to evaluate performance data: absolute vs. relative; peers vs. benchmark
Adherence to stated style or objective
Conflicts of interest
Investment process
Consider alternative investments
Averaging vs. lump sum, indexing vs. active management, international?
Guaranteed Investment Contracts (GICs), Variable Annuities

Step 5. **Monitor**/*Performance Monitor*
Determine monitoring frequency—quarterly vs. annually
Compare managers/funds to benchmark, peer group and policy statement objectives
Verify comfort with risks taken, measure risks vs. return, short and long term
Check fees and expenses against plan
Monitor all policy and procedural provisions

Step 6. **Re-balance**/*Tactical Asset Allocation*
Adjust allocations to reflect current reality: low interest rates, high or low equity valuations
Decide on re-balancing time interval or size of performance determined imbalance
Remember that re-balancing costs money

Bold title of each step used in Trone, Allbright, and Taylor (1996)
Italicized title of each step used in Winks (2001)

Some advisors will take different approaches than the process we describe here. Some will add steps and suggest additional lines of inquiry and analysis. Others will bypass some of the steps described here. The reader should think twice before discarding whole sections of Exhibit 9-3. Each step should be relevant to most individual investors' financial planning. Of course, if you decide to work without an advisor, these steps describe what you should be doing by yourself.

Analysis/*Asset Study*

This first step in the planning process is designed to make sure that the investor and the advisor have a clear understanding of the investor's current situation and, to the extent possible, the investor's prospects. Some individual investors are quite well organized and have most of their raw financial data at their fingertips. More commonly, an investor will start with good intentions and, as time passes and his responsibilities multiply, the effort to keep close tabs on his personal financial situation will slide. While not everyone can keep his records up to date at all times, periodic reviews are essential and the start of a relationship with a new advisor is an ideal time for an update. The experience of most advisors and their clients is that this step alone is often worth the cost and effort of engaging an advisor. The perspective it provides and the fresh look at one's financial situation can be invaluable in approaching a variety of future issues ranging from investment to employment to personal lifestyle decisions. A growing number of advisors use and provide statements compatible with one or both of two popular programs, Money and Quicken. An investor will find that he can save his own time and an advisor's time by using one of these systems for record keeping. Automatic and semi-automatic links to these programs take time to set up, but it is often time well spent.

Optimize/*Diversify/Strategic Asset Allocation*

This step is in many respects the heart of the investment process. As the text box beginning on page 272 indicates, financial advisors routinely emphasize the critical importance of asset allocation. Asset allocation is probably less of a factor in determining investment results than it is often described as being; but it is, nonetheless, extremely important and worth any effort expended on it. An advisor and/or in some cases software programs like Financial Engines' or Fidelity's, which are offered to many 401(k) plan participants, or Financeware.com, which is offered to and through advisors, can be of considerable value in helping an investor evaluate the risk and return features of assets and asset classes considered for inclusion in the portfolio. An experienced advisor can help by putting the investor's attitude toward risk and expectations for possible returns in the context of personal experience and in the context of the decisions and experiences of other clients.

The asset allocation process gives the investor and the advisor an opportunity to understand each other's perspectives better and should give the investor a better understanding of the mechanics and limitations of diversification. The advisor and investor will learn about any strong feelings the other has on the attractiveness and desirability of various assets and asset classes. Among the topics the parties should discuss are (1) the range of possible investment strategies, (2) investment tactics, (3) realistic expectations as to how specific asset classes fit and their expected contributions to results, (4) the significance of an investor's employment and possible employer stock and stock option plans for the diversification of financial risk, (5) the effect of any high-value but low-cost-basis asset like an employer's stock or real estate that may affect your flexibility in asset allocation, and (6) the appropriate time horizon—20 to 40 years or longer for a young investor, but a shorter period for an investor nearing or past retirement. Most importantly, both parties should have similar expectations for the level and variability of returns from various asset classes.

How Important Is Asset Allocation?

It has become a mantra among many financial advisors that "Asset allocation accounts for 90% (or more) of portfolio performance." This conclusion stems primarily from two *Financial Analysts Journal* articles which attempted to find the "determinants of portfolio performance": Brinson, Hood, and Beebower (1986) and Brinson, Singer, and Beebower (1991). Almost from their first appearance, these articles drew both praise and criticism—praise for the simplicity and elegance of the analysis, criticism from the intuitive reaction that ascribing so much importance to a single high-level portfolio allocation decision did not make sense. When the conclusion is examined from various performance perspectives, a lower dependence on asset allocation seems more defensible. Among the sternest critics of the original papers was Jahnke (1997); but other academics and practitioners, including Loeper (1999, 2000a), have joined the controversy—on both sides.

While the precise importance of asset allocation has not been resolved to everyone's satisfaction, a consensus has begun to form around a re-examination of the Brinson, et al. papers and a reformulation of the questions they asked. Specifically, when Ibbotson and Kaplan (2001) redid the Brinson, et al. studies with more recent data and formulated the question in the same way Brinson, et al. had stated it, they, too, found that about 90% of the *variability of returns across time* (the funds' pattern of ups and downs) was explained by asset allocation policy. However, when the question was reformulated to ask how much of the *variation in returns among funds* is explained by differences in policy, the result was quite different. In answering this question, Ibbotson and Kaplan found that asset allocation policy accounted for about 40% of the differences between two funds' performance.

The latter question—and result—is closer to the issue and to the intuitive expectations of those who had questioned the original Brinson, et al. studies on the basis that 90% was simply too much of the return variation to attribute to the asset allocation decision.

While a definitive analysis of this issue is beyond the scope of the present volume, it is interesting to step back and consider the calculation of R^2—which in a study of this kind is referred to as the co-efficient of determination because it generally shows how much of a phenomenon is accounted for or "determined" by a specific independent variable. In many financial time series, it is possible to achieve a high rate of price or return correlation (R) and still have quite different return levels. The returns over each time period tend to move *in the same direction* for all portfolios, even if the *magnitude* of the moves is quite different in different portfolios. The high values of R and R^2 for portfolios with very different returns are much like the case of broad-based equity market indexes. These indexes are highly correlated, but they often produce significantly different returns when used as templates for index funds. In other words, the correlation is high because the portfolios are nearly always moving in the same direction, but the tracking error is also high because the magnitude of the movements varies significantly among the indexes. A similar phenomenon seems to be at work in the attempt to measure the importance of asset allocation.

> Asset allocation is clearly important, but the 40% weight accorded it by the more recent Ibbotson and Kaplan study is almost certainly a more appropriate number for most purposes than the older 90% figure. The good news is that an investor does not have to ignore almost everything other than asset allocation. The bad news is that the investor *cannot* ignore everything else.

On the latter point, the technology boom of the late 1990s created some unrealistically high common stock returns in many portfolios, and those same portfolios suffered substantially in 2000 and 2001 unless they were substantially reconstituted. Other investors underperformed in the late nineties but enjoyed relative prosperity from their stock investments in 2000 and 2001. Obviously, no investor or advisor should expect or promise (respectively) such results for a future period, but questions of style, approach to risk, and expected returns should elicit compatible responses from both parties. Any investor who questions the importance of continuing to move asset allocation in the direction of achieving and maintaining the highest degree of diversification consistent with the undiversifiable positions found in some portfolios should periodically re-examine Exhibits 1-2 and 1-3 and reread the discussion of risk and diversification in Chapter 1.

A topic which is rarely discussed in sufficient depth at the beginning of a relationship is the investor's and the advisor's attitudes toward taxes. Different approaches to taxes can be the basis for as much controversy—and as much ill will between an investor and an advisor—as any other issue. Accepting the risk of injecting a personal value judgment, the most constructive attitude toward taxes is that the fundamental policy objective should be to maximize the assets and cash flow that an investor and the investor's family will have at their disposal to accomplish their personal financial objectives. Whether these objectives emphasize a high level of consumption or a high level of charitable contributions, is a decision for the investor, and the role of the advisor should be to help in the implementation.

Some investors and some advisors take extreme attitudes toward taxes: either that taxes should be ignored or that the principal objective of any investment policy should be to minimize taxes even if that occasionally entails a sacrifice in after-tax return. Failure of the investor and the advisor to agree on how tax issues should be addressed is a cause of many investor/advisor divorces. Ironically, the complexity of many tax issues makes the inability of some parties to determine an optimal tax policy inevitable. A disagreement on the approach to taxes need not be fatal to an advisor-investor relationship, but if there is a distinct difference in approach, the parties need to be prepared to look for and work on developing a consensus both can live with. As with every other issue under discussion here, the final call belongs to the investor. A good advisor will accept that, but she will try to change your mind if she is convinced you are wrong. You are paying for this advice, so listen carefully.

Development of well-articulated investment objectives is particularly important. Is the investor interested in absolute returns or relative returns? In other words, will the investor be happy with a 10% return year after year when investors in the latest hot sector are earning 30% in the current year? It is important to agree in advance whether a manager should be evaluated on absolute or relative performance, and whether a relative performance comparison should be to a money manager's peers or to an agreed-upon performance benchmark index. The parties will generally examine a manager's or a fund's adherence to a stated style objective, evaluate the manager's investment process, and try to eliminate possible conflicts of interest.

There are a wide variety of investment choices to consider and evaluate in addition to the perennial issue of indexing versus active management discussed later in this chapter. The parties should examine the role of international investments, alternative investments such as hedge funds, etc. If the value of an investor's assets are likely to be essentially static, apart from investment gains, the asset allocation will be relatively simple and periodic re-balancings can be used to bring assets back into line if they get out of line as a result of superior or inferior performance in one asset or another. On the other hand, if an investor has a substantial cash flow—either in or out—decisions will have to be made as to how assets are going to be allocated in the period ahead or how obligations are going to be covered through liquidation of assets.

An investor who wants maximum involvement in the investment process and maximum control of her investment destiny will find frequent reviews of asset allocation and portfolio management software in a wide range of publications. For example, Braham (2001) features a review of some asset allocation programs that are often available as part of a financial planning package from your 401(k) service provider. Publications of the American Association of Individual Investors such as the *AAII Journal* and *Computerized Investing* and Walter Mossberg's columns in the *Wall Street Journal* and *Smart Money* often feature excellent software and hardware reviews. More specialized software is reviewed in Fazzi (2001).

Very few types of investments should carry generic red warning flags to keep investors away. Two products which should generally be avoided but which are too often found in investor portfolios are guaranteed investment contracts (GICs) and variable annuities (VAs). Guaranteed investment contracts are common in 401(k) plans. They are basically pooled debt instruments issued by insurance companies with certain commitments to interest rate payments and restrictions on sale or liquidation designed to protect the issuer from losses on a high-yield bond portfolio that generates returns for the GICs. In general, the lure of unrealistically and unsustainably high returns from GICs should be resisted by most investors. A stable value fund which holds a diversified bond portfolio is usually a better way to obtain some of the high-yield features associated with GICs. The stable value fund will usually offer a reduction in some kinds of risk and significantly lower embedded costs.

Variable annuities tend to be oversold to investors who are highly sensitive to taxes. Variable annuities have a few useful applications because of their insurance features; but ETFs eclipse them on all cost comparisons and most tax comparisons because of the combination of tax deferral, capital gains rates on eventual distributions, and potential step-up of basis at death with the ETF. Any variable annuity investments should be done with one of the lower-cost providers of such annuities—Vanguard and Fidelity come to mind, but there are other relatively low-cost providers.

Formalize/*Investment Policy Statement*

This step is the outcome of the previous step. As the word *formalize* suggests, it involves the production of a document which outlines individual responsibilities and spells out the decision reached in the asset allocation process. The formal statement will include specific decisions often glossed over in a broad asset allocation plan, such as the level of cash reserves to be maintained, a formal statement of the attitude toward taxes to be adopted in the management of the investor's assets, and guidelines on things as diverse as when the asset allocation will be re-evaluated, when the portfolio will be re-balanced, and what securities and other instruments such as futures and options are appropriate, either to make allocation adjustments in the portfolio or to accomplish other objectives.

If the primary advisor is going to be one of several or, alternately, the sole money manager, a set of guidelines and responsibilities needs to be spelled out. If the advisor's responsibility is to help find and engage other money managers, procedures and responsibility for management policies need to be stated. Accounting and auditing functions—to the extent the parties believe these necessary in the context of the relationship with specific money managers—should be part of the formal financial plan. One thing which nearly all advisors emphasize is that the plan should be clear enough that another advisor could take over implementation of the plan, if necessary.

Implement/*Manager (Fund) Search and Selection*

An investor may engage one or a number of managers to help implement the asset allocation process or the management of one or more asset classes. Most advisors have worksheets and questionnaires designed to elicit the information on which to base selections. Many investors find aspects of the manager or fund selection decision to be difficult to get their arms around because they do not see clear criteria for selection.

As one example of a complex decision, choosing a manager or a fund to implement an asset class allocation is not just a case of selecting last year's top performer. The consensus of most serious studies is that a manager's past performance is not an ideal guide to the future, but it is slightly better than nothing. An extraordinarily high return in an unusual market period or with an unusual investment technique should lead the investor and her advisor to approach a top-performing money manager with caution. The selection procedure should be formalized and followed consistently, but this does not mean that a process that does not seem to be working cannot be modified or even abandoned. As noted elsewhere, we expect the growth of ETFs to lead to major changes in the way investors and fund analysts approach the fund selection process.

Monitor/*Performance Monitor*

This should be a relatively simple step. It should be designed to occur regularly and systematically. If the process is not designed to be efficient, there will be a tendency to put it off and to run the risk of unsatisfactory results going unrecognized and uncorrected. The investor and the advisor need to agree on a monitoring frequency. Obviously, quarterly monitoring gives more frequent results and analysis than annual monitoring, but it also engages more of the advisor's time and will increase costs. For most investors, a full-scale annual portfolio review is probably most appropriate. Funds and managers will be compared to appropriate benchmarks—either indexes or peer groups or both—and to the policy statement objectives. The parties should verify everyone's comfort with the risks taken, compare the risks with returns, and determine that the investor is still comfortable with the asset allocation and not unpleasantly surprised by how the portfolio behaved in the context of the period's market environment.

Someone—probably the investor's tax preparer or accountant—should check fees and expenses against the plan, and the procedures of all service providers should be checked for compliance with adopted policies.

Re-balance/*Tactical Asset Allocation*

This is a simple step, usually done as a result of and in connection with the performance monitoring process. Allocations need to be adjusted for recent portfolio behavior and current market realities such as the level and term structure of interest rates, the level of equity market valuations, etc. The investor and advisor should discuss and agree upon a re-balancing time and/or on the size of any performance-determined imbalance that will trigger re-balancing.

It is important that the investor and advisor pay attention to the costs of re-balancing. Transaction costs are more a function of market impact than of commissions—which are nominal or even non-existent for most advisor-managed accounts. Market impact is an important consideration in any re-balancing involving less liquid securities. Re-balancing will usually have a tax impact if taxable accounts are involved. The tax impact of the re-balancing should be carefully evaluated. It might be a good trade-off to defer re-balancing if the tax and transaction costs of re-balancing are large relative to the size of the imbalance to be corrected. For example, if your current allocation to small growth stocks is too high by 1% of the value of the portfolio and you estimate the tax, commission, and market impact cost of bringing the allocation into line to be one-quarter of 1% of the value of the portfolio, it probably does not make sense to re-balance. There is no bright line test for deciding when to re-balance, however.

INCORPORATING ETFs INTO THE FINANCIAL PLAN

Rather than highlight the virtues of ETFs at every opportunity in the previous section, it seems more appropriate to deal with the attractions and the role of ETFs in the implementation of a financial program in a separate section. We have implicitly assumed that the investor who has read this far shares our enthusiasm for the virtues of ETFs as an important part of most individual investment portfolios, particularly in the portion of those portfolios that are subject to taxation on realized capital appreciation.

Cost and Tax Savings in Asset Allocation

We anticipate that many asset allocation decisions will center on which ETFs to use or what manager or advisor who uses ETFs in portfolios or fund-of-fund applications to employ. The diversity of ways to achieve effective diversification with ETFs, the tax efficiency of well-managed equity ETFs when held very long-term in a taxable portfolio, the transaction and management cost control they permit in the hands of a skilled asset allocation practitioner, and the growing availability of different asset classes and sub-classes embodied in ETFs, all make extensive use of ETFs a natural process. Once actively managed ETFs are available, their variety and flexibility will further increase opportunities to use ETFs, especially in taxable accounts. Assuming that the investor and the advisor have a similar view of the virtues of ETFs to that espoused in these pages, there are a number of money managers who use ETFs extensively in asset allocation programs; there are a number of advisors of all kinds who have developed specialties and subspecialties in ETFs. ETF knowledge and skills are increasingly important, and an investor should expect to find some knowledge of ETFs on the part of most advisors she will be interviewing. The investor and the advisor should explicitly consider how ETFs can efficiently replace other portfolio segments and how a portfolio of specialized ETFs can offer some of the tax loss harvesting opportunities usually associated only with individual stocks. Aggregating a desired portfolio exposure with an ETF can reduce the market impact component of trading costs and save some of the advisor's time to focus on other important issues—or to permit a fee reduction.

What to Avoid

This is a good spot to offer some generalizations on what to look for and what to avoid in selecting specific ETFs. Many of these suggestions appear elsewhere in the text, but it makes sense to summarize them in a single location. These cautions were written with index funds in mind, but a number of them will be equally applicable to actively managed funds.

Avoid equity ETFs that:

- Use representative sampling to manage an index portfolio solely because the index itself is not RIC compliant. Representative sampling can be effective in reducing costs if there are more than, say, 500 names in the index. If the index has 100 or fewer stocks, the index should be fully replicated and the index should be naturally RIC compliant. This means that the Sector

SPDRs are the only U.S. sector funds available at this writing that should be used without a close look at the specific underlying sector index. (Issues: tracking, transaction cost control, performance measurement.)

- Require the fund to use more than two or three national or international clearance and settlement regimes. This rule is proposed to disqualify most multinational funds until at least 2003. (Issues: costs incurred by Authorized Participants (dealers), fund costs not reflected in the expense ratio, tax efficiency.)
- Use inefficient (high-trading-cost) indexes. This makes S&P 500 funds far more costly than they appear and Russell 2000 funds probably unacceptable. The best choice for a broad-market U.S. fund given choices available in late 2001 is the Vanguard Total Market Index VIPERS. (Issues: high trading costs not reflected in the expense ratio).
- Use global indexes where foreign securities will not be more than half of the portfolio. (Issues: tax inefficiency, clearing and settlement inefficiencies not reflected in the fund expense ratio.)
- Do not manage to avoid capital gains distributions. (Issues: poor fund management, poor index, or both.)
- Fund analysts criticize for high transaction costs. (Issues: This is not an easy call for most fund analysts to make, and few would make it lightly, so the investor should believe the analyst unless the fund offers compelling evidence to the contrary. Remember, the most important transaction cost internal to the fund is usually market impact, not commissions or ordinary trading spreads.)

Avoid both equity and fixed-income ETFs that:

- Display a large or consistently unfavorable tracking error relative to their index before expenses. (Issues: poor index, poor fund management, or both.)

In general, an ETF manager should be able to avoid taxable capital gains distributions in an equity fund without incurring extra costs that unfairly penalize non-taxable investors. Barring an unanticipated change in the tax law, this should be as true for actively managed funds as for index funds. Capital gains distributions in an equity ETF are evidence of problems in the index or, more likely, in the ability and commitment of the portfolio manager to tax efficiency. An equity ETF issuer with a history of capital gains distributions should be used with caution. Avoiding realized capital gains in a fixed-income ETF can require artificial and expensive techniques to deal with situations where each of a large number of transactions realizes a small capital gain as interest rates decline gradually. Some fixed-income ETFs may be able to avoid capital gains distributions without extra costs, but it can be harder to accomplish and has a larger element of randomness than tax efficiency in an equity ETF. A better strategy is to try to hold positions in the fund for long-term gains, if possible.

ETF Derivatives

It is probably appropriate to include a word or two on ETF derivatives, specifically options on funds and single-stock futures contracts physically settled into an ETF. The latter product is not yet available as this is being written, but we expect it to be available in the United States by early 2002. The former product, options on funds, is not available on all funds as a result of licensing issues involving the purveyors of certain benchmark indexes that have historically licensed their indexes for index options under exclusive agreements which do not permit licenses on options on fund products. We would expect that two types of derivatives will be developed for most successful equity ETFs: one type with the asymmetric payout structure associated with options and the other type with the symmetric payout structure associated with single-stock futures contracts. Thus, there will be two ways to modify an investor's exposure to the underlying ETF. Not every investor or advisor will feel the need to use these derivatives, but some will find them extremely useful at times to provide a temporary and tax-efficient adjustment to an asset allocation. Under certain circumstances, however, purchase or sale of an option or a single-stock futures contract to reduce exposure to a position held as a long-term capital asset may trigger a tax event, so professional tax advice is essential.

This is particularly true with these ETF-linked derivatives instruments because there are some unresolved tax questions, largely in connection with risk-reducing transactions, that may trigger realization of a capital gain.

Without elaborating extensively, unwanted tax events usually can be avoided by using ETF futures and options on *broadly similar* indexes or portfolios that are part of the same asset class rather than an ETF derivative on the fund held by the investor. For example, an investor long an S&P 500 index fund might buy a put on a Russell 1000 index fund to reduce downside risk while retaining upside exposure. Exposure both on the upside and the downside could be reduced by the sale of a Russell 1000 fund futures contract. The possibilities are extensive and they can be extremely attractive to both tax-sensitive and tax-insensitive investors under appropriate circumstances. These derivatives will undoubtedly be the subject of at least a few articles and perhaps some books of their own.

INDEX FUNDS VERSUS ACTIVELY MANAGED FUNDS

Most equity investors are familiar with the fact that in most annual performance comparisons, the majority of actively managed funds (whether measured by a body count or weighted by assets) underperform index funds. This should come as no surprise. Actively managed funds usually have higher expense ratios and higher transaction costs than index funds. The *average active fund almost has to fall behind the average index fund.* A closely related issue has pitted indexers against active managers in discussions that occasionally pass into incivility.[5] The principal subject of this related debate is: *Can an active manager add value?* Since the numbers suggest that the average manager appears to add value less than half the time, and most managers have occasional bad years, establishing that a particular manager adds value requires (1) a long trial period, (2) statistical tests that measure expected deviations from the mean, and (3) consistent favorable deviations by active managers with the best records. Indexing advocates dismiss the records of legendary active managers as the expected favorable extreme values generated by an essentially random process. Besides, they ask, how does an investor find the legendary manager before the record has been established?

Active managers and their academic supporters (not *all* academics advocate indexing) answer that tests for consistency in year-to-year performance indicate that prior performance is at least a weak indicator of future performance and that their tests can detect some anomalies that will help find top managers relatively early in their runs. Unfortunately, the statistical tests a specific manager must pass to establish unquestionable portfolio management superstar qualifications are inconsistent with biology and psychology (the length of most managers' careers as managers of portfolios for public investors) and the effect of compounding a high return (the change in size of the portfolio from the beginning to the end of a manager's career). On the latter point, the manager's job is different when it consists of managing a few million dollars early in a career than it becomes after high returns and publicity have attracted a hundred billion dollars. In wrapping up their case, the supporters of active management point to specific managers and to studies that confirm the existence and support the detectability of valuation anomalies, however ephemeral, that can serve as the basis of successful active management.

Both sides make good points, and the investor should consider the applicability of all the arguments to his own situation before committing money to either an index fund or an active manager. Economically, the resolution is straightforward. Added costs are a handicap to an active manager just like extra weight is a handicap to the strongest horse in some races. *The investor and his advisor should attempt to evaluate the incremental return value of the active manager's strategy and capability relative to the size of his cost handicap.* On the surface this sounds too easy. It is not easy, but at least it is essentially the right question. Most fund purchase decisions are made on less solid ground than this. If the investor and advisor are not satisfied that the manager's approach gives the manager a likely edge over an index fund after higher costs, they should go with the index fund or a mix of index funds.

In Chapter 1, we pointed out that active traders trading in relatively small sizes have a much smaller handicap today than similar traders had 25 years ago. This is not a suggestion that the reader become an active trader. It is simply a statement that a modest edge in understanding the investment characteristics of a company or the significance of a macro investment issue is easier to turn into a trading profit than it has ever been before. It is still not easy in an absolute sense.

We can make a similar case for active management. The reductions in trading costs when the trade is small enough to limit market impact makes small-scale active management more likely to succeed than it has been in the past. A number of studies have concluded that a skilled active manager may add value.[6] Other recent studies have found pockets of inefficiency in securities markets, suggesting at least a few opportunities for systematic return enhancement and lending credibility to the quantitative analysts who offer enhanced index strategies.[7] Of greater importance, the use of indexes that are not fund-friendly and the growing market impact costs associated with changes in portfolios based on popular benchmark indexes like the S&P 500 and the Russell 2000 makes the small-scale active manager's handicap relative to funds based on these indexes smaller than that handicap has been. In addition, the ETF structure will help remove some of the historic tax penalties associated with active management inside an investment company structure.

The preceding paragraph *is not* a call to abandon indexing for active management. It *is* a strong argument that the historic (1) cost and (2) tax disadvantages of active management relative to indexing are increasingly manageable. It is also a strong statement to most of the index fund industry that it is collectively on the wrong track. Index managers have dissipated a significant fraction of their cost advantage over active management. They rely on inefficient indexes, on indexes *managed* by committees, and on a small number of major indexes that lead most index funds with similar objectives to buy and sell at the same time. These features of contemporary indexing are all contrary to the original principles of indexing. Investors and advisors should hold index fund managers to higher standards than many of them have been meeting in recent years.

In closing this topic, a paragraph from a recent article in the *The New York Times* on index funds versus actively managed funds strikes a resonant chord:

A. Michael Lipper, president of Lipper Advisory Service, also said index funds made particular sense for investors who also own more aggressive, expensive funds. "The nice thing about mutual funds is that you don't have to draw a firm conclusion," he said. "You can mix index and actively-managed funds and hedge your bets. And it doesn't have to be 50-50," he added, without quite tipping his hand.[8]

SOME GENERALIZATIONS ON INVESTMENT SUCCESS

As we near the end of this book—and the end of this chapter devoted to the investment process and investment policy—I would like to take advantage of an author's position to offer a few observations on ways to increase your chances of investment success.

Do Your Homework

Although the emphasis in much of this volume has been on the specifics of ETFs and the desirability of having help from a capable advisor in using them, the investors who do best usually understand their investments most thoroughly. While many advisors say that they would like an investor to simply turn his affairs over to them, the same advisors tend to perform best when challenged in a constructive relationship with an astute investor who knows as much as possible about investments and how to invest successfully. Usually, the best investors are those who understand investments very well themselves and can enhance their own effort with the skills of an appropriate advisor. Doing your homework and understanding the instruments and companies you are investing in is an important part of investment success. At first, your interest in understanding your investments may take more of an advisor's time than a client with less interest would require. Try to use the advisor's time well and ask for reading material rather than a "class session" with the advisor whenever possible. Formal investment classes can be an organized way to expand your own knowledge.

Be Patient

For many individuals, the decision to spend time and effort on their personal investments is a decision to do some active trading. As we have seen, execution of transactions has increasingly become a commoditized process. With the exception of situations when an investor is disadvantaged by being on the same side of the market as everyone else, small scale execution costs should be lower today than ever before. As long as there is no time-sensitive information content motivating your trade, patience in execution is usually rewarded.

Patience with a fund or with an advisor is generally a good policy as well. Even more important than patience with instruments or individuals is patience with the market. In general, the best strategy, particularly with an extremely tax-efficient vehicle like an equity ETF, is to stay with a profitable position.

Be Tax Sensitive

As this is written, statutory capital gains tax rates are at low levels. Nonetheless, tax deferral is more important than a low tax rate on capital gains for most investors. The appearance of the alternative minimum tax (AMT) on more tax returns means that the effective tax rate on long-term capital gains for many investors is often notably higher than the statutory rate. As long as the structure and tax treatment of ETFs is consistent with the current tax model as described in Chapter 4, most taxable investments in ETFs should be managed with sensitivity to the tax advantage of sticking to profitable positions in well-managed ETFs for the very long term—unless the case for change is compelling.

Pay Attention to Costs, but Don't Chase False Economies

Perhaps the best illustration of this point is the almost compulsive attention to fund expense ratios by some users and analysts of exchange-traded funds. As noted in Chapters 4 and 6, it is far more important to *look at the total costs* of using the fund, including the transaction costs of tracking an inappropriately chosen index and other costs associated with inefficiencies in the fund structure or with inefficient management—*costs that do not show up in the expense ratio*. Unfortunately, most of these costs do not show up in the work of most fund analysts—at least not yet. The general guidance provided in Chapters 4 and 6 should be useful until systematic internal transaction cost analysis of ETFs is readily available.

SOME CONCLUDING OBSERVATIONS ON ETF EVALUATION

The focus on stated expense ratios which has characterized the early years of open ETFs is unlikely to disappear. Fund managers are going to have to live with the idea that investors and their advisors are looking more closely at all fund expenses than they have ever looked before. There will be a great deal more information available on ETF trading spreads and market quality. We would expect leadership to come from advisors because they are going to be making recommendations to their clients in terms not only of which funds to use, but how the orders should be executed. Evaluation of market quality will be an ongoing issue.

There will be more comprehensive and more useful evaluations of ever more complex ETFs. The initial oversimplified evaluations of broad market index funds based solely on expense ratios will be replaced by much more sophisticated analysis. As time goes by and additional tools are developed, the evaluation processes will extend to actively managed funds and, eventually, to fund-of-funds products. We expect part of the mantle for evaluation of exchange-traded funds to pass eventually from the brokerage firm researcher back to the independent fund evaluation services, but these services are unlikely to dominate fund selection as thoroughly as they have in the past.

A fund analyst needs to dig deeper and become at least passingly familiar with some of the nuances of trading and execution if he or she is to provide useful advice to exchange-traded fund clients. One area in which we expect independent mutual fund analysts to reassert their historic role is performance attribution and evaluation of the quality of fund management, particularly active management. To do so, they will use the greater transparency of active ETFs relative to most active funds to analyze the ratio of good decisions to bad decisions. They will measure the cost of mistakes and they will measure the value added by good calls—mistake by mistake and good call by good call. A star rating based on past peer group performance or an interview with the fund manager as she is leaving the office to volunteer in a homeless shelter may still mark the manager as, respectively, a generally capable manager and a "good" person. Neither will do much to retain subscribers to a fund evaluation service—and to attract fund buyers. For the first time analysts will have timely access to fund portfolio contents and portfolio changes. Their clients will expect them to make effective use of this bounty. Of course, more effective fund evaluations will not come at all unless investors support providers of sound analysis and insist that less effective analysts improve their product.

As focus for the management of ETFs moves increasingly beyond traditional indexing to enhanced indexing and active management, the role of the management company will become increasingly important, though still not as important as the trading and advisory functions in terms of financial service industry revenue generation.

ENDNOTES

1. The growth in custom separate account management, partly at the expense of conventional mutual funds, has been chronicled at length in specialized publications for financial advisors, but Lauricella and O'Brian (2001) brought the discussion to the pages of the *Wall Street Journal*. Other comments on the need for help and the issue of separate account management include Clements (2001), McNamee (2001), and Rottenberg (2001).

2. Not all advisors are registered investment advisors, nor are they required to be. The fact that someone who describes herself as an advisor does not have an ADV Part II should not disqualify an individual or firm from consideration as an advisor. The ADV Part II is prepared and filed with regulators by registered investment advisors, an industry specialty that usually involves hands-on management of investment portfolios for a management fee. The ADV Part II can be

a source of useful information if you are dealing with a registered investment advisor.

3. Go to www.oag.state.us, the Maryland Attorney General's website. Click on "Securities Division" then "Publications." Download "How to Choose a Financial Advisor," and "Financial Advisor Interview Checklist." Go to www.investoradvice.org, The Forum for Investor Advice, and click on "The Scorecard." The styles of these questionnaires are very different from each other. Both contemplate their completion in a face-to-face interview, but that is not essential.

4. For which he humbly begs forgiveness from the cited authors.

5. Some of the more civil (though hardly low-key) discussions are reprised in Bogle (1999), (2001a), and (2001b); Legomsky (2001); Malkiel (2000); and Grinold, et al. (2000).

6. See Baks, et al., (2001), Chevalier and Ellison (1999), Elton, et al. (1996), Goetzmann and Ibbotson (1994), Bergstresser and Poterba (2000), Black (1973) and Marcus (1990). Also see Gruber (1996), Siegel, et al. (2000), Phillips and Kaplan (2001), and Wermers (2001). Identifying the successful manager in advance is still difficult.

7. See Lo and MacKinlay (1999) and Lo (2001). See also TIAA-CREF (2001), p. 15, for a discussion of that manager's Dual Investment Management Strategy^{SM}, which includes a quantitatively enhanced index fund segment.

8. Legomsky (2001).

Appendix

Getting Information on ETFs— Where to Look and What to Look For

I n this Appendix, we provide an indication of where an investor might look for ETF information. Rather than attempt to suggest sources for a particular piece of information which might be found in a variety of locations, we describe some of the potential information sources which an active user of ETFs should examine and what might be found in each of them. The information provided here will be updated from time to time on www.etfconnect.com.

ISSUERS

The issuer of any open ETF is required to publish a number of documents and to make the documents available to essentially anyone who requests a copy. In most cases, the issuers prefer that investors who seek this information download a copy in electronic form from the fund's website to save printing and postage costs. Among the documents available are prospectuses, simple product descriptions, and brochures. Product descriptions will increasingly be the principal document an investor will receive automatically upon the purchase of ETF shares. Fund investors are used to seeing prospectuses; so one would expect that a large proportion of investors will ask to see a prospectus as part of the sales process or request one before or after a transaction in ETF shares.

Another useful document which might be available for electronic download on an issuer's website is the Statement of Additional Information, or SAI, which is the second part of the prospectus for a mutual fund–type ETF. (The mutual fund type of ETF includes all 40

Act ETFs except the original 500 SPDR, the Midcap SPDR, the DIA-MONDS, and the NASDAQ 100 Trust). Theoretically, an investor can get a hard copy of the SAI from the issuer, but relatively few investors request them, the companies print only a few, and it may take a long time and several calls to an 800 number to obtain one. Downloading the SAI from the website may be your best source—if it is posted there.

Most issuers publish educational material on ETFs. Some chapter segments from this book will be available on the www.etfconnect.com website, and additional material not available in time for the book's publication will be posted there from time to time. Brad Ziegler, director of education for Barclay's Global Investors, has written a number of worthwhile short pieces under the sobriquet of "Dr. Index." Some of these are available in hard copy by mail or may be downloaded from the iShares website.

The issuer websites serve as important sources for a variety of different kinds of information on each individual fund or ETF family. The material on the websites changes over time, so the interested investor should visit the web addresses from time to time and stay alert to information about new web locations.

www.HOLDRs.com

Information about HOLDRs Trusts on various sectors and special portfolios. Detailed information on market data feeds, news, and component stock lists as well as spin-offs and changes, investment strategies, a cost-basis calculator, and downloadable prospectuses. HOLDRs are trust-issued receipts that represent an investor's beneficial ownership of a specified group of stocks. HOLDRs allow an investor to benefit from the ownership of the stocks in a particular industry, sector, or group. Sponsored by Merrill Lynch.

www.iShares.com

Information about the iShares family of index funds. iShares are U.S. registered index funds. Each iShare represents a portfolio of stocks designed to track one specific index. The iShares News column offers news on iShares, the financial markets, and some charts. The site also includes decision-making tools such as quotes and charts, an index tracker, an ETF allocator to create a portfolio of

ETFs based on the Dow Jones US Sector and Total Market Indexes, a Premium/Discount Chart, and a Tracking Error Chart. The "My Portfolio" feature, which requires registration and sign-in, enables the user to customize a watch list for stocks, iShares, and other securities and to track an unlimited number of portfolios with up to 30 securities each. The "My Broker" feature enables an investor to link to his/her broker's website automatically whenever he/she is logged in to iShares.com, and thus buy and sell shares without further thought. Sponsored by Barclays Global Investors.

www.spdrindex.com

Informational site about the Select Sector SPDRs funds available in sectors such as Basic Industries, Consumer Services, Consumer Staples, Cyclical/Transportation, Energy, Finance, Industry, Technology, and Utilities. Select Sector SPDRs hold sector-based equity portfolios of companies in the S&P 500. Detailed fund descriptions, index components, tradability, creation units, dividends, standardized performance data, charts, and a downloadable prospectus are available at the site. State Street Bank and Trust Company serves as advisor, administrator, and custodian; ALPS Mutual Fund Services is the distributor.

www.streetTRACKS.com

Site containing information about the streetTRACKS family of funds. streetTRACKS funds are based on indexes published by a number of organizations: Dow Jones and Company, FORTUNE, Morgan Stanley, and Wilshire. The site has a section explaining generally what exchange-traded funds are and outlining what their benefits are, how to buy and sell, index performance, tradability, and tax efficiency. The "Using ETFs" tab covers asset allocation, cash equitization, hedging risks, and transition management. There is also a "Top Questions" tab which gives further elaboration on the advantages of ETFs and a mechanism to obtain a prospectus once certain requisite information is provided. Managed by State Street Global Advisors.

www.etfconnect.com

Sponsored by Nuveen Investments, this is the first comprehensive ETF site providing industry information on exchange-traded funds

(ETFs), closed-end funds (CEFs), Preferred Shares, and HOLDRs. There are multiple search functions, including a Multifund search and a Find-a-Fund search whereby information can be obtained for a product by entering the CUSIP, ticker, fund name, or asset class. Search results allow a user to view pricing and performance information for multiple funds side by side. Detailed fund performance information is provided for the ETF and CEF sub-categories, including prices, premiums and discounts, net asset values, dividends, market performance histories, and recent developments. Links for industry news, exchanges, specialists, trade groups, fund sponsors, and index providers are available on easy-to-navigate pages.

Under the Education Center tab, there are overviews on Exchange-Traded Funds, Closed-End Funds, and Preferred Shares. The FAQs are broken down into instrument-specific categories. There is an industry research function, a glossary of terms, links to ETF articles, and Tools. Under the Tools heading, there is a portfolio tracker to track funds and stock holdings, access current market summaries, monitor intra-day market charts, and read the latest financial news. Registration and log-in is required to utilize this free feature.

THE AMERICAN STOCK EXCHANGE AND OTHER EXCHANGES

The AMEX and, to a limited extent, other exchanges where ETFs are listed or traded publish required and supplementary material on ETFs in hard copy and on their websites. Some of the broader discussions provide good introductory material on ETFs, on special ETF topics such as premiums and discounts on ETF shares, and other issues which have attracted regulatory or press attention.

www.Amex.com
The website of the American Stock Exchange provides news, quotes, and real-time updates of market activity. Performance and component securities information on listed option products such as equity, index, put and call (LEAPs), and ETF options is also provided. There is an options tutorial defining options and option types, pricing, buy-

ing and selling, benefits, and risks. There is a section devoted exclusively to exchange-traded funds and in-depth information about the underlying indexes. There is detailed fund information including trust components, facts, holdings, sectors, performance charts, and total returns. There is a separate HOLDRs section providing specifics on the HOLDRs Trust, Index Notes, Equity Notes and other products. The portfolio tracking feature allowing a user to set up a private portfolio and track investments is accessible only after providing a name and e-mail address. Stock Screening enables a user to find price, capitalization, risk, revenue, and earnings data for up to 100 Amex, NASDAQ and NYSE stocks using specific industry and/or stock symbol criteria. The Earnings section lists weekly earnings surprises for listed companies, analyst activity, analyst forecast change tables for fiscal quarters/years, and an earnings calendar. A future highlight of the Amex website will be access to an online version of the *Dictionary of Financial Risk Management*. A hotlink to the Dictionary will also be available through www.etfconnect.com.

www.cboe.com

The website of the Chicago Board Options Exchange provides real-time market quotes (paid subscriptions are required to receive different levels of service, except for the 20-minute delayed quotes, which are free), market statistics, intra-day and average daily volume reports, most active listings, volatility indices and historical stock indices, index settlements, and dividend yields. The section on options products provides details on product specifications, including structured products, index funds and exchange-traded funds, such as the iShares S&P 100, S&P 500, and NASDAQ 100 (QQQ). Product specification information includes fund descriptions, administration, trading unit, price quotations, dividends and distributions, net asset value, margin and short sales, creations and redemptions, and where to get additional information. There is a Trading Tools section, which has a symbol directory, news on stock splits and new listings, index overflows, an options calculator, big charts, U.S. company news, company research center, and commentary from theStreet.com. The Institutional section features links to educational materials and products for institutional investors such as Institutional white papers with overviews of strategies and regulatory considerations for mutual funds, corporations, individual retirement accounts (IRAs and Keogh plans), ERISA pension funds, hedge funds, and high-net-worth investors. There are also links to information on single-stock futures, FLEX options, margin, and escrow receipts.

www.nyse.com

The website of the New York Stock Exchange provides real-time market and quick quote information for all listed companies, index and exchange-traded funds and bonds, in-depth market performance, current and historical data, a roster of NYSE listed companies, members and institutional investors, regulations governing trading, and a searchable archive of statistics and share volume records. The section devoted to Indices and ETFs gives an overview of what ETFs are and their advantages. Specific funds are cited such as the S&P Global 100 with links to real-time indices, performance charts, fact sheets, and information brochures in pdf format. The Your Portfolio feature, which requires registration, allows the user to track up to 20 stocks and five leading indices and check their performance anytime.

www.nasdaq.com

The website of the NASDAQ stock market provides news headlines, up-to-the-minute quotes, and information on market activity, major indices, sector overviews, flash quotes and portfolio tracking. Information is also provided on global markets, IPOs, new SEC filings, upcoming splits, earnings forecasts, analyst recommendations, upgrades, and downgrades. There is a section devoted to exchange-traded funds including a general introduction explaining what ETFs are and a "heatmap" which helps a user spot significant price changes as they occur in individual exchange-traded funds. There is a Most Active chart, a NASDAQ Market Indices Chart, a sector overview, and a ticker.

The NASDAQ 100, NASDAQ Biotech Index, Broad-Based, Sector, and International indexes are covered extensively. Information about NASDAQ index-based ETFs includes fact and spec sheets, infoquotes, lists of companies, options, and a link to obtain downloadable prospectuses.

INDEPENDENT WEBSITES ON ETFs, INDEXES, AND INVESTING

ETF and Fund Websites

www.etfinternational.com

Site of ETF International Associates, a private firm providing consulting services to financial institutions in the conceptualization and implementation of both indexed-based (IB) and actively managed exchange-traded funds and foreign exchange–based and indexed-based structured products. Introductory and advanced information is provided on domestic and international ETFs. There are articles about ETFs, links to research sites, ETF events, and conferences.

www.exchangetradedfunds.com

Exchangetradedfunds.com is the website for ETF.Com Inc., whose primary business will be to provide information regarding all product aspects of exchange-traded funds through its website, exchangetradedfunds.com. The site is still under development as of this writing.

www.indexfunds.com

With open, comprehensive, and independent information on index investing, this site serves as an advocate for investors. Contains educational information on index funds under the Index Funds University heading. The ETF Zone features the latest ETF news and articles, top 10 ETFs, ETFs basics and how to use them, frequently asked questions, types of ETFs, domestic and foreign, recent launches, an ETF screener, current fund performance data, a discussion board, and ETF-related links. An essential checkpoint for every ETF investor.

www.morningstar.com

Independent site providing current market quotes, news, charts, fund ratings and analyst research. Also contains information on bonds, funds, exchange-traded funds, portfolios, a wealth management center, tutorials on investing, and discussion boards. The ETF Center has ETF news, most popular ETFs by trading volume, a limited-function ETF cost analyzer to compare costs between ETFs and a portfolio of stocks. A tutorial section explains what ETFs are, how they can be used, premiums and discounts, and a glossary of ETF terminology with definitions provided at fund-specific links. There are links to other ETF sites as well as an ETF discussion board.

www.worldlyinvestor.com

Independent site which publishes a newsletter featuring stories and information about financial markets, stocks, bonds, and mutual funds with the intent of educating and advising retail investors. In addition to news stories related to finance and investing and links to its newsletter, the site contains some information on mutual funds and exchange-traded funds.

www.vanguard.com

Select "Personal Investors" and click on the VIPERs link. Information provided on Vanguard's exchange-traded funds, VIPERs (Vanguard Index Participation Equity Receipts), includes a summary describing each fund, links to performance data, distributions, holdings, management, and frequently asked questions. There are also links to order literature tailored for individual or institutional investors such as product brochures, annual and semiannual reports, and a prospectus.

Index Websites

www.djindexes.com
www.msci.com
www.russell.com
www.ryanindex.com
www.standardpoor.com

Investing Websites

www.bloomberg.com
www.cbsmarketwatch.com
www.cnnfn.com
http://finance.yahoo.com
www.forbes.com
www.motleyfool.com
www.smartmoney.com

Other Websites of Interest

www.appliederivatives.com

This is primarily a derivatives product and market website. It is useful to ETF users for its information on ETF development and extensive coverage of single-stock futures.

SPECIALIZED PUBLICATIONS

Academic Journals

Major finance journals, have published a number of articles on exchange-traded funds and related topics. Many articles published before the present volume went to press are listed in the bibliography. Academic journals to watch for ETF and related articles include:

> *Financial Analysts Journal*
> *Journal of Business*
> *Journal of Finance*
> *Journal of Index Issues*
> *Journal of Investing*
> *Journal of Portfolio Management*
> *Journal of Private Portfolio Management*

Specialized Journals

American Association of Individual Investors (AAII) Journal
Computerized Investing

The American Association of Individual Investors publishes a number of special publications for the do-it-yourself investor. The two journals listed here regularly cover topics of interest to ETF investors. Professor Albert Fredman's articles on ETFs in the *AAII Journal*, for example, Fredman (2001a, 2001b), are particularly worthwhile.

Books (scheduled for publication, except as indicated)

How to Be an Index Investor—Max Isaacman*
Exchange-Traded Funds and E-Mini Stock Index Futures—David Lerman
Exchange-Traded Funds—Al Neubert
Exchange-Traded Funds—Jim Wiandt, Will McClatchy, Indexfunds.com*

Exchange-Traded Funds—Brad Zigler
* currently available

Press Coverage

Many finance columns in local newspapers have provided ETF information from time to time and some columnists write regularly about ETFs. Because Canadians have been exposed to ETFs (e.g., TIPs) for longer than U.S. residents, Canadian newspapers and financial publications provide particularly good ETF coverage. Many general-interest and finance-oriented publications have carried articles on ETFs. These columns and articles vary greatly in usefulness, sophistication—and even accuracy. A list of some publications to watch includes:

> *Barron's*
> *Bloomberg Personal Finance*
> *Business Week*
> *The Economist*
> *Forbes*
> *Fortune*
> *Money*
> *Mutual Funds*
> *Newsweek*
> *The New York Times*
> *Smart Money*
> *Time*
> *USA Today*
> *Wall Street Journal*

ANALYST COVERAGE FROM MAJOR BROKERAGE/ INVESTMENT BANKING FIRMS

Some of the best—and certainly the most regularly updated—source material on ETFs is produced by analysts in the research departments of major brokerage firms. Any list of individuals, firms, and report topics would be out of date long before this book's publication process was complete. We suggest the reader check the websites listed in this chapter and contact major brokerage firms for ETF material. A group of friends who share an interest in ETFs but who use different brokers, might find that collectively they have access to a great deal of useful material.

TRADITIONAL MUTUAL FUND SERVICES

Lipper—www.lipper.com
Morningstar—www.morningstar.com
Value Line—www.valueline.com
Wiesenberger—www.wiesenberger.com

The traditional mutual fund services got a relatively slow start on ETFs, primarily because the original UIT structures were not considered funds, and this fact provided an excuse for ignoring the category in its early years to avoid a commitment of resources. Now, the fund services have begun to provide an increasing amount of information. In general, their current level of coverage is less comprehensive, less sophisticated, and less useful than the material provided by the better brokerage firm research publications and websites. Most of the fund services continue to upgrade their efforts and, while they tend to evaluate ETFs in much the same way as they evaluate traditional conventional mutual funds, they are beginning to recognize that there are specific ETF issues that cannot be treated as a simple extension of their conventional mutual fund coverage.

Glossary

The terms in this glossary are fund and portfolio basket-related terms from the *Dictionary of Financial Risk Management*. In some cases the formal definition has been modified slightly to focus on funds. An updated online version of the entire dictionary will be available on *www.amex.com* and by hotlink to the AMEX site from *www.nuveen.com*. Please send suggestions for terms to be added to Gary.Gastineau@nuveen.com.

12b-1 Fee: A mutual fund fee, named for the SEC rule that permits it, used to pay for distribution costs, such as advertising and trailer commissions paid to brokers. If the 12b-1 fee exceeds 0.25% of assets, the fund is characterized as a load fund.

12(d)(1) Limit: Section 12(d)(1) of the Investment Company Act of 1940 limits the ability of registered investment companies to invest in other investment companies. Without specific exemptions from this section, no registered investment company may acquire more than 3% of the outstanding stock of another investment company, or acquire securities from a single investment company with an aggregate value of more than 5% of its total assets, or acquire securities from multiple investment companies with an aggregate value in excess of 10% of its total assets. For example, a fund could not hold more than 3% of all outstanding Qubes (QQQ). Certain funds-of-funds have obtained exemptions from these limits.

40 Act: *See Investment Company Act of 1940.*

401(k) Plan: A defined contribution, income tax-deferred retirement plan under which employees of a corporation may elect to make pre-tax contributions to an employer-sponsored plan in lieu of receiving currently taxable income. In some plans, part or all of the employee contribution is matched by an employer contribution.

403(b) Plan: A defined contribution, income tax-deferred retirement plan similar to a 401(k) plan for employees of certain not-for-profit organizations.

457 Plan: A defined contribution, income tax-deferred retirement plan similar to a 401(k) plan for employees of state and local government and tax-exempt organizations. 457 Plans are not subject to ERISA. The funds belong to the employer and are subject to the claims of the employer's general creditors.

A Shares: In a multiclass mutual fund structure, this class is usually the front-end load class.

Account Registration: The name(s) that appear on an investor's account statement.

Accrued Interest: Interest that accumulates on a fund's investments, but has not yet been paid.

Active Management: An investment process that attempts to outperform the average or benchmark return in an asset class at a specific level of risk through the use of superior information and judgment in portfolio construction. Active management may be based on some combination of traditional security analysis and research, technical analysis, macroeconomic forecasts and application of various fundamental quantitative tools. *Contrast with Passive Management.*

Active Manager: A portfolio manager who takes an active role in any aspect of the investment process—including some or all of asset allocation, style exposures, security selection, and risk management—in an attempt to improve a portfolio's risk-adjusted return.

Adjustable-Rate Instrument: Any of a wide variety of fixed principal obligations whose periodic payout is set relative to a reference index rate (such as LIBOR) to create a longer-term fixed principal obligation with a floating-rate interim cost.

Advisor/ Adviser: (1) An organization employed by a mutual fund's board to give professional advice on the fund's investments and asset management practices. See also *Registered Investment Advisor*. (2) A trained investment counsellor who assists investors in the establishment and execution of an investment program. The advisor's firm is compensated by commissions or a fee.

Advisory Fee: (1) The amount a fund pays to its investment advisor for the investment management associated with overseeing a fund's portfolio. *Also referred to as Management Fee*. (2) The compensation of some investment counsellors.

Affiliated Company: An intercorporate relationship in which one company owns an interest in another company. Also refers to companies that are related to each other in some way. An affiliated company is sometimes referred to as a subsidiary if its shares are owned by another company.

After-Hours Trading: The buying and selling of financial instruments outside what, until recently, have been considered normal trading hours (e.g., weekdays, 9:30 to 4:00PM E.T. for stock exchanges in the United States).

Aftermarket: The market for a security after an initial public offering. The aftermarket (or secondary market) may be over-the-counter or on an exchange.

After-Tax Contribution: Investment in a retirement plan from the taxed portion of an employee's pay. These contributions are treated differently from the more common pre-tax contribution when they are distributed. All contributions to Roth IRAs are after-tax contributions.

After-Tax Return: The return from an investment after all income taxes have been deducted. By comparing after-tax returns an investor can determine which investment makes the most sense based on his or her tax bracket.

Agency Debt: Obligations issued by an agency of the U.S. government and benefiting from government credit. In the United States, debt of certain former agencies such as Fannie Mae and Freddie Mac is still referred to as agency debt because it retains implied government support.

Agency Transaction: A transaction in which the executing brokerage firm acts as an agent and usually charges a commission for its services. *Contrast with Principal Transaction.*

Aggressive Growth Fund: A mutual fund that seeks maximum long-term capital gains. Such funds often invest in stocks of small and mid-sized companies, though company size is not always a selection criterion.

Alpha: A measure of the incremental return generated from active portfolio management.

Alternative Investments: Any asset category that is not used by a large number of investors or investment managers, usually because it cannot absorb large amounts of money or requires uncommon analytical or management attention. Examples include hedge funds, managed loan funds, and venture capital.

Alternative Minimum Tax (AMT):   A tax calculation made as a supplement to the standard income tax calculation for individuals and corporations in the United States. It is designed to insure that wealthy individuals and successful corporations pay a minimum percentage of their income in taxes in spite of any tax shelters or tax-exempt investments they may have. The AMT, which can make certain standard tax benefits unattractive to taxpayers affected by it, has begun to affect the tax returns of less affluent taxpayers than those it was designed to tax.

AMT Bonds: Types of municipal bonds whose income is subject to the alternative minimum tax (AMT). AMT Bonds include those issued to finance such private purpose activities as industrial redevelopment and sports stadium construction.

American Depositary Receipts (ADRs):   Certificates traded in U.S. markets representing an interest in shares of a foreign company. ADRs were created to make it possible for foreign issuers to meet U.S. security registration requirements, and to facilitate dividend collection by dollar-based investors. Some ADRs sold in the United States under Section 144(a) exemptions are not readily resalable to all U.S. investors; but most ADRs are nearly as freely traded in the United States as domestic issues.

American Stock Exchange (AMEX):	A securities exchange located in downtown Manhattan that is noted for the variety of its listings. Companies with shares traded on the AMEX are generally smaller than those listed on the New York Stock Exchange. The AMEX is the listing exchange for most U.S. registered exchange-traded funds (ETFs) and a variety of listed derivative securities, including equity and index options.
Analyst:	Also called a Financial Analyst or Security Analyst. Analysts train to use a variety of tools and techniques to evaluate investments. Analysts are employed by brokerage firms and investment advisors to develop, buy, sell, and hold recommendations on securities and to answer questions from their firm's staff and clients on specific investments or proposals. Experienced analysts often hold the CFA designation, which is evidence of systematic study and certification by satisfactory scores on a series of three annual tests.
Angels:	Venture capital investors or—in some circles—investors in Broadway plays.
Annualized Rate of Return:	The average return over a stated number of years, taking into account the effect of compounding. For example, a 100% return over five years is equivalent to an annualized rate of return of 18.2% per year.
Annualized Return:	The rate of return that would occur on average per year given a cumulative multi-year return or a fractional year return and taking into account compounding and discounting. The formula for annualizing a return is:

$$R_a = (1 + R_u)(1/n) - 1$$

where R_a equals the annualized return, R_u equals the unannualized return, and n equals the number of years over which the cumulative return is calculated. When reporting investment performance, it is inappropriate to annualize returns calculated over periods of less than one year.

Annual Percentage Rate (APR): The total cost of a loan, expressed as a yearly interest rate. The annual percentage rate is often not the same as the stated interest rate since it depends on the amount that has been financed, the finance charges, and the term of the loan. Calculated as the periodic (monthly or quarterly) rate times the number of periods in a year. Not compounded each period. *Compare to Annual Percentage Yield (APY).*

Annual Percentage Yield (APY): The true annual rate of return. The actual rate earned in one year after compounding. The APY is one plus the periodic rate raised to the power of the number of periods in a year, all minus one; If r is the quarterly return, APY $= (1 + r)^4 - 1$. *Compare to Annual Percentage Rate (APR).*

Annual Report: A legally required document that every fund or publicly held corporation sends to its shareholders within 60 days after the end of the fiscal year. The annual report describes the fund's or firm's financial condition and performance and includes an audited financial statement.

Annuitant: The recipient of benefits from an annuity contract.

Appreciation: Increase in value of an asset.

Arbitrage: (1) Technically, the action of purchasing a commodity or security in one market for immediate sale in another market (deterministic arbitrage). (2) Popular usage has expanded the meaning to include any attempt to buy a relatively under-priced item and sell a similar, relatively over-priced item, expecting to profit when the prices resume a more appropriate theoretical or histori-cal relationship (statistical arbitrage). (3) In trad-ing options, convertible securities, futures, and exchange-traded funds, arbitrage techniques can be applied whenever a strategy involves buying and selling packages of related instruments. (4) Risk arbitrage applies the principles of risk offset to mergers and other major corporate develop-ments. The risk-offsetting position(s) do not insu-late the investor from certain event risks (such as termination of a merger agreement or the risk of delay in the completion of a transaction), so the arbitrage is incomplete.

Asked Price: Price at which an instrument is offered for sale. Often abbreviated as Ask Price. *Also called Offer or Offered Price.*

Asset Allocation: (1) Dividing investment funds among markets to achieve diversification and/or a combination of expected return and risk consistent with the investor's objectives. (2) A value-oriented invest-ment strategy that attempts to take long positions in markets or market sectors where prices appear to be low and to reduce positions, or take short positions in markets or market sectors where prices appear to be high. Tactical (TAA) or strate-gic (SAA) asset allocation advocates and value-seeking portfolio managers often use similar techniques and policies. In contrast to momentum investors, who accentuate market trends, most asset allocators' trades tend to offset destabilizing market movements and counteract price and rate fluctuations. The asset allocator tends to buy when prices decline and sell when prices rise.

Asset Allocation Fund: A fund that invests its assets in a wide variety of investments that may include domestic and foreign stocks and bonds, government securities, gold or other precious metals, and real estate. Some asset allocation funds keep the proportions allocated among different investments relatively constant, while others alter the mix as market conditions change.

Asset Class: A grouping of investable assets with the following characteristics: (a) non-zero exposure (positive or negative) has the potential to raise the utility of a portfolio; (b) its risk-return characteristics cannot be duplicated by some combination of other assets; (c) it is relatively homogeneous internally; and (d) it has the capacity (size) to absorb a meaningful fraction of portfolio assets. Recently, there has been a tendency toward asset class pollution—a tendency to divide the world of investments into more alleged asset classes than are warranted or useful.

Asset Manager: A portfolio manager, corporate treasurer, or other individual responsible for management of the risks and returns associated with a portfolio of securities or other instruments.

At the Bell: Time and/or price at the close of the market.

At the Opening: (1) Time and/or price at the market opening. (2) A market or limit-price order to be executed at the opening or not at all; all or part of any order not executed at the opening is treated as canceled.

Auction Rate Preferred Stock (ARPS): A floating-rate preferred with the dividend rate reset by Dutch auction, typically every forty-nine days. The interest rate is usually subject to a maximum, and the issue is putable at each auction.

Auction/ Remarketed Notes: A note with essentially the same features as an Auction Rate Preferred Stock (ARPS).

Automatic Reinvestment: A mutual fund service giving shareholders the option to purchase additional shares with cash from dividend and capital gains distributions.

Average Annual Return (AAR): The most common basis for stating the historical return of a mutual fund, AAR is stated after expenses.

Average Down or Up: Purchasing a security at various levels to establish a lower or higher average cost. *See Dollar Cost Averaging.*

Average Effective Maturity: For a bond fund, the average maturity dates of the fixed-income securities in the fund's holdings. A bond's effective maturity takes into account the possibility that it may be called by the issuer before its stated maturity date. In this case, the bond trades as though it had a shorter maturity than its stated maturity.

Average Maturity Date: The average length to maturity of all bonds held in a fixed-income fund.

Average Portfolio Maturity: The weighted average maturity of all the bonds in a bond fund's portfolio.

B Shares: In a multiclass mutual fund structure, this class is usually the back-end load or contingent-deferred sales charge class.

Back-End Load: A mutual fund sales charge imposed when an investor sells fund shares rather than when he purchases them. The back-end load generally decreases the longer the investor holds the shares because an annual fee charged to the account covers the commission paid the salesman, usually in about 5 years. *Also called Contingent Deferred Sales Charge.*

Back Office: Brokerage house and investment management firm sales, trading support, and record keeping operations.

Back Testing: The practice of applying a valuation or forecasting model to historical data to help appraise the model's possible usefulness when current and future data are used.

Backup Servicing Arrangement: An agreement for a replacement servicing agent to assume responsibility for servicing (collecting payments on) a pool of securitized loans. "Hot" backup arrangements require the replacement servicer to be prepared to act quickly.

Balanced Fund: An investment company (mutual fund) that invests in a mix of stocks, bonds, and/or money market instruments to meet some combination of growth, income, and conservation of capital investment objectives.

Bank Debt (or Bank Loans): Loans made by banks to corporations, partnerships, and other entities. Such loans may finance leveraged buyouts or merger and acquisition activity, as well as general corporate activities.

Basis Point (BP, BIP): 1/100 of a percentage point, also expressed as 0.01%. The difference between a yield of 7.90%

and 8% is 10 basis points. When applied to a price rather than a rate, the term is often expressed as annualized basis points.

Basket:

A set of related instruments whose prices or rates are used to create a synthetic composite instrument that trades as a unit or serves as the underlying for an exchange-traded fund or a derivative instrument.

Basket Deposit Receipt (BDR):

See Exchange-Traded Fund (ETF).

Basket Trade:

See Portfolio Trade.

Bear Market:

A prolonged period of declining stock prices, typically defined as a decline of 20% or more from the market high.

Before-Tax Contribution:

The portion of an employee's salary contributed to a retirement plan before federal income taxes are deducted. This contribution reduces the taxpayer's gross income for federal tax purposes. Generally, any withdrawal from an account funded with before-tax contributions will be taxable at the time of withdrawal.

Benchmark:

A standard, often an unmanaged index, used for comparative purposes in assessing an investment's performance.

Beneficial Owner:

The person or firm that will benefit from owning an asset even though they may not be registered as the owner.

Beneficiary:

A recipient of proceeds from a qualified retirement plan, a will or a trust, or insurance policy upon the death of the registered owner.

Bequest: Property left to an heir under the terms of a will.

Beta: A measure of the variability of a fund's share price in relation to the Standard & Poor's 500 Index. Securities with betas higher than 1.0 have been and are expected to be more volatile than the S & P 500. Securities with betas lower than 1.0 have been and are expected to be less volatile than the S & P 500.

Bid: The price at which a trader is willing to buy a security.

Bid-Asked Spread: The difference between the bid and offer price or rate. The most widely used comparative measure of market quality.

Blue-Sky Laws: State securities laws that require funds to register their shares and to provide details on each share class so that investors can base their investment judgments on relevant data. The purpose of the laws is to prevent securities fraud—in other words, to protect investors from inadvertently buying a piece of "blue sky." Exchange-traded funds are not subject to state registration.

Bond: A type of IOU issued by corporations, governments, or government agencies. The issuer makes regular interest payments on the bond and promises to pay back the face value of the bond at a specified point in the future, called the maturity date. Bonds may be issued for terms of up to 30 years or more.

Bond Anticipation Notes: Short-term debt issued by states and municipalities as interim financing for projects to be funded by anticipated bond issues.

Bond Fund: A fund that invests in bonds: generally corporate, municipal, or U.S. Government debt securities. Bond funds generally emphasize income rather than growth.

Bond Insurance: Insurance as to timely payment of interest and principal of a bond issue.

Bond Trustee: A fiduciary agent for the holders of a debt instrument. Bond trustee functions include certifying the validity of the bond when it is issued; ensuring that the indenture provisions are met; checking payment of interest and principal and the status of any assets pledged as collateral; periodically reporting to bond holders; and maintaining records.

Book Value: The net worth, or liquidation value, of a business. Calculated by subtracting all liabilities, including debt and preferred stocks, from total assets and dividing by the number of shares of common stock outstanding.

Bottom-Up Investing: Approach to investing that identifies individual securities likely to perform well before considering broad economic trends.

Bracket Creep: Occurs when inflation pushes income into higher tax brackets. The result is no increase in real purchasing power but an increase in income tax payable.

Breakpoint: The size of an open-end mutual fund purchase that entitles the buyer to a lower sales charge.

Broad-Based Index   An index designed to reflect the movement of the entire market or stocks in a specific capitalization range.

Broker-Dealer: A securities firm that sells funds or other securities to the public.

Bull Market: A prolonged period of rising security prices. While the general trend of prices is positive, prices on any given day will fluctuate and may decline.

Business Cycle: The regular ebb and flow of economic conditions over time, characterized by fluctuating employment levels, industrial productivity, and interest rates.

C Shares: In a multiclass mutual fund structure, this class is usually the level load class with a permanent sales charge component of the expense structure.

Callable Bond: A bond whose issuer reserves the right to redeem (or "call") it before it is due. This feature represents a risk to the investor in that bonds are generally called when interest rates fall and, thus, usually cannot be replaced with a similar yielding issue of the same quality.

Call Features: Terms in a bond indenture that give the issuer the right to call the bond for redemption at certain prices and at certain times.

Call Protection: Provisions in a bond indenture or preferred stock that designate a period of time during which the issuer cannot call an issue or during which the issuer must pay a premium over parity to retire the issue.

Call Risk: The possibility that callable bonds held by a fund will be redeemed prior to maturity. The risk to the investor is that if bonds are redeemed early, it may be impossible to reinvest the funds in a similar instrument with a similar yield.

Capital Gain/ (Loss): The difference between the sales price of a capital asset, such as an exchange-traded fund, mutual fund, stock, or bond, and the cost basis of the asset. If the sales price is higher than the cost basis, there is a capital gain. If the sales price is lower than the cost basis, there is a capital loss. Short-term capital gain refers to a gain on assets owned for one year or less. Long-term capital gain generally refers to a gain on assets owned for more than one year. Net capital gains generated by a fund from the sale of securities in its portfolio are distributed to shareholders, usually once a year in December.

Capital Gains Distribution: A distribution from a mutual fund or an exchange-traded fund of taxable long-term capital gains, usually from the sale of common stocks held for more than a year. Note that short-term capital gains are included with the income distributions of a regulated investment company. Capital gains distributions are taxed at long-term capital gains rates no matter how long the shareholder owned shares in the mutual fund. Capital gains distributions are taxable in the year in which they are declared, which is not necessarily the same as the year in which they are paid.

Capital Gains Overhang: The accumulated unrealized capital gains (market value MV minus cost basis CB when MV>CB) in a mutual fund which are likely to lead to future taxable capital gains distributions.

Capital Growth: A rise in the value of a fund's securities, reflected by the appreciation of its net asset value per share.

Capitalization: The market value of a company's outstanding securities, excluding current liabilities. Under $250 million is generally considered small cap; $250 million to $2 billion is mid cap; and over $2 billion is large cap.

Cash: In discussing financial instruments, generally used to include the value of assets that can be converted to cash immediately without a material price impact.

Cash Drag: *See Dividend Drag.*

Cash Equivalent: A readily marketable financial instrument with a highly stable value.

Cash Management Account (CMA): A consumer account offered by a brokerage firm—initially in cooperation with a bank, but increasingly with a money market mutual fund providing deposit and checking privileges. These accounts have simplified consumers' management of their cash balances and have been a significant factor in disintermediation of retail bank deposits in recent years.

Cash Management Bill: Non-standard bills that the Treasury occasionally sells to help it match its cash inflows and outflows.

Cash Reserves: Cash deposits as well as short-term bank deposits, money market instruments, and U.S. Treasury bills.

Central Securities Depository (CSD): An institution which holds immobilized or dematerialized securities in book entry form and is responsible for the centralized transfer against payment by entries on its books. Depositories are responsible for safekeeping the physical certificates that have been issued for equities and bonds. *See, for example, Depository Trust Company (DTC).*

Certificate of Deposit (CD):   An insured, interest-bearing debt instrument issued by a bank, which requires the depositor to keep the money invested for a stated period of time.

Certified Financial Planner (CFP):   A person who is certified by the Institute of Financial Planners to give financial advice. CFPs take exams in financial planning, taxes, insurance, estate planning, and retirement. Continuing education credits are required each year to maintain the certification.

Certified Investment Management Consultant (CIMC):   CIMC's complete course work and pass NASD-proctored examinations for Levels I and II of the Institute for Certified Investment Management Consultants' course. CIMCs must have industry experience, adhere to a code of ethics and satisfy continuing education requirements.

Check Writing Privilege: A feature of some types of brokerage accounts and mutual funds. The owner of the account receives a checkbook and can write checks against the account value or balance. *See also Cash Management Account.*

Circle: A customer willing to buy a security in an underwriting will ask a salesman to "circle" some amount at a specified price. If the security is issued at that price or better, the customer has committed to buy.

Classes of Shares: (1) Mutual funds can have multiple classes of shares with claims on a single portfolio. Each class permits investors to purchase the portfolio in a different way. Class A shares might give investors the option of paying a front-end sales load while Class B shares give investors the option of paying a contingent-deferred sales charge. In a few cases, a fund may have both conventional and exchange-traded share classes. (2) Corporations can have different classes of shares based upon voting rights (Class A shares might have one vote for each share and Class B shares might have one vote for each ten shares) or participate in different components of the company's earnings, as in the case of target stock. *See also Target Stock.*

Cliff Vesting: Full vesting in a benefit after a specified length of service with no vesting prior to that time.

Clone Fund: An investment company which follows the same policies or is benchmarked to the same index as another fund. The clone may be offered because the cloned fund has been successful and is closed to new money, or because of restrictions on ownership of funds used by retirement plans.

Closed-End Fund: An investment company with a fixed number of shares outstanding. After the initial offering of shares is completed, a new investor buys shares from another shareholder rather than from the fund. In contrast to shares in an open-end mutual fund, which can usually be redeemed at net asset value, a closed-end fund's shares can trade in the market at a premium or discount to their net asset value. *Compare to Exchange-Traded Fund.*

Commercial Paper: Corporate promissory notes issued to provide short-term financing, sold at a discount and redeemed at face value. A principal component of money market fund portfolios because of its high yield.

Commission: The fee an investor pays a broker to buy or sell a fund or other security, typically assessed on a per-trade basis. No commission is charged for no-load, open-end mutual funds, giving them a cost advantage over exchange-traded funds for investors who trade frequently.

Common Stock: A security that represents ownership in a public corporation.

Compounding: The growth that comes from investment income and gains on both the original principal and the previously reinvested income and capital gains of an investment.

Confirm: A printed record of a transaction sent to an investor when distributions are paid or other business is transacted.

Constructive Receipt: The date that IRS regulations determine a taxpaying entity received an income payment or realized a gain.

Consumer Price Index (CPI): The change in consumer prices determined monthly by the U.S. Bureau of Labor Statistics, often cited as a general measure of inflation.

Contingent Deferred Sales Charge (CDSC): A fee imposed when mutual fund shares are redeemed (sold back to the fund) during the first few years of ownership. The CDSC declines over time and is usually eliminated after, say, 5 years. *Also called Back-End Load.*

Continuous Net Settlement (CNS): The National Securities Clearing Corporation's (NSCC's) automated accounting system that clears and guarantees settlement of compared security transactions. CNS nets each participant's security obligations into one net position for each issue, and one overall net cash position. NSCC becomes the contra-party to each trade and guarantees settlement. The system plays an important role in reducing each participant's risk and their customers' risk exposure to failure of a trade counterparty to perform.

Convertible Bond: A bond, preferred stock, or warrant that is convertible into the common shares of a corporation or into some other security under specific circumstances.

Core/Satellite Investment Strategy: An exchange-traded fund asset allocation program using broad index fund (core) and style and sector funds (satellites) in an attempt to enhance overall performance.

Corporate Action: An event or resolution approved by a corporation's board of directors that changes the corporate capital structure or financial condition. Examples include full or partial call of securities; maturation and repayment of debt or preferred stock; conversion of debt; exchange, tender or spin-off of securities; split or reverse split of shares; securities offerings; liquidation or name change.

Corporate Bond: A type of IOU issued by corporations. The issuer makes regular interest payments on the bond and promises to pay back, or redeem, the face value of the bond at a specified point in the future, called the maturity date.

Correction: A relatively short-term drop in stock prices, usually defined as a decline of 10% or more from the market's high.

Cost Basis: The adjusted cost of a security or physical asset that is used for tax calculations. Adjustments include depreciation expense and capital gains on which tax payments have been made.

Coupon: (1) The nominal annual rate of interest on a bond or note, usually expressed as a percentage of the face value. (2) A piece of paper detached from a bearer bond and exchanged for a quarterly, semiannual, or annual interest payment.

Coupon Rate: The interest rate that an issuer promises to pay periodically over the life of a bond or other debt security, expressed as a percentage of notional value.

Creation Unit: The minimum module for issue or redemption of shares in an open exchange-traded fund (ETF), usually between 25,000 and 300,000 fund shares, depending on the fund's policy. Existing ETFs issue their shares in return for portfolio deposits of securities in multiples of the creation unit basket specified by the fund's advisor. With minor exceptions related primarily to accrued dividend payments and cash balancing amounts, creations and redemptions are in kind, not in cash. ETF trading on the secondary market on the exchange is in the individual fund shares issued in the creation, not in Creation Units.

Credit Rating: An evaluation of the credit-worthiness of a debt security by an independent rating service.

Credit Risk: The potential for default by an issuer on its obligation to pay interest or principal on debt securities. Most U.S. government securities are considered to have very little credit risk.

Cumulative Discount Privilege: A way for a fund shareholder to qualify for a reduced sales charge by combining investments in different funds made at the same time into a single transaction.

Current Yield: Annual dividend or interest divided by the current price of a stock or bond.

CUSIP: A nine-digit identifier (called a CUSIP number) used to uniquely identify every security publicly traded in the United States. CUSIP stands for Committee on Uniform Securities Identification Procedures.

Custodian: A financial institution that holds securities in safekeeping for clients.

Cyclical Stocks: Stocks of companies whose main business experiences regular ebbs and flows in activity due to changes in the economy. The auto, chemical, paper, and steel industries, for example, are considered cyclical, since their earnings tend to fall when the economy slows. Food and drug stocks are generally considered to be non-cyclical, since food and medical care needs continue no matter what economic conditions are.

Debt Security: *See Fixed-Income Security.*

Decimalization: The process of changing the prices that securities trade at from fractions to decimals. Decimalization of equity securities is complete in the United States. The bond market continues to trade in fractions.

Declaration Date: (1) The date the Board of Directors of closed-end, exchange-traded, and preferred funds announce the amount of the dividend and/or capital gains distribution to be paid to shareholders. (2) The date a corporate board declares a cash or stock dividend.

Default Risk: *See Payment Default Risk.*

Defaulted Securities: Typically fixed-income securities (or any fixed dividend-paying securities such as preferred stock) that are unable to make their interest rate payments and/or unable to repay their principal.

Defined Benefit Pension Plan: A pension plan in which the employer commits to specified dollar payments to qualifying employees. The pension obligations are ultimately debt obligations of the plan sponsor.

Defined Portfolio: A fixed basket of securities underlying some limited function unit trusts and trust-issued receipts. The basket is held for a fixed term set by the requirements of the investment and does not change except as a result of certain corporate actions. Positions will be eliminated from the basket under certain circumstances, but new positions will only be added if they arise from mergers or spin-offs involving the original positions.

Deflation: A decline in the prices of goods and services. The opposite of inflation.

Demutualization: The process of changing corporate structure from mutual or "member" ownership to some other form. Recent examples include mutual insurance companies such as Metropolitan and Prudential, which have converted or are converting from policy holder ownership to publicly owned companies, and a number of stock markets which have converted from membership organizations to publicly held companies.

Depository Trust Company (DTC): A corporation owned collectively by broker-dealers and banks responsible for holding securities owned by its shareholders and their clients and for arranging the receipt, delivery, and monetary settlement of securities transactions. Once securities are on deposit, further transfers within the system can be accomplished electronically at low cost. DTC has merged with the National Securities Clearing Corporation (NSCC) to form the Depository Trust and Clearing Corporation (DTCC). DTC now exists as an operating unit of DTCC.

Developed Nations: These are countries that have economically mature economies. General characteristics include major industrial production and high political stability.

Developing Nations (or Developing Markets): Typically, these are countries that are in the early stages of economic development. General characteristics include a high demand for capital investment, a high dependence on export markets, a need to develop basic economic infrastructures, and low political stability.

Derivative: A financial security or arrangement whose value is based on, or "derived" from, a traditional security, asset, or market index.

DIAMONDS: An exchange-traded fund based on the Dow Jones Industrial Average.

Direct Rollover: A distribution from a qualified plan or IRA account that is sent directly to the custodian of an IRA account and is reported to the IRS as a rollover.

Disclosure Statement: A document which describes the terms of an IRA. All investors who open an IRA account receive a copy of the current disclosure statement.

Discount: Amount (stated in dollars or as a percent) by which the selling or purchase price of a security is less than its face amount or net asset value.

Discount Bond: (1) A debt instrument, such as a Treasury bill or a coupon or principal payment stripped from sovereign or other debt, that pays no periodic interest but trades at a discount from its ultimate settlement value at maturity. (2) A coupon debt instrument that sells below its value at maturity because market interest rates are higher than its coupon rate.

Discount Rate: The interest rate charged by the Federal Reserve to member banks. Basically, the floor rate for interest rates in the economy.

Disinflation: A slowing of the rate at which prices are increasing. Not the same as deflation, when prices actually drop.

Distribution: (1) The payment of dividends and/or capital gains by a fund to its shareholders. (2) The payment of dividends or spinoff of shares in an affiliated company to a corporation's shareholders.

Distribution-in-Kind: The receipt of underlying securities when redeeming a creation unit of a fund instead of receiving cash.

Distribution Schedule: The schedule describing when throughout the year a closed-end, exchange-traded, or preferred fund makes income, principal, dividend, and/or capital gains distributions.

Diversifiable Risk: *See Non-Systematic Risk.*

Diversification: An approach to investment management analyzed and popularized by Harry Markowitz and encouraged by widespread acceptance of the usefulness of the capital asset pricing model (CAPM). With diversification, asset-specific risk can be reduced relative to the average return of a portfolio by investing in a variety of asset classes, such as stocks, bonds, money market instruments, and physical commodities, as well as by diversifying within these categories and across international boundaries. Diversification usually reduces portfolio risk (measured by return variability) because the returns (both positive and negative) on various asset classes are not perfectly correlated.

Diversified Common Stock Fund: A mutual fund that invests its assets in a wide range of common stocks. The fund's objectives can be growth, income, or a combination.

Dividend: A distribution of earnings to shareholders of a corporation or an investment company. Investment company dividends are usually paid out of investment income, including net short-term capital gains. Investment companies also make distributions of net realized long-term capital gains, typically once a year.

Dividend Drag: One major issuer of exchange-traded funds has attempted to make a *bête noire* of the evil sounding "dividend drag." Dividend drag is attributed primarily to several of the older, unit trust-based ETFs (SPDRs, MidCap SPDRs, and DIAMONDS). Because of the passively invested nature of these unit trusts, the SEC initially required that cash dividends received by the trust could not be reinvested in portfolio stocks. Dividends were to be accumulated and paid out periodically to investors. During the accumulation period, dividend cash could be invested by the trustee. Any interest earned (at a short-term rate) would be applied to the expenses of the trust. During a rising market, a dividend paying portfolio using the unit trust structure will lag behind a comparable fund based on a mutual fund structure which can equitize dividends (invest in stocks) until the fund is ready to pay the net dividends to shareholders. Furthermore, because the unit trusts are not permitted to lend securities, an additional opportunity to enhance portfolio returns is not available to them.

The cost disadvantage of these unit trust features is debatable. The value of dividend equitization depends in large part on what the market does. Equitizing dividends will be undesirable during a period of declining markets. Of course, the period when exchange-traded funds have been growing most rapidly has been a period of generally rising markets. The value of dividend equitization ranges from a negative value in a declining market to as much as five or six basis points per year on an S&P 500 portfolio (the 500 SPDR) in the better years of the 1990's. Stock lending opportunities are rare in Dow Jones Industrial Average stocks and only slightly more common in stocks in the S&P 500. In the best of circumstances, stock lending might add a few basis points to an S&P Mid-Cap or NASDAQ 100 portfolio.

Regardless of the course of the markets in the period ahead, the issue of dividend drag should soon disappear. At least one of the trustee-custodians of the unit trust structure ETFs has applied to the SEC for permission to take the steps necessary to equitize dividends and engage in stock lending. SEC statements indicate that the Commission will approve these requests in time. The other unit-trust trustee is prepared to make a similar application promptly upon publication of a notice that the Commission is preparing to grant the initial request. There is every reason to believe, therefore, that the phrase "dividend drag" will disappear from ETF vocabularies before it makes it into standard dictionaries. *Also called Cash Drag.*

Dividend Rate: The most recent rate at which a fund is distributing dividend and interest income earned on the fund's investment portfolio, usually expressed in cents per share.

Dividend Yield: The most recent rate at which a fund is distributing dividend and interest income earned on the fund's investment portfolio, usually expressed as an annualized percentage of the fund's offering price per share.

Dollar-Cost Averaging: An investment strategy of making investments of equal amounts at regular intervals in the same fund. Because the shareholder buys more shares at lower prices and fewer shares at higher prices, the average cost of the shares purchased will generally be lower than the average price over the investment period. However, dollar-cost averaging does not ensure a profit or protect against a loss in a declining market, and an investor may have to pay a commission with every purchase.

Domestic Company: Refers to a corporation that is headquartered in the United States. Although many domestic corporations conduct a majority of their business and receive a majority of their revenues from operations in the United States, many of these same corporations have significant operations abroad and receive significant revenue from overseas.

Dow Jones Industrial Average ("The Dow"):   The most commonly used indicator of stock market performance, based on the prices of 30 major U.S. companies.

Downtick: A transaction executed at a lower price than the preceding transaction in that security, or a new quote registered at a lower price than the preceding quote in that security.

Duration: A mathematical measure of the price sensitivity of a bond fund's portfolio to changes in interest rates. Duration is stated in years; the shorter the duration, the less price variability you can expect in the fund's price per share.

Dutch Auction: An auction system where the price of the item being auctioned is gradually reduced until it elicits a responsive bid. Dutch auctions are used to sell U.S. Treasury bills and to set rates on some remarketed floating-rate debt instruments and preferred stocks.

Earnings Growth Rate: Typically, the average annual rate of growth in earnings per share over the past five years.

Earnings Per Share: A measure of a company's financial performance, calculated by dividing a company's earnings by the number of common shares outstanding. This is an important figure for investors who are looking for stocks they consider to be undervalued in price.

Education IRA: Not actually a retirement account; rather, it is established to pay for a child's post-secondary education.

Emerging Market Fund: A mutual fund investing a majority of its assets in the financial markets of one or more developing countries, typically small markets with a short operating history. Such funds usually take higher risks in exchange for higher potential returns.

Employer Matching Contribution: A company's contribution to an employee's retirement account.

Enhanced Indexing: A modified indexing strategy that attempts to exceed the total return of the benchmark index.

Equity Fund: A mutual fund that invests primarily in stocks.

Equity Security: A type of security representing ownership in a corporation. Common stock, preferred stock, and convertible securities are all equity securities. Nonconvertible debt securities do not represent ownership.

Equity Unit Investment Trust: A portfolio of selected common stocks that provide either the potential for above-average capital appreciation or income.

ERISA: The Employee Retirement Income Security Act of 1974 that created rules covering qualified retirement savings plans.

Estimated Current Return (ECR):   The estimated annual net interest income per unit divided by the current offering price.

Estimated Long-Term Return (ELTR): This return is calculated according to SEC mandated formulas for a unit investment trust. The estimated return is projected over the estimated life of the trust and is not guaranteed. The calculation is based on an average of the yields to maturity of the bonds held in the unit investment trust, which are adjusted to reflect the sales charge and estimated expenses.

Ex-Dividend: The status of shares during the time between the dividend record date and the payment date of a corporate or fund dividend or capital gain distribution. When a security is trading ex-dividend, a purchaser is not entitled to the distribution.

Ex-Dividend Date: The date on which the buyer of a stock is no longer able to purchase the stock the regular way and still receive a specific dividend payment. A holder of the stock who sells on the ex-dividend date is entitled to retain the dividend when it is paid.

Exchange Fund: Investment vehicle which allows investors to exchange their low basis stock holdings for shares in a diversified portfolio of stocks in a tax-free transaction. Opportunities to create exchange funds have been reduced by Internal Revenue Service actions. *Also called Swap Funds. Contrast with Exchange-Traded Fund (ETF).*

Exchange of Futures for Physicals (EFP): A technique (originated in physical commodity markets) whereby a position in the underlying is traded for a futures position. In financial futures markets, the EFP bypasses any cash settlement mechanism built into the contract and substitutes physical settlement. EFPs are used primarily to adjust underlying cash market positions at a low trading cost. An EFP by itself will not change either party's net risk position materially, but EFPs are often used to set up a subsequent trade that will modify the investor's market risk exposure at low cost. *Occasionally called Against Actuals (AA), Cash-Futures Swap, Ex-Pit Transaction.*

Exchange Privilege: A mutual fund option permitting shareholders to transfer their investments from one fund to another within the same fund family.

Exchange-Traded Fund (ETF): A modified unit trust or investment company characterized by a dual trading process. Fund shares are created or redeemed in large blocks through the deposit of securities to, or delivery of securities from, the fund's portfolio. Secondary trading, in lots as small as a single fund share, takes place on a stock exchange. The dual trading process permits (and potential arbitrage requires) the fund shares to trade close to net asset value at all times. ETFs trade at prices very close to their current underlying value throughout the trading day and are usually more tax efficient than comparable conventional funds. HOLDRs and Folios, two alternative basket or portfolio products, are sometimes compared to ETFs. In contrast to HOLDRs and Folios, ETFs are subject to investment company regulation and regulated investment company tax treatment, and the product structures are quite different.

Expense Ratio: For a mutual fund or other investment company, the charge to fund assets for investment management, marketing, custody, administration, and other related costs, but not for unusual outlays for law suits or for trading expenses like brokerage commissions. Usually expressed in basis points or as a percentage of net assets.

Face Value: A bond's stated redemption value at maturity. Most bonds have a face value, or par value, of $1,000. *Also called Notional Value.*

Family of Funds: A group of mutual funds, usually with different investment objectives, that are managed and distributed by the same company.

Federal Funds Rate: The interest rate charged by banks to lend to other banks needing overnight loans; this figure is the most sensitive indicator of the direction of interest rates.

Federal Reserve System: The central bank of the United States, which has regulated credit in the economy since its inception in 1913. Includes the Federal Reserve Bank, 14 district banks, and the member banks of the Federal Reserve.

Fee-Only Advisor: A financial advisor who charges only a set hourly rate or a percentage of assets under management for a financial plan. The fee-only advisor does not charge transaction-based sales commissions, or else credits such commissions against scheduled fees.

Fiscal Year: An accounting period of 365 days (366 in leap years) for which a fund or operating corporation prepares financial statements and performance data. Not necessarily the same as the calendar year.

Fixed-Income Fund: A fund whose objective is to provide current income by investing in fixed-income securities.

Fixed-Income Security: An investment that provides a return in the form of fixed periodic payments and/or scheduled payment of a preset principal amount at maturity.

Flexible Fund: A mutual fund or exchange-traded fund that can invest in stocks, bonds or other financial instruments in proportions determined by the fund manager. The manager is responsible for the fund's asset allocation, and its investment policy statement is usually very broad.

Float: In equity markets, the number of shares of a corporation that are available for trading by the public. Float estimates usually exclude large insider positions and intercorporate control or strategic holdings.

Floating-Rate Securities: Bonds, bank loans, or other securities with coupon rates that adjust periodically based on a specified reset mechanism.

Folio: An unstructured basket of common stocks that may represent a stock index, a sector or theme, or even an actively managed portfolio at inception, but which may be modified by an investor or an advisor to meet the tax and spending needs of its owner. The rationale for the folio is to take advantage of diversification and the ability to realize tax losses in a separately managed account. In general, an investor will have to devote a fair amount of time to the folio or engage the services of a specialized advisor.

Forward Commitment: A purchase or sale of a security at a specified price with delivery and cash settlement at a specified future date.

Forward Pricing: The valuation process for a conventional mutual fund transaction. All orders to buy or sell shares are based on the next net asset value calculation.

Front-End Load: A sales commission charged at the time of purchase of some mutual funds and other investment products.

Full Faith and Credit: An unconditional commitment to pay interest and principal on debt securities, usually securities issued or guaranteed by the U. S. Treasury or tax-exempt general obligation bonds of a state or local government.

Fundamental Analysis: The study of a company's business and financial condition to help forecast future movements in its stock price. Analysts consider the company's past record of earnings and sales as well as company assets, management, and markets to predict trends that could affect a company's stock.

Fund Abbreviation: An abbreviation of a fund's name, commonly used in newspaper listings. Distinct from the three- to five-character "ticker" symbol.

Fund Family: A group of funds with different investment objectives, offered by the same management company.

Fund Net Assets: The total value of a fund's securities, cash, and other holdings, minus any outstanding debts.

Fund of Funds: A financial intermediary organized as a corporation, business trust, or partnership that accepts equity investments and buys shares of other funds that, in turn, hold securities or commodities.

Fund/SERV: A service of the National Securities Clearing Corporation (NSCC) that automates and standardizes the processing of mutual fund purchase and redemption orders, settlements, and account registrations. Fund/SERV is integrated with the continuous net settlement (CNS) system in contributing to a daily net money settlement with each firm.

Futures: Agreements to buy or sell specific amounts of financial instruments or physical commodities for an agreed upon price at a certain time in the future.

General Obligation (GO) Bond: A municipal bond backed by the general credit of the issuing organization. General obligation bonds are more secure than revenue bonds and thus trade with a slightly lower yield.

Global Fund: A mutual fund that invests in stocks of companies based in the U.S and in foreign countries. Taxable U.S. investors should usually own domestic securities and foreign securities in separate funds to take advantage of the foreign dividend withholding tax credit.

Government Bond: A type of IOU issued by governments. The issuer makes regular interest payments on the bond and promises to pay back, or redeem, the face value of the bond at a specified point in the future, called the maturity date. Bonds may be issued for terms of up to 30 years or more.

Grantor Trust: A legal structure that is a security, although it is not issued by a company that has been registered with the SEC under the Investment Company Act of 1940. Holding a grantor trust is substantially similar to holding a basket of securities. The trust passes along all the voting rights and dividends associated with the underlying securities. HOLDRs use the grantor trust structure.

Growth: An investment style that seeks higher returns than a broad market equity index with equal or less risk. Growth funds primarily invest in a diversified portfolio of stocks of established, well-known companies.

Growth and Income: An investment style that attempts to provide attractive total returns from a balanced portfolio of stocks, bonds, and cash equivalents, emphasizing capital appreciation in up markets and capital preservation in down markets. Growth and Income funds invest primarily in stocks of well-known companies with a secondary emphasis on U.S. Treasury and quality corporate bonds.

Growth and Income Fund: A fund that seeks a combination of long-term growth of capital and current dividend income.

Growth Fund: A fund that holds stocks of companies with above-average prospects for growth and, usually, low-dividend yields.

Guaranteed Fund: An investment company that offers a minimum performance guarantee. In the most common type of guaranteed fund, the sponsor of the fund promises that the investor will receive at least his original principal back at the end of 5 or 7 years if none of his shares are redeemed over the period. Any positive return belongs to the investor. The guarantee is funded by a higher management fee than a fund without the guarantee would carry. A similar structure is available in equity-linked notes.

Harvesting Losses: A euphemism for tax-loss-motivated sales of securities to offset gains realized on other positions.

Hedge: A strategy used to manage investment risk. In portfolio investing, hedging involves the purchase of an offsetting position, such as a put option or futures contract, to guard against the risk of a market decline.

Highest In, First Out (HIFO):   Accounting: A principle of tax efficiency in a conventional mutual fund that defers taxes as much as possible by selling the highest cost lot of a particular stock first and then others in sequence until the lowest cost lot is sold last. *See also Lowest In, First Out (LIFO)*.

High-Yield Bonds: Bonds that are rated below Baa, the lowest investment grade bond rating.

High-Yield Bond Fund: A fund that invests in bonds rated below Baa, the lowest investment-grade bond rating.

HOLDRs: Shares in a grantor trust which represent an interest in a specific portfolio of stocks, usually in a particular industry, sector or group. HOLDRs were developed by Merrill Lynch to allow an investor to own a moderately diversified group of stocks in a single investment that is transparent and liquid. HOLDRs are characterized by low ongoing expenses, a high degree of tax flexibility, which leads to tax-efficiency as long as the investor does not sell the HOLDRs' highly appreciated component shares. The holder of HOLDRs can separate the portfolio into its component securities at modest cost to realize losses. The principal disadvantage of HOLDRs is that an investor who breaks them up will find that keeping track of the tax basis and tax consequences associated with subsequent transactions in the component securities may be relatively complex.

Holding Period Return: Income plus price appreciation or less price depreciation during a specified time period divided by the cost or market value of the investment.

Income:

An investment strategy that seeks to provide attractive after-tax returns with moderate risk from a balanced portfolio of government, corporate, or municipal bonds, stocks, and cash equivalents. Income funds invest primarily in quality bonds, with a secondary emphasis on stocks of established well-known companies.

Income Dividend:

Payments to fund shareholders of dividends and interest earned by securities held by a fund. Income dividends are paid after deducting operating expenses.

Income Fund:

A fund that invests largely in investment-grade bonds and dividend-paying stocks.

Income Risk:

The possibility that the income provided by a fund or a floating rate instrument will fluctuate due to changing interest rates. Money market funds and short-term bond funds are most subject to income risk.

Indenture:

The formal contract governing a corporate bond that explains the bond's maturity, coupon rate, call privileges, and other terms.

Index:

Usually, a number calculated by weighting or linking a number of prices or rates according to a set of predetermined rules. A financial market index is a statistical construct that measures relative or absolute price changes and/or returns in stock, fixed income, currencies, or futures markets. The purpose of the index calculation is usually to provide a single number whose behavior is representative of the movements of a variety of prices or rates and indicative of behavior in a market. Indexes serve as the underlyings for a number of products, particularly in equity and fixed-income markets.

Index Fund: A fund designed to track the performance of a market index. Most common among stock funds, but used in fixed-income markets as well.

Index Shares: A subset of exchange-traded funds (ETFs), index shares are based on an index and implemented by holding an index portfolio.

Index Tracking: A reference to the correlation between a portfolio's return and the return on a benchmark index, or, alternately, to the portfolio's tracking error relative to the index. Many equity index funds and enhanced index portfolios are managed with close attention to index tracking. See also Tracking Error.

Indexation: (1) A relatively passive investment strategy that attempts to replicate the return of a benchmark index in a fund. (2) The practice of linking the coupon on a debt security to an index of inflation.

Indexing Plus: *See Enhanced Indexing.*

Indicated Dividend: Total of dividends that would be paid on a share of stock or a fund over the next year if each dividend were equal to the most recent dividend.

Indicated Yield: Yield of a stock, bond, or fund at its current price if the total of dividends or interest that would be paid over the next year were equal to the most recent dividend or interest payment.

Individual Retirement Account (IRA):   An investor's tax-deferred retirement account, established and funded by deposits with a financial intermediary. The investments range from insured bank deposits and fund shares to individual stock positions. The investor can also roll a 401(k) position from a former employer into an IRA without immediate tax effect.

Inflation: A rise in the prices of goods and services, often equated with loss of purchasing power.

Initial Offering Date: The date a fund is first available for sale.

Initial Public Offering (IPO):   A company's first public offering of common stock.

Initial Sales Charge: The sales charge paid by the investor at the time of purchase of fund shares on the primary market.

In-Kind: *See Distribution-In-Kind.*

Institutional Investors: Entities such as banks or insurance companies that purchase and sell large blocks of securities for their own and for client accounts.

Insurance: (1) An arrangement under which one party to a contract (the insurer) in return for a consideration (the premium) indemnifies another party (the insured) against a specific loss, damage, or liability arising from specified, uncertain events. (2) A risk/return pattern characteristic of options that limits (or insures against) price or rate movements through a predetermined (strike) price or rate in exchange for the explicit or implicit payment of an option (insurance) premium. (3) The component of an option or of a more complex instrument that provides this risk limitation feature. In contrast to a straight hedging transaction that eliminates risk symmetrically over all prices ranges, an insurance position creates an asymmetric risk/return pattern.

Insured Bond: A municipal bond backed by the credit of the issuer and by a commercial insurance policy.

Interest: Money paid for the use of borrowed funds.

Interest-Only Obligation: A tranche of mortgage-backed securities whose owner receives only the interest (or a portion of the interest) on the underlying mortgages. During a period of falling interest rates, rapid repayments of principal by mortgage holders reduces the value of interest-only obligations.

Interest Rate Risk: The risk that a security or fund will decline in price because of changes in market interest rates.

Internal Revenue Service (IRS): The Internal Revenue Service was created in 1913 to administer the collection of federal income taxes.

International Company: Refers to a corporation that is headquartered outside of the United States. Although many international corporations conduct a majority of their business and receive a majority of their revenues from operations outside the United States, many of these same corporations have significant operations in the United States and receive significant revenue from the United States.

International Fund: A mutual fund that holds securities of issuers domiciled outside of the United States.

Investment Adviser (Advisor): Individual or entity providing investment advice for a fee. Registered Investment Advisers must register with the SEC or State securities commissions and abide by the rules of the Investment Advisers Act.

Investment Club: A group of investors who pool their money and knowledge to make investments, learn about investing, and diversify their portfolios.

Investment Company: The technical name for many closed-end, exchange-traded, and preferred funds, which are governed by rules established in the Investment Company Act of 1940.

Investment Company Act of 1940 (or 40 Act): Legislation enacted in 1940 (with subsequent amendments and regulations under the legislation) which governs the operation of the fund (mutual, closed-end, exchange-traded, preferred) and investment advisory industries. This act stipulates the conditions that funds and investment advisors have to meet in order to distribute their products and services to the general public.

Investment Company Shares: The formal name for many closed-end fund, open exchange-traded fund, and preferred fund shares, which are governed by rules established in the Investment Company Act of 1940.

Investment Grade: Bonds whose issuers are judged by an independent rating service such as Standard & Poor's or Moody's Investors Service to be very able to pay interest and repay principal. Standard & Poor's and Moody's Investors Service designate bonds in their top four categories (AAA/Aaa, AA/Aa, A, and BBB/Baa) as investment grade.

Investment Horizon: The length of time an investor expects to keep a sum of money invested.

Investment Manager: Individual or entity responsible for the selection and allocation of securities for a portfolio.

Investment Objective: (1) The goal that a mutual fund pursues on behalf of its shareholders. (2) Less formally, the goal of an individual investor.

Investment Policy: A formal statement outlining broad investment objectives.

Investment Style: A broad indicator of a fund's investment emphasis. For stock funds, the investment style indicates whether a fund emphasizes stocks of large-, medium-, or small-capitalization companies, and whether it emphasizes stocks with growth or value characteristics or a blend of these characteristics.

ISIN Number (International Securities Identification Number): A code that uniquely identifies a specific securities issue. The organization that allocates ISINs in any particular country is the National Numbering Agency (NNA). CUSIP numbers are the principal securities identifiers in the U.S.

Joint Account: An account registered to two or more adult shareholders.

Joint Tenants with Right of Survivorship (JTWROS): A form of account registration in which two or more individuals share an undivided interest in an account. In the event of one tenant's death, the surviving tenant(s) automatically inherits the property without the necessity of court proceedings. A minor may not be a joint tenant.

Jumbo CD: A certificate of deposit issued by a bank in amounts of $1 million to $5 million and paying a higher rate of interest than smaller-denomination certificates. The ability to participate in jumbo CD purchases is one of the advantages of investing in a money market fund.

Junk Bonds: Lower-rated, higher-yielding bonds with a credit rating of BB or lower.

Keogh Plan: A retirement plan for self-employed individuals and their employees.

Large Cap Stock: Usually a reference to the shares of a company with an equity market capitalization of more than $2 billion.

Letter of Intent (LOI):   A way for a shareholder to qualify for a reduced sales charge by promising to invest a certain amount within a specified time.

Level Load: *See Load Fund.*

Leverage: An investment or operating position subject to a multiplied effect on profit or position value from a small change in sales quantity or price. Leverage can come from high-fixed costs relative to revenues in an operating situation, or from debt or an option structure in a financial context.

Leveraged Fund: A method to potentially generate a higher level of income for shareholders. A fund may issue preferred stock that pays generally lower short-term rates to investors seeking short-term liquidity. The proceeds are used to buy additional investments in the fund portfolio. Common shareholders may earn extra income from the difference between the rates earned on the fund's long-term bond portfolio and the short-term rates paid to preferred shareholders. As long as short-term yields are lower than those for long-term bonds in the portfolio, the income received by common shareholders of leveraged funds will be higher than it would be if the funds were un-leveraged. At the same time, the net asset value per common share will be more volatile than those of comparable un-leveraged funds, since the increases or decreases in the total portfolio value are all attributed to the common shares.

Leveraged Loan: A bank loan to a below-investment-grade-borrower traded in a secondary loan market. The quality of the loan may be enhanced by a collateral deposit.

Liquidation Price: The bid price of a unit investment trust minus the deferred sales charge.

Liquidity: The ability to turn assets into cash easily. An investor should be able to sell a liquid asset quickly with little effect on the price. Liquidity is a central objective of money market funds.

Load: An amount charged for the sale of some fund shares.

Load Fund: A fund that levies a sales charge when shares are bought (a front-end load) or sold (a back-end load). A level load fund charges a sales fee each year, possibly with an eventual cutoff.

London InterBank Offered Rates (LIBOR):   The primary fixed-income index reference rates used in the Euromarkets. Most international floating rates are quoted as LIBOR plus or minus a spread. In addition to the traditional Eurodollar and sterling LIBOR rates, yen LIBOR, Euro LIBOR, Swiss franc LIBOR, etc., are also available and widely used.

Long-Term Capital Gain (LTCG): A profit on the sale of a security or fund share that has been held for more than one year. Generally LTCGs are taxed at a preferential rate in the United States.

Long-Term Investment Strategy: A strategy that looks past the day-to day fluctuations of the stock and bond markets and responds to fundamental changes in the financial markets or the economy.

Loss Harvesting: Selling enough loss positions from a portfolio to eliminate taxable gains. In a separate account portfolio, the investor's total gain and loss position will be considered in deciding what losses to harvest.

Lowest In, First Out (LIFO): Accounting: With respect to exchange-traded funds (ETFs), a principle of securities delivery that removes the lowest cost securities lots first in filling a redemption request to increase the average cost basis of a fund in its portfolio securities. An important feature in an ETF's tax efficiency. *See also Highest In, First Out (HIFO).*

Low-Load Fund: A fund that charges a sales commission of 3.5% or less for the purchase of its shares.

Lump-Sum Distribution: A single payment that terminates an employee's interest in a retirement plan account.

Management Company: The firm that organizes, manages, and administers a fund.

Management Fee: The amount a fund pays to its investment advisor for supervising the fund's holdings and operations. *Also called an Advisory Fee.*

Management Investment Company: A mutual fund.

Market Maker: A trader who enjoys certain trading privileges in exchange for accepting an obligation to help maintain a fair and orderly market.

Market Risk: The possibility that stock or bond prices will fluctuate adversely to an investor's interest.

Market Timing: An investment strategy based on predicting market trends. The goal is to anticipate trends, buying before the market goes up and selling before the market goes down.

Maturity: The date on which the life of a financial instrument is scheduled to end through cash, physical settlement, or expiration with no value.

Median Market Cap: The middle stock in a stock fund's portfolio in terms of market capitalization.

Micro Cap Stock: Micro cap stocks are issued by companies with very small or "micro" capitalizations, usually less than $100 million.

Mid Cap Stock: Usually a reference to the shares of a company with a market capitalization of between $500 million and $2 billion.

Minimum Investment: The smallest investment permitted when opening a new fund account or making an additional purchase.

Momentum Fund: A fund that attempts to achieve above-average results by following what its manager discerns as an established trend in securities process.

Money Market Fund: A fund designed to provide safety of principal and current income by investing in securities that mature in one year or less, such as bank certificates of deposit, commercial paper, and U.S. Treasury bills. The price per share is usually fixed at $1.00.

Mortgage-Backed Security: Debt instruments that are guaranteed (or collateralized) by residential, commercial, or industrial real-estate mortgages.

Municipal Bond: An IOU issued by a state, city, or other sub-sovereign government unit to finance public works such as the construction of roads or schools. The interest is usually free from federal income tax and may be free from certain state and local taxes as well.

Municipal Bond Fund: A fund that seeks to provide income exempt from federal income tax, consistent with preservation of capital and the fund's risk characteristics, by investing in a portfolio of municipal bonds.

Mutual Fund: A diversified, managed portfolio of securities that pools the assets of individuals and organizations to invest toward a common objective such as current income or long-term growth.

Mutual Fund Liquidity Ratio: The ratio of cash (and equivalents) to total assets held by mutual funds (excluding money market funds) is often used as an indicator of potential demand for stocks and the degree of bullishness/bearishness of mutual fund managers.

NASD: The National Association of Securities Dealers, an industry organization charged by Congress with standardizing investment practices and establishing high ethical standards in the financial industry.

NASDAQ: A nationwide electronic automated quotation system established by the NASD for up-to-the-minute price quotations and trading on over 5,000 OTC stocks.

Net Asset Value (NAV) Per Share for a Fund: The total assets (securities, cash, and accrued earnings) of an open-end, closed-end, exchange-traded or preferred fund, minus the fund's liabilities, divided by the number of shares outstanding.

New York Stock Exchange (NYSE): The oldest (since 1792) and largest stock exchange in the U.S.

No-Load Fund: A mutual fund whose shares are sold without a sales commission and without a 12(b)(1) fee of more than 0.25% per year.

Non-Investment Grade Bond: Bonds whose issuers are judged by an independent rating service, such as Standard & Poor's or Moody's Investors Service, as unable to pay interest and repay principal reliably. Standard & Poor's and Moody's Investors Service designate bonds rated below BBB/Baa as non-investment grade. *Also called High Yield Bond or Junk Bond.*

Non-Systematic Risk: An element of price risk that can be largely eliminated by diversification within an asset class. In factor models estimated by regression analysis, it is equal to the standard error.

Offering Price: *See Asked Price.*

Offshore Fund: A mutual fund or, more commonly, a hedge fund domiciled outside the United States.

Open-End Investment Company: Technically, a mutual fund that constantly offers new shares for sale and undertakes to redeem outstanding shares on any business day at their NAV. Participants can buy and sell shares on any business day and the size of the fund is not limited. Open-end exchange-traded funds are a variant of the traditional open-end company, but their shares are not individually redeemable.

Optimized Tracking Portfolio: *See Representative Sampling.*

Option: The right to buy or sell a given security within a particular time at a specified price. The right to buy is a call; the right to sell is a put. Unlike a futures contract, owning an option does not obligate the investor to perform the transaction; the obligation is only on the part of the seller of the option.

Over the Counter (OTC): A market, regulated by the NASD, for securities that are not traded on any organized stock exchange, as well as some listed securities traded off those exchanges. Most government, municipal, and corporate bonds are also traded over the counter. The trades take place by telephone or by computer network.

Par Value: The face value or notional value of a bond or stock as printed on the certificate. Bonds generally have a par value of $1,000.

Part B Prospectus: *See Statement of Additional Information.*

Passive Investing: Investing in a fund or other pooled investment vehicle that attempts to match the risk/return pattern of a market index. The term passive investing is, perhaps, somewhat misleading in describing the activities of the manager of an index portfolio. While the manager may not engage in active management in the sense of picking stocks or determining wide-ranging investment policy, the method in which some index changes are handled places a premium on an aggressive, active response by the index fund manager.

Passive Management: Most commonly, indexation of a portfolio. Indexation means giving up the opportunity for superior performance within an asset class in return for protection from inferior performance. The word "passive" suggests a more relaxed approach than the successful managers of such portfolios adopt. *Contrast with Active Management.*

Passive Structured Portfolio Management: Use of quantitative tools to track an index closely while maximizing the tax efficiency of a fund. If a trade-off is necessary, the choice usually will be to stress tax efficiency.

Payable Date: The day on which a fund or corporation pays its distributions to shareholders.

Payment Default Risk: Although bond issuers promise to make regular interest payments on the bond and promise to pay back, or redeem, the face value of the bond at the maturity date, some issuers may fail to meet these obligations. Payment default risk refers to the risk that a specific issuer may not be able to meet these obligations.

Phone Switching: The ability to transfer cash between mutual funds in the same family with a telephone call.

Physical Assets: Agricultural, industrial, or natural resource products that underlie commodity futures.

Plan Administrator: Organization responsible for administration of a pension or profit sharing plan.

Portfolio: A collection of securities and/or other financial instruments under common ownership and management.

Portfolio Allocation: The proportion of a fund's assets invested in each of stocks, bonds, and cash equivalents.

Portfolio Diversification: *See Diversification.*

Portfolio Manager: An investor of institutional funds or manager of accounts for multiple individuals.

Portfolio Trade: The purchase or sale of a basket of stocks. By NYSE definition, a portfolio trade (or program trade) includes more than fifteen different stocks with a total value of $1 million or more entered as a coordinated transaction. Portfolio trades may be undertaken to increase or reduce market exposure in a portfolio or as one side of an EFP or index arbitrage trade. *Also called Basket Trade.*

Portfolio Turnover Rate: An indication of trading activity, typically for a year. Turnover is usually measured as: (purchases plus sales)/(beginning value plus ending value). Portfolios with high turnover rates generally incur higher transaction costs than portfolios with lower turnover.

Preferred Stock (or Preferred Shares):   A class of stock usually with a fixed- or floating-rate linked dividend that has preference over a company's common stock in the payment of dividends and the liquidation of assets. There are several kinds of preferred stock, among them adjustable-rate preferred and convertible preferred.

Preliminary Prospectus: *See Red Herring.*

Premature Distribution: A distribution from an IRA made before the owner reaches age 59½. Such a distribution is generally subject to a 10% penalty tax.

Premium: Amount (stated in dollars or percent) by which the selling or purchase price of a security is more than its face amount or net asset value.

Pre-Refunding: A procedure used by state and local governments to refinance municipal bonds to lower interest expenses. The issuer sells new bonds with a lower yield and uses the proceeds to buy U.S. Treasury securities, the interest from which is used to make payments on the higher-yielding bonds. Because of this collateral, pre-refunding generally raises a bond's credit rating and thus its value.

Price (or Market Price): The monetary amount that a financial instrument can be purchased or sold for on a financial market.

Price/Book Ratio: The market price per share of a stock divided by its book value (i.e., net worth) per share. For a fund, the ratio is the weighted, average price/book ratio of the stocks in the fund's portfolio.

Price/Earnings Ratio (P/E Ratio): The ratio of a stock's current price to its per-share earnings (P/E) over the past year. For a fund, the ratio is the weighted average P/E of the stocks in the fund's portfolio. P/E is an indicator of market expectations about corporate prospects; the higher the P/E, the greater the expectations for a company's future growth in earnings.

Prime Rate: (1) The interest rate a bank charges on loans to its most creditworthy customers. Frequently cited as a standard for general interest-rate levels in the economy. (2) A lending rate offered to a bank's better retail customers.

Primary Market: The primary market is the market for new issues of securities. The primary market is distinguished from the secondary market, where previously issued securities are bought and sold with investors and market makers participating in trades. The issuer of the securities.

Principal Only (PO Obligation): A tranche of mortgage-backed securities whose owner receives only principal payments made by the underlying mortgages. During periods of falling interest rates, rapid repayments of principal by mortgage holders increases the value of the principal-only obligations. During periods of rising interest rates, principal payments may slow down and the value of the principal-only obligations will decline.

Principal Transaction: A transaction between a retail or institutional customer and a financial intermediary in which the financial firm acts as a principal, i.e., trades for its own account. *Compare to Agency Transaction.*

Private Placement: The sale of securities to a limited number of investors at the initial stages of a company's operations, a private placement allows selected investors to invest in attractive companies before the company sells stock to the public. Of course, the risk of investing is also higher at the early stage of operations.

Prospectus: Formal selling document for offerings of mutual funds, corporate securities, and some other securities.

Proxy: A written authorization that allows one person to act for another. For example, shareholders who are unable to attend an annual meeting may mail in their ballots and vote by proxy.

Proxy Statement: Document providing shareholders with background information on management and large shareholders, and on matters to be voted on by shareholders.

Public Offering Price (POP): The purchase price of one share on the primary market, including any up-front sales charge.

Q's, QQQ, or Qubes: Nicknames for the NASDAQ 100 Index Tracking Stock Index Shares. Their stock symbol is QQQ.

Qualified Retirement Plan: A retirement plan established by employers for their employees meeting the requirements of Internal Revenue Code Section 401(a) or 403(a). Plan assets and earnings are not taxed until they are paid out as benefits.

R^2 (Pronounced R-squared): A measurement of investment risk that shows how closely the portfolio's performance correlates with the performance of a benchmark index (such as the Standard and Poor's® 500 Index), and thus indicates how closely that performance is linked to the broad market. A high R^2 signifies that the portfolio's fluctuations generally reflect market moves, while a low R^2 indicates that other factors tend to drive fund performance.

Real Rate of Return: The return on an investment after it is adjusted for the effect of inflation.

Rebalancing: Periodic revisions to a portfolio necessitated by the effect of the passage of time on asset and liability duration, changes in the constitution of an index, portfolio cash flows, or market-driven departures from a target allocation.

Record Date: The date that determines which shareholders will be paid a dividend or other distribution, or will be entitled to vote at the annual meeting.

Redeem: To cash in or exchange fund shares for liquid assets.

Redemption: The process of turning or exchanging fund shares for cash or a basket of the fund's securities.

Redemption Price: The price at which a holder can sell (redeem) a fund's shares, determined by deducting any applicable sales charge from the net asset value (NAV) per unit/share.

Red Herring: A preliminary prospectus for a securities offering in the U.S. The red herring usually has full details of the offering except price and, perhaps, size. It has comprehensive financial data on the issuer. The name comes from a required note usually printed in red ink stating that the issue cannot yet be sold because the registration statement is not yet effective.

Registered Investment Company: A fund company that is registered with the SEC. *Not the same as Regulated Investment Company (RIC).*

Regulated Investment Company (RIC): A reference to income pass-through provisions for investment companies in the Internal Revenue Code. In addition to SEC registration, an investment company must meet IRS diversification requirements to avoid taxation at the fund level. *Not the same as Registered Investment Company.*

Reinvestment Privilege: The right of shareholders to use income and/or capital gain distributions to purchase additional shares of their fund.

Replicating Portfolio: A portfolio constructed to match the performance of an index or benchmark as closely as practicable. An exchange-traded fund with a replicating portfolio will usually track its index more closely and trade at a tighter bid-asked spread than a fund with a representative sampling portfolio. *Contrast with Representative Sampling or Optimized Tracking Portfolio.*

Representative Sampling: A technique used to create a benchmark tracking portfolio when the benchmark is not naturally compliant with rules governing portfolio structure, such as the regulated investment company diversification requirements for a U.S.-based investment company. Representative sampling is also used when certain securities are not readily available to match the benchmark. *Compare to Replicating Portfolio.*

Repurchase Agreement (Repo): A purchase of U.S. government securities from a bank or broker made under the stipulation that the seller agrees to buy back or repurchase the securities at a fixed price on a future date. Repos usually mature in a week or less.

Retail Investor: A private investor that typically purchases and sells securities in smaller quantities than institutional investors.

Revenue Bond: A municipal bond that is backed by revenue from the project being financed. Revenue bonds are usually less securely backed than general obligation bonds, and thus may trade at higher yields.

Reverse Repurchase Agreement (Reverse-Repo): A sale of U.S. government securities by a bank or broker made under the stipulation that the buyer agrees to sell back the securities at a fixed price on a future date. Reverse-repos usually mature in a week or less.

Rights of Accumulation (ROA): A way for a shareholder to qualify for a reduced sales charge by adding the value of shares already owned to the amount of a new purchase.

Rights Offering: Primarily used for closed-end funds. Fund management can raise additional capital by issuing shareholders rights to buy new common shares at predetermined prices. These offerings often involve substantial discounts to net asset value to encourage participation, which dilutes common shareholder ownership in the fund.

Rollover: A tax-free transfer of cash or other assets from one retirement plan to another. An IRA holder may shift assets from his or her present IRA to another. Distributions from a qualified retirement plan may also be rolled over to an IRA or to another employer's plan.

Rollover IRA: An individual retirement account that holds assets from a qualified retirement plan. If these assets are not mixed with other tax-sheltered retirement contributions, they can be rolled over to another qualified plan.

Roth IRA: A retirement plan created by the Taxpayer Relief Act of 1997. Contributions to a Roth IRA are made from after-tax income. Distributions from the Roth IRA are tax-free if they meet certain requirements (income, time since the Roth IRA was established, age of the owner, etc.).

Sales Charge: A fee that investors may pay when purchasing funds, (i.e., from the fund itself) on the primary market. Fund management companies typically use this fee to cover their selling and distribution costs. Closed-end funds, exchange-traded funds, and preferred funds do not have a sales charge for shares purchased on the secondary market, although investors must pay the normal brokerage fee associated with the purchase and sale of these shares.

Secondary Market: In contrast to the primary market, where new security issues are sold to investors, the secondary market is the traditional exchange or over-the-counter market where previously issued securities are bought and sold by individual and institutional holders with brokers and dealers as intermediaries.

Sector Diversification: Indicates the percentage of a portfolio's total net assets invested in each of the major industry classifications that comprise the market in which the fund invests.

Sector Fund: A specialized fund that invests exclusively in a related group of industries to potentially better opportunities for capital appreciation. Sector portfolios/funds are often more volatile than those which invest in a more diversified range of industries.

SEC Yield: A standardized measure of the current net market yield on a fund's investment portfolio. The SEC yield calculation is made in an unusual way, based on a 30-day (or one month) period ending on the most recent balance sheet date:

$$\text{Yield} = 2\left[\left(\frac{a-b}{cd} + 1\right)^6 - 1\right]$$

Where

a = dividends and interest earned during the period.

b = expenses accrued for the period (net of reimbursement).

c = the average daily number of shares outstanding during the period that were entitled to receive distributions.

d = the maximum offering price per share on the last day of the period.

Securities and Exchange Commission (SEC): The federal agency created by the Securities and Exchange Act of 1934 that administers the laws governing the securities markets. The SEC also regulates the registration and distribution of unit investment trusts, exchange-traded fund shares, and mutual fund shares.

Securities Lending: A carefully collateralized process of loaning portfolio positions in securities to custodians, dealers, and short sellers who must make physical delivery of fungible positions. Securities lending can reduce custodial costs or enhance annual returns by a full percentage point or more in some markets at some times, although revenue from this source is usually much smaller. Improvements in securities settlement procedures and systems to facilitate securities lending have tended to reduce lending premiums over time.

Senior Loans: *See Bank Debt.*

Series Fund: A group of different mutual funds, each a "series" with its own investment objective and policies, structured as a single corporation or business trust.

Series 7 License: A general securities registered representative license, entitling the holder to sell all types of securities products.

Settlement Date: The date on which the exchange of cash, securities, and paperwork involved in a transaction is completed. Usually one day after the trade date ($T+1$) in conventional funds and fixed-income markets, and three days after the trade date ($T+3$) in exchange-traded funds and equity markets.

Short Sale: The sale of a security or other financial instrument not previously owned by the seller in the expectation that it will be possible to repurchase that instrument at a lower price some time in the future. The term "short sale" is ordinarily applied only to the sale of securities, but an equivalent synthetic short position can be attained through the sale of an uncovered call option and the purchase of a put or by selling a forward or futures contract.

Short Sale Rule: A mildly controversial requirement imposed by the SEC, requiring that short sales can only be made on a plus tick or zero plus tick (a price higher than the last sale at a different price). Supporters of this rule argue that it prevents bear raiders from selling short to drive a stock down.

Short-Term Capital Gain: A profit on the sale of a security or fund share held for one year or less.

Short-Term Tax-Free Income: An investment style that seeks capital preservation while providing attractive tax-free income. Short-term tax-free funds invest in diversified portfolios of quality municipal bonds with a weighted-average maturity between one and seven years.

Signature Guarantee: A stamp or seal by a bank or member of a domestic stock exchange (or other acceptable guarantor) on correspondence that authenticates a signature. A notary public cannot provide a signature guarantee.

Small-Capitalization Stocks: The stocks of companies whose market value is less than $250 million. Small-cap companies tend to grow faster than large-cap companies and typically use any profits for expansion rather than for paying dividends. They also are more volatile than large-cap companies and have a higher failure rate. *Also referred to as Small Cap.*

Specialist: A floor member of an exchange that accepts primary responsibility for making a fair market in securities at all times that the exchange is open for business. The specialist may take positions in these securities for their own account.

Specie, In Specie: (1) In coin as opposed to paper money. (2) In-kind, as in the "in-kind" exchange of securities for fund shares in the creation and redemption of exchange-traded funds. This archaic usage, more common in the medieval church and courts than in commerce, has been revived in connection with ETFs in Europe.

SPDRs (or Spiders): Standard & Poor's 500 Depositary Receipts. A warehouse receipt unit investment trust structure that provides the investor with an interest in the holdings of a trust designed to track the return of the S&P 500 index. SPDRs were introduced by the American Stock Exchange in 1993. They became one of the fastest growing "fund" products in history and launched the open exchange-traded fund (ETF) market. The acronym is also part of the name of other ETFs, the MidCap SPDRs, and nine Sector SPDRs.

Standard & Poor's 500 Index: A daily measure of stock market performance, based on the performance of 500 major companies. Though it does not include transaction or management costs, the S&P 500 is often used as a yardstick for equity fund performance.

Standard Deviation: A measure of the degree to which specific observations varied from an average over a certain period. The smaller the difference, the lower the standard deviation will be—and the greater the degree of stability one might expect over the period.

Statement of Additional Information (SAI): A supplementary document to a fund prospectus that contains more detailed information about the fund. *Also known as a Part B Prospectus.*

State Municipal Bond Fund: Municipal bond fund whose objective is to provide current income that is exempt from regular federal, state, and, in some cases, local income taxes by investing in a portfolio of municipal bonds from a single state.

Street Name: A reference to securities registered in the name of a broker or a nominee such as a clearing house instead of in the name of the beneficial owner. Street name registration facilitates securities transfers and has grown in popularity since the move to three business day settlement for stocks.

Street Name Account: An investor's account which is held in the name of a brokerage firm (in part to facilitate payment and delivery of securities).

STRIPS: An acronym for Separately Traded Registered Interest and Principal Securities. These zero-coupon notes and bonds are created by trading note and bond coupon and principal payments stripped from Treasury securities.

Syndicated: Often used to refer to investments in the primary market that are underwritten, sold, or distributed by multiple securities dealers, where a group of firms (i.e. a syndicate) guarantee the sale of an issue/loan by purchasing it for subsequent resale to investors at a higher price.

Synthetic: A financial instrument that is composed of other financial instruments. A synthetic instrument may be composed of a single security or a variety of instruments whose combined features are comparable to the instrument it replicates.

Systematic Investment Plan: An arrangement which permits regular investments in a fund through payroll deductions, automatic transfers from a checking account, or automatic exchanges from another fund.

Swap Fund: *See Exchange Fund.*

Target Stock: A special class of common or preferred shares with dividends and/or earnings participation linked to a specific segment of the issuer's business.

Taxable Equivalent Yield: The yield on a taxable bond that would produce the same after-tax return for a taxpayer as a specific tax-exempt issue. It is always a good idea to ask about the tax rate assumptions in the calculation. *Also called Equivalent Taxable Yield.*

Taxable Fixed-Income Fund: A portfolio of corporate or U.S. Treasury debt that provides monthly, quarterly, or semi-annual income.

Tax-Aware Portfolio Management: A commitment to exercise a reasonable effort to achieve fund tax efficiency by a portfolio's advisor. Less commitment than an investor would expect in a *Tax Managed Fund.*

Tax-Deferred: Income on which taxes can be postponed until a later date. Contributions to a 401(k) plan, for example, are not taxed until they are withdrawn from the account, but when withdrawn, they are fully taxed at the applicable tax rate.

Tax-Deferred Income: Ordinary income and capital gains from investments in a qualified retirement plan. This income is not subject to taxation until a withdrawal is made.

Tax Efficiency: A characteristic of a financial instrument that permits a dealer or an end user to establish or modify a position in a way that requires lower tax payments than an alternate similar position or instrument. Mutual funds are frequently evaluated on the basis of their ability to defer capital gains taxes for their shareholders.

Tax-Exempt Bond: *See Municipal Bond.*

Tax-Free Income: An investment strategy that seeks to provide high levels of attractive tax-free income while also preserving capital. Tax-free income funds invest in diversified portfolios of quality municipal bonds with a weighted-average maturity between 15-30 years.

Tax-Free Fixed-Income Fund: A portfolio of federally tax-exempt (and for some state-specific portfolios, state and local tax-exempt) municipal bonds that provide monthly, quarterly, or semi-annual income.

Tax Loss Carry-Forward: A tax benefit that allows an individual, a corporation or a fund to offset past losses against future profits.

Tax-Lot Accounting: A record keeping technique that traces dates of purchase and sale, cost basis, and transaction size for each lot of each security in a portfolio.

Tax-Managed Fund: An open-end mutual fund managed with the objective of minimizing taxes even at the expense of benchmark tracking, diversification, or even pre-tax return. More tax-focused than a fund under *Tax Aware Portfolio Management*.

Tax Year: The 12-month period used by an individual to report income for income tax purposes. For most individuals, their tax year is the calendar year.

Technical Analysis: Analysis of the supply and demand for securities using charts and graphs to identify price trends that may forecast future price movements.

Ticker (or Ticker Symbol): The ticker is a security's trading symbol, such as QQQ for the NASDAQ 100 Trust.

Top-Down Investing: An investor first looks at trends in the general economy, and then selects industries and finally companies that should benefit from those trends.

Total Return: Usually expressed as income plus any principal gain or minus any principal loss during a measurement period divided by principal (investment) and expressed as a percent.

Tracking Error: Used to describe the volatility of returns of a portfolio relative to the returns of its benchmark portfolio, typically expressed in terms of the standard deviation of the differences between the portfolio and index returns over a specific horizon (such as a year). Net-asset-value tracking error is the difference between the net-asset-value of the fund or trust and the return of the index or strategy on which the fund is based. Price-to-index tracking error is the difference between the returns based on the closing market prices for a fund or trust and the returns based on the closing market prices of the underlying index.

Trade Date: The date on which all the terms and methods for resolving any remaining contingencies in a financial instrument are agreed upon.

Traditional IRA: A personal, tax-deferred retirement account that allows you to make contributions from your current income. Your contributions may be tax-deductible subject to certain earned-income limitations and age restrictions.

Tranche: One of a related series of security issues (typically interest-paying fixed income securities) that are created from underlying cash flows to meet the risk/return demands of different investors.

Each tranche may have a different cash flow, strike price, and expiration date.

Transfer Agent: An institution, usually a bank, used by an issuer of shares to maintain its shareholder records and perform all account transactions.

Transfer of Assets: Refers to an IRA being transferred directly from one custodian or trustee to another. The IRA holder does not actually receive the funds. All IRA transfers are non-reportable transactions to the IRA holder and the IRS.

Treasury Bill, Bond, Note: Negotiable debt obligations issued by the U.S. government and backed by its full faith and credit. Treasury bills are short-term securities with maturities of one year or less. Treasury notes are intermediate-term securities with maturities of 1 to 10 years. Treasury bonds are long-term securities with maturities of 10 years or longer.

Treasury Interest STRIPS (TINTS) STRIPS based only on interest coupons stripped from Treasury notes or bonds, not on principal payments.

Triple Tax-Exempt Fund: A municipal bond fund whose dividends and interest are exempt from regular Federal, state, and local income taxes affecting an investor resident in the designated locality.

Turnover: (1) In a portfolio, usually calculated as (Purchases + Sales)/(Beginning Value + Ending Value). If a portfolio has an average turnover of 50% by this measure, approximately half the securities (in a portfolio with modest contributions and withdrawals) are replaced with new positions each year. (2) In the U.K., trading volume.

Turnover Rate: *See Portfolio Turnover.*

Umbrella Fund: The high level fund in a fund-of-funds structure.

Underwriter: (1) An investment banker that purchases securities for his own account with the express intention of reselling them in the open market. (2) An insurer that undertakes to furnish an insurance contract in exchange for a premium. (3) The organization that sells a mutual fund's shares to broker/dealers.

Undistributed Net Investment Income (UNII):   Represents the life-to-date balance of a fund's net investment income less distributions of net investment income. UNII appears as a line item on a fund's statement of changes in net assets.

Uniform Gift to Minors Act (UGMA):   State law that allows any adult to contribute to a custodian account in a minor child's name without having to name a legal guardian or establish a trust.

Unit Investment Trust (UIT):   An investment company that usually buys and holds a fixed portfolio until the trust's termination date. When the trust is dissolved, proceeds are paid to shareholders. Like a mutual fund, shares of a UIT can be redeemed on any business day. Other UITs serve as the structure for some early exchange-traded funds (ETFs).

Universal Stock Futures: The brand name Liffe gives to its version of cash-settled single-stock futures contracts.

Unrated Securities: Typically, fixed income securities are rated for creditworthiness and repayment risk by independent rating services such as Standard & Poor's or Moody's Investor Services. However, not all securities are rated by these services, perhaps due to the size of the security issue, or perhaps because the issuing company is not able to provide the prerequisite information to the rating services.

Value Investing: A strategy for equity investing that emphasizes stocks with below-average price-to-book ratios, but above-average dividend yields.

Value Stocks: Stocks that have relatively high dividend yields and that sell at relatively low prices in relation to their earnings or book value.

Volatility: The fluctuations in market value of a fund or other security. The greater a fund's volatility, the wider the fluctuations between its high and low prices. Usually measured by annualized standard deviation of stock price or return.

Warrant: An option to purchase or sell the underlying security at a given price and time or at a series of prices and times outlined in the warrant agreement. A warrant differs from a put or call option in that it is ordinarily issued for a period in excess of one year. Ordinarily, exercise of a common stock warrant sold by the issuer of the underlying increases the number of shares of stock outstanding, whereas a call or a covered warrant is an option on shares already outstanding.

Wash Sale: The sale and repurchase of the same asset within 30 days. The IRS does not allow an investor to claim a tax loss on a wash sale.

When-Issued Securities: Refers to a transaction made conditionally because a security, although authorized to be issued, has not yet been issued. New issues of stocks and bonds, stocks that have split, and Treasury securities are traded on a when-issued basis.

X: Appears next to a fund's listing in the newspaper to indicate that the fund recently paid a capital gain dividend. This amount was previously included in the fund's net asset value and is deducted from the net asset value when it is paid out. The "x" stands for "ex-dividend."

Yield: *See Dividend Yield and SEC Yield.*

Yield Curve: A graph or "curve" that depicts the yields of bonds of varying maturities, from short-term to long-term. The graph shows the relationship between short- and long-term interest rates.

Yield Spread: The variation between yields on different types of debt securities. This variation is generally a function of supply and demand, credit quality, and expected interest-rate fluctuations. Treasury bonds, for example, because they are so safe in terms of credit risk, will normally yield less than corporate bonds. Yields may also differ on similar securities with different maturities. Long-term debt, for example, carries more risk of market changes and issuer defaults than shorter-term debt, and thus usually yields more.

Yield to Maturity: The annual return on a bond, assuming the bond is held until its maturity date. Unlike current yield, this takes into consideration the purchase price, redemption value, time to maturity, coupon yield, and time between interest payments.

Z: Appears after a fund's name in the daily newspaper if the price isn't available in time to meet the

NASDAQ reporting deadline, usually due to an extremely tight reporting schedule.

Zero Coupon Bond: A security that pays no interest but is instead sold at a discount from face value. The holder receives the rate of return through gradual appreciation of the security, which is redeemed at maturity for the full face value.

Bibliography

1. Arnott, Robert D., Andrew L. Berkin, and Jia Ye, "The Management and Mismanagement of Taxable Assets," *The Journal of Investing*, Spring 2001, pp. 15–21.

2. Arnott, Robert D. and Ronald Ryan, "The Death of the Risk Premium: Consequences of the 1990s," *Journal of Portfolio Management*, Spring 2001, pp. 61–74.

3. Arnott, Robert D. and Peter L. Bernstein, "What Risk Premium Is "Normal"?" forthcoming in the *Journal of Portfolio Management*.

4. Baca, Sean P., Brian L. Garbe, and Richard A. Weiss, "The Rise of Sector Effects in Major Equity Markets," *Financial Analysts Journal*, September/October 2000, pp. 34–40.

5. Baks, Klaas P., Andrew Metrick, and Jessica Wachter, "Should Investors Avoid All Actively Managed Mutual Funds? A Study in Bayesian Performance Evaluation," *The Journal of Finance*, February 2001, pp. 45–85.

6. Banc One Investment Advisors Corporation, One Group Mutual Fund Family Prospectus, November 1, 2000.

7. Barnes, Mark A., Anthony Bercel, and Steven H. Rothmann, "Global Equities: Do Countries Still Matter?" *The Journal of Investing*, Fall 2001, pp. 43–49.

8. Bary, Andrew, "The Trader—Indexers Trounce Active Managers and Roil Market, Too," *Barron's*, January 4, 1999, p. MW3.

9. Bary, Andrew, "The Trader—Wow! '98 Had Enough Thrills for Several Years," *Barron's*, December 28, 1998, p. MW3.

10. Bergstresser, Daniel and James Poterba, "Do After-Tax Returns Affect Mutual Fund Inflows?" Working Paper 7595, National Bureau of Economic Research (March 2000).

11. Bernstein Investment Research and Management, Tax Management Essays, www.bernstein.com, 2000.

12. Bernstein, Peter L., *Capital Ideas*, Free Press, 1992, pp. 233–252.

13. Black, Fischer, "Yes, Virginia, There is Hope: Test of the Value Line Ranking System," *Financial Analysts Journal*, September–October 1973, pp. 10–14.

14. Black, Fischer, "The Tax Consequences of Long-Run Pension Policy," *Financial Analysts Journal*, July–August 1980, pp. 21–28.

15. Blitzer, David M., "Here At The S&P 500," *Journal of Index Issues in Investment*, Jan.–Mar. 2000, pp. 1–5.

16. Bodie, Zvi, Allen Marcus, and Alex Kane, *Investments*, 5th Edition, McGraw-Hill, 2001.

17. Bogle, John C., *Common Sense on Mutual Funds*, Wiley, 1999.

18. Bogle, John C., *John Bogle on Investing—The First 50 Years*, McGraw-Hill, 2001.

19. Bogle, John C., "The Twelve Pillars of Wisdom," speech given to The Arizona Republic Investment Strategies Forum, Phoenix, Arizona, April 27, 2001, http://www.vanguard.com/bogle_site/april272001.html.

20. Braham, Lewis, "Who Gives the Web's Best 401(k) Advice?" *Business Week*, July 30, 2001, pp. 88–90.

21. Brenner, Lynn, *Smart Questions to Ask Your Financial Advisers*, Bloomberg, 1997.

22. Brenner, Lynn, "What Goes Where?" *Bloomberg Personal Finance*, September 1998, pp. 121–122.

23. Brenner, Lynn, "The Right Advice," *Bloomberg Personal Finance*, September 2001, pp. 64–71.

24. Brinson, Gary P., L. Randolph Hood, and Gilbert L. Beebower, "Determinants of Portfolio Performance," *Financial Analysts Journal*, July–August 1986, pp. 39–48.

25. Brinson, Gary P., Brian D. Singer, and Gilbert L. Beebower, "Determinants of Portfolio Performance II: An Update," *Financial Analysts Journal*, May–June 1991, pp. 40–48.

26. Campbell, John Y., Martin Lettau, Burton G. Malkiel, and Yexiao XU, "Have Individual Stocks Become More Volatile? An Empirical Exploration of Idiosyncratic Risk," *The Journal of Finance*, February 2001, pp. 1–43.

27. Carty, Michael C., "Favored Large-Cap Barometer Will Change," *Pensions & Investments* 36, November 1, 1999.

28. Cavaglia, Stefano, Christopher Brightman, and Michael Aked, "The Increasing Importance of Industry Factors," *Financial Analysts Journal*, September/October 2000, pp. 41–54.

29. Chevalier, Judith and Glenn Ellison, "Are Some Mutual Fund Managers Better Than Others? Cross-Sectional Patterns in Behavior and Performance," *The Journal of Finance*, June 1999, pp. 875–899.

30. Charron, Terry Sylvester, "Tax-Efficient Investing for Tax-Deferred and Taxable Accounts," *The Journal of Private Portfolio Management*, Fall 1999, pp. 31–37.

31. Clash, James M., "401(k) Tax Strategy," *Forbes*, August 26, 1996, p. 114.

32. Clements, Jonathan, "Now You've Retired, Bring In the Help," *Wall Street Journal*, August 28, 2001, p. C–1.

33. Clifford, Lee, "The Island of Misfit Stocks," *Fortune*, Sept. 4, 2000, pp. 356–8.

34. Cramer, James, "The Index Game," *Time*, December 20, 1999, p. 117.

35. Currier, Chet, "To Avoid Taxes, Investors Pay Elsewhere: A Law Deferring Levies on Capital Gains Distributions Is The Only Real Answer," *The Washington Post*, May 6, 2001, p. H03.

36. Cushing, David and Ananth Madhavan, "Stock Returns and Trading at the Close," *Journal of Financial Markets*, 3 (2000) pp 45–67.

37. Damato, Karen, "Mutual Funds: Life Cycle Choices Offer Simple Path," *Wall Street Journal*, June 22, 2001, pp. C1 and C17.

38. Davidson, R.B., III, "The Value of Tax Management for Bond Portfolios," *The Journal of Private Portfolio Management*, Spring 1999, pp. 49–55.

39. Deliva, Wilfred L., "Exchange-Traded Funds Not for Everyone," *Journal of Financial Planning*, April 2001, pp. 110–124.

40. Dickson, Joel M., "Tax-Efficient Mutual Funds," *Investment Counseling for Private Clients II*, Association for Investment Management and Research (2000), pp. 39–49.

41. Dickson, Joel M. and John B. Shoven, "Ranking Mutual Funds on An After-Tax Basis," Center for Economic Policy Research, Publication No. 344, Stanford University, 1993.

42. Dickson, Joel M. and John B. Shoven, "A Stock Index Mutual Fund Without Net Capital Gains Realizations," Working Paper 4717, National Bureau of Economic Research, April 1994.

43. *The Economist*, "Flotsam and Jetsam," May 26, 2001, p. 73.

44. Ellis, Charles D., "The Loser's Game," *Financial Analysts Journal*, July–August 1975, pp. 19–26.

45. Elton, Edwin J., Martin J. Gruber, George Comer, and Kai Li, "Where Are the Bugs?" forthcoming in *The Journal of Business*.

46. Elton, Edwin J., Martin J. Gruber, and Christopher R. Blake, "The Persistence of Risk-Adjusted Mutual Fund Performance," *The Journal of Business*, April 1996, pp. 133–157.

47. Fazzi, Raymond, "In Search of the Holy Grail," *Financial Advisor*, September 2001, pp. 68–83.

48. Fidelity Investments, Fidelity Freedom Fund Family Prospectus, May 29, 2001.

49. Frankel, Tamar, *The Regulation of Money Managers, The Investment Company Act and the Investment Advisers Act*, Volume I, Little, Brown and Company, 1978.

50. Frankel, Tamar, *The Regulation of Money Managers*, Supplement, Volume I, Aspen Law and Business, 2000.

51. Fredman, Albert J., "An Investor's Guide to Analyzing Exchange-Traded Funds," *AAII Journal*, May 2001, pp. 8–13.

52. Fredman, Albert J., "Sizing Up Mutual Fund Relatives: Low-Cost Alternative Investing," *AAII Journal*, July 2001, pp. 9–14.

53. Garnick, Diane M., John Davi, Steve Kim, and Silvio Lotufo, "Index Dynamics: S&P Turnover Accelerated in Y2K," Merrill Lynch, January 11, 2001.

54. Gastineau, Gary L., *The Options Manual*, 3rd Edition, McGraw-Hill, 1988.

55. Gastineau, Gary L., "Beating the Equity Benchmarks," *Financial Analysts Journal*, July/August, 1994, pp. 6–11.

56. Gastineau, Gary L. and Mark P. Kritzman, *Dictionary of Financial Risk Management*, Frank J. Fabozzi Associates, 1999.

57. Gastineau, Gary L., "Exchange-Traded Funds—An Introduction," *The Journal of Portfolio Management*, Volume 27, Number 3, Spring 2001, pp. 88–96.

58. Goetzmann, William N., Takato Hiraki, Toshiyuki Otsuki, and Noriyoshi Shiraishi, "The Japanese Open-End Fund Puzzle," *The Journal of Business*, Volume 74, Number 1, 2001, pp. 59–77.

59. Goetzmann, William N. and Roger G. Ibbotson, "Do Winners Repeat?" *The Journal of Portfolio Management*, Winter 1994, pp. 9–18.

60. Gordon, Robert N., "Hedging Low-Cost-Basis Stock," *AIMR Conference Proceedings*, Number 4, 2001, pp. 36–41 and 42–44.

61. Gotoh, Masaki, "Change in Australian SPI 200 Settlement Methodology: Potential Implications on Expiration," *Global Equity Index/Equity Derivatives Report—Goldman Sachs*, September 11, 2001, pp. 1–6.

62. Gramm, Phil, "Gramm Outlines Committee Agenda for the 107th Congress," January 22, 2001 Press Release from the Senate Banking Committee, www.senate.gov.

63. Grinold, Richard C. and Ronald R. Kahn, *Active Portfolio Management*, McGraw-Hill, 2nd Edition, 2000, especially pp. 559–571.

64. Gruber, Martin J., "Another Puzzle: The Growth in Actively-Managed Mutual Funds," *Journal of Finance*, July 1996, pp. 783 - 810.

65. Harper, Richard, "Two is Better than One," Nuveen Investments Publications, January 2001.

66. Hellerstein, Judge Alvin K., Memorandum and Order of Judgement in "The McGraw-Hill Companies vs. Vanguard Index Trust, *et al.*," 00 Civ. 4247 (AKH), United States District Court, Southern District of New York, April 25, 2001.

67. Hervey, Richard, M., "Taxation of Regulated Investment Companies," *Tax Management Portfolios*, Number 740, 1999.

68. Hopkins, Peter J.B. and C. Hayes Miller, *Country, Sector and Company Factors in Global Equity Portfolios*, AIMR-Blackwell, 2001.

69. Ibbotson, Roger G. and Paul D. Kaplan, "Does Asset Allocation Policy Explain 40, 90, or 100 Percent of Performance?" *Financial Analysts Journal*, January–February 2000, pp. 26–33.

70. Jaffe, Charles A., *The Right Way to Hire Financial Help*, MIT Press, 1998.

71. Jahnke, William W., "The Asset Allocation Hoax," *Journal of Financial Planning*, February 1997, pp. 109–113.

72. Jankovskis, Peter, "Will the Real Style Please Stand Up," *Journal of Index Issues in Investment*, April–June 2000, pp. 9–15.

73. Jeffrey, Robert H., "Reflections on Portfolio Management After 25 Years," *The Journal of Investing*, Spring 2001, pp. 9–13.

74. Jeffrey, Robert H. and Robert D. Arnott, "Is Your Alpha Big Enough To Cover Its Taxes?" *The Journal of Portfolio Management*, Volume 19, Number 3, Spring 1993, pp. 15–25.

75. Julian, Bill, "Catching the Winners," *Salomon Smith Barney Portfolio Strategist*, August 23, 2001, pp. 8–11.

76. Kim, Steve, Mike Troikka, Pankaj Patel, Kevin Chang, and Edward Tom, "Index Watch—Style Dissonance Between Russell and S&P," Credit Suisse First Boston, Quantitative Analysis, August 19, 2001.

77. Kliesen, Kevin L., "The Switch to NAICS," *National Economic Trends*, The Federal Reserve Bank of St. Louis, August 2001, p. 1.

78. Kliesen, Kevin L. and Daniel L. Thornton, "The Expected Federal Budget Surplus: How Much Confidence Should the Policymakers Place in the Projections?" Federal Reserve Bank of St. Louis Review, March/April 2001.

79. Kritzman, Mark P., *Puzzles of Finance*, John Wiley & Sons, Inc., 2000.

80. Lauricella, Tom and Bridget O'Brian, "Getting Personal: Popularity of Managed Accounts Grows," *Wall Street Journal*, August 6, 2001, pp. C1 and C17.

81. Legomsky, Joanne, "Active Managers Await the Verdict," *The New York Times*, April 8, 2001, p. Bu–30.

82. Levy, Robert J., Tracey Longo, Andrew Rafalaf, Jennifer Stathis, and Barbara Mlotek Whelehan, "100 Great Financial Planners," *Mutual Funds*, October 2001, pp. 48–53.

83. Litt, David M. and Yigal D. Jhirad, "MSCI iShares and Their Relationship to Net Asset Value," Morgan Stanley Dean Witter Quantitative Strategies, August 2000.

84. Lo, Andrew W., "Personal Indexes," *The Journal of Index Issues*, 3rd Quarter 2001, pp. 26–35.

85. Lo, Andrew and Craig MacKinlay, *A Non-Random Walk Down Wall Street*, Princeton, N.J., Princeton University Press, 1999.

86. Loeper, David B., "The Asset Allocation Myth," Financeware.com Industry White Paper, August 3, 1999.

87. Loeper, David. B., "Asset Allocation Math, Methods and Mistakes," Financeware.com Editorial Commentary, June 1, 2001.

88. Loeper, David. B., "The Concentration Crisis—Risk Without Reward," Financeware.com Editorial Commentary, July 29, 2001.

89. Longo, Tracey, "How to Pick a Planner," *Mutual Funds*, October 2001, pp. 44–47.

90. Lucchetti, Aaron and Tom Lauricella, "Vanguard and S&P Seem Such a Nice Pair; Why the Nasty Spat?" *Wall Street Journal*, August 23, 2001, pp. A–1 and A–18.

91. Maier, Jon, "A Discussion on Index Ratios," Paine Weber Research Notes, 2000.

92. Malkiel, Burton, G., *A Random Walk Down Wall Street*, Norton, 7th Edition, 2000.

93. Marcus, Alan J., "The Magellan Fund and Market Efficiency," *The Journal of Portfolio Management*, Fall 1990, pp. 85–88.

94. Markowitz, H.M, *Portfolio Selection: Efficient Diversification of Investments*, Cambridge, MA: Basil Blackwell, 2nd Edition, 1991.

95. McNally, Kevin and Dennis Emanuel, "Fundamental Ideas for Exchange-Traded Funds," Salomon Smith Barney, October 18, 2000, pp. 12–19.

96. McNamee, Mike, "How To Get Back On Track," *Business Week*, July 30, 2001, pp. 81–83.

97. Michaud, Richard O., "Risk Policy and Long-Term Investment," *Journal of Financial and Quantitative Analysis*, June 1981, pp. 147–167.

98. Miller, Merton H., "Financial Innovation: The Last Twenty Years and the Next," *Journal of Financial and Quantitative Analysis*, Volume 21, Issue 4, December 1986, pp. 459–471.

99. Morgenson, Gretchen, "What the Sales Brochure Didn't Tell You," *Forbes*, April 7, 1997, pp. 90–96.

100. Moriarty, Kathleen, "Examining Exchange Traded Fund ("ETF") Structures in the United States," Unpublished ABA Business Law Presentation Memorandum, 2001.

101. Pachetti, Nick, "The Best Advice Money Can Buy," *Money*, August 2001, pp. 61–66.

102. Phillips, Don and Paul D. Kaplan, "The Greatest Return Stories Ever Told: Comment," *The Journal of Investing*, Fall 2001, pp. 94–95.

103. Phipps, Melissa, "The Best Advisers' Best Advice," *Worth*, September 2001, pp. 70–82.

104. Plexus Group, "Is Eliminating Tracking Error Hazardous to Your Client's Wealth?" Commentary 64, January 2001.

105. Poterba, James M., "Prescriptions for Tax-Efficient Investing," *The Journal of Investment Consulting*, December 2000, pp. 18–24.

106. Poterba, James M., "Estate Tax Avoidance by High Net Worth Households: Why Are There So Few Tax-Free Gifts?" *The Journal of Private Portfolio Management*, Summer 1998, pp. 1–9.

107. Price, T. Rowe and Associates, "Taxable vs. Tax-Deferred Accounts," *AAII Journal*, October 1996, pp. 11–12.

108. Rattray, Sandy, "REITs are Common Stocks—It's Official!" Goldman Sachs Index and Perspectives Supplement, October 2001, pp. 19–22.

109. Revell, Janice, "Recovery Is Sweet," *Fortune*, August 13, 2001, pp. 66–84.

110. Rottenberg, Dan, "Personal Wealth," *Bloomberg*, October 2001, pp. 90–95.

111. Rutter, James, "The A–Z of Exchange-Traded Funds," *Global Investor*, July/August 2001, pp. 36–41.

112. Ryan, Ron, "ETFs as a Dynamic Asset Allocation Tool," *ETFs—A Guide to Exchange-Traded Funds*, Institutional Investor, Fall 2001, pp. 95–97.

113. Samuelson, Paul A., "Challenge to Judgment," *Financial Analysts Journal*, Fall 1974, pp. 17–19.

114. Saxton, Jim, "Mutual Fund Shareholders Tax Relief Bill Introduced Today," Joint Economic Committee Press Release, June 22, 2000, www.house.gov/jec/press/2000/06-22-0.htm.

115. Schoenfeld, Steven, "The Multiple Dimensions of Global Equity Risk Management—A Practitioner's Perspective," *Global Investment Risk Management*, Ezra Zask, Ed., McGraw-Hill/Irwin, 2000, pp. 45–65.

116. Schoenfeld, Steven, Peter Handley, and Binu George, "International Equity Benchmarks for US Investors—Assessing the Alternatives, Contemplating the Tradeoffs," *Investment Insights*, Barclays Global Investors, Volume 3, Number 4, December 2000.

117. Schwartz, Robert A. and Ben Steil, "Controlling Institutional Trading Costs: "We Have Met The Enemy, and They Are Us," Forthcoming in *The Journal of Portfolio Management*.

118. Serwer, Andy, "Ready For the Big Leagues," *Fortune*, October 16, 2000, pp. 385–386.

119. Sharpe, William F., "Asset Allocation Management Style and Performance Measurement," *The Journal of Portfolio Management*, Winter 1992, pp. 7–19.

120. Sharpe, William F., "The Sharpe Ratio," *The Journal of Portfolio Management*, Fall 1994, pp. 49–69.

121. Shoven, John B. and Clemens Sialm, "Long Run Asset Allocation for Retirement Savings," *The Journal of Private Portfolio Management*, Summer 1998, pp. 13–26.

122. Siegel, Laurence B., Kenneth F. Kroner, and Scott W. Clifford, "The Greatest Return Stories Ever Told," *The Journal of Investing*, Summer 2001, pp. 91–102.

123. Smith Barney Mutual Funds, Smith Barney Allocation Series Prospectus—Class A, B, L and Y Shares, May 31, 2001.

124. SPDR Trust, Series 1 Prospectus, "Adjustments to the Portfolio Deposit," January 31, 2001, pp. B–53–B–56.

125. Stein, David M., "Measuring and Evaluating Portfolio Performance After Taxes," *The Journal of Portfolio Management*, Winter 1998, pp. 117–124.

126. Stein, David M. and Premkumar Narasimhan, "Of Passive and Active Equity Portfolios in the Presence of Taxes," *The Journal of Private Portfolio Management*, Fall 1999, pp. 55–63.

127. Stein, David M., Andrew F. Siegel, Premkumar Narasimhan, and Charles E. Appeadu, "Diversification in the Presence of Taxes," *The Journal of Portfolio Management*, Fall 2000, Volume 27, Number 1.

128. Stevenson, Richard W., "Surplus Magic: It Works Both Ways," *The New York Times*, July 8, 2001, p. Bu–4.

129. Teitelbaum, Richard, "The Greatest Hits of the Index King," *The New York Times*, October 8, 2000, p. 24.

130. Tergesen, Anne, "What Doesn't Belong in Your 401(k)," *Business Week*, July 30, 2001, pp. 84–86.

131. TIAA-CREF Institutional Mutual Funds Prospectus, February 2001.

132. Topkis, Maggie and Andrew Rafalaf, "Secrets of Indexing," *Mutual Funds*, October 2001, pp. 54–62.

133. Trone, Donald B., William R. Allbright, and Philip R. Taylor, *The Management of Investment Decisions*, McGraw-Hill, 1996.

134. Updegrave, Walter, "This Is a Test," *Money*, October 2000, p. 71.

135. Updegrave, Walter, "Foreign Concepts," *Money*, September 2001, pp. 67–72.

136. The Vanguard Group, Vanguard Life Strategy Fund Family Prospectus, April 27, 2001.

137. Wagner, Wayne H., "Defining Best Execution," *AIMR Conference Proceedings*, 2001, Number 2, pp. 13–24.

138. Wagner, Wayne and Al Winnikoff, *Millionaire*, Renaissance Books, 2001.

139. Welch, Scott D., "Diversifying Concentrated Holdings," *AIMR Conference Proceedings*, 2001, Number 4, pp. 30–35 and 42–44.

140. Wermers, Russ, "The Greatest Return Stories Ever Told: Comment," *The Journal of Investing*, Fall 2001, pp. 92–93.

141. Wilcox, Jarrod W., "Risks and Benchmarks," *The Journal of Index Issues*, 3rd Quarter 2001, pp. 54–62.

142. Winks, Steve, "The Center for Fiduciary Studies Proposes Practice Standards, SEC and DOL Very Receptive," *Senior Consultant*, December/January 2001, Volume 4, Number 1, pp. 1 and 13–20.

143. WM Advisors, WM Group of Funds Prospectus, March 1, 2001.

144. Woolley, Suzanne, "Advice Worth the Price," *Money*, August 2001, pp. 69–84.

145. Young, Patrick and Thomas Theys, *Capital Market Revolution: The Future of Markets in an Online World*, Prentice Hall, 1999.

146. Zigler, Brad, "More on Exchange-Traded Funds," *Journal of Financial Planning*, August 2001, p. 12.

147. Zweig, Jason, "Is the S&P 500 Rigged?" *Money*, July 2001, pp. 84–89.

Index